‖‖ ‖‖‖‖‖ ‖‖‖ ‖ ‖‖‖‖‖‖‖‖‖‖ ‖‖ ‖‖
W9-ASG-444

DEATHLY DECEPTION

Denis Smyth studied for his Ph.D. in History at the University of Cambridge under the supervision of Sir Harry Hinsley, official historian of British intelligence in the Second World War. He lectured in Modern European History at University College, Cork from 1976 to 1985, and has been a Professor in the Department of History, and in the International Relations Programme, at the University of Toronto since 1985. His previous publications have dealt with the diplomacy and strategy of the Great Powers during the twentieth century and he has edited a number of volumes in the *British Documents on Foreign Affairs* series.

To Gayle & Joseph,

With very best wishes,

Denis

Praise for Deathly Deception:

'Captivating'
Military Review: The Professional Journal of the U.S Army

'Superlative . . . Readers are likely to find this book impossible to put down once started and impossible to forget once finished.'
Roland Green, *Booklist*

'This is another fascinating and very readable book on the most brilliantly tangled web of deception spun in the Second World War.'
History Today

'Smyth's book gives an engaging picture of an exceptionally intricate, exceptionally secret piece of military deceit . . . He scores over Macintyre on one important point: he has done a lot of work on the archives of the Special Operations Executive.'
M. R. D. Foot, *Literary Review*

'This fascinating story is told with new thoroughness. Recommended for all studying World War II intelligence activities.'
Library Journal

'An important, well-written and soundly documented history of Operation Mincemeat.'
Hayden B. Peake, *Studies in Intelligence*

'Fascinating stuff, much like a police procedural on television, and more than a little ghoulish.'
HistoryNet.com

'[Denis Smyth] now graces the University of Toronto, which surely must treasure his grasp of the complexities and the falsehoods surrounding secret intelligence and its vital role, properly deployed by the quick and the dead, to ensure the survival of our way of life.'
William Stevenson, *Literary Review of Canada*

DEATHLY DECEPTION

THE REAL STORY OF
OPERATION MINCEMEAT

DENIS SMYTH

OXFORD
UNIVERSITY PRESS

OXFORD
UNIVERSITY PRESS

Great Clarendon Street, Oxford OX2 6DP

Oxford University Press is a department of the University of Oxford.
It furthers the University's objective of excellence in research, scholarship,
and education by publishing worldwide in

Oxford New York

Auckland Cape Town Dar es Salaam Hong Kong Karachi
Kuala Lumpur Madrid Melbourne Mexico City Nairobi
New Delhi Shanghai Taipei Toronto

With offices in

Argentina Austria Brazil Chile Czech Republic France Greece
Guatemala Hungary Italy Japan Poland Portugal Singapore
South Korea Switzerland Thailand Turkey Ukraine Vietnam

Oxford is a registered trade mark of Oxford University Press
in the UK and in certain other countries

Published in the United States
by Oxford University Press Inc., New York

© Denis Smyth 2010

Crown copyright material is reproduced under
Class Licence Number CPOIP0000148 with the permission
of OPSI and the Queen's Printer for Scotland.

The moral rights of the author have been asserted
Database right Oxford University Press (maker)

First published 2010
First published in paperback 2011

All rights reserved. No part of this publication may be reproduced,
stored in a retrieval system, or transmitted, in any form or by any means,
without the prior permission in writing of Oxford University Press,
or as expressly permitted by law, or under terms agreed with the appropriate
reprographics rights organization. Enquiries concerning reproduction
outside the scope of the above should be sent to the Rights Department,
Oxford University Press, at the address above

You must not circulate this book in any other binding or cover
and you must impose the same condition on any acquirer

British Library Cataloguing in Publication Data

Data available

Library of Congress Cataloging in Publication Data

Library of Congress Control Number: 2010923437

Typeset by SPI Publisher Services, Pondicherry, India
Printed in Great Britian on acid-free paper by
Clays Ltd., St Ives plc

ISBN 978-0-19-923398-4 (Hbk.)
ISBN 978-0-19-960598-9 (Pbk.)

1

For Margaret and in memory of Sir Harry Hinsley
and Professor T. Desmond Williams

Acknowledgements

Historians are not always high-flyers but they are usually high-maintenance. Getting this particular historical project airborne required a collective effort from a substantial ground crew and, once aloft, careful guidance from an expert team of air traffic controllers to arrive at the desired destination.

The individuals to whose memory this book is dedicated initiated me into the ways and wiles of international relations. Professor T. Desmond Williams of University College, Dublin, enlightened my undergraduate mind with his profound insights into the nature of statecraft and strategy. Professor Sir Francis 'Harry' Hinsley of the University of Cambridge fostered my postgraduate understanding of the phenomenon of war in international history with his blend of scholarly expertise and personal experience. I was privileged to come under his doctoral supervision at the time he was embarking upon the writing of his magisterial, multi-volume official history of British secret intelligence during the Second World War. Sir Harry's pioneering work on the secret war against Nazi Germany and Fascist Italy had an early impact upon my academic career. It prompted me to present a senior-level seminar course on the clandestine dimension of the Second World War to undergraduate students at the University of Toronto. The unflagging enthusiasm of my Toronto students for such a course—which I have now offered for two decades—has sustained my own interest in the secret intelligence history of the Second World War. Moreover, the pedagogical need to keep abreast of current scholarship in this field has kept me informed on the progressive opening-up of significant archival collections—particularly in the United Kingdom and the United States—relating to the covert history of the period. The abiding influence of my original mentors, the unfailing interest of my students and the scholarly opportunities offered by access to previously sealed, 'top-secret' records, have led me to undertake my own study of one of the more celebrated covert operations mounted during the Second World War.

In working on this book, I have been helped by old friends and new. Once more, Professors Desmond Dinan, Paul Preston, and Angel Viñas gave personal encouragement, professional advice, and practical assistance. Two successive Chairs of the Department of History at the University of Toronto, Professors Ron Pruessen and Jane Abray, also lent generous moral and material support to my project. I deeply appreciate their consideration in view of their heavy administrative responsibilities. Two Spanish historians, Dr Manuel Ros Agudo and Dr Jesús Ramírez Copeiro del Villar, were kind enough to provide me with copies of their own books on aspects of the clandestine competition between the belligerent camps inside Franco's Spain during the Second World War. In actually conducting the archival research for this work I was fortunate enough to be able to draw on the kind assistance of former students of my seminar course at the University of Toronto. Chantal Aubin, Alexandra Luce, and Dr Mathilde von Bülow were unstinting in their efforts to track down my documentary desiderata. The following graduates of the University of Toronto also pitched in to feed my insatiable archival appetite: Lorne Breitenlohner, Dr Joseph Maiolo, and Dr Hilary Earl. Another Toronto alumnus, Vasilis Dimitriadis, proved his worth, as a true friend and colleague, by devoting many hours to tracing recondite published sources on my behalf. To all of these selfless individuals, I owe a very considerable debt of gratitude.

My professional research assistant, Dr Kevin Jones, also rendered sterling service to the project. His archival investigations combined industry and intuition in equal measure. He identified key sources, examined them critically and reported his findings with clarity and concision. Moreover, his enthusiasm for the work never dimmed, even when I set him on the trail of elusive documents which had utterly defeated my own efforts to track them down. Needless to say, he got them by hook or by crook.

There was one form of expertise which this study required and which I could not readily find amongst my existing circle of personal friends and professional colleagues, namely, an understanding of forensic pathology. In deciding to write about *Operation Mincemeat*—a strategic deception scheme which sought to pass misleading information to the enemy through the medium of a dead body—I badly needed the professional advice of an expert who could guide me through the complex medical issues involved in such a covert plan. I found just such an individual in the person of Dr Noel McAuliffe, a forensic pathologist in the Office of the Chief Coroner for Ontario. In addition to being a master of his medical speciality,

Dr McAuliffe has a natural talent for explaining its subject matter to a lay person like myself. Such light as I have been able to shed in the following pages on the medical aspects of *Operation Mincemeat* primarily derive from my illuminating discussions with him. Dr Lorraine Philp and Dr Lesley Douglas also helped with this facet of the project.

As my librarian wife never fails to remind me, the keepers of the written (and spoken) word also make an indispensable contribution to the completion of any work of history. Amongst the librarians and archivists who have rendered me priceless assistance are the following individuals: Ms Lara Andrews of the Library of the Canadian War Museum, Ottawa; Ms Margaret Brooks, Keeper of the Sound Archive at the Imperial War Museum, London; Ms Phyll Melling, Printed Books Department, Guildhall Library, London; and Mr Matthew Sheldon, Head of Curatorial Department, Library of the Royal Naval Museum, Portsmouth. Many other members of staff at the following institutions have also greatly facilitated the research upon which this work is based: the National Archives of the United Kingdom, Kew, Richmond, Surrey; the United States National Archives and Records Administration, College Park, Maryland; the Department of Documents and the Sound Archive at the Imperial War Museum, London; the British Library, London; the Library of the Royal Naval Museum, Portsmouth; Toronto Public Library; the University Library, Cambridge; and University of Toronto Libraries.

Permission to quote from the typescript memoirs of Rear Admiral David Scott has been kindly granted by the Head of Curatorial Department, Library of the Royal Naval Museum, Portsmouth.

I am also very grateful to Mr Nicholas Reed for permission to include the photograph of his father, Major Ronnie Reed, in the illustrations for this book. His generosity has allowed the reader to compare that photograph with the official snapshot of 'Major Martin' affixed to the latter's identity card. Mr Nicholas Reed's help in this regard is all the more appreciated in the light of his intention to publish his own book on his late father's life and fascinating times in secret service.

My editor at Oxford University Press, Matthew Cotton, also deserves special acknowledgement for his wise counsel and courteous attention throughout our partnership in the production of this book. He kept me on an even keel with his steady hand and congenial manner. I am also grateful to Ms Deborah Protheroe, Senior Picture Researcher at Oxford University Press, for her invaluable work on the illustrations for this book and to Ms Claire Thompson, my Production Editor, for seeing the work through to publication with every proficiency. My thanks are also due to Ms Luciana O'Flaherty, a Senior Commissioning Editor at OUP, for taking the book on in the first place. I am also deeply appreciative of Mr Jeremy Langworthy's highly professional copy-editing of my text. He performed his delicate surgery with a lightness of touch and an endless concern for the general welfare of the patient.

Finally, I want to thank Margaret for her constant support during every twist and turn of this book's evolution. I cannot imagine how I could have completed the work without her sympathy and solidarity.

Naturally, in spite of all the help I have received from the individuals and institutions mentioned above in the writing of this book, any inaccuracies and imperfections it contains are mine and mine alone.

Toronto   Denis Smyth
January 2010

Foreword

Operation Mincemeat was a 'wizard wheeze': the scheme to pass strategic misinformation to Nazi Germany's warlords in 1943, via a dead body, was imaginatively conceived, ingeniously implemented and audaciously executed. Therefore, my first priority has been to tell this gripping tale in all its exotic and poignant detail. By drawing upon a comprehensive collection of documentary and published materials—in English, German, and Spanish—it has proved possible to recount this extraordinary exploit in unprecedented depth. Yet, any account of *Operation Mincemeat* must acknowledge that it was more than a macabre intrigue. This deathly deception was undertaken in deadly earnest, so as to inflict mortal injury on the fascist powers in the Mediterranean. To achieve that ambitious aim, British deception planners had to succeed where so many of their predecessors in the long history of attempts to mislead an opponent in war had failed: they had to deceive the enemy's High Command into the strategic misdeployment of their forces across whole theatres of war and not merely on a given battlefield. Only if Britain's secret warriors could convince the Third Reich's senior intelligence appraisers and military authorities of the reality of the Allied threat to invade Greece (outlined in the forged letters carried by *Operation Mincemeat*'s dead messenger), could they fool the foe into diverting his forces away from the real Anglo–American objective—Sicily—and towards the false target. Thus, my second major priority has been to explain how British deception planners sought to exert a decisive influence over German troop dispositions during the crucial run-up to the Allied invasion of Sicily on 10 July 1943, by transmitting a credible and consistent, but entirely fictitious version of Allied offensive intentions to the enemy, throughout that period.

For a start, before *Operation Mincemeat* could even be contemplated, British code-breakers had to disclose Hitler's preoccupations to their deception planners to enable them to prey upon the Fürher's pre-existing anxieties. Prior knowledge of the German leader's belief that Greece was the Achilles' Heel of the Axis Alliance in the Mediterranean prompted the British to focus *Mincemeat*'s seeming revelations about the forthcoming Allied offensive on that country. The *Mincemeat* letters appeared all the more genuine because they confirmed Hitler's worst fears. British code-breakers also contributed in another vital manner to this effort to mislead the German Supreme Command into making strategic errors in the Mediter-ranean. By cracking the various cipher machines used by the German Armed Services (and their Supreme Command's secret intelligence service, the Abwehr), they allowed the British planners and senior Allied com-manders to monitor the digestion by the German intelligence agencies of the *Mincemeat* papers, and to measure the extent to which their misleading contents were influencing German troop dispositions from May to July 1943. This book's analysis of the receipt by, and reaction of, the German Armed Forces to these deceptive documents is informed by a consideration of every relevant radio message sent by enemy spies or soldiers, which the British managed to intercept and decrypt, when their *ruse de guerre* was hitting home.

Of course, if *Operation Mincemeat*'s message had to seem credible to the Germans, so did its dead messenger. Although it might seem surprising that the Spanish pathologists (who conducted an autopsy on the body when it was plucked from their coastal waters), as well as German intelligence agents and appraisers, were prepared to accept that *Mincemeat*'s corpse-courier had recently died by drowning, there is no real mystery here. The medical advice of the day, according to which *Operation Mincemeat* was implemen-ted, turned out to be sound, and can even impress by today's scientific standards. Neither the real cause of the deceased's demise (the ingestion of rat poison containing phosphorus), nor the mode of his dying (consequent liver damage) were likely to be detected in a significantly decomposed body just pulled from the sea. By consulting medical textbooks published at the time, and more recently, and by canvassing contemporary expert opinion, I have been able to explain why *Operation Mincemeat*'s moribund messenger was not exposed as bogus when subjected to foreign scrutiny.

This work also accounts for the remarkable staying-power of *Operation Mincemeat* in holding the Germans' attention right up to the invasion of Sicily, on 10 July 1943, and even beyond. The stamina of their stratagem exceeded even the hopes of Britain's top-level deception planners, because they expected that the Anglo–Americans' own preparations for the actual invasion of Sicily would become so obvious to the Axis powers by mid-June 1943, that *Mincemeat*'s warning about a British incursion into Greece would be discredited, by then. To try and sustain their deception's capacity to mislead the enemy for as long as possible, the British Chiefs of Staff ordered their military mission to Greece to mount a coordinated campaign of sabotage, code-named *Operation Animals*, against German communications inside that occupied country, during later June and early July 1943. Of course, that was just the kind of irregular military action likely to precede an actual British invasion of Greece, and it did the trick in resuscitating all the German Supreme Command's fears about the imminence of an Allied attack there. In examining *Operation Animals'* critical role in reviving German strategic apprehensions about Greece in the immediate run-up to the Anglo–American landings in Sicily, I have drawn on the records of the Special Operations Executive (Britain's agency for fostering resistance and sabotage inside Nazi-occupied Europe), British strategic intelligence reviews, and high-level German command communications.

The real story of *Operation Mincemeat* is certainly a dramatic saga, but it is also the record of one of the most complex stratagems ever attempted in the annals of war.

Contents

List of Plates

1. Lieutenant Commander Ewen Montagu, © Bettman/Corbis.
2. Sir Bernard Spilsbury, © National Portrait Gallery, London.
3. W. Bentley Purchase, © National Portrait Gallery, London.
4. Corpse of Glyndwr Michael, National Archives (WO106/5921).
5. Major Martin's ID card, National Archives (WO106/5921).
6. Major Ronnie Reed, courtesy of Nicholas Reed.
7. Lieutenant General Sir Archibald Nye, Imperial War Museum (BH10075).
8. Pam, National Archives (WO106/5921).
9. Letter from Pam, National Archives (WO106/5921).
10. Major Martin's belongings, National Archives (WO106/5921).
11. Flight Lieutenant Charles Cholmondeley and Lieutenant Commander Ewen Montagu posing before the van transporting the corpse, courtesy of Jeremy Montagu.
12. Lieutenant N. L. A. Jewell and officers on board HMS *Seraph*, Imperial War Museum (A21112).
13. Major Martin's death notice, © The Times Newspapers/NI Syndication Ltd, 1943/John Frost Newspapers.
14. Allied leaders at the Algiers conference, June 1943, © Hulton Archive/Getty Images.
15. British troops landing in Sicily, July 1943, Imperial War Museum (NA4193).
16. Major Martin's tombstone, National Archives (WO106/5921).

List of Abbreviations

Abwehr	*Amtsgruppe Auslandsnachrichten und Abwehr* (Secret Intelligence Service of the German Supreme Command)
AEM	*Alto Estado Mayor* (Supreme General Staff of the Spanish Armed Forces)
AFHQ	Allied Force Headquarters (Mediterranean Theatre)
B1A	Section of MI5 which ran double agents
C	Head of the British Secret Intelligence Service (SIS/MI6)
CCO	Chief of Combined Operations
CIGS	Chief of the Imperial General Staff
COPPS	Combined Operations Pilotage Parties
COS	Chiefs of Staff
DMI	Director of Military Intelligence
DNI	Director of Naval Intelligence
EAM	Greek National Liberation Front
EEF	Egyptian Expeditionary Force
ELAS	Greek National Liberation Army
FHW	*Fremde Heere West* (Foreign Armies West—an intelligence evaluation department of the Germany Army's High Command, which also served the OKW)
FOS	Flag Officer, Submarines
GC&CS	Government Code and Cypher School (Bletchley Park)
GSO	General Staff Officer
ISK	Intelligence/Illicit Services, Knox
ISOS	Intelligence/Illicit Services, Oliver Strachey
ISSB	Inter-Services Security Board
IWM	Imperial War Museum
JIC	Joint Intelligence Sub-Committee
JPS	Joint Planning Staff
KKE	Communist Party of Greece

KO	*Kriegsorganisation* (Abwehr station operating within a foreign neutral, or pro-German country during the Second World War)
LCS	London Controlling Section
MI5	Security Service
MI6/SIS	Secret Intelligence Service
MOD	Ministry of Defence
NID	Naval Intelligence Division
OKM	*Oberkommando der Kriegsmarine* (High Command of the German Navy)
OKW	*Oberkommando der Wehrmacht* (Supreme Command of the German Armed Forces)
RIS	Radio Intelligence Service
RNVR	Royal Naval Volunteer Reserve
RSHA	*Reichssicherheitshauptamt* (Central Office for Reich Security)
SIGINT	Signals Intelligence
SIM	*Servizio de Informazione Militare* (Italian Military Intelligence Service)
SOE	Special Operations Executive
VCIGS	Vice-Chief of the Imperial General Staff
W/T	Wireless Telegraphy

Yes, but wait a moment. We must be practical.
The important bee to deceive is the Queen Bee.

A. A. Milne, *Winnie-the-Pooh*
(London: Methuen, 1926), 14

Prologue

At eleven minutes past ten on the night of 29 April 1943, the fishing fleet from the port of Huelva, in south-western Spain, was sailing out into the Gulf of Cadiz. Intent on tracking the local shoals of sardines, none of the crews noticed the additional roiling of the waters in their boats' wake as His Majesty's submarine *Seraph* broke through the surface of the Atlantic Ocean behind them.[1] With its low silhouette and operating in conditions of patchy visibility on a moonless night, HMS *Seraph* was able to sail out to sea for some twelve miles without being detected. This was so despite the steady throb of the submarine's diesel engines, a mode of propulsion which allowed the boat to recharge the batteries of its electric motors, while it travelled seaward. However, around 1.00 a.m. the following morning and before the batteries were fully charged, HMS *Seraph* turned coastwards and also switched to her electric motors. So powered, the British submarine was able to 'run silent' through 'the large number of small fishing boats which were working in the bay', off the mouth of the Río Tinto.[2] As the *Seraph* glided unseen and unheard towards the Huelvan shoreline, her sailors were free to go about their business under the expert eye of their 29-year-old commander, Lieutenant N. L. A. ('Bill') Jewell, a decorated veteran and future naval aide-de-camp to the Queen. They manhandled a cylindrical container, which was over six feet long and just under two feet wide, through the submarine's torpedo hatch on custom-made slides. Jewell then instructed his submariners to lash the container securely to the rail surrounding their craft's gun platform. That done, he ordered that the vessel be 'trimmed down', namely that its buoyancy be reduced to the point where it was sailing virtually awash. Next, Jewell cleared the submarine's deck of all but the officers on board—five in all, including himself.[3]

This move must have puzzled the rest of the crew, since a container marked 'Optical Instruments' hardly seemed to deserve such special treatment.[4] Jewell's brother officers, however, were not quite as perplexed as their men by these unusual proceedings, for their skipper had revealed to them on the night of 28 April, while they were closeted together out of earshot of the rest of the crew, the nature of the 'mysterious task' which the Admiralty had assigned to them. One of those present later recalled the impact the captain's revelation made upon his subordinates:

> We sat round the Wardroom table as Jewell opened a large buff coloured envelope. Now we learned, with something of a shock, that there was a dead body in the canister which was lying in one of the torpedo reload racks in the Fore Ends. Sailors had been sleeping alongside it, possibly using part of it as a pillow. We were to land this body on the beach at the Spanish port of Huelva.[5]

However, Jewell was unable to divulge to his officers the true purpose which the clandestine cargo they had transported from Scotland to Iberian waters was meant to serve. Even he had not been briefed fully about the secret scheme in which HMS *Seraph*'s mute passenger was to be a passive participant.[6] So sensitive was the mission being executed by Lieutenant Jewell and his crew that none of them was allowed to know its real character and precise goal, in case they compromised its security by careless word or deed. So, instead of being able to put them in the exact picture, Jewell was directed to tell his subordinates a carefully prepared cover story: 'it was that we suspected the Germans of getting at papers on bodies washed ashore and therefore this body was going to be watched'. If the British could confirm their suspicions, then they should be able to pressure the Franco regime into expelling the Nazi spies from Spanish soil. For the mission to succeed, however, 'absolute secrecy' was essential, since 'if anything leaked out about this operation not only would the dangerous German agents not be removed, but the lives of those watching what occurred would be endangered'.[7]

With his sailors safely below decks, and his fellow officers already sworn to secrecy, Lieutenant Jewell could set about discharging his covert commission, in the early hours of 30 April 1943. First, he allocated the necessary duties. He put Lieutenant David Scott, the *Seraph*'s first officer, in charge of the bridge, where Lieutenant Ralph Norris, the boat's gunnery and torpedo officer was placed on watch to guard against a chance encounter with a German U-boat or a Spanish vessel (be it a naval craft or a fishing boat). Then, Lieutenant John Davis, the submarine's navigator, was also assigned to act as a look-out, but from the boat's deck or 'casing', where he could lend a helping hand when the time came to lower the body into the water.

The remaining two members of this exclusive officers' watch tackled the grim task of opening the canister and removing the corpse lying within it. Jewell was acutely conscious of the youth of his comrades-in-arms (the average age of the *Seraph*'s officers was twenty-four years), and the fact that most of them had not encountered a dead body up close. So, he selected the submarine's warrant engineer, Lieutenant Dickie Sutton, as the officer least likely to be squeamish and most likely to be helpful in handling these delicate jobs on the lurching deck of HMS *Seraph*. 'Chiefie' Sutton was 'an old-timer in submarines with a twinkle in his eye who fixed all sorts of gadgets for everybody'. He had impressed all on board, as 'not only an efficient and hard-working engineer' but also as 'a jack-of-all-trades able to make almost anything with his capable hands'.[8] That manual dexterity was put to good use on the moving deck of the *Seraph*, just after 4.00 a.m., as Sutton assisted Bill Jewell in loosening the bolts on top of the canister-cum-coffin with a box spanner attached to its lid.

Ten minutes later, at 4.15 a.m., they had the lid off the air-tight container from which they gingerly extracted a blanket-covered body. Then Jewell knelt down to undo the knotted tapes binding the army blanket enshrouding the corpse.[9] When he had them untied and had thrown the blanket open, the naval officers' senses and sensibilities were promptly assailed by palpable signs of bodily decomposition—a gruesome fact that the professional tone of Jewell's post-operational report to British naval intelligence could not conceal:

> The face was heavily tanned and the whole of the lower half from the eyes down covered with mould. The skin had started to break away on the nose and cheek bones. The body was very high.[10]

However, Jewell showed no signs of being unnerved by this sorry sight. Instead, he proceeded to follow his operational orders calmly and conduct a careful inspection of the cadaver to ensure that it was suitably outfitted to achieve its secret goal. Thus, Jewell verified that the Mae West life jacket, which had been placed on the body back in Britain, was still inflated properly. He also checked that the body's military uniform, with its insignia, was in a presentable state. Finally, he made sure that a black briefcase, bearing the British 'Royal Cypher', was securely attached to the person of the deceased.[11]

Throughout this harrowing process, Jewell's young associates maintained an admirable sangfroid, in spite of being so brusquely exposed to such corruption of the flesh. Their subdued manner apparently derived not from indifference to this sad spectacle, but rather from innate reverence for the dead. Their captain, too, instinctively did the decent thing; for, as the other officers bared and bowed their heads, Jewell said aloud those parts of 'The Order for the Burial of the Dead' from the *Book of Common Prayer* which he could recall, including the following lines from Psalm 39:

> I will keep my mouth as it were with a bridle: while the ungodly is in my sight.
>
> I held my tongue, and spake nothing: I kept silence, yea even from good words; but it was pain and grief to me.[12]

Yet, the dead man was not bound for the silence of a watery grave. True, Jewell and company, their respects duly paid, did lower the body into the sea at exactly 4.30 a.m., where its life-jacket kept it afloat. Indeed, the cadaver began to drift towards a beach about 1,600 yards away on the Spanish coast. Once Jewell ordered the *Seraph* to quit the scene at 'full speed' astern, the wake from the boat's twin screw propellors helped push the body further and faster inshore. Still, the submarine had not yet fully completed its top-secret operation. After sailing for a half mile south of the point where the body had been deposited, *Seraph* slowed once more. This was to enable her officers to drop another item into the sea—a rubber dinghy, inflated but turned upside down, and with only one of the standard issue set of two paddles. Finally, Jewell sailed his craft a considerable distance back out to sea. There a last object was dumped overboard. This time it was the canister-casket, now pre-filled with water and containing the blanket and tapes (which had enveloped the corpse), as well as the rubber dinghy's packaging. However, to Jewell's alarm, the container-coffin proved remarkably seaworthy. As the unwanted object bobbed up and down in the sea water near his submarine, he decided to resort to force of arms. He had a Vickers gun brought up on the bridge and the container was sprayed with machine gun bullets. Still, however, it would not go under and the *Seraph's* skipper came to the conclusion that only point-blank gunfire would send it to the bottom. So, he had a .455 service revolver fetched from below and handed it to his first officer. He then ordered Lieutenant Scott to go forward and stand on one of their boat's bow-planes. Next, Jewell manoeuvred the submarine skilfully into position right alongside the container, so that Scott was standing, however precariously, on the fore-plane directly above it. From that perch, he was able to empty the revolver's chamber of six shots right into the top of the canister, causing it to sink into waters fully 310 fathoms deep.[13]

Jewell's very anxiety to leave no physical traces, save the floating corpse and capsized dinghy, on the sea's surface must have revealed the intended effect—if not the actual aim—of their macabre mission to his accomplices. Clearly, they were simulating the aftermath of a plane crash, and in a region of Spanish coastal waters where the real thing had happened seven months before.

I

Accidental Conception

A violent thunderstorm broke over the southern coast of Spain, near the ancient port of Cadiz, in the afternoon of 26 September 1942. As local people gazed at this spectacular sound and light show, a mechanical mishap augmented nature's fireworks. An aircraft plummeted from the sky around 3.30 p.m. and exploded upon hitting the surface of the Atlantic Ocean, just offshore. The plane turned out to be a Catalina flying boat (F.P.119) from 202 squadron of the Royal Air Force's Coastal Command. The seaplane had been en route from Plymouth in England to join its squadron at their base in Gibraltar, when it came to grief. All seven members of the aeroplane's crew perished in the crash, as did the three passengers whom they were transporting to the Rock.[1] The accidental death of these individuals would have attracted little attention in a world at war, but for the fact that two of them were bearers of top-level military secrets. One of these couriers was Paymaster-Lieutenant J. H. Turner, a junior staff officer in the Royal Navy, who was returning to his post at Gibraltar. The other was Louis Danielou Clamorgan (travelling incognito as 'Charles D. Marcil'), a French naval officer bound for North-West Africa, where he was to carry out a covert mission on behalf of General de Gaulle's 'Fighting France' movement.[2] In the hours following the crash, the bodies of Turner and Clamorgan—along with other corpses and additional wreckage from the aircraft (including two dinghies)—were recovered from the sea off Cadiz. Although the Spanish authorities quickly impounded the deceased and their belongings, rumours soon spread locally to the effect that the flotsam from the ill-fated Catalina contained top-secret documents.[3]

These rumours were well founded. Paymaster-Lieutenant Turner, in particular, had been carrying on his person documents which seriously threatened to compromise a major forthcoming Allied offensive, if they fell into the wrong hands. The operation in question, code-named *Torch*, was to be an amphibious assault of a size and complexity never before attempted in the history of war and for which secrecy was absolutely crucial. The British and Americans intended to steer large fleets of troop transports and warships through thousands of miles of hostile waters to mount a surprise attack on the colonies ruled by Vichy France (a satellite regime of the Italo-German Axis) in North Africa.[4] The *Torch* plan envisaged an initial landing of 107,000 troops (three-quarters of them American) at separate points on the coasts of Morocco and Algeria, in early November 1942. The invasion force, which was to grow to a quarter-of-a-million strong within three weeks of the first landings, would make an early thrust, also, to seize the remaining French North African colony, Tunisia. This country was geopolitically significant because it was the French possession nearest to the home territory of one of the Axis partners: the Italian islands of Sardinia and Sicily lie due north and due east, respectively, of Tunisia's northern coastline. Beyond these operational goals, however, the *Torch* plan was meant to achieve far-reaching strategic aims. A successful occupation of French North Africa would end the virtually unbroken sequence of military disasters suffered by the Allies since mid 1941. The thunderclap of victory there would resound on both sides of the Atlantic, renewing British determination and American resolve to fight European fascism to the finish. Last but not least, increased Anglo–American pressure on the Axis in the Mediterranean theatre should divert German resources from the most crucial battlefield of the Second World War, the Eastern Front, where the great bulk of the German armed forces were locked in mortal combat with the Red Army.[5]

Indeed, the issues riding on the success of *Operation Torch* were sufficiently critical to persuade the British Prime Minister, Winston Churchill, that his own political survival might depend on its outcome. 'If Torch fails', he confided to the Foreign Secretary, Anthony Eden, on 1 October 1942, 'then I'm done for and must hand over to one of you.'[6] Of course, Churchill was not by nature a quitter, but he was ready to fear the worst by early October 1942. His anxiety arose from his acute awareness that Britain and its Allies stood at one of the most decisive junctures of the global conflict, when 'the Hinge of Fate' (as he later put it) was about to turn, perhaps irreversibly, in favour of one of the warring camps.[7] What precisely concerned the Prime Minister was the imminent unfolding of the Western Allies' ambitious pincer attack in Africa—a military move designed to crush the life out of the Axis power on that continent.[8] In fact *Operation*

Torch's assault on the western end of the North African coastline, in early November, was to be preceded by another large-scale onslaught at its eastern end, in late October. At El Alamein in Egypt, the British Eighth Army would launch a methodically prepared offensive to repel, once and for all, the Axis threat to the Suez Canal and the Middle East's oilfields. The British intent was to destroy the main Axis fighting force in North Africa, Field Marshal Erwin Rommel's *Panzerarmee Afrika* (a mixed formation comprised of both German and Italian divisions) which had surged into Egypt, to within striking distance of the Nile delta, by early July 1942. Any enemy units which might escape destruction at the hands of the Eighth Army would have only one line of retreat: right into the unwelcoming arms of the *Torch* invaders as they drove eastward from their beachheads.[9] So, if all went according to plan, the Western Allies should be masters of the southern Mediterranean shore by the coming winter of 1942–3. Moreover, if Anglo–American victory in North Africa coincided with a Soviet triumph in the ferocious battle of Stalingrad (well under way by October 1942), then the 'Hinge of Fate' might well be about to shift decisively towards the anti-Nazi Grand Alliance. Certainly, the Allies should be in a position to wrest the strategic initiative in the global contest from their foes. Having scrambled for months—and in Britain's case for years—to keep pace with the serial shocks and lightning strikes of their adversaries, the UK, the USA and the USSR soon might be able to call the shots and spring the surprises. On the other hand, if the Anglo–American attacks scheduled to begin at opposite ends of North Africa from late October to early November 1942 failed, then all might be lost. With such substantial stakes involved in the forthcoming operations, it is no wonder that Winston Churchill should remember the weeks of September and October 1942, immediately prior to the opening of the Alamein and *Torch* assaults, as the most stressful time he had to endure during the entire Second World War.[10] He subsequently described 'the period of waiting', at this vital stage of the worldwide war, as 'one of suppressed but extreme tension'.[11]

Thus, it was into an atmosphere, already charged with great apprehension about the impending twin offensives in the Mediterranean, that there arrived 'alarming information of loss of a Catalina between Lisbon and Gibraltar, and bodies washed up at Cadiz with letters in their pockets, containing details of North (-West) African attack' (to quote the summary of the bad news made by the Chief of Britain's Imperial General Staff, General Sir Alan Brooke, in his diary entry for 29 September 1942).[12]

Many other Anglo–American officers and officials were dismayed at this potentially catastrophic breach of security surrounding *Operation Torch*. However, it was Churchill who had impressed an American officer, the day before, as being the 'chief worrier' over the loss of top-secret documents relating to *Operation Torch*.[13]

The document whose loss most disturbed the Allied authorities was one carried, along with other papers, by Paymaster-Lieutenant Turner in the inner pocket of his naval uniform. It was a letter from General Mark Clark, the American Deputy Commander of the Allied Expeditionary Force for *Operation Torch* to General Noel Mason-MacFarlane, Governor and British Commander-in-Chief of Gibraltar. In this letter, dated 14 September 1942, Clark mentioned that his superior, General Dwight D. Eisenhower (the American Commander-in-Chief of the *Torch* force) would arrive in Gibraltar, on or about the eve of the 'target date' of '4 November'. The obvious implication—that 'Ike' would be journeying to the Rock to take charge of an imminent large-scale amphibious operation—was confirmed by another document on Turner's person. This item was identified as originating from 'H.Q. Naval Commander-in-Chief, Expeditionary Force' and referred, inter alia, to a 'combined Headquarters'.[14] So, even though the documents in Turner's possession did not disclose the exact location of the *Torch* invasion, they were sufficiently revealing to warrant serious concern. Certainly, enemy intelligence analysts should have had no difficulty in deducing from such clues the Allies' imminent intention to launch a major amphibious assault on the western mouth of the Mediterranean, where the most obvious target was Vichy French-ruled North Africa. In these troubling circumstances, 'the vital question' that the Anglo–American authorities had to address was 'whether the letter (from Clark to Mason-MacFarlane) had been tampered with'—a point emphasized by Churchill's chief military staff officer, General Hastings 'Pug' Ismay, to General Eisenhower on 29 September.[15] The fact that this crucial document had lain, along with Turner's body, in official Spanish custody for at least twenty-four hours before being handed over to the British, conveyed no reassurance on this critical matter.[16] For a start, the Franco regime was an ideological soulmate of the fascist powers, having won the Spanish Civil War of 1936–9 largely thanks to assistance from Germany and Italy.[17] Moreover, as the British in particular knew by this stage of the Second World War, Generalissimo Franco—despite his formal status as a 'non-belligerent' in the global contest—was prepared to render many clandestine services to his fellow dictators, even if he had been unable to agree terms with Hitler, during 1940–1, for Spain's open engagement in the conflict.[18] General Clark's letter could slip all too easily through such accommodating fingers into the grasp of Nazi agents.

Faced with the distinct possibility that the Catalina crash might have delivered *Operation Torch*'s secrets into hostile hands, Britain's pre-eminent strategic counsellors took immediate action: the Chiefs of Staff (COS, whose committee comprised Generals Alan Brooke and Ismay, as well as the service heads of the Royal Navy and the Royal Air Force—Admiral Sir Dudley Pound and Air Chief Marshal Sir Charles Portal, respectively) ordered an immediate inquiry into the incident, on 29 September.[19] The natural body to undertake this task was the Inter-Services Security Board (ISSB, composed of representatives from each of the armed forces' departments and Britain's Secret Intelligence and Security Services), which had overall responsibility for safeguarding the secrecy of pending military operations. Actually, bureaucratic competition and confusion had prevented the ISSB from functioning properly as the keeper of British operational secrets during the Second World War, until the preparations for *Torch* in the autumn of 1942.[20] Now, however, that long-awaited opportunity to prove its worth seemed jeopardized by the fallout from the aviation accident at Cadiz. Understandably, then, a senior figure in Britain's Security Service (MI5), found the ISSB to be 'in a great flap', on 1 October 1942, 'as to whether Torch has been compromised' by 'the Catalina which crashed off the Spanish coast'.[21] Certainly, it is true that the ISSB did move with remarkable speed to assess the damage done to *Torch*'s operational security by the temporary loss of Turner's documents. However, their review was not an ill-considered rush to judgement.

On 30 September—the very day after being commissioned to investigate the episode, the ISSB judged that 'on the information at present available Operation TORCH had not been compromised as a result of the loss of this aircraft'.[22] The Board's members were able to reach such a prompt preliminary conclusion because of the exceptionally thorough examination which Paymaster-Lieutenant Turner's corpse, clothing and other personal effects underwent, upon their return to British custody on 27 September. British experts combed over the body and its possessions, once they reached the Rock of Gibraltar, for the slightest sign of search or interference by third parties. However, both an RAF intelligence officer and an RAF medical officer determined that the deceased and his documents remained inviolate.[23] Still, it was a minute amount of an extraneous substance detected on Turner's uniform which did most to dispel the ISSB's alarm over the air crash. The Board highlighted this key finding, in their subsequent report to Churchill and the COS, when reviewing the condition in which General Clark's letter to General Mason-MacFarlane had been found:

> (its) inner envelope was secured by two very small blobs of sealing wax but without impress of any seal. It has since been confirmed that the envelope was so sealed before dispatch. There is no evidence of the seals having been lifted or the envelope slit. Sand in the button holes of the clothing indicated that it was unlikely that the coat had been opened to reach the inner pocket. If the letter had been tampered with, all traces of the fact had been most carefully concealed.[24]

In a sense, therefore, in reaching the more studied conclusion in its official report on the Catalina crash that 'it was very unlikely that the operation [*Torch*]' had been 'in any way compromised as a result of this accident', the ISSB was resting its case on foundations of sand—or at least those grains of sand embedded in the buttonholes of Turner's naval uniform and which had seemed undisturbed by prying fingers.[25]

However, when the British Chiefs of Staff came to consider the ISSB's report on 3 October, they heard rather more substantial evidence which corroborated its reassuring conclusion. On that occasion, Admiral Pound 'read out a report from a most secret source' to his colleagues, which provided irrefutable proof that Turner's papers had not fallen into the wrong hands.[26] Pound's evidence was incontrovertible because it came from the proverbial horse's mouth. The designation 'most secret source' was one of the stock phrases employed to conceal the 'Ultra Secret', i.e., the intelligence produced by the code-breakers of Britain's Government Code and Cypher School (GC&CS) at Bletchley Park. There, intellect and imagination united in a relentless effort to break the high-grade ciphers used by the Nazis to scramble their radio communications: powerful mathematical brains exposed the inner workings and inherent vulnerabilities of the seemingly impregnable German cipher machines; acute analytical intelligence probed the Achilles' heel—human operator error—of the theoretically impenetrable German encryption systems, to produce 'cribs', or clues, which reduced the astronomical odds against reading the enemy's encoded messages and, finally, immensely inventive minds developed code-breaking machines to determine, within a finite time, the daily changes the Germans made to their encryptions.[27] From a modest start in the spring of 1940, the boffins of Bletchley Park pressed home their cryptanalytical attack on German radio communications with such success that, by the close of 1942, they were reading as many as 4,000 of the Nazis' high-grade secret wireless messages every single day.[28] The scale of the British code-breakers' triumph was all the more remarkable in that they had to direct their efforts against multiple targets. This was so because the various components of the Nazi war machine used different devices to render their radio messages incomprehensible to enemy eavesdroppers. Thus, as the Second World War progressed, Hitler and his High Command increasingly communicated with their senior military commanders in the various theatres of war via the international teleprinter code. A machine—which the British dubbed 'Tunny'—masked such strategically important messages by generating a 'stream of obscuring letters' to cloak their content.[29] It took some of Bletchley Park's very best minds and some of its most sophisticated machines (including even 'the world's first semi-programmable computer', code-named 'Colossus') to prise open the 'Tunny' system.[30] However, another high-grade encryption mechanism, employed by all three German armed services during the Second World War, also presented formidable challenges to GC&CS. The 'Enigma' machine was an electro-mechanical apparatus designed to encipher the text of messages, prior to their transmission in morse code over the air waves.[31] The German Army, Navy, and Air Force used Enigma extensively for communications at the operational level, but its messages could also convey tactical and/or strategical information.[32] In principle, Enigma was an extremely secure cipher system, as long as it was operated properly (which it generally was within the German Army). In practice, however, Enigma operators, who experienced too much pressure or too continuous monotony, failed to take the steps necessary to guarantee secure encryption via the device. In this regard, German Air Force signallers were a godsend to British code-breakers, who regularly exploited their constant sins of omission and commission, to read the *Luftwaffe*'s Enigma ciphers.[33] Still, even the German Navy, which developed the most complex Enigma machine of all those used by the Third Reich's armed forces, and also adopted the most complex encryption procedures, eventually succumbed to the brilliance of Bletchley Park's code-breaking efforts, spearheaded by the mathematical genius, Alan Turing.[34]

Of course, the volume and variety of the enemies' codes and ciphers (with their many separate networks) meant that Bletchley Park had to evolve into a cryptanalytical enterprise on a truly industrial scale. Barely employing a hundred workers at the start of the Second World War,

GC&CS would have a complement of nearly 9,000 by its end.[35] Moreover, this factory-style system of signals intelligence (SIGINT) production required an intense division of labour. Specialization of function promoted efficiency, while compartmentalization of task improved security for the top-secret endeavour.[36] Yet, not all those who experienced the transformation of Bletchley Park from an institution with a scholarly mindset and modus operandi 'into a bustling headquarters with multiple assembly lines' welcomed this change in their circumstances.[37] Thus, late in 1941, Britain's foremost veteran cryptanalyst, Alfred 'Dilly' Knox, denounced the 'monstrous theory' which confined him to the task of producing decrypts for others to assess and analyse. Such a state of affairs Knox judged to be 'impossible for a scholar', who was 'bound to see his research through to the final text'. The individual to whom this protest was directed was Alastair Denniston, then head of Bletchley Park. Denniston and Knox had been colleagues in the pioneering British efforts to break the codes of the Imperial German Navy during the First World War. However, he defended the new order at GC&CS for the Second World War, in his response of 11 November 1941 to Knox's *cri de coeur*, pointing out that the exploitation of Dilly's breakthroughs by lesser brains would leave his uniquely intuitional mind free to roam over fresh cryptanalytical realms.[38]

Knox's brain certainly was a rare instrument. It induced the most profound introspection, when seized of a particular problem. Once, a young colleague, who had waited with growing alarm outside the door of a bathroom for 'Dilly' to emerge, burst into a singular scene: there stood Knox transfixed in thought while water gushed from both taps into a plugless bath.[39] Indeed, the celebrated code-breaker actually seemed to find the clammy heat and steamy atmosphere conducive to cryptanalysis. He had been happy to perform his code-breaking during the First World War in a closet-sized office which doubled as his section's bathroom. Yet, his most spectacular feat of code-breaking during that war was the product of neither abstraction nor abstractions. In 1917 he managed to break into the high-level flag code used by the German admiralty through a combination of literary erudition and psychological intuition. Presented with an intercepted message, of whose text only the recurring word-ending 'en' had been decoded, Knox (classical Greek scholar that he was) detected poetic rhythm and rhyme. Further inferring that only a romantically inclined soul would be likely to use lines of poetry for a test transmission, he deduced that one of the words in the text was probably *Rosen* (roses). This inspired guess was sufficient to allow one of Knox's fellow code-breakers to identify the couplet as written by Friedrich von Schiller. This exercise in literary detective work produced a thirteen-word crib which greatly facilitated the British break into the high-grade code used by the German Navy's Command to conduct its campaign of unrestricted submarine warfare against Britain's transatlantic lifeline, during 1917–18.[40]

True, Dilly Knox remained, throughout his illustrious career in crypt-analysis, the very model of an academic amnesiac. He forgot to invite his own brother to his wedding; his distracted driving was a menace to himself, to his passengers and to all other road users; and, on occasion, his subor-dinates would have to abandon their attack on Nazi Germany's codes and ciphers to tackle an even more elusive target, the whereabouts of Dilly's cherished pipe. Yet, even when they located this indispensable tool of Knox's cryptanalytical craft, his assistants' mission was not fully accom-plished: they still had to make sure that he filled its bowl with tobacco rather than bits of stale sandwich.[41] Only then could Dilly Knox surround himself with the external fug which seemed to complement perfectly the internal fog in which his mind operated. Yet, behind this smokescreen a mighty spirit was abroad, as his niece, the eminent novelist, Penelope Fitzgerald, came to realize: 'the borderland where the mind, prowling among misty forms and concepts, suddenly perceives analogies with what it already knows, and moves into the light—this was where Dilly was most at home'.[42] Moreover, Knox's mental meanderings in the twilight zones of cryptography yielded illuminations of the greatest practical value to his country in a time of total war. Denniston acknowledged his sterling service in the letter mentioned above: 'You are Knox, a scholar with a European reputation, who knows more about the inside of a machine than anyone else.'[43]

For the most extraordinary aspect of Knox's intuitive style of code-breaking was that it allowed him to discern the innards of enemy cipher machines. Indeed, he was in the process of achieving his most important success of this kind at the time of his correspondence with Denniston in late 1941. In August of 1941, Dilly Knox had been presented with the formidable challenge of breaking a version of an enemy cipher apparatus which he had never even seen—the Enigma machine used by the German military intelligence service, the *Amtsgruppe Auslandsnachrichten und Abwehr* (secret intelligence service of the German Supreme Command, known simply as the Abwehr). Knox was not alone, however, in tackling this difficult task. He had the critical assistance of two young women, Mavis Lever and Margaret Rock. 'Give me a Lever and a Rock and I will move the Universe', he quipped and, by October of the same year, he had delivered on his promise. Focusing upon peculiarities in the encrypted text produced by the Abwehr Enigma machine (which was significantly different in make-up from those used by the other branches of the German armed forces), Knox came to understand that it worked by multiple turnovers of its 'encrypting wheels'. With this understanding, Knox and his colleagues could exploit the same kind of mistakes made by Abwehr personnel in operating their Enigma, which had opened up other versions of the device to regular penetration by British code-breakers.[44] Bletchley Park produced its first complete decrypt of an Abwehr Enigma message on Christmas Day, 1941. It was the first in a series, called after its instigator 'Intelligence Services Knox' (ISK), that would amount to 140,000 decrypts by the end of the Second World War.[45]

Other hands and minds presided over this vast expansion and exploitation of the original break into the Abwehr Engima because Dilly Knox was unable to return to work at Bletchley Park after October 1941. He was stricken with a recurrence of the stomach cancer that would kill him, eventually, in February 1943. However, characteristically, Knox worked until the end, at home—in his sick room and even on his death bed—to help keep open the vital window on the operations and organization of the Abwehr, which the ISK product provided.[46] The official history of *British Intelligence in the Second World War* rightly acclaims Knox's breaking of the Abwehr Enigma as the 'most fundamental' contribution made by Bletchley Park to Britain's security during the entire Second World War.[47] In Spain alone, for example, ISK helped the British to build up 'an encyclopaedic knowledge' of the Abwehr's spy networks and their clandestine activities. Thus, as early as the spring of 1942, British security and counter-intelligence authorities had established that the main centre of German espionage in Spain—the Abwehr section in Madrid, or *Kriegsorganisation* (KO)—had a staff of twenty officers to supervise the operation of ten outstations, includ-ing those at Cadiz and Huelva in south-western Spain.[48] The Abwehr's spy centre in the Spanish capital also had Engima machines (as did the outsta-tions situated around Gibraltar) with which to encrypt secret intelligence reports for subsequent transmission by radio, from or via Madrid, to Ber-lin.[49] In fact, the ability of British counter-intelligence to monitor the radio communications of Nazi spies at work in 'neutral' countries like Franco's

Spain had begun as early as 1940. In particular, in December of that year, an elite team at Bletchley Park, initially led by another veteran code-breaker, Oliver Strachey, had broken the Abwehr's main hand cipher (used by agents in the field and most outstations to encode their radio signals).[50]

With access to both the Abwehr's machine and hand ciphers, Bletchley Park seemed well placed to inform on the extent to which the Nazis had penetrated the secrets of *Operation Torch*, as a result of the Catalina crash. Indeed, the vigilant British did intercept and decipher an exchange of radio messages between KO Madrid, the Abwehr's outstation in Cadiz and its Berlin headquarters, about the 'plane crash at CADIZ and salvaging of important documents'. One of the intercepted items—a communication, dated 29 September, from the chief Abwehr agent in Cadiz, codenamed *Gitano* ('Gypsy'), to KO Madrid—contained the following frank admission: 'I know nothing about documentation.'[51] Since, as noted above, the most sensitive documents temporarily lost in the air crash—those carried by Paymaster-Lieutenant Turner—had been restored to British possession by 27 September, it did appear that the Germans had missed a heaven-sent opportunity to find out about the forthcoming Allied landings. Certainly, it is understandable that Admiral Pound should cite such authoritative 'Ultra' intelligence at the COS meeting on 3 October, to corroborate the independent conclusion of the ISSB that *Operation Torch* had not been compromised as a result of the aviation accident. The equally reassuring contents of the ISSB and SIGINT reports were communicated promptly to the prime minister. A doubtless relieved Churchill noted their receipt on 7 October.[52] However, it soon turned out that his worries about *Torch*'s security were far from over, as 'Ultra' provided further revelations about the Catalina crash. The additional cause for concern came from an Enigma-enciphered message, transmitted by KO Madrid to Berlin on 30 September, but not deciphered and distributed by Bletchley Park to interested parties until 16 October. It now transpired that another batch of secret documents had been salvaged from the sea. Moreover, police officers of the Franco regime had not only shown these papers to German spies in Madrid but also, subsequently, had provided the local Abwehr with 'photographic copies' of all of them.[53] The ISSB received this bad news on 20 October, while General Alan Brooke alerted the COS, on 22 October, to this fresh menace to *Torch*'s security.[54] Once more, the ISSB had to assess a potential threat to the secrecy of *Operation Torch*. Their key responsibility this time around, as one of their number put it, was to determine 'the interpretation put upon the documents by the enemy'.[55]

In fact, all the missing documents had originated from General de Gaulle's 'Fighting France' movement and had been recovered from a suitcase belonging to the French agent, Clamorgan. He had been travelling, under the cover-name of 'Marcil', to North Africa to liaise with pro-Allied and anti-fascist elements there and, consequently, had been provided, inter alia, with lists of Free French agents in Morocco and of Gaullist sympathizers there and in Tunisia.[56] Armed with this insider information, the Germans would be able to pressure the Vichy administration in North Africa into proceeding against these unfortunate individuals. However, it was not the counter-intelligence harvest the Axis might reap from the Catalina crash but, once again, its possible strategic fallout that preoccupied the ISSB, as it sought to assess the real damage done by the leakage of the Marcil documents to the Abwehr. In that regard, the Board decided that only one of the lost papers (which totalled eighteen in number) was of potential concern. This was the record of a meeting held amongst military members of the Fighting French Committee in London, on 22 September 1942. The official minute made mention of an Allied landing in French Morocco. Since landings on the Atlantic coast of French Morocco (along with others on the Mediterranean coast of Algeria) were an integral part of *Operation Torch*, this document might seem to have given the Allies' game plan away. However, the chief of de Gaulle's secret intelligence bureau, Colonel Passy (the *nom de guerre* of André Dewavrin), was not fazed when taxed with this breach of security by a representative from MI6, Britain's espionage service. Instead, the Free French spymaster was inclined to 'dismiss the matter lightly', maintaining that the document in question merely referred to an Allied incursion into Morocco as a 'possible project for the future'. Indeed, the ISSB had to admit that although the compromised minute did mention a landing in Morocco, it did not specify at which locations, on what date, or by which Allied forces.[57]

As a result of these measured considerations, the ISSB gave carefully qualified advice to the COS, on 29 October 1942, about the risks involved in pressing ahead with *Torch*, now the enemy might know about one of its component attacks: 'We submit that although, in our view, the Operation has not necessarily been jeopardized by the contents of this document, the element of tactical surprise in Morocco may have been endangered.'[58] In light of such a limited counsel of caution and, in view of the fact that the

revised D-Day of 8 November 1942 for launching *Operation Torch* was only
ten days away, Allied commanders had little choice but to grit their teeth
and proceed with their mighty enterprise. Too many military wheels were
in motion for a halt to be called, unless clearer signs emerged that the enemy
had deduced what was underway. Of course, Allied analysts carefully
reviewed reports from all their intelligence sources—espionage, code-
breaking, and aerial photo-reconnaissance—to determine Axis appreciations
of the strategic situation at the western mouth of the Mediterranean, during
the first week of November. This systematic surveillance discovered no
obvious comprehension, on the part of Nazi Germany's warlords, of the
precise purpose of the Allied forces converging on the Strait of Gibraltar.
Thus, Britain's central intelligence-evaluation body, the Joint Intelligence
Sub-Committee, were able to calm their superiors' nerves on 3 November:
'Our conclusion is still that the Axis, although suspicious of an Allied attack
on French West Africa (particularly on Dakar) and/or French North Africa,
have not yet appreciated the exact destination, timing or scale of the [*Torch*]
attack.'[59] In reality, the inaccuracy and imprecision of most German intelligence reports relating to Allied intentions in the Mediterranean theatre,
contaminated as they were by Allied misinformation, prevented Berlin
paying proper attention to the few genuine revelations about *Torch* (including the Free French document) it received.[60]

So, in the heel of the hunt, the alarms raised over the repercussions of
the Catalina crash off Cadiz for *Operation Torch* turned out to be false.
That amphibious assault proceeded under cover of 'amazing secrecy', as a
mightily relieved British Prime Minister acknowledged.[61] *Torch* caught the
Germans off guard and by surprise. However, as it happened, this near
miss for the security of *Operation Torch* would not be without considerable
consequence for the Allies, but of a kind that greatly benefited the anti-
fascist cause. This happy turn of events was due to the intrepid imaginings
of a British secret warrior, Flight Lieutenant Charles Cholmondeley of the
Royal Air Force. While others in the know brooded over the dangers
arising from the Cadiz plane crash, Cholmondeley preferred to explore
the possibilities the incident pointed up for active deception of the enemy.
Proverbially, dead men are meant to tell no tales, but the aftermath of that
accident suggested that a corpse might be made to speak very persuasively
to a select audience, namely, the Third Reich's intelligence and military
chiefs. After all, the Abwehr had displayed a keen interest in gaining access
to the documents in the possession of both the deceased English and

French couriers, a fact which showed that a dead body might serve as a reliable instrument for the premeditated leaking of further papers to the Nazis. Only next time, these documents could be fabricated so as to deliver seriously misleading information to the German High Command from an apparently top-level British quarter, through the good offices of the predeceased courier.[62] Having derived this inspiration from the Catalina episode, Flight Lieutenant Cholmondeley now developed the idea into a formal 'plan for introducing documents of a highly secret nature into the hands of the enemy'. Thus, on 31 October 1942, while all about him still fretted over the risks to *Torch* posed by the loss of Marcil's documents, Cholmondeley outlined his proposal, which he named *Plan Trojan Horse*, for his colleagues:

> A body is obtained from one of the London hospitals (normal peace time price £10), it is then dressed in Army, Naval or Air Force uniform of suitable rank. The lungs are filled with water and the documents are disposed in an inside pocket. The body is then dropped by a Coastal Command aircraft at a suitable position where the set of currents will probably carry the body ashore in enemy territory. On being found, the supposition in the enemy's mind may well be that one of our aircraft has either been shot or forced down and that this is one of the passengers.

Cholmondeley did concede that there was no absolute guarantee that the message carried by such a courier would 'get through' to the enemy. However, he also observed that such a scheme would permit the transmission of information of an apparently 'far more secret' (i.e. top-level) kind than could be passed, credibly, by other channels to the Nazis.[63]

Actually, in suggesting this ambitious design for duping the Germans, Cholmondeley was only doing his job, for his role in Britain's secret war effort was 'largely as an ideas man', as his section head later acknowledged.[64] Another of Cholmondeley's wartime colleagues subsequently paid a rather backhanded compliment to the brain which had conceived this audacious deception, describing it as 'one of those subtle and ingenious minds which is for ever throwing up fantastic ideas—mostly so ingenious as either to be impossible of implementation or so intricate as to render their efficacy problematical, but every now and again quite brilliant in their simplicity'. Yet, *Plan Trojan Horse* was far from being either 'wild' or woolly at its moment of conception.[65] In fact, Cholmondeley's own proposal enumerated a whole series of issues requiring further examination before the project could be realized in practice:

1. Medical advice with regard to possible autopsy by the enemy and the obtaining of a suitable body.
2. Enquiry as to whether any signs would be apparent showing that the body had in fact been dropped into the water from a height.
3. The choice of points where the currents are suitable.
4. The nature of the documents to be carried and rank and Service of the uniform chosen for the body.
5. The possibilities of making the body 'double' for an actual officer.
6. Other persons or departments who might have to be taken into our confidence.
7. The possibility of the enemy picking up the plane which carries out the drop.[66]

The colleagues whose advice Cholmondeley sought on the feasibility of his audacious deception plan were members of the 'Twenty Committee', on which he also sat as a representative of Air Intelligence. That body supervised the operation of the 'double-cross' system (hence its designation as the 'Twenty Committee', after the Roman numerals—XX—for that number). Under the 'double-cross' system, German agents were played back, primarily by section B1A of MI5, against their Nazi spymasters. Initially, this systematic hijacking of the entire Nazi espionage campaign against Britain, and the conversion of its spies into British double agents, had served security and counter-intelligence purposes: to protect British secrets and to learn about German efforts to penetrate them.[67] However, the use of the double-cross agents as conduits of deception became possible from mid 1942 on, thanks to the opening up of the Abwehr's secret radio communications by Dilly Knox and company. Now, British security and counter-intelligence officers were able to confirm that the Germans accepted the bona fides of the British-controlled double agents and almost certainly had no independent espionage networks active inside Britain able to contradict and/or check up on the 'turned' spies.[68] So, the Twenty Committee had had some experience already of practising deception against the Germans—particularly in the implementation of cover plans for *Operation Torch*—when it came to consider *Trojan Horse* on 5 November 1942.[69] However, it is also true that such a scheme as Cholmondeley was proposing 'had nothing directly to do with the work of double agents', as the chairman of the Twenty Committee, Major John C. Masterman, later admitted. Still, as he also noted, at that stage of the war in later 1942, the Twenty Committee was 'the focal point of all information and misinformation which was allowed to go to the Germans' and, therefore, 'it was natural for it to discuss and further plans of this kind, especially at a time when deception control had hardly got fully into its stride'. Again, the Twenty Committee, as an inter-service and inter-departmental outfit, could both draw on the separate specializations and resources of the Army, Navy, and Air Force necessary for execution of the planned deception, and ensure the requisite coordination of their respective contributions to the joint enterprise.[70]

Thus, in presenting his *Plan Trojan Horse* for consideration by the Twenty Committee, Cholmondeley was inviting criticism from a panel of real experts, well versed in the ways of counter-intelligence and deception. They were adept at shooting holes in kites that would not fly with the Germans' secret intelligence services and High Command, and were bound to subject a subterfuge as bold and bizarre as Cholmondeley's latest brainwave to intense scrutiny. True to form, in the course of a 'long discussion' on 5 November, members of the Twenty Committee identified 'various practical difficulties' (doubtless, similar to those highlighted by Cholmondeley in his submission of 31 October) in the proposed project. Consequently, they declined to approve *Trojan Horse*, even in principle, concluding that 'a good deal of further examination' was necessary 'before any decision could be reached' on its feasibility. Still, at least the majority on the Twenty Committee had not insisted on killing off the project altogether. Indeed, Cholmondeley was commissioned, along with two other colleagues from the Committee, to investigate the possible impediments in the way of implementing *Plan Trojan Horse*.[71] It was the most modest of beginnings for what the sometime secret warrior and noted historian, Hugh Trevor-Roper, would come to acclaim as 'the most spectacular single episode in the history of deception'.[72]

2

Medical Consultation

The affection with which Charles Cholmondeley was regarded by his colleagues inside Britain's security and counter-intelligence community probably explains why the Twenty Committee was prepared to indulge his latest fancy, *Plan Trojan Horse*. It was hard to say 'no' to a man whom his fellow deception planners found to be 'charming' and congenial, however outlandish his proposals might appear initially.[1] Yet, if Cholmondeley's affability earned his audacious scheme a second look, his other predominant trait—although no less endearing—promised to serve it less well; for he also impressed his contemporaries as a 'self-effacing' and 'retiring' individual, possessed of an 'innate modesty'.[2] This personal diffidence, combined with his relative youth and lowly military rank, meant that he might not possess the necessary personal assertiveness, professional authority, and social connections to press the case for such an unorthodox plan as *Trojan Horse* successfully against the reservations of more experienced colleagues, or the doubts of less imaginative top brass.

Indeed, this ambitious deception would have to find a more qualified champion, in one of the other two officers charged by the Twenty Committee with conducting the feasibility study of the plan, if it were to stand any real chance of being put into practice. One of this duo might have seemed the natural candidate to espouse Cholmondeley's project. Major Frank Foley sat on the Twenty Committee as the representative of Britain's spy service, MI6. He had been appointed to that committee, in May 1942, to replace an individual whose hypersensitive security consciousness and bureaucratic parochialism had threatened to paralyse and, perhaps, even wreck the double-cross system. Foley's cooperative spirit ensured that the Twenty Committee was no longer working at cross-departmental purposes. Henceforward, the double agents could be groomed as effective instruments of national security and credible channels of deception in a coordinated campaign drawing on the resources of all Britain's clandestine services.[3] However, Foley brought more than a healing touch to this joint venture. He also lent considerable expertise to the collective effort to feed the German appetite for Britain's wartime secrets. In the guise of Chief British Passport Control Officer he had worked as MI6's head of station in Berlin throughout the 1920s and the 1930s. Thoroughly conversant with the turbulent politics of interwar Germany, he was appalled by the Third Reich's treatment of its Jewish citizens. So, he went to extraordinary lengths to assist their flight from Nazi persecution, saving thousands of lives in the process. Foley bent Britain's visa rules, falsified documents, and even personally browbeat concentration camp officials into transferring some of their victims to his custody. Again, at considerable risk to himself—since he did not enjoy diplomatic status and, therefore, immunity from arrest by the German authorities—he sheltered Jews on the run in his own house until some, at least, could make good their escape from 'the Fatherland'.[4]

Duly warned by intelligence sources of the imminent outbreak of war, Foley quit Berlin in late August 1939 and also managed to elude the Nazis' clutches when they invaded Norway (where he had been posted) in April 1940. Indeed, he played a not insignificant role in facilitating and firming up the Norwegian will to continue the fight against the German invaders, initially at home and then from abroad.[5] Moreover, his services as someone who 'knew the Germans backwards' (to quote the opinion of a fellow MI6 officer) were even more highly prized after the fall of France in June 1940, when Britain was fighting for its very life.[6] Official recognition of his unrivalled understanding of the Nazis' mindset came in May 1941, when the Prime Minister ordered MI6 to assign its leading expert on the Third Reich to debrief Rudolf Hess. So, Foley found himself closeted for hours on end with the Deputy Führer of the Nazi state, after he had flown to Britain on a quixotic personal mission to propose a compromise peace. Although the prolonged interrogation merely led to the conviction that Hess was deranged—a judgement which led the British authorities to incarcerate their uninvited guest in a mental asylum—the episode at least confirmed Foley's reputation as the most respected 'old hand' on Germany within the British secret intelligence community.[7] Certainly, he seemed the obvious person to whom to turn 'if people wanted to know how the Germans would react to any particular deception plan', as his MI6 colleague again noted.[8]

Yet, Foley, too, for all his experience of, and expertise on, Germany was not the ideal person to promote the official adoption of *Plan Trojan Horse*.

The problem was that, despite his status as Britain's greatest expert on the inner workings of the Third Reich, he was essentially a secret intelligence field officer. His support for the proposed deception scheme and, even more, his considered advice on how best to pitch its misleading message to the Nazi spymasters and warlords, would prove invaluable as and when the project was given the go-ahead from on high. However, before Cholmondeley's daring conception could reach the stage at which Foley's technical counsel could advance its cause, the plan would have to negotiate the treacherous corridors of power in London, where sceptics and naysayers abounded. The novelist and sometime military staff officer, Anthony Powell, discerned the inherent tendency of Britain's Second World War bureaucracy to erect 'a really impregnable system of obstruction and pre-clusion'—as he put it in his novel, *The Military Philosophers*.[9] Indeed, Churchill himself denounced Britain's inter-service Joint Planning Staff as 'the whole machinery of negation'. They had incurred his wrath because of their habit of raising practical objections to the succession of pet military projects with which he bombarded them.[10] Major Frank Foley, who in the estimate of another of his professional peers was 'not a member of the establishment clique', lacked the personal contacts inside the political and military elite to overcome the instinctive resistance such an unconventional proposal as *Trojan Horse* was likely to provoke among them.[11] Indeed, Britain's most senior wartime military bureaucrat, General Ismay, consid-ered Cholmondeley's daring design to be a 'somewhat startling cover plan' when he encountered it, and entertained real doubts about 'whether it would work'.[12] What *Trojan Horse* sorely needed was an advocate conver-sant with the ways of Whitehall, familiar with its senior ranks and confident enough to urge the merits of this highly unorthodox operation upon them. The plan found just such a champion in the person of Lieutenant Com-mander the Honorable Ewen S. Montagu, Royal Naval Volunteer Reserve (RNVR).

Ewen Montagu was the third member of the triumvirate the Twenty Committee selected from its ranks to investigate whether Cholmondeley's proposal could be turned into a practical proposition. Although Montagu would later describe himself as 'a mere Lieutenant Commander R.N.V.R.' attempting to 'persuade all these very senior officers to co-operate' in the development of a deception which might never be implemented, in fact he was an ideal candidate for the job.[13] For a start, he enjoyed the social cachet of having been born into the Anglo-Jewish aristocracy on 29 March 1901, as the second son of Baron Swaythling, a prominent merchant banker. His uncle was Edwin Samuel Montagu, the Liberal MP and Cabinet minister, whose most important government post was as a moderately progressive Secretary of State for India from 1917 until 1922. Ewen Montagu also availed himself of the educational opportunities open to those of his class and wealth: he attended Westminster Public School and the universities of Harvard and Cambridge. Moreover, although the undergraduate degree he earned at Cambridge was not particularly distinguished, it did enable him to embark upon professional legal studies. These culminated in his qualification as a barrister in 1924. Montagu then devoted himself for the next decade and a half to practising at the bar on England's western circuit before 'taking silk' (i.e., becoming a King's Counsel) in 1939, only six months before the outbreak of the Second World War.[14]

However, despite his elevated social status and his learned profession, he hoped to see active service in the war. To this end, he had enrolled in the supplementary reserve of the RNVR as early as 1938, his choice of the senior service being determined by his self-confessed 'mania' for sailing. As an accomplished yachtsman, with a working 'knowledge of seamanship, boat handling and navigation', he was rapidly called to arms—once war broke out—at the ripe old age of thirty-eight. Yet, his training as a 'Probationary Temporary-Acting-Sub Lieutenant' ('the lowest-known form of marine life', according to Montagu's Petty Officer instructor) was soon interrupted, when the naval authorities tumbled to the fact that they had a King's Counsel amongst their apprentice junior officers. He was reassigned, immediately, to specialized study and then appointed as an assistant staff officer (in Intelligence) to the Royal Navy's Humberside headquarters at Hull. There, his initiative in establishing an intelligence-gathering system targeting the crews of neutral merchant ships and trawlers earned him promotion to rank of Lieutenant Commander and also caught the eye of Rear Admiral J. H. Godfrey, the overall director of Naval Intelligence. Godfrey was a driven and exacting taskmaster but, as Montagu also quickly understood, he was an intelligence chief of real genius too. 'Uncle John', as Godfrey was known, ironically, to his underlings (since he was far from avuncular in his dealings with them) had two personal assistants (one of them being Ian Fleming, the future creator of the fictional spy extraordinaire, James Bond) and a personal administrative Section 17, within the Naval Intelligence Division (NID). Having summoned Montagu in November 1940 to work in the NID on a trial basis, Uncle John was sufficiently impressed by the barrister turned covert warrior to put him in charge of a small, separate sub-section, designated 17 M, within his own department, to deal with all non-operational 'special intelligence', i.e., 'Ultra' material. In the early days of 1941 the decrypts which fell into that category were largely the result of Bletchley Park's successful attack on the Abwehr's hand ciphers. Access to such secret information naturally qualified Montagu to liaise with Section B1A of MI5 and other parties involved in the development of the double-cross system. So, he was the obvious choice to represent the NID on the Twenty Committee, on which he served continuously from its very inception in January 1941 until its 226th and final meeting in May 1945 (save for a three-month mission to the United States from December 1941 to February 1942). In the end, Godfrey was so pleased with his subordinate's work that, in July 1942, he established a new 'Section 12' within the NID to supersede 17 M and function 'as a combined special intelligence and deception section with Montagu in charge'.[15]

What had brought Montagu to the centre of Britain's double-cross and deception campaigns against the Third Reich was a combination of natural ability, innate inclination, and formal education. Godfrey recognized that Montagu possessed 'the sort of cork-screw mind' required for this 'most complicated' business.[16] However, the latter also had an instinctive liking for the dark arts of intrigue and deceit. Thus, the way he came to regard *Plan Trojan Horse* as 'in essence a large-scale fraud' explains the relish with which he set about its promotion:

> my first excursion into crime gave me an understanding of how fascinating a criminal's life can be, and why some men and women prefer it to any other . . . [17]

Such gusto for the game of double-cross, allied to his imaginative flair, certainly prepared Montagu to play an effective part in that subtle sport. What turned him into one of its most accomplished exponents, however, was his education and subsequent career as a barrister. Professionally formed in the adversarial tradition of the English common law, Montagu was accustomed to pitting his wits against opposing counsel in courtroom duels. In that arena of legal combat, he had become adept at fathoming his antagonist's mindset and manipulating it to his advantage. Having 'to learn throughout our career to put ourselves in our opponents' place and try to anticipate what he will think and do on *his* information', as Montagu later put it, was a far better training for the practice of deception against the enemy in wartime, than even the most successful military career could provide. Again, the lawyer's imperative need to master a given brief thoroughly, with meticulous attention to telling details, further equipped Lieutenant Commander Montagu for the task of duping the enemy with convincing, comprehensive, and consistent cover stories.[18]

So innate aptitudes, in tandem with acquired skills, propelled Montagu into what he himself described as a 'fascinating job' at 'the real centre of things'.[19] Indeed, in the course of his duties, he liaised with senior levels of command in both the British and American navies.[20] He was also inducted into some of the most sensitive secrets of the entire Allied war effort, like 'Ultra' and the construction of the atomic bomb.[21] Moreover, his personal background and elite education imbued him with the confidence to move in such elevated military circles. Admittedly, on occasion, Montagu's assertiveness got the better of his sense of decorum. One such episode occurred as a result of a ham-fisted attempt involving General Mason-MacFarlane, the Governor and GOC Gibraltar, to help sell one of the cover plans for *Operation Torch* to the Germans. 'Mason-Mac', in a move approved by deception authorities in London, sought to persuade the Germans that the military build-up at the Rock was part of a large-scale endeavour to relieve the heavily bombed island of Malta. He did so by exhorting the Rock's garrison, via a supposedly 'closed broadcast', to spare no effort in the bid to assist the beleaguered British forces on Malta. Of course, that clumsy intervention had the exactly opposite effect to what 'Mason-Mac' and the London-based deception planners had intended. The Abwehr station in Madrid immediately assured Berlin that Malta could not be the object of the Allies' military build-up at Gibraltar, since no one in their right mind would announce to an entire garrison, in advance, the real target of a military operation. Montagu was so incensed by this ill-considered move that he personally demanded there be no repetition of such follies in the future, lest they undermine Britain's best efforts at double-cross and deception. Unfortunately, the NID officer to whom he entrusted the duty of conveying the gist of this urgent request to the War Office was so impressed by Montagu's protest-cum-plea that he handed its actual text over to them. The Director of Military Intelligence, Major General F. H. N. Davidson, was less than amused by Montagu's call for 'half-witted generals' to be 'henceforward prevented from butting in as amateur deceivers into an art they didn't understand'. Indeed, the Director of Military Intelligence (DMI) demanded that the upstart naval intelligence officer be disciplined for this brazen show of disrespect to his military superiors. Ironically, it fell to 'Uncle John' Godfrey—whose own legendary tactlessness and talent for plain speaking would cost him his job as head of Naval Intelligence, within a few weeks (in late November 1942)—to remind Montagu of the need to be more circumspect in the drafting and distribution of official documents.[22] Yet, Montagu's healthy irreverence for the established chain of command would prove of vital service in the promotion of the unconventional plan to use a dead body to pass misleading documents to the enemy. A less assertive or more deferential advocate could hardly have prevailed against the efforts of his military superiors to dilute or downgrade the project.

So, it was just as well that Montagu backed Charles Cholmondeley's *Trojan Horse* plan right from the beginning. He did this because he realized that the Allies would need cover plans for future operations in the Mediterranean, after *Torch* had been successfully completed. Accordingly, he 'strongly supported' Cholmondeley's unorthodox suggestion when the Twenty Committee considered it on 5 November 1942. He was particularly attracted by the prospect Cholmondeley's scheme offered of planting 'a really convincing "high level" document which would mislead the enemy' as to the Allies' next major target in that region of conflict.[23] That is to say, Montagu had grasped, immediately, that *Plan Trojan Horse* actually held out the possibility of affecting the Axis High Command's deployment of their forces across a whole theatre of war. So, this deception might achieve what was virtually unprecedented in the entire history of warfare, namely, the misdirection of the enemy on the grand strategic plane, where the decisions are made which settle the outcomes of campaigns and wars.[24] No wonder, then, that Montagu was an instant convert to the project and promptly put himself forward 'to go into the question of obtaining the necessary body, the medical problems and the formulation of a plan'.[25] Doubtless, the other members of the Twenty Committee appreciated that if anybody could make a go of this vastly ambitious strategic deception it was the dynamic and determined Commander Montagu. However, in directing that an officer from the Royal Air Force (Cholmondeley) and another from the British Army (Foley, who was also, of course, in MI6) join Montagu in investigating the feasibility of *Plan Trojan Horse*, his colleagues, likely, were not just agreeing with their chairman that it 'was essential to the scheme that it should be worked out by the different services'.[26] They probably understood, too, that Flight Lieutenant Cholmondeley and Major Foley could act as buffers between Montagu's buccaneering style and the more staid service bureaucracies.

If Masterman ensured that Montagu had suitable partners in promoting *Trojan Horse*, then he was careful, also, to give the latter the benefit of his considerable experience of institutional politics, as an academic administrator and history don at Oxford. Masterman's former pupil, Second World War colleague in British Intelligence, and later fellow historian at Oxford, Hugh Trevor-Roper (who was not known for holding many people in high esteem) came to regard 'J.C.' with a grudging respect, as this post-war assessment shows: 'he is a skilful operator, a man of great, not to say excessive prudence' who 'prefers to lead his followers' at 'a gentle pace, towards attainable ends'.[27] In fact, Montagu, himself, had been impressed, already, by 'the supreme tact, equanimity and common sense' with which Masterman presided over the deliberations of the Twenty Committee. So, he was prepared to pay close attention to practical advice from that quarter, on how best to obtain the approval of his superiors for the planned deception. Masterman's suggestion was to present the top brass with a virtual fait accompli. He reasoned thus: since the Chiefs of Staff's reflex reaction would be to reject such a fantastical scheme as inherently impractical, the 'only hope was to provide them with everything ready and completely convincing'.[28]

The most obvious problems that had to be solved, before *Plan Trojan Horse* could be passed on to the Chiefs of Staff as a practical project were medical ones. Even assuming a suitable corpse could be found to serve as the notional victim of an accidental drowning in foreign waters, could it be presented in such a condition as to pass muster in a post-mortem examination conducted by hostile hands?[29] Only an expert could answer that crucial question, upon which the whole fate of this audacious deception depended. Accordingly, Montagu sought the advice of Britain's most eminent forensic pathologist, Sir Bernard Spilsbury, on this vital matter. Spilsbury had earned a legendary reputation, not only within medico-legal circles but also amongst the wider British public, as an apparently infallible authority on the causes of death—especially in suspicious circumstances. Certainly, his fame rested on a foundation of hard work: he would perform more than 25,000 autopsies during his career, managing to conduct as many as 1,000 a year when he was in his professional prime.[30] Again, he appeared as an expert witness for the prosecution (he made many fewer courtroom appearances for the defence) in almost 200 murder trials.[31] Not content with clocking up long hours analysing specimens in his laboratory, he also undertook detailed, on-the-spot investigations of crime scenes, often under the grimmest conditions. He also personally arranged ballistic and other experiments to try and determine fatal sequences of events.[32] Still, it was the quality of his interventions in a series of sensational murder trials, rather than the sheer quantity of his labours in the field of forensic pathology, that did most to establish that branch of medical science as a legitimate source of evidence for British criminal prosecutions and his own renown as its most credible exponent.

In his celebrated essay on the 'Decline of the English Murder' (published first in *Tribune* in February 1946), George Orwell defined the golden age of homicide in Britain, its 'Elizabethan period' as it were, as lasting from roughly '1850 to 1925'. Within that 'great period', Orwell identified eight individuals and one duo as killers 'whose reputation has stood the test of time'. Dr Bernard Spilsbury served as a key expert witness in all five of these capital crimes which had been committed after the commencement of his career as a forensic pathologist. Of the other four cases, three were brought to trial before Spilsbury was born, whilst the fourth—the notorious case of 'Jack the Ripper'—occurred whilst the future pathologist was still a youngster and, in any event, never led to any prosecution.[33] Still, the cases from Orwell's hall of homicidal infamy in which Spilsbury did become involved, along with some others, were more than sufficient to make him a household name throughout the United Kingdom. In February 1935, readers of the mass-circulation *Daily Express* newspaper nominated stories about Sir Bernard, alongside those about such famous personalities as the US President Franklin D. Roosevelt and the screen goddess Greta Garbo, as among their favourites.[34] Nor was this celebrity a flash in the pan; for in the previous decade, Spilsbury had been voted, regularly, on to the list of the twenty most famous living Englishmen.[35] Spilsbury's attainment of a public renown not enjoyed by any medico-legal expert before or since was a function, to some extent, of the classic age of capital crime in which he lived and worked. During the first forty years of the twentieth century, a number of social and cultural factors coalesced to produce a unique popular interest in murder stories and the courtroom dramas in which they usually culminated. A mass readership avidly digested the extensive coverage of murder trials which not only scandal sheets like the *News of the World* but even serious newspapers like *The Times* provided.[36] Moreover, such newspaper accounts could be as graphic as they were comprehensive, in an era when reporting restrictions were unknown.[37] Yet, if Spilsbury was paraded before a mass audience, so were his professional peers, and none of them came to command the same national acclaim. Indeed, Bernard Spilsbury's fame spread far beyond Britain's own shores, with the *Washington Post* hailing him, in March 1938, as 'England's modern Sherlock Holmes'.[38]

What initially won Spilsbury the kind of popular admiration later ages would accord to stars of show business and the sports field was his seeming technical brilliance. This was perhaps most dazzlingly displayed in what one of his biographers calls 'one of the most ghastly dismemberments in forensic history'.[39] In a determined effort to obliterate all physical traces of his victim (one Emily Beilby Kaye), her assailant (Herbert 'Pat' Mahon) 'had variously burnt, boiled, chopped up and pulverised' her remains.[40] In an exercise he himself likened to 'building up a jigsaw puzzle', Spilsbury managed to reconstruct the deceased's skeleton (minus its missing skull) from upwards of 1,000 fragments of bone. The pathologist also succeeded in identifying sufficient of the butchered body parts to discover that the dead woman had been between three and four months pregnant. This medical finding supplied a motive for a murderous attack by the already married Mahon.[41] Moreover, Spilsbury also copper-fastened the Crown's case against Mahon by stoutly maintaining in court, contrary to the accused's assertions, that Emily Kaye could not have suffered a fatal injury in accidentally falling and striking her head against a coal scuttle.[42] So grateful was the Home Office for Spilsbury's exceptional services to the prosecutors on this occasion that—in a rare gesture—it awarded him an *ex gratia* payment of fifty guineas.[43]

This was only the latest in a series of honours bestowed by a grateful British establishment on the man whom the press had already crowned as 'the undisputed superstar of British legal medicine'.[44] Other tokens of official appreciation predated his spectacular contribution to the successful prosecution of Herbert Mahon. Thus, at the start of 1911—when he was still only thirty-three years of age—Spilsbury was appointed Honorary Pathologist to the Home Office, an onerous position he would retain until 1934.[45] Again, in January 1923, he became the first forensic pathologist to receive a knighthood, once more at the relatively young age of forty-five.[46] Whilst all of these signs of official pleasure, undoubtedly, were rewards for his forensic services rendered to the Crown, it was his professional demeanour in public trials that really explains his rapid preferment. Indeed, it was his courtroom manner, even more than the matter of his testimony as an expert witness, which swayed judges, juries, and journalists in case after case. For a start, Spilsbury cut an elegant figure in the witness box: tall and austerely handsome, he always made sure that he was immaculately attired for his courtroom appearances, even to the last detail of a daily fresh, floral buttonhole.[47] Still, clothes were insufficient to turn Spilsbury into what one prominent English judge termed 'the ideal scientific witness'.[48] It was his comportment under oath that most impressed all who witnessed it. He communicated his evidence and opinions with concision and conviction, taking care to express them in clear and non-technical language. Again, he remained so preternaturally calm and composed under critical cross-examination that the best efforts of defence counsel to question Spilsbury's conclusions often only tightened the pathologist's hold over the juries in murder cases.[49] Indeed, Mr Justice Darling, who presided over the trial in 1922 of Major Herbert Rouse Armstrong (one of Orwell's 'immortals') for the murder of his wife, was so captivated by Spilsbury's self-assured performance as a prosecution witness in the case, that he paid the pathologist an almost lyrical tribute in his judicial summing-up:

> Do you remember Dr Spilsbury? Do you remember how he stood and the way in which he gave his evidence? . . . Did you ever see a witness who more thoroughly satisfied you that he was absolutely impartial, absolutely fair, absolutely indifferent as to whether his evidence told for the one side or the other . . . You should recollect and consider the demeanour of every witness . . . and when you consider Dr Spilsbury, when you have to say whether you trust the opinion that he gave, you are entitled then to remember his demeanour . . . and to act accordingly.[50]

With such extravagant appreciations of Spilsbury's apparent impeccability as an expert witness a matter of legal record, no wonder that lesser mortals came to quail at the prospect of questioning his professional judgement in court. One defence counsel was seemingly so daunted by the task as to address Spilsbury as 'Saint Bernard', when cross-examining the famous figure.[51] Moreover, while Spilsbury himself denied any pretensions to omnipotence, his alleged disavowal smacked more of self-esteem than self-deprecation: 'I have never claimed to be God, but merely His locum on His weekends off.'[52]

Of course, Sir Bernard's reputation for virtual infallibility in the field of morbid anatomy and forensic pathology made him appear to be the ideal expert to whom to turn for advice on the medical feasibility of *Plan Trojan Horse*. Certainly, Britain's most pre-eminent pathologist should be able to offer the best-informed opinion available on the medical aspects of the proposed deception. Again, medical approval from such a canonical—if not formally canonized—authority should make quite an impression on Britain's warlords—whose imprimatur was also necessary before *Plan Trojan Horse* could be launched. Finally, Spilsbury's natural discretion should ensure that he would not seek to learn more about the top-secret scheme than he needed to know, and also, that what he was told would go no further. In Montagu's estimate the distinguished pathologist was 'closer to being an oyster' than anybody he had ever encountered, even during his wartime career as a naval intelligence officer.[53] Sir Bernard could be relied upon to clam up where *Trojan Horse* was concerned. Admittedly, there were other aspects of Spilsbury's personality which made the prospect of approaching him, personally, over the covert project rather less attractive. He had impressed even his fellow doctors as an essentially 'retiring and outwardly frigid' individual, who 'disliked visits from strangers' and who could seem 'somewhat distant', even to 'casual professional acquaintances'.[54] Still, Montagu knew that he could appeal to Sir Bernard's pride, professional and patriotic, in consulting him on such weighty business of the state. Spilsbury had revealed how intertwined personal and national self-esteem were in his outlook, in an affirmation he made concerning the desirability of establishing a centralized 'Medico-Legal Institute' in London in the early 1930s:

> [The Institute] should be entirely British; there is no need to seek enlightenment from other countries as to our requirements ... the study of pathology in this country needs no guidance ... from other nations.[55]

Spilsbury did answer his own nation's call, even if somewhat belatedly. He proved elusive, initially, when Montagu—in furtherance of his brief from the Twenty Committee of 5 November to inquire into the practicality of *Plan Trojan Horse*—tried to pin him down to meet at a particular time and place.[56] However, after a couple of frustrating weeks, Montagu did succeed in arranging an appointment with the man he considered to be a 'great pathologist'.[57] So, some time between 20 and 25 November, there occurred the medical consultation which determined the fundamental feasibility of employing a dead body to transmit misleading information to the enemy. Montagu and Spilsbury met in one of the latter's clubs, the Junior Carlton, in Pall Mall. As they sipped sherry in that rather palatial setting, the naval intelligence officer who had no time for small talk, and the forensic pathologist who had no talent for it, promptly got down to business.

Without divulging any of the wider operational details or the strategic stakes involved in the planned *ruse de guerre*, Montagu informed Spilsbury of the military need to plant a corpse on the enemy through the unneutral offices of Franco's Spain. He then raised the critical question of whether the Germans and Spaniards could be induced 'to accept a floating body as that of a victim of an aircraft disaster'.[58] Spilsbury's response to this key inquiry, which he delivered after only a short pause for thought, was characteristically concise and confident:

> if the body of a man who had died from suitable natural or other causes was washed ashore in Spain, no one could tell, without a first class post mortem, that he had not died in an aeroplane crash. Victims of a crash very often died from shock and no water would be present in the lungs: Spaniards, as Roman Catholics, were averse to post mortems and did not hold them unless the cause of death was not only of great importance but was, on the face of it, doubtful: in addition, they had no really good pathologists.[59]

This categorical pronouncement by the celebrated pathologist on the possibility of using a corpse as an instrument of deception in the planned circumstances, was doubly welcome to Montagu and company. First, Sir Bernard's emphatic assurance that there were no insuperable medical barriers to the scheme smoothed the way for *Trojan Horse*'s immediate elaboration and future implementation. Secondly, Spilsbury's practical medical advice also made a material contribution to the deception's further development. He was undoubtedly correct in the opinion, which he gave to Montagu at the Junior Carlton club, on the vexed question of determining death by drowning. Even today, the medical profession has no infallible tests or procedures to prove that an individual has perished through drowning— not least because it is not uncommon for a person's lungs to engorge with fluid and become heavy, when the heart is failing terminally.[60] So, as Spilsbury noted, it would be inordinately difficult for any Spanish pathologist to affirm, with absolute certainty, that a body which had turned up in their coastal waters had not died due to drowning. However, as the British pathologist also observed, even if a Spanish post-mortem examination did arrive at that negative conclusion, there were plenty of other possible causes of death—serious accidental injury, exposure, and shock—compatible with the notion that a corpse, found adrift in the ocean, was the victim of a recent air crash.[61] Such inherent medical ambiguities not only helped protect the planted corpse from being unfrocked as a fraud; they also ensured that the search for likely candidates to play dead for *Trojan Horse* need not be confined only to those who had expired through ingesting sea water.[62] Moreover, Spilsbury also supplied Montagu with an invaluable contact to help him to locate the right dead man for the job. He referred the naval intelligence officer to his friend, William Bentley Purchase, HM Coroner for London's Northern District, who had qualified both as a medical doctor and as a barrister-at-law, as was usual for the holders of such an office in Britain's capital city. The procession of deceased individuals through the coroner's court, over which Bentley Purchase presided at St Pancras, did seem a good place to start the search for a corpse which might be pressed into his country's clandestine service.[63]

Greatly relieved by Sir Bernard Spilsbury's assurances about the medical feasibility of *Plan Trojan Horse*, Montagu hastened to give the good news to his colleagues. At their meeting in the afternoon of 26 November 1942, he reported on his conversation with the distinguished pathologist, 'from which it appeared that there were no medical obstacles to the plan'. Montagu also relayed Spilsbury's suggestion that Bentley Purchase would be the best person with whom to arrange 'the supply of a suitable body'. Buoyed by this encouragement from such an eminent medical authority, the Twenty Committee not only directed Montagu to approach the said coroner with a view to procuring the necessary corpse, but also authorized him to 'give Mr. Purchase some idea of the true reason for his request'.[64] Once more, Montagu found his quarry rather elusive at first, but he did manage to meet up with him in the second week of December 1942.[65] In consulting Bentley Purchase, as it happened, Montagu was addressing his unconventional proposal not just to a greatly respected medico-legal expert but also to a decorated hero of the First World War. His bravery under fire, while serving with the Royal Army Medical Corps, had earned him the Military Cross.[66] So, when requested by Ewen Montagu (who was also a friend) to aid in the acquisition of a dead body for a covert military purpose, he readily bowed to the demands of a country once more at war, stating that 'there would be no difficulty in providing a suitable corpse'. Indeed, he did not question the legality of such an exercise, even if he did allude to 'certain technical difficulties' that might arise 'with regard to the official disposal of the corpse'. Still, Bentley Purchase assured Montagu that he was confident about resolving such problems and, by the time of his next meeting with Montagu in mid December, he had decided how to proceed. Not only had he set in motion the arrangements for 'getting hold' of a suitable corpse, he had also devised an appropriate procedure for its formal disposal: he would issue a certificate stating that the body was 'being "removed out of England" for burial'.[67]

Yet, before a body could be subjected to such official process, it had to be found in the first place. Moreover, the search for a suitable corpse for treatment according to the needs of *Plan Trojan Horse* proved to be more protracted than the deception planners and their medical counsellors had imagined.

This was primarily because of the rather precise requirements which Montagu had stipulated to the Coroner as essential for the chosen corpse to meet: the 'body had to be that of a man who could pass as a Staff Officer who had no friends or relatives to claim him and who had died from reasonably undetectable causes'.[68] Montagu got the impression from the Coroner that satisfying the second of these conditions should not be too difficult, as a number of corpses turned up every year with no proof of identity or traceable relations.[69] However, the weeks crept by and the Old Year turned into the New, without Bentley Purchase receiving into his mortuary and/or coroner's court (both situated right next to St Pancras Hospital in Camden Town) a qualified candidate for the mission. Either the deceased had met his end in a manner all too inconsistent with death by drowning, exposure, or both, or he was mourned by concerned relatives, who might be reluctant to allow their dear departed one to be 'recycled' for an unspecified military project, and who also might be too indiscreet to be trusted in such a secret affair. As their fruitless quest dragged on, Montagu, Cholmondeley, and the other officers involved in the development of the deception grew increasingly exasperated at their paradoxical plight. There they were, caught up in the middle of humanity's greatest self-inflicted slaughter, the Second World War, and yet they still could not find a single cadaver to fit their bill. As Montagu later lamented, 'we felt like the Ancient Mariner—bodies, bodies, everywhere, nor any one to take!' Indeed, the deception planners got so desperate, as the weeks rolled by, that they even contemplated doing a 'Burke and Hare', i.e., robbing the grave of some freshly interred likely prospect for their purpose.[70] It was all to the good that they resisted this macabre temptation since a recently embalmed body was unlikely to convince even supposedly slipshod Spanish post-mortem examiners that it had met its demise in a plane crash out to sea. Injection marks from a wide-bore needle, the strong chemical odour of formalin-based embalming fluid and the firmness of the bodily flesh which such a solution causes would be dead giveaways.[71]

Of course, what certainly complicated the deception planners' task was the fact that they could not afford—for operational security reasons—to advertise even their search, let alone its purpose.[72] Still, when Bentley Purchase's own steady supply of 'customers' failed to produce a suitable candidate for the job, they realized that they would have to accept the risks involved in casting their net more widely. So, doubtless with the Coroner's cooperation, they spread a discreet word around London's hospitals and mortuaries, and one of these institutions finally delivered up the goods, on 28 January 1943. On that day, Glyndwr Michael, a 34-year-old Welsh labourer of no fixed abode passed away in St Stephen's Hospital, on the Fulham Road in Chelsea. Michael's death was due to the damage he had done to his liver, by swallowing rat poison containing phosphorus, in a suicide attempt two days earlier.[73] These medical circumstances of Michael's death seemed to match the deception planners' specification that the deceased should have 'died from reasonably undetectable causes' more or less perfectly. Thus, although the poison which Michael had taken had fatally impaired the functioning of his liver, Bentley Purchase did not believe that the real cause of death in this instance (i.e., the ingestion of phosphorus) would be uncovered in any subsequent post-mortem. This was so for three reasons: first, the deceased had only swallowed a small dose of the poison— an amount which had been insufficient to kill him outright; second, phosphorus is usually present in the human body—so the mere presence of this substance in the dead man's remains would not of itself signify anything medically abnormal; finally, immersion in sea water—the notional element in which the protagonist of *Trojan Horse* was meant to perish— often leads to a body's absorbing chemicals in quantities over and above its normal fair share.[74] The worst that could be detected would be 'faint traces of chemical action in the liver', which, as just noted, could be attributed to the body's immersion in the ocean.[75] Bentley Purchase's view of the difficulty of detecting phosphorus poisoning in a post-mortem reflected authoritative, contemporary opinion, as may be seen in the following statement made by Dr Sydney Smith (Regius Professor of Forensic Medicine at the University of Edinburgh, and an expert witness who had crossed swords with Sir Bernard Spilsbury in a number of celebrated murder trials) in the eighth edition of his reputed text-book, *Forensic Medicine*, published in 1943: 'the diagnosis of phosphorus poisoning is by no means easy'. Smith drew on his own considerable experience to support this judgement: 'I have seen cases of phosphorus poisoning which have been attended by skilled physicians, have been admitted to and have died in hospital, and on whom the autopsy has been performed by a skilled pathologist without the diagnosis of phosphorus poisoning having been made'.[76] Again, Bentley Purchase also understood that if and when Glyndwr Michael's thawed remains were subjected to a foreign post-mortem examination, they would be in the process of decomposition. This fact should both mask any symptoms of phosphorus poisoning and account for the absence of any of the usual signs associated with death by drowning.[77] So, allowing for the medical condition of the Welshman's corpse, and for the carefully staged way in which it was planned to present the cadaver to the Francoist authorities and their Nazi accomplices, it did not seem impossible to persuade them that this lost soul died as a result of drowning, exposure, or shock, after the aircraft on which he had been travelling crashed into the sea.

If Glyndwr Michael satisfied the deception planners' need for a person who 'had died from reasonably undetectable causes', he also appeared to fulfill their other requirements, too. Admittedly, this individual was hardly at the peak of physical fitness when he died by his own hand in London, in late January 1943. He had made his suicide attempt (which was to kill him two days later) in a common lodging house, apparently 'while temporarily insane' and, doubtless, in despair at the privations of his lonely existence as a homeless labourer.[78] This hard life had left him with a gaunt physique, which hardly equipped him to play even the posthumous part of a fit, active-service officer. However, Montagu was not dismayed when a senior British military figure questioned whether such a scrawny specimen could be passed off to the enemy as officer material. Montagu responded to this critical query by pointing out that the chosen corpse did not have to resemble the athletic officer-types prevalent on the front line, but rather their more ascetic counterparts rife within staff-officer circles.[79] After all, it was from within staff-officer ranks that a courier would be selected to carry top-secret documents, of the kind envisaged in *Trojan Horse*, on an overseas assignment. Within this less muscle-bound and more cerebral group, one might well encounter a 'wizened' staff officer of just the sort Anthony Powell depicts in his novel, *The Military Philosophers*, a work whose finely observed characters reflect, if they do not exactly replicate, the author's own real-life experiences and encounters while serving in Britain's wartime military bureaucracy.[80]

If Glyndwr Michael's somewhat emaciated frame did not disqualify him from serving as a passive agent for the planned *ruse de guerre*, then another legacy of his vagabondish existence positively fitted him for the part. By the time he took his own life, he was a desperately solitary soul, with no friends to speak of. He also seems to have lost all contact with his family. They were members of a mining community in South Wales and, at the time of Glyndwr's birth on 4 January 1909, they had resided at 136 Commercial Street, Aberbargoed. His father, Thomas Michael, was a colliery haulier in the local pit, whose slag heap loomed over the town. Thomas never married his son's mother, Sarah Ann Chadwick, who also bore him a daughter, Doris, in 1911. Such humble origins are no automatic barrier to personal development. However, his mother's illiteracy may have constituted an additional obstacle to Glyndwr's vocational advancement. Moreover, mental illness also seems to have blighted his career prospects. Indeed, the very fact that he could be described on his death certificate as 'a labourer of no fixed abode', in the middle of the Second World War, probably means that he had been declared unfit for military service—and very likely on grounds of mental incompetence.[81] In any case, the inner demons that drove Glyndwr Michael to take his own life also, apparently, prompted him to lose touch with the surviving members of his own family and much of the wider community. Such a socially isolated individual must have seemed an answer to the *Trojan Horse* planners' prayers.

Yet, for all that, when he came to publish his account of *Operation Mincemeat* a decade after it was staged, Ewen Montagu maintained that frantic efforts were made to inquire about the chosen corpse's past life and extant relatives. Montagu also noted in his book, entitled *The Man Who Never Was*, that the most anybody could be told about the dead man's proposed mission was that it would be of real service to his country, that it would be sanctioned by the topmost level of government and that the deceased would be given a decent burial, albeit under a *nom de guerre*, once his posthumous duty was done. Montagu then records that 'permission, for which our indebtedness is great, was obtained on condition that I should never let it be known whose corpse it was'.[82] However, the source of that authority to use a particular dead body for *Operation Mincemeat* is not specified in Montagu's text. Family assent is implied rather than explicitly stated and it is possible that approval actually came from an official quarter.

Certainly, the sequence of events which immediately followed on from Glyndwr Michael's death, afforded little enough time to trace and consult his kith and kin. Hardly had the deceased breathed his last in St Stephen's Hospital, Fulham, on Thursday 28 January 1943, than Bentley Purchase was called upon to assess the fitness of the mortal remains for the intended covert purpose. Having satisfied himself on that count, the Coroner had to arrange for the transportation of the body to the mortuary attached to his own court at St Pancras. Once the body was resting safely there, Bentley Purchase was able to make the necessary medical and legal arrangements for its processing, in accordance with the deception planners' desiderata. First, he made sure that no post-mortem examination, and particularly, no autopsy was performed on Glyndwr Michael's corpse, lest it leave traces which might come to light in a future investigation of the remains by foreign hands.[83] Then, on Thursday 4 February, Bentley Purchase presided over an inquest in his coroner's court at St Pancras, which officially concluded that the deceased 'did kill himself while of unsound mind' by 'phosphorus poisoning' in the form of 'rat poison'.[84] These proceedings might have given Montagu the only opportunity to consult members of the Michael family—always assuming any of them had actually attended the inquest.[85] However, this possibility can be virtually ruled out because of the contents of an outline plan for the deception which Montagu and Cholmondeley had typed up and circulated to their colleagues on the Twenty Committee for, and almost certainly in advance of, their meeting at 2.30 p.m. on the same Thursday, 4 February. In that five-page document it is categorically stated that 'a suitable body has been obtained and is now available'.[86] So, it seems fairly clear that Glyndwr Michael's posthumous fate had already been sealed by the time the coroner's court was held.

However, Michael's afterlife was also of finite duration, as Montagu and Cholmondeley emphasized in their submission to the Twenty Committee on 4 February; for they noted that, whilst the corpse was currently 'available', it would have to be 'used within the next three months or so'.[87] Bentley Purchase made sure that it would remain usable during that three-month period by preventing its immediate interment and keeping it preserved in a refrigerator in his mortuary. As pre-arranged with Montagu, he also dealt with the legal niceties by informing the registrar of the Metropolitan Borough of St Pancras that the body was going to be sent out of England for burial.[88] So, only a week elapsed, in all, between Michael's death and the conclusion of the formalities which allowed his cadaver to be placed in cold storage, pending developments, in St Pancras Mortuary. Again, even if those proceedings did take place with the approval of a member (or members) of Glyndwr Michael's family, the British authorities remained reluctant for a long time afterwards to admit the part they played in them. They were particularly anxious to avoid giving the impression that the British government had acted improperly in getting hold of a body to use in *Operation Mincemeat*. This concern was evident in the response of the British Ministry of Defence to the stated wish of Ewen Montagu to be allowed 'publish a true account of Operation MINCEMEAT'. In explaining to the Foreign Office the reasons for his opposition to Montagu's suggestion, Sir Harold Parker, Permanent Secretary to the Ministry of Defence (MOD), raised the following objection, among others, on 8 December 1950:

> any true account which commanded respect would have to show how, with the connivance of Mr. Bentley Purchase, a London coroner (who, I believe is still in office), those responsible for the deception were able to manipulate the law so as to secure possession of the body of a suicide.[89]

The same official informed Montagu on 20 December 1950, of the ministry's decision that 'publication of the facts of the operation would not be in the public interest', once more placing the necessary revelation of 'how the law was manipulated to secure possession of a corpse' at the top of the list of reasons for this conclusion. He also cited a more general principle to justify the MOD's opposition to disclosures about such covert actions:

> Activities of this kind may be necessary in the stress of war but I am sure that, on reflection, you will agree that Government ought to preserve a decent reticence about them, and that it would be wholly contrary to the public interest to disclose them, except for compelling reasons of State.[90]

In his reply to Parker's letter, Montagu denied that any law had been manipulated for the sake of *Operation Mincemeat*, maintaining that all the actions undertaken on its behalf were completely lawful.[91] However, after a conversation with Montagu, on 29 October 1952, Britain's post-war deception chief, John A. Drew, reported him as acknowledging that 'it would not enhance his prestige at the Bar if it were publicly known that he had been concerned with an operation such as "Mincemeat" which, inter alia, involved manipulation of the law in respect of the burial of corpses'.[92] Moreover, even when in 1953 the British government changed its mind about keeping a cloak of secrecy over this episode and permitted the publication of Montagu's *The Man Who Never Was*, along with another book about *Operation Mincemeat* (Ian Colvin's *The Unknown Courier*), official sensitivity on some issues had not diminished. The Joint Intelligence Committee refused to declassify any documents relating to certain specifics of the scheme. Pride of place among the points still to be considered as 'top secret' was given, once more, to 'the true means by which the corpse was obtained and any details from which the man's real identity could be inferred'.[93] Indeed, if by the start of 1953 the Ministry of Defence had resolved to give official leave to Montagu to publish his version of the *Mincemeat* deception, it was because he was officially regarded as 'a responsible person', fully aware of 'all the delicate points' and 'prepared to accept official guidance on particular facets of the story'.[94] The following excerpt from a letter sent to MI5's Guy Liddell, reveals how this guidance was given:

> As promised I send you herewith a copy of Montagu's first rough draft . . . The draft contains certain amendments which I have made and in particular you will see that there is no reference whatsoever to the Security Service as having had any part in the operation . . . or to the real source of the corpse. By making him an anonymous officer of one of the Services we avoid a great many difficulties. We also made the officer an only son and killed off his parents so that there is nobody to whom inquiries can be directed.[95]

Of course, the 'murder' of the corpse's notional parents was a purely literary execution. However, in the final text of Montagu's *The Man Who Never Was*, published in later 1953, its subject is stripped down to even barer bones than in the streamlined version being foisted on the author by British bureaucrats earlier that year. In the published work, the posthumous protagonist has also lost his social and professional status, with the removal of references to him, in the first draft, as 'an officer' and as belonging to an 'old service family'.[96]

However, perhaps the most significant officially inspired amendment to Montagu's earlier drafts of *The Man Who Never Was*, was the removal of any mention of Bentley Purchase's crucial role in making a suitable body available to play the part of the dead messenger in the deception plan. This enforced omission, in what another MOD official called 'Montagu's controlled version, in which delicate points had been modified', was a pity, not least because one of the author's earlier drafts recorded the Coroner who assisted the deception planners, as making a most cogent case for using an unclaimed dead body for purposes of state during a world war.[97] In that suppressed passage, the Coroner contends that to give the deceased a respectful burial, after he had rendered great posthumous service to his nation, was surely better than planting him in a pauper's grave or placing him on a dissection table. Indeed, he would receive a more honourable interment than many members of the armed forces or even unfortunate civilians caught up in the carnage of total war.[98] Despite such reassurance from Bentley Purchase, a much published authority in the field of medical jurisprudence, Montagu and his colleagues would experience pangs of conscience as they disturbed Glyndwr Michael's final repose to prepare him for his part as the deceased courier in *Operation Mincemeat*.[99] Such scruples proved that their moral sensibilities had not been degraded by combat with a foe as barbaric as Nazi Germany. Yet, the overriding necessity of defeating Hitler's murderous and merciless regime clearly justified, in the deception planners' minds, the enlisting of a dead body for the covert project. Still, they treated the dead Welshman with as much respect as possible during the development and execution of the secret scheme. Moreover, if all went according to the deception plan, Glyndwr Michael would be buried with full military honours in Spanish earth—the kind of dignified funeral denied by the Third Reich to millions of its victims.

With the requisite body now placed in cold storage, Montagu and Cholmondeley were free to draw up an outline plan for the operation and request official authority to proceed with its implementation. Before presenting such a document to the Twenty Committee, Montagu had one final duty to perform, however. He had to obtain a new code name for the project. This had to be done not only to avoid an appellation like *Trojan Horse* giving too much of the covert game away, but also because official code names were allocated centrally by the ISSB, on lists distributed to the various armed services.[100] When Montagu went to consult the latest list of code names approved by the ISSB for Admiralty use, he found one to be irresistible: it both appealed to his 'somewhat macabre' sense of humour and seemed so gruesomely apt, as to augur well for the success of the enterprise.[101]

So it was under the code name *Operation Mincemeat* that Montagu and Cholmondeley submitted their plan for consideration by the Twenty Committee, on 4 February. Its stated purpose was to pass to the Axis apparently top-secret documents, relating to a forthcoming Anglo–American offensive in the Mediterranean, 'in such circumstances that they will regard them as the orders for the next operation to be carried out by the Allies'.[102] The authors of the *Mincemeat* plan also showed how profoundly they appreciated the essential aim of such a strategic deception: it should affect enemy actions (and their troop dispositions, above all), not merely shape their attitudes. The object of the exercise would be to persuade the enemy High Command to deploy their forces to counter the notional threat conjured up by *Mincemeat*, rather than concentrate in defence of the real target to be assaulted by the Western Allies in the Mediterranean Sea later in 1943.[103] The means envisaged for duping the Axis remained the same as in Cholmondeley's original suggestion for this covert operation:

> A dead body, dressed in Officer's uniform, and carrying [misleading] ... papers, should be dropped from an aircraft, together with some portions of wreckage from a suitable aircraft, in a position whence it will probably wash ashore on Spanish territory. The impression to be conveyed being that a courier carrying important 'hand of officer' documents was en route for Algiers in an aircraft which crashed.[104]

Naturally, the plan's promoters were also careful to reassure their colleagues on the Twenty Committee that earlier concerns about the feasibility of *Operation Mincemeat*, from the medical viewpoint, could be discounted:

> Expert opinion has been taken and it is not thought that the enemy would be able to discover that the body had died in some other way. This is made the more probable as the Spaniards will not be likely to hand the body over to the enemy (but to a British Consul) and do not approve of post mortems.[105]

They were also anxious to persuade their peers that this venture, for all its unorthodox aspects, was not a mission impossible, but rather had every chance of succeeding. Indeed, Montagu and Chomondeley rated *Mincemeat*'s 'prospects of success' as high. They did so for two reasons: first, 'from experience' they knew that the Spaniards would 'probably allow the Germans to have photographs or copies of the documents' (as they had done, of course, with some of the papers lost in the Catalina crash of September 1942); secondly, because they reckoned, again in the light of their considerable experience in matching wits with the Nazis, that the Germans would find it impossible not to take such a documentary windfall at face value.[106]

The only difficulties which Montagu and Chomondeley contemplated at this stage of *Mincemeat*'s development were practical matters that could be solved by appropriate care and attention. Thus, in addition to stressing that the available body would not keep longer than three months on ice, they issued another caution:

The body must be dropped within 24 hours of its being removed from its present place in London. The flight, once laid on, must not be cancelled or postponed.[107]

So, the deception planners, it seemed, would have to have cast-iron arrangements in place to ensure the prompt delivery of the body to its destination. Otherwise, the rapid onset of decomposition, after the body had started thawing, could endanger the whole credibility of the deception. Again, the British armed service in whose uniform it was decided to dress the cadaver, would have to be prepared to handle potentially awkward questions about the identity of the deceased and the circumstances of his death.[108]

Actually, at the meeting of the Twenty Committee where the Montagu–Cholmondeley plan for *Operation Mincemeat* was discussed, it seems to have been assumed by all present that the Army was the natural service to which the corpse could be 'called' to do his duty as a courier of top-secret documents. Thus, the War Office representative on the Committee was directed 'to go into the question of providing the body with a name, necessary papers, etc'. However, the Twenty Committee still regarded the cooperation of Britain's other armed services as indispensable for the implementation of the planned deception: Air Intelligence would have to get their ministry to lay on an aircraft to transport the body and to drop it into the sea off the Spanish coast, at a spot which Naval Intelligence should get the Admiralty to pinpoint.[109]

Still, the Twenty Committee did not wait until all these practical details were settled and all the administrative arrangements made before officially endorsing *Operation Mincemeat*. Instead, they formally adopted the Montagu–Cholmondeley plan at their early-February meeting and thereby initiated the bureaucratic procedure for obtaining approval from Allied grand strategists for the deception.[110] The readiness of the Twenty Committee's members to champion a scheme still in process of elaboration probably stemmed from their understanding that the venture was a timely one. Montagu and Cholmondeley had identified Sicily in their outline plan as a likely 'real target' for Allied invasion in 1943, as indeed it was.[111] Anglo–American agreement had been reached at the Casablanca conference, a couple of weeks earlier, to attack Italy's largest Mediterranean island, not later than 'the favourable July moon period' of the forthcoming summer.[112] Such an ambitious amphibious assault could turn into a bloody catastrophe if the island were packed with defenders—especially well-equipped and well-led German ones. So, all concerned with the planning of what was to be the largest seaborne assault in the history of human warfare to date appreciated that enemy forces had to be spread-eagled across the Mediterranean by Allied feints at other targets, for the invasion of Sicily to have any chance of success. Clearly, the Twenty Committee concluded that in *Operation Mincemeat* it had come up with just the ruse required to divert German forces in the Mediterranean away from Sicily. Accordingly, they also made sure, at their 4 February meeting, to arrange that Colonel John Bevan, head of the London Controlling Section—Britain's central body for the overall planning of coordination and implementation of strategic deception plans—should be brought into the picture. It would be Bevan's task to approach the Inter-Service Directors of Plans (who reported to the Chiefs of Staff) and press the virtues of *Operation Mincemeat* upon Britain's warlords.[113]

Consequently, an awesome weight might be placed upon the brittle shoulders of Glyndwr Michael—not just the lives of those tens of thousands of Allied soldiers set to storm the Sicilian shore in mid summer 1943, but also the fate of millions of people whom the invasion might help liberate from Nazi Germany's brutal tyranny. Whether the chosen corpse would really get the chance to have posthumous greatness thrust upon him, however, was still in the laps of the gods—or at least within the gift of one of their number.

Only if *Mincemeat*'s backers could placate and persuade what Anthony Powell calls 'the Voodoo deity of the whole Civil Service', that 'mystic holy essence incarnate of arguing, encumbering, delaying, hair-splitting, all for the best of reasons', would Glyndwr Michael be called to arms.[114]

3

Grand Stratagem

At first, it seemed as if *Operation Mincemeat*'s advocates should find a receptive audience in the Western Allies' councils of war during early 1943. After all, the proposed deception plan appeared well suited to the purposes of the strategy agreed by Anglo–American warlords (including the British Prime Minister and the American President) at the Casablanca Conference, in January of that year. Their grand design was calculated to take the fight to their enemies on a truly global scale. In this strategic scheme the early seizure of Sicily was given precedence: it should contribute to 'making the Mediterranean lines of communication more secure' and also diminish German strength on the Russian front, whilst increasing Allied pressure on Mussolini's Italy.[1] Admittedly, Anglo–American accord at Casablanca on a joint strategy for the worldwide fight against the Axis and Japan had not been easy, because of divergent priorities between the UK and the USA. There had been free and frank exchanges between the American Joint Chiefs of Staff and the British Chiefs of Staff before their differences of opinion could be reconciled, at least up to a point.[2] Yet, General George C. Marshall, the US Army's Chief of Staff, and his colleagues had conceded, reluctantly, that operational and logistical realities ruled out a full-scale invasion of North-Western Europe for 1943. So, the Americans eventually agreed to mount *Operation Husky* (code name for the Allied invasion of Sicily in July 1943) instead, despite their concern that such an additional Mediterranean campaign might act as 'a suction pump' draining men and *matériel* away from 'the main plot', to use Marshall's critical phraseology.[3] Undoubtedly, the planned investment of human and material resources in the attack on Sicily was on the grandest scale: the invasion fleet of 3,200 vessels would be the largest armada the world had ever seen and it would transport a total of 180,000 troops along with 18,000 military vehicles and 1,800 artillery pieces to the Sicilian shore, during the

initial invasion. *Operation Husky*, in fact, would amount to the larges
amphibious assault in the history of warfare, up to that time.[4] Yet, eve1
such a formidable force might not prevail in this most daunting an(
disaster-prone form of warfare. Certainly, the storming of a hostile shore
the seizure of beachheads and their expansion for a concerted drive inlan(
would all be jeopardized by concentrated resistance from units of th(
German Army, which had already impressed US military intelligence a
'strictly hot mustard'.[5] The Supreme Allied Commander for *Husky*, General Eisenhower, overtly warned the Anglo–American strategists o1
20 March, 1943 about this very danger:

> There is unanimous agreement among all commanders ... that if substantial
> German ground troops should be placed in the region (of Sicily) prior to the
> attack, the chances for success become practically nil and the project should
> be abandoned.[6]

Given this appreciation by Allied senior commanders of the need to kee[
German reinforcements well away from Sicily, British deception planners—
to whom responsibility for cover plans in the Mediterranean was assigned a1
Casablanca—had to develop 'a plan within a plan'. In fact, they had beer
charged, by the British Chiefs of Staff, on 29 January 1943, with formulating
an overall deception strategy, designed to present the Axis with apparen1
menaces on all sides. Seemingly threatened on many fronts, the enem)
could be expected to retain their forces more or less in position and no1
heavily reinforce the Russian one, in particular. However, at the same time
British deception planners were exhorted by their military chiefs to do al
they could to retard the flow of enemy reinforcements to the island o1
Sicily.[7] This last assignment was a particularly tall order. The problem wa:
one of geo-strategic logic: in view of the imminent expulsion of Axis force:
from North Africa—although stubborn German resistance would delay the
inevitable end in Tunisia until mid May 1943—at the hands of the converging Eighth Army and the *Torch* forces, the Allies' next offensive move
seemed all too obvious. The Italian island of Sicily lay only ninety miles of1
the Tunisian coast.[8] Accordingly, the British cover planners did not attemp1
the impossible task of trying to persuade the enemy High Command that the
Allies had no intention of ever moving against Sicily. Instead, they sought to
convince Hitler and his advisers that—for logistical and strategic reasons—
the Western Allies would attack the Axis forces in the Eastern Mediterranean
and the Balkans first and, only later, descend upon the territory of fascist

Italy.[9] Yet, any attempt to plant a fear of this kind 'out of the blue', as it were, in the consciousness of the enemy's commanders would have been unlikely to succeed, as the in-house history of British deception in World War Two notes:

> Strategic deception can seldom claim, by some brilliant coup, to cause the enemy to change his mind or do something on the spur of the moment which he had no intention of doing, but it can play up to his fears or his pre-conceived ideas, and give in his mind reality to these pre-conceived ideas.[10]

Of course, a deception deliberately fashioned so as to prey upon the target's secret strategic preoccupations should be cost-effective too. It should be able to summon phantom armies from within the enemy warlord's psyche to amplify the relatively modest means employed to support the subterfuge. Indeed, the Allies were especially fortunate in having Adolf Hitler as their primary antagonist, for the Führer turned out to be constitutionally incapable of making any rational, objective calculation of the forces opposing him—a fact which Allied deception planners came to comprehend, to their considerable advantage:

> The risk was taken that Hitler's world strategy complex and the anxieties caused by it would outweigh with him the probability, and it should have been the certainty, that the Allies had not the resources to undertake many of the operations against which he felt compelled to insure himself.[11]

Still, the notional threats posed by Allied feints, however impractical in reality, had to seem plausible to Hitler and his confidants. Only, when the Nazi leader's particular worries had been pinpointed, could they be exploited so as to entice him into making military mistakes and mis-deployments. 'Knowledge of the trend of enemy anxiety', as another British post-war assessment put it, was the key to success in strategic deception; for on that 'foundation of fear' it became possible 'to build up a ficticious and misleading structure and to represent Allied capabilities and intentions as very different from what they really were'. Moreover, as the same appraisal noted, 'the principal channel through which such knowledge became available was ULTRA'.[12] So, it was the code-breakers of Bletchley Park who ultimately enabled British deception planners to tune their siren songs precisely into Hitler's mental frequency.

Yet, however obvious it might seem that Ultra's secrets should have guided Allied deception strategy from the very beginning, this point had

eluded the British Chiefs of Staff when they established the London
Controlling Section (LCS) in June 1942. Although the brief of this body,
which reported directly to the COS, was 'to prepare deception plans on
a world-wide basis with the object of causing the enemy to waste his
military resources', no one in high authority had seen fit to arrange
automatic access for any of its personnel to Ultra material. Such a state of
affairs could have deprived the LCS of the most reliable secret intelligence on the Nazis' strategic concerns and calculations.[13] Indeed, had
that situation been allowed to continue, it could have robbed Britain's
central strategic planners of the ability to batten on to their foe's pre-
existing fears, all the better to misinform and mislead them. It was 'the
only deceptioneer in daily contact with the whole of Special (i.e. Ultra)
Intelligence' as the irrepressible Ewen Montagu later described himself,
who rectified this serious systemic sin of omission. He approached the
head of Britain's spy service, Brigadier Sir Stewart Menzies (who exercised authority over Bletchley Park and the distribution of its precious
cryptanalytical product) for permission to pass on to the LCS's Controlling Officer, Colonel John Bevan, any items of Ultra intelligence of
potential importance to strategic deception efforts. Having been given
the go-ahead by 'C' (as MI6's chief was traditionally called), Montagu
proceeded to transfer just over 200 'Reference Sheets' containing 'Special Intelligence' to Bevan between September 1942 and March 1943.
These documents primarily consisted of reports about German intelligence on, and their assessments of, Allied strategic intentions. Then, in
March 1943, Bevan managed to open a direct channel to Menzies which
yielded occasional deliveries at first and, eventually, a steady stream of
information from this most secret of sources.[14]

Still, Montagu's help in facilitating LCS's first vital access to Ultra
intelligence should have been conducive to an harmonious working relationship between its staff and the veteran covert warriors of the Twenty
Committee, as they came to cooperate in the crucial mission of dissuading
the Germans, via *Operation Mincemeat*, from reinforcing Sicily. Certainly,
the first meeting between the interested parties, over the implementation
of the operation, which was held in 'Tar' Robertson's office in the late
afternoon of 10 February 1943, went smoothly enough. In addition to
Robertson, the Twenty Committee was represented by *Mincemeat*'s original champions, Cholmondeley and Montagu, and by that Committee's
secretary, J. H. Marriott, a civilian solicitor. This foursome outnumbered

but did not outgun the single LCS representative at the meeting: that organization's Controller, Colonel John Bevan. Still, crucially, the latter raised no objections in principle to the bold venture and agreed to 'proceed with the plan'. He also promised to try and get official approval for the execution of the operation using either an aircraft or a submarine to transport the corpse to its destination. Bevan's willingness to urge the merits of *Mincemeat* upon his military superiors doubtless derived from his instant appreciation of its utility as a means of deterring German reinforcement of Sicily—exactly the immediate priority of current British strategic-deception planning, as defined by the COS in their prescription of its goals for 1943, on 29 January.[15]

Having achieved rapid and ready consensus on the advantages of *Operation Mincemeat* as a grand stratagem, Bevan and the team from the Twenty Committee devoted the rest of the meeting to considering some of the practical issues involved in its implementation. Prominent amongst these problems was how to convey the misleading 'operational plans' to the enemy in a manner that was simultaneously reliable, accessible, and credible. In considering this conundrum—at once technical and psychological—those present clearly remembered the Spaniards' earlier failure to discover the secret documents on Paymaster-Lieutenant Turner's person. Indeed, one of their number thought he knew the reason why: the alleged 'Roman Catholic prejudice against tampering with corpses'. Consequently, he warned that 'any papers actually placed on the body would run a grave risk of never being found at all'. Accordingly, the participants agreed that 'the carrying of operational plans in a dispatch or brief case' appeared to be a better bet: it would seem 'plausible' to the Spaniards and they should also not suffer any religious scruples about interfering with an inanimate object. On the other hand, there was a disadvantage involved in attempting to convey *Mincemeat*'s misleading documents in a bag or case, as opposed to putting them in the pockets of the deceased's uniform: the receptacle might get separated from its 'owner', while the body was floating towards the Spanish coast. One obvious solution, that of fastening the case to the corpse with the kind of security chain used by messengers, was ruled out. Such a device was not used by military couriers and its exceptional employment in *Mincemeat* 'might endanger the whole operation'. So, 'Tar' Robertson and his B1A section of MI5 were directed 'to experiment with the flotation qualities of various sorts of bags', especially those equipped with a shoulder strap.

Other matters addressed had to do with the form and content of the documents to be included in the batch of papers, and the professional character of their courier. One suggestion was that it would be a good idea to include some 'purely private letters to and from individuals using this channel to avoid censorship'—an authentic touch that might dispel suspicions. On the message to be delivered to the Nazis through Francoist 'good' offices, and its bearer, the meeting reached ready agreement. The misleading operational plan would identify Sardinia as the actual target of the Mediterranean assault to be mounted by the Allies in the summer of 1943 and also reveal Marseilles and Sicily as the alleged cover targets for the real attack. It was also resolved that the individual bearing *Mincemeat*'s deceptive tidings should appear to be an army officer, suitably attired for his part in battledress.[16] Over the next couple of months, many of the specific decisions reached at this first interdepartmental meeting on *Operation Mincemeat* would be revised or even reversed, but Montagu and Cholmondeley had good reason to be satisfied with their afternoon's work on 10 February. After all, their pet project had been taken on board, it appeared, as a central element in the overall deception strategy the LCS was developing for 1943. Moreover, that organization's controller, Colonel Bevan, was now personally pledged to winning the assent of the elevated command circles, within which he moved, to the launching of *Operation Mincemeat*. Yet, far from remaining satisfied with this state of affairs, Ewen Montagu soon made it abundantly clear to his colleagues in the Naval Intelligence Division that he had begun to doubt seriously whether Bevan and company were really up to their vital job.

What apparently crystallized Montagu's concerns about the fitness of Bevan and his colleagues in the LCS for their task of conducting strategic deception against the enemy was a high-level German radio communication intercepted by the British on 26 February 1943 and, subsequently, decrypted at Bletchley Park. The message had been dispatched from the *Oberkommando der Wehrmacht* (OKW—Supreme Command of the German Armed Forces) to German headquarters in Tunisia and when its text, duly decoded and translated, was distributed to the NID on 27 February, Montagu found that it contained the following unwelcome revelations about Nazi appreciations of Allied offensive intentions:

> From reports coming in about Anglo–American landing intentions it is apparent that the enemy is practising deception on a large scale. In spite of this a landing on a fairly large scale may be expected in March. It is thought

the Mediterranean is the most probable theatre of operations, and the first operation to be an attack against one of the large islands, the order of probability being Sicily first, Crete second, and Sardinia and Corsica third.[17]

Montagu was naturally alarmed that Sicily had been 'allowed to become' the Allies' 'most probable target', an impression that would 'be hard to remove from the enemy's minds'. The fact that the German Supreme Command expected the next Allied blow to be struck in March, several months ahead of the actual date for the *Husky* landings, was of little comfort. Indeed, in view of the seemingly impossible task he—and his fellow British deception planners—now had to tackle, of diverting German strategic focus in the Middle Sea away from Sicily, Montagu proceeded to alert senior NID officials, including the new Director of Naval Intelligence, Commodore E. G. N. Rushbrooke, to 'the grave danger' inherent in the existing Allied arrangements for practising strategic deception.

With his usual lack of respect for the chain of command, Montagu proceeded to lambaste the professional failings and personal shortcomings of the controller and staff of the London Controlling Section, in a 'personal memo' which he circulated within the NID on 1 March 1943. Montagu concentrated his criticism on Colonel John Bevan, in particular:

> He is almost completely ignorant of the German Intelligence Service, how they work and what they are likely to believe. He is almost completely inexperienced in any form of deception work. He has a pleasant and likeable personality and can 'sell himself' well. He has not a first grade brain. He is extremely ambitious and is not above putting up to the Chiefs of Staff a report which he must have known presented an entirely false picture of his work in connection with TORCH. He can expound imposing platitudes such as 'we want to contain the Germans in the West' with great impressiveness. I have dealt with his character in this way as I am sure he will not improve with experience.[18]

The exasperated naval Lieutenant Commander then turned his fire on Bevan's departmental colleagues, whom he damned as 'either unsuited to this sort of work (in which they are all wholly inexperienced)' or as 'third rate brains'.[19]

To justify his accusation that Bevan's incompetence had 'culminated' in the accurate German estimate of Anglo–American offensive plans and deception ploys revealed in the Ultra decrypt of 27 February, Montagu provided a whole catalogue of the controller's sins of commission and omission in the recent past and present. Thus, he charged that LCS's deception efforts for *Torch* had been inept, ill-timed, and ineffective. He particularly ridiculed the fact that Bevan had agreed to General Mason-MacFarlane's self-defeating attempt to promote Malta as an alternative target for *Torch* through a public address to the Gibraltar garrison (see p. 27 above).[20] Montagu certainly had a point. *Operation Torch* had achieved surprise, but primarily thanks to the success of the efforts at keeping the assault secret. As Masterman later noted, the critical factor for *Torch* was '*not* that the cover plans were successfully planted on the Germans but that the real plan was not disclosed or guessed'. In short, *Torch* was 'a triumph of security', not of strategic deception.[21] Nor, in Montagu's stern view, was the LCS's more recent record any more impressive. Thus, he heavily criticized Bevan's slowness in winning approval from the Anglo–American military authorities for deception plans and policies during the winter and early spring of 1942–3.[22] With his own interest in *Operation Mincemeat* and the wider Mediterranean deception schema into which it would have to be integrated, Montagu literally underlined what seemed to him to be Bevan's most damaging deriliction of duty: 'Why even now weeks after HUSKY has been laid on, have we got no deception plan drafted, much less approved and started, for HUSKY?'[23]

In another paragraph of his memo, Montagu actually supplied at least a partial explanation for Bevan's apparent reluctance to promote deception plans with the necessary dispatch and determination. The problem, it seemed, was a lack of confidence, as much as competence:

> Col. Bevan, in spite of all efforts by those who have experience in deception to co-operate with him, persists in devising plans and papers, and submitting them to the D[irector]'s of P[lans] or the Chiefs of Staff either before mentioning them to 'the experts' or without ever mentioning them at all...He can do practically nothing without drawing up long documents...which delay action (but look well if shown to superior officers). He will never do anything without authority from the highest possible level (who are of necessity so busy that he either takes no action, or is too late).[24]

Montagu acknowledged that the questions he was raising—of whether and how the LCS might be reformed so as to avoid a 'complete failure' of all British efforts to deceive the Germans—were ones that could be settled only by senior authorities.[25] Still, the rocket he had launched was also a distress signal: it was a *cri de coeur* to his superiors in British Naval Intelligence to rescue not only *Operation Mincemeat*, but the whole British strategic deception endeavour in the Second World War from what he saw as the fatally inept hands of Bevan and the LCS. Of course, it would be up to the new Director of Naval Intelligence, Commodore Rushbrooke, to decide whether to answer Montagu's call to bureaucratic battle. Certainly, Rushbrooke was not lacking in personal courage. His distinguished service on board destroyers during the First World War had won him both the British DSC and the French *Croix de Guerre*. Most recently, he had commanded the British aircraft carrier HMS *Eagle* from April 1941 until June 1942. Under his captaincy, the *Eagle* had sailed with two convoys to resupply Malta, both to provide air cover for other vessels and to transfer fighter planes from its flight deck to air bases on the besieged Mediterranean island. During the second of these voyages, from 11 to 15 June 1942, Rushbrooke had brought his ship safely through a veritable hail of enemy torpedoes and bombs. In fact, HMS *Eagle* was sunk by a German U-boat, a couple of months later, whilst en route once more to Malta as part of yet another relief convey. However, by then, Rushbrooke had been transferred to shore duties, whence he was summoned to replace Godfrey as Director of Naval Intelligence (DNI) in late 1942.[26]

Yet, for all his warrior spirit, such arduous active service must have taken a toll on Rushbrooke, and Montagu, for one, remembered him as 'not a fit man' who 'had had an exhausting war', before assuming the post of DNI.[27] However, Rushbrooke's ultimate reluctance to declare administrative war on Bevan and the LCS probably owed less to battle fatigue and more to rational calculation than the ebullient Montagu might have cared to admit. After all, any seasoned campaigner is likely to become adept at weighing the odds in a looming fight and deciding whether, in a given instance, discretion might not be the better part of valour. When it came to a potential confrontation with Bevan, Rushbrooke—who had also seen some service as a senior naval staff officer in the early 1930s and was, therefore, not completely unversed in the ways of Whitehall—surely knew that the bureaucratic big guns would all be on the other side.[28] Johnny Bevan may not have impressed Ewen Montagu in their early months of contact, but he did turn out to be genuinely gifted at what one of his staff called the 'extremely uphill work' of ' "selling" deception' to many senior commanders.[29] Montagu, of course, had conceded in his critical memo that Bevan could 'sell himself well', but he had also deprecated the Controller's apparently incorrigible habit of consulting his superiors at every turn. Yet, in working 'in close cooperation with the Joint Planning Staff', in keeping

'the Chiefs of Staff informed regarding all matters of deception both at
home and abroad', and in maintaining regular contact with the Joint
Intelligence Sub-Committee (JIC), MI6, and other relevant official bodies
and departments, Bevan was actually following orders. The COS's 'Directive to Controlling Officer' of 21 June 1942, had enjoined Bevan to keep in
close touch with Britain's strategic planners and decision-makers.[30] However, Dennis Wheatley, one of Bevan's senior assistants, and a popular
author of adventure stories and supernatural thrillers, claimed later that
Bevan himself had largely drafted the very COS 'Directive' purporting to
guide and govern his deception work. So, the injunction to liaise regularly
with senior executive echelons of the British war effort was no unwelcome
imposition from on high. It, however, did confer a licence to roam Whitehall's corridors of power at virtual will. Indeed, the specific proviso in the
'Directive' which 'authorised' the Controller 'to report' to the COS 'direct
insofar as this may be necessary', was clearly crafted with careful fore-
thought: it guaranteed Bevan automatic access to Britain's primary council
of professional grand strategists.[31] Much as Montagu might rail against
Bevan's constant consultations with the top brass, these senior commanders
were precisely the people who could make or break a deception project like
Operation Mincemeat.

Of course, familiarity can breed contempt rather than collaboration but,
as it transpired, the LCS possessed a triumvirate of talents adept at grooming such powerful figures as constructive partners for strategic deception
efforts. Bevan, himself, certainly seemed to belong within such elevated
circles. He had been educated at Eton and Oxford and had served both on
the front line (where his bravery had won him the MC) and was a sector
intelligence staff officer in the First World War. He also married into the
aristocracy where he acquired not only the daughter of an Earl as his wife,
but also a sister-in-law who was wed to a soldier—General (later Field
Marshal) Sir Harold Alexander, one of Britain's most senior commanders
in the Mediterranean during the Second World War.[32] However, it was
not just his social cachet which won over hearts and minds inside Britain's
ruling elite. Bevan also had winning ways. Dennis Wheatley remembered
the latter's 'extraordinary ability to charm and interest men of great
intellect and power which won for him the complete confidence of the
Chiefs of Staff and the personal friendship of the CIGS, General Sir
Alan Brooke'.[33] As fellow birdwatchers, the Controller and the Chief of
the Imperial General Staff were able to meet regularly over dinner

without 'talking shop' all the time.[34] Bevan's success in infiltrating the charmed circles of power within wartime Britain would prove critical for the success of deception on the strategic plane. This was because, as Bevan soon discovered after being appointed to overall control of Britain's strategic deception effort, his authority essentially consisted of the power to persuade his superiors to endorse and execute any given cover plan. The Chiefs of Staff explicitly refused the request he made in early September 1942 for adequate means to implement deception schemes. Instead, they told him that he should be 'directly responsible to the Directors of Plans', who would help him implement 'such plans as might be approved by the Chiefs of Staff'.[35]

So, in constantly consulting Britain's top military planners and decision-makers, Bevan was not only doing his job, but also doing it in the only way he could ever hope to get anything done, i.e., with the practical assistance of those authorities who controlled the resources required for the implementation of strategic deception projects. Yet, Montagu continued to argue, even after the end of the war, that the 'need for high level approvals hamstrung' British efforts at strategic deception:

> Not all of the Joint Planners and certainly few of the High Level authorities really understood what deception was, how it was carried out or what it could do. How could they? It needed careful study and they certainly had not the time—it is unlikely that many of the people who approved or turned down plans knew how a double agent worked or what our organisation comprised or could do.[36]

However, given the high stakes involved in strategic deception—nothing less than the possibility of decisive victory or defeat in an entire theatre of war—the unwillingness of Allied commanders to surrender their ultimate say in such weighty affairs seems understandable. Clearly, some overall authority had to ensure a proper coordination of real and feigned dispositions and preparations, otherwise there was a real danger that some contradiction between the actual plans and the cover ones would give the game away. On the other hand, the Chiefs of Staff's insistence that deception targets must have the approval of themselves and their planners placed the Controller in the position of permanent petitioner for their grace and favours. In the view of the official historian of British deception during the Second World War, Sir Michael Howard, this stipulation 'laid a heavy burden on Bevan's personality and persuasiveness'.[37]

Happily, however, Bevan did not have to bear this onus alone, for some of his subordinates turned out to be prize assets for LCS in its missionary work amongst the agnostics of the senior planning and command echelons. Thus, the man formally appointed as Deputy-Controller of the LCS in March 1943, Major Sir Ronald Wingate, provided a powerful reinforcement for Bevan's charm offensive.[38] Wingate impressed his colleague, Dennis Wheatley as a *bon viveur*, who 'had a great self-assurance and a delightful sense of humour'. This personality 'opened all doors to him' and made Wingate a most valuable recruit to the deception planners' cause.[39] Again, Wheatley himself, as one of the most popular mystery writers of his day and as someone who had a well-deserved reputation for keeping a fine table amidst the short rations of wartime Britain, was able to cultivate a wide range of influential military figures, to LCS's considerable advantage.[40] Moreover, those who came to enjoy the deception planners' company were persuaded as much by their substance as their style, for Bevan and his compact group of colleagues were far from being the dunces Montagu had made them out to be. In fact, after winning the MC on the Western Front in 1917, Bevan himself had served with distinction as a senior intelligence analyst during the last year of the First World War, supplying accurate appreciations of enemy intentions to the British High Command. Bevan had also mastered the complex Danish language, while working at Hambro's bank in Copenhagen for a spell during the 1920s. Then he had returned to London to work—again very successfully—in his own family's stockbroking firm, until he was called back to military service in 1939.[41] Montagu's assessment of Wingate's mental ability was even further off the mark. Perhaps a Cambridge man like Montagu was bound to be unimpressed by Wingate's double first from Oxford (even if the former's own degree from 'the other place' had been a rather less distinguished second-class honours, grade two). However, the Lieutenant Commander was also clearly inclined to discount Wingate's illustrious career in the Imperial Civil Service, which had culminated in the latter's appointment as Governor of Baluchistan in India.[42] Indeed, Montagu was ready to write off the deputy-controller as just another member of the LCS's staff whom he regarded as temperamentally unsuited or intellectually unfit for deception work. However, Wingate made quite a different impression upon his colleagues in the LCS. Dennis Wheatley, for one, found the Deputy-Controller to be 'as cunning as seven serpents' and completely conversant with the niceties of bureaucratic protocol and governmental rank. Consequently, 'he was often able to achieve results which would have been beyond the scope of anyone lacking such highly specialized knowledge coupled with his particular form of guile'.[43] So, why had Montagu so badly misjudged the calibre and competence of the LCS team?

In fact, what seems to have blinded Montagu to the virtues of the LCS as an ideal lobby group for such projects as *Operation Mincemeat* was his growing frustration with another problem: the cumbersome nature of the British and Anglo–American strategic decision-making process, with which he—and all of his fellow deception planners—had to deal. What doubtless crystallized his concern about his superiors' stately pace of policymaking progress in the spring of 1943 was his awareness that time was pressing if *Operation Mincemeat* was to be mounted with any chance of success. Glyndwr Michael's all too mortal remains could not be kept on ice indefinitely, while protracted consultations were held between Allied headquarters in London and Washington, and amongst those in Cairo, Algiers, and Rabat. Yet, two problems now threatened to delay the implementation of *Mincemeat* to beyond the 'shelf life' of Glyndwr Michael's corpse as a credible candidate for the role of a recently deceased courier envisaged for him in the deception scheme. One arose from operational concerns, the other from organizational complications. The two issues had been pinpointed at successive meetings of the Twenty Committee in later February, 1943.

On 18 February, Montagu had informed his colleagues on that committee that, while progress had been made with the practical arrangements for *Mincemeat*, the plan could not be initiated any earlier than the end of April.[44] The Directors of Plans had imposed this restriction. Moreover, they had chosen the date for the earliest possible launching of *Mincemeat* carefully, for 30 April was the deadline fixed by the Anglo–American warlords at the Casablanca Conference for the final defeat of the Axis forces in North Africa.[45] This projected schedule would allow the Allied forces up to two months' respite within which to regroup for the invasion of Sicily the following summer. The Directors of Plans had been 'attracted by [*Mincemeat's*] possibilities' when briefed about it by Bevan in the second week of February, but they were also conscious of the contingency of the timetable for the launching of *Husky* and how it might be affected by the unfinished military business on the Mediterranean's southern shore. So, they warned Bevan 'that it would be unwise in view of possible changes in real strategy to carry out the operation [*Mincemeat*] more than two months prior to the real operation [*Husky*], which it is to cover'.[46] Indeed, by the time Montagu informed the Twenty Committee, on 18 February, about the ban on any premature execution of *Operation Mincemeat*, the planners' caution seemed justified fully by unfolding events in Tunisia. There, Anglo–American forces were struggling desperately to contain powerful surprise assaults unleashed by the German commanders von Arnim and Rommel four days earlier.[47]

Contrary to the Allies' pre-*Torch* expectations, Hitler's response to the Anglo–American thrust into Tunisia had been fast and furious. Already by December 1942 there were sufficient Axis reinforcements of tanks and troops on the ground to repel two separate Allied drives towards the city of Tunis.[48] Moreover, by the end of January to early February, 1943, Rommel's *Panzerarmee* had arrived in Tunisia—after its long retreat from El Alamein—to bolster the defences of this last bastion of Axis power in Africa.[49] Nor were the Germans content to wait passively for the Allies to build up sufficient strength to roll over the Axis forces. They launched robust counter-attacks against the *Torch* forces to the west in February, and against the newly arrived Eighth Army, on the southern Tunisian front in early March. An inexperienced and disorganized Allied command did just manage to parry the Germans' westward lunge in February, while Montgomery—duly alerted by Ultra—comprehensively defeated Rommel's southern thrust on 6 March.[50] Even then, the Axis troops conducted a stubborn fight to hold their steadily shrinking defensive perimeter in Tunisia until 13 May 1943.[51]

Understandably, Allied commanders in North Africa remained pre-occupied with these ongoing operations in Tunisia until well into April, leaving the staff planners working on *Operation Husky* without clear directions or definite decisions on many aspects of the invasion of Sicily, including the exact date for the projected assault in the following summer.[52] However, this distraction of the Anglo–American High Command in the Mediterranean theatre of war by their unexpectedly protracted battle with the Axis forces for total control of North Africa, did more than lead to a sense of drift amongst *Husky*'s planners. It also threatened to upset the even more delicate timetable for implementing *Operation Mincemeat*. After all, Glyndwr Michael had been granted a decidedly short stay of entombment: he had only three months from the original refrigeration of his corpse within which to pose credibly as the victim of a recent air crash. Yet, in their understandable anxiety to avoid prejudicing Mediterranean operations by any premature instigation of deception schemes, the Directors of Plans had already postponed the initiation of *Operation Mincemeat* until the expiration of that three-month period, at the earliest.

If this intractable timetable were not enough to dismay Montagu, the laborious style of Anglo–American strategic deliberation simultaneously imperilled the whole progress of Allied deception planning in the spring of 1943. *Pace* Montagu, Bevan, and the LCS had responded with remarkable promptness to an order from the Chiefs of Staff on 29 January 1943 to prepare strategic deception plans for Europe and the Mediterranean (defined as the British deception planners' exclusive preserve by the Casablanca Conference) and to coordinate worldwide deception plans with their American counterparts. Drawing on earlier proposals, the LCS submitted, on 2 February, a draft deception policy, to cover military moves against Germany and Italy during 1943, for consideration by their military masters.[53] Their grand deceptive design proposed that the Allies should menace the Axis on any and all fronts where such threats could be 'plausibly' posed, with the overall purpose of 'containing enemy forces and discouraging their transfer to the Russian front'. In particular, they should project invasion threats against Norway, Northern France, Southern France, and the Balkans. With the need to deter the Germans from strengthening the Axis garrison in Sicily clearly in mind, Bevan and his colleagues suggested that Allied deception policy in the Mediterranean should try and induce 'the enemy to give first priority to the maintenance and reinforcement of the south of France and the Balkans'.[54] The Chiefs of Staff readily endorsed this master plan for deceiving the Axis on a grand scale. However, the proposal then stalled as it was caught up in the slow-moving machinery of transatlantic strategic coordination; for such a far-reaching deception blueprint required approval from the US High Command through the mechanism of the Anglo–American Combined Chiefs of Staff Committee, which was based in Washington. The LCS plan was dispatched to the United States by secure means on 10 February 1943, but it was not until 3 April that the Combined Chiefs gave formal approval—with a few minor amendments—to the overall deception strategy formulated by the British specialists for the European and Mediterranean theatres in 1943.[55] Once more, the operational uncertainty prevailing within the Anglo–American camp throughout the spring months of 1943 had paralysed the inter-Allied planning process. This uncertainty was caused by both the protracted battle for Tunisia and the persistence of divergent strategic priorities between and, even within, the respective British and American commands. In this climate, it was virtually impossible to make a definite decision about the cover plans for real military moves which themselves might have to be reversed or rescheduled.[56] Thus, General Eisenhower warned Prime Minister Churchill, on 17 February (amid the fierce German counter-attack) that, while he recognized 'the extreme importance of launching HUSKY at the earliest date possible', it now seemed 'doubtful' whether the Allied armies in Tunisia could achieve 'the final destruction of the Axis forces (there) before the end of April'—and it might take even longer to finish them off.[57] Of course, such an open-ended military schedule would render *Mincemeat* unworkable for the purposes of strategic deception relating to *Operation Husky*.

Admittedly, such organizational complications and operational contingencies, which were threatening to make *Mincemeat* a non-starter, were above and beyond Bevan's control. However, since the Controller was frequently the bearer of bad news from on high, Montagu apparently came to regard him as the actual source of the delays and difficulties afflicting the development of strategic deception policy, during the spring of 1943. Indeed, so jaundiced had Montagu's view of Bevan and the LCS become by the time he penned his diatribe of 1 March against them, that he failed to acknowledge one solid success they had achieved in their initial lobbying on behalf of *Operation Mincemeat*. Thus, although the Directors of Plans had prohibited the launching of *Mincemeat* before the end of April at the earliest, Bevan won from them the critical concession that the preparations for this particular deception scheme could continue.[58] This permission was crucial, because it allowed Montagu, Cholmondeley, and their collaborators to work out the myriad practical details that had to be settled in advance, if *Mincemeat* were to be ready for instant implementation once it got the green light. Still, Montagu was unimpressed by the Controller's good work in this regard, not least because he remained unsure that all the effort being invested in preparing *Mincemeat* would not go to waste. For there remained one critical administrative hurdle to clear before this ingenious scheme, conceived in London to cover the main Allied offensive in the Mediterranean for the summer of 1943, could become a practical proposition. This obstacle consisted of the need to obtain approval for the project from yet another interested party. The problem was that the Mediterranean was neither *mare incognitum* to Britain's community of deception planners, nor a *tabula rasa* upon which its London-based members were free to trace designs purely of their own choosing. As Major Wingate had reminded his colleagues on the Twenty Committee at their meeting on 25 February, 'the Mediterranean [deception] policy was entirely in the hands of Colonel Dudley Clarke'.[59]

4

A Sea of Troubles

I n his 1 March critique of LCS and its Controlling Officer, Montagu had also condemned Bevan for his willingness to defer to Britain's legendary deception planner in the Mediterranean theatre of war: 'he (Bevan) still has no deception plan for HUSKY; he will not attempt to devise one until he has met Col. Dudley Clarke in Algiers'.[1] Yet, even Montagu, himself, in this same damning document was prepared to concede that Dudley Clarke had 'done brilliant tactical deception in his area of the Middle East'. However, Montagu also maintained that the great deception planner's efforts on the level of strategic deception had been 'rather less successful'.[2] In fact, Dudley Clarke—who had begun his deception work in 'a converted bathroom' in Cairo, in December 1940, under the imaginative patronage of the taciturn but cerebral British GOC, Middle East, General Sir Archibald Wavell—soon developed his covert commission into an enterprise of very considerable scope and scale.[3] His brief, as he recalled it, was 'to deceive the enemy on a systematic, continuous and theatre-wide basis', so as to help keep the Suez Canal and the Middle East's oil from falling into hostile hands. Clarke also recollected how sorely his deceptive services had been required in the late spring to early summer of 1941, when Wavell 'was striving with pitifully inadequate forces simultaneously' to evacuate a beaten British army from Greece and Crete, to seize the vast expanse of Italian East Africa, to occupy Vichy-French-ruled Syria, to quell pro-Axis insurgents in Iraq, and to mount a counter-attack against the Italo–German forces in the Western Desert.[4]

In such straitened military circumstances deception could act as a force multiplier, dissuading the enemy from assaulting a particularly weak point in British defences. Such was the island of Cyprus in June 1941. Its entire garrison amounted to barely 4,000 troops of less-than-front-rank quality and it was all too vulnerable to a German *coup de main* launched from the newly won Nazi springboard on the adjacent island of Crete. Dudley Clarke and his small band of deception planners, now installed with the title of 'A' Force in new premises which they shared with a high-class Cairo brothel, responded to Wavell's urgent pleas that Cyprus's defences be bolstered by sleight of hand—since the GOC could spare no men or *matériel* to augment them. What Clarke and company sought to do was to persuade the Germans that Wavell actually did have an extra unit, the notional '7th Division', which could be assigned to reinforce Cyprus. From 13 June on, 'A' Force employed a whole battery of bogus means to sell this fictitious formation to German intelligence. They expended considerable effort on false visual display—from fake divisional signs and headquarters to dummy tanks and decoy transport—to deceive watchful enemy agents and German reconnaissance aircraft. Such visual evidence was corroborated by generating sufficient radio traffic to maintain the illusion that the 7th Division was up and running in Cyprus. 'A' Force also spread rumours, throughout Egypt and Palestine especially, about the 7th Division's transfer to Cyprus, in the confident expectation that Axis sympathizers would relay this 'news' to the enemy. Finally, to make sure that the deceptive message about the 7th Division got through loud and clear, an apparently 'top secret' plan detailing the island's defences and defenders (with the 7th Division most prominent amongst them) was leaked deliberately to a woman who was known to be in contact with German and Japanese spies.[5]

As it happened, the Germans had never planned to invade Cyprus, but this deceptive effort turned out to be far from a vain one. For the British made several captures of enemy documents, during the second half of 1942, which confirmed that the Axis High Command had been led to believe completely in the existence of the entirely fictitious 7th Division.[6] This fact was to have the most momentous consequences for the outcome of the Second World War. This was because, as Thaddeus Holt notes, 'it was around this nucleus that Clarke's great accomplishment in strategic deception, the long-term bogus order of battle was formed'.[7] It took time for the seed sown in Cyprus to blossom into what Dudley Clarke himself described as 'the first comprehensive "Order of Battle" Deception Plan', code-named *Cascade*. This scheme was the fruit of Clarke's gradual 'realisation that no deceptive threat to any chink in the enemy's armour can be made effective unless he is also persuaded that ample reserves are in hand to implement it'. What was needed, in effect, was a two-stage approach: 'the creation of imaginary troops by deception methods in order to sustain the very threat it sought to establish'.[8] *Plan Cascade*, initiated in March 1942, sought to gather previously separate efforts—to insinuate fictitious formations into enemy appreciations of Allied strength—together in one 'permanent comprehensive scheme. Its immediate purpose was to inflate the Allied order of battle in the Middle East by 30 per cent, so as to deter the enemy from making an additional attack in the region during 1942, over and above Rommel's thrust to Libya.' The efforts to exaggerate British numbers in German eyes succeeded ever beyond their best hopes. The victory of Montgomery's Eighth Army, in November, at El Alamein, netted a rich haul of top-level German army intelligence staff documents, which overestimated British tank strength by 40 per cent and infantry strength by 45 per cent.[10] However, *Cascade* was destined to brim over the levees of the Levant and spread across the earth: it became the primary element in all subsequent Anglo–American strategic deceptions across the entire Eurafrican theatres of war. For, by exploiting enemy fears about the apparent capacity of the Western Allies to launch relatively simultaneous amphibious assaults against Greece, as well as Sardinia or Sicily in 1943, or against the Pas de Calais, as well as Normandy in 1944, deception planners could critically dilute the concentration of defenders around their actual targets—and even deter their rapid reinforcement once the blow had fallen. In truth, the Allies did not have the surplus forces necessary to mount further seaborne attacks in the immediate aftermath of the invasion of Sicily in 1943 and of Normandy in 1944. Remarkably, however, British deception planners managed by painstaking and persistent labour to persuade the OKW that Allied commanders did have just such a strategic reserve of troops at their disposal. Thus, the bogus units which 'A' Force managed to foist on German military intelligence in 1942 remained embedded in their estimates of Allied military manpower, along with many later additions, right up to the end of the Second World War.[11]

Of course, once a comprehensive, inflated order-of-battle plan was initiated, it required careful tending: for the illusion of truth depended on a multitude of details which had to be kept mutually consistent and constantly updated. If neglected or forgotten, Clarke warned, the order-of-battle deception could 'imperil both military plans and delicate Deception machinery'.[12] In part to ensure that this 'all-important and never-ending' commitment was maintained and, in part, to brief deception staffs attached to Allied operational headquarters scattered across the Mediterranean and the Middle East, Clarke began issuing, from March 1942, a top-secret 'Strategic Addendum'. This document informed these deception planners in the field on policy in general, and also about the particulars of current cover plans.[13] As Clarke himself noted, it was 'Part Three' of the 'Strategic Addendum' which contained the most vital material:

> In it there appeared the 'Story' of each plan in operation, broken down into single sentences and transposed in such a manner as to form the meaningless pieces of a jig-saw puzzle which would show the coherent picture only when fitted together in some centre of the enemy's Intelligence.[14]

Clearly, it would take a singular brain to compose such a misleading manual: a mind disciplined enough to manage a grand deceptive design, while still adverting to so many component (and moving) parts and, yet, also devious enough to outwit the enemy with its innate penchant for intrigue. Fortunately, 'A' Force found just the right man for this demanding job in its own commanding officer, Dudley Wrangel Clarke. It was he who drafted all fifty-seven of 'A' Force's strategic addenda during the Second World War, drawing on a rare combination of mental powers to do so.[15] Thus, one of his subordinates, Major Oliver Thynne, remembered his commanding officer as possessing 'the most all-containing brain' he had ever encountered. At any given moment, Clarke seemed to be capable of entertaining 'complete deception orders of battle and battle plans for say two particular situations', while incubating 'another six embryo plans in his mind'.[16] Moreover, an extraordinary escapade in which Clarke got himself involved in later October 1941 provided incontrovertible proof of his penchant for cloak-and-dagger work. In an apparent attempt to pass misleading military information to a German contact in Madrid, Clarke had donned female attire to carry out his mission. Whilst still so clad, he had been detained by the Spanish police.[17] Clarke's arrest in these sensational circumstances confounded many of Britain's secret warriors. Guy Liddell of MI5's 'B' Division wondered why it was even necessary for Clarke to go to Spain, in person, let alone turn up there disguised 'as a woman complete with brassiere, etc.'[18] The communist double agent, Kim Philby, who was then head of the Iberian section of MI6's counter-intelligence Department, Section V, also clandestinely confessed his perplexity over this bizarre episode to his Soviet spymasters. He informed them, on 31 October, that 'so far, no reason has reached London as to why he (Clarke) was found in women's clothes'.[19] In the event, Clarke was able to talk his way out of Spanish custody—ironically, it seems, with the help of the ever gullible German spy service.[20] Clarke had a more difficult task convincing Britain's astonished warlords that he could be trusted to return to his highly sensitive and responsible duties, coordinating Allied deception throughout the Mediterranean and Middle East. In the end, however, after a high-level investigation, they let him resume his deception work, persuaded that he was 'just the type who imagines himself as the super secret service agent'.[21] They clearly hoped that the sobering effects of incarceration in a Francoist jail and an official British reprimand would curb his inclination towards such reckless behaviour in the future.

Certainly, Dudley Clarke, once back in harness in Cairo, proceeded to repay his superiors' act of faith with compound interest. As already noted, even the hyper-critical Montagu was ready to acknowledge, in the spring of 1943, that 'A' Force's commanding officer had performed exceptionally well in misleading the enemy on the tactical/operational level, by then.[22] On that plane of warfare perhaps Clarke's greatest contribution had been the way in which he facilitated the Eighth Army's assault at El Alamein, in late October 1942. There, he sought to persuade *Panzerarmee Afrika* that Montgomery's forthcoming attack would come at a later date, and from a different direction than actually planned. This message was successfully communicated to Axis commanders—including Rommel—through dummy military displays and extensive use of camouflage, wireless deception, and double agents. So, the Eighth Army was able to achieve total surprise with its critical blow against an un-concentrated enemy on 24 October.[23] Moreover, at the strategic level as already mentioned, 'A' Force had been practising a comprehensive Middle East order-of-battle deception again as early as March 1942—a *ruse de guerre* which would become the vital precondition of all subsequent strategic deception schemes implemented by the Western Allies in their Eurafrican campaigns during the war. Indeed, Clarke, himself, noted that there was an added advantage to such a systematic endeavour to exaggerate the size of Allied forces in the Mediterranean and Middle East: it provided a constantly repeated stock of intelligence on which Allied double agents could draw to maintain credibility with their notional Axis spymasters.[24] This state of affairs conformed exactly to Clarke's conception of how strategic deception should be done:

> By thus feeding the enemy continually with scraps of information from a dozen different sources, we hoped to enable him to piece together in time the whole bogus picture . . . [25]

This incrementalist approach to misleading the enemy also seemed to justify Clarke's claim to control British deception policy in the Mediterranean.

Occupying his commanding height at the apex of 'A' Force, only he could be expected to discern 'the essentials of the wide overall picture'.[26] Later in the war, Clarke even argued that running deception as a one-man show was actually an ideal set up. He advised the US Army in October 1944 that 'one brain—and one alone—must be left unhampered to direct any one deception plan'. This was desirable because a deception was 'after all little more than a drama played upon a vast stage, and the author and producer should be given as free a hand in the theatre of war as in the other theatre'.[27] Both the British and Americans had granted Dudley Clarke official responsibility for all deception efforts within the Mediterranean and the Middle East (as well as East and South Africa) by December 1942.[28] So, it had taken Clarke not much more than a year of hard labour, after his madcap adventure in Madrid, to rescue his reputation and restore his pre-eminence in his chosen field of covert operation. With his status recently confirmed as Allied deception supremo within the Mediterranean, no wonder that LCS was inclined, in the spring of 1943, to defer to Colonel Dudley Clarke's authority—both in terms of judgement and jurisdiction—when it came to proposing projects like *Operation Mincemeat*, which clearly encroached on both. Yet, to Montagu, such deference on the part of Bevan and his colleagues meant conceding a veto over the plan to someone likely to regard Cholmondeley's brainchild as an intrusion into his own preserve, and as incompatible with his own proven methods.

It should be understood that there was no real disagreement among the Twenty Committee's *Mincemeat* team, the LCS, and 'A' Force over the goal of Allied strategic policy towards the Mediterranean during the spring and summer of 1943. 'A' Force readily accepted the strategic sense of the main deceptive line laid down by London, i.e., that they should induce the Axis to focus on their defences in the south of France and the Balkans, whilst discouraging the Germans from reinforcing Sicily.[29] Accordingly, Clarke and company drew up a grand schema, *Plan Barclay*, between 15 and 21 March 1943, which sought to attain both aims with a single deceptive stroke.[30] It sprang from their comprehension of the elementary point that Nazi forces detained or diverted to the south of France or the Balkans, could not swell the ranks of Sicily's defenders.[31] In fact, the main notional threat envisaged in *Barclay* was one defined by 'A' Force planners several months earlier and which was now integrated into their grand cover plan for 1943:

To persuade the enemy that we intend to invade the Peloponnese simultaneously with a landing in Western Crete, using a newly created 'Twelfth
Army' of approximately ten Divisions plus one Division of the Eighth Army
from Malta.[32]

Such false invasion threats would appear genuine to the German High
Command precisely because they capitalized on prior successes of the
British secret war effort against the Nazi warlords. The main formation
allegedly about to descend on southern Greece and Crete was entirely a
product of Dudley Clarke's fertile imagination. This phantom force notionally consisted of two army corps (each comprising one armoured division and three infantry divisions), two additional armoured divisions and an
extra tank brigade, as well as an airborne division.[33] Implanting the bogus
'Twelfth Army' into the collective psyche of the Axis command in the
Mediterranean represented a triumph not only of substance but also of style
for Clarke's way of doing deception; for it both justified the painstaking
effort Clarke and his colleagues invested in sustaining a long-term order-of-
battle deception and vindicated the former's technique of drip-feeding
individual items of information to the enemy's intelligence services—a practice
which encouraged them to leap to erroneous and exaggerated conclusions.

Moreover, Dudley Clarke and company had good reason to believe that
the enemy High Command would take the military spectres, which 'A'
Force was conjuring up, very seriously—especially in the Eastern Mediterranean, for to menace the Axis there made all sorts of strategic sense. Allied
landings in Greece could subvert the entire southern flank of the Nazi forces
fighting in Russia, and sever Axis lines of communication between the
Mediterranean and the Black Sea.[34] An Anglo–American incursion into
the Balkan peninsula could also threaten to interdict the flow of critical raw
materials from the region—especially that along the river Danube—to the
German war economy. Vital sources of bauxite in Yugoslavia, Romania,
and Greece; of chrome in Yugoslavia and Bulgaria; and—above all—of oil
in Romania, might be cut off by this single Allied offensive move.[35] Indeed,
assessments by both Britain's Joint Planners (in February 1943) and Joint
Intelligence Sub-Committee (in March 1943) highlighted the Third Reich's
dependence upon Balkan supplies of raw materials and its consequent
vulnerability to Allied military actions in the south-eastern corner of Europe.[36]
British deception planners, however, had been aware for quite some time
about Germany's sense of insecurity in this key area.

For, thanks to the window opened up into the enemy's troubled soul by the boffins of Bletchley Park, the British were able to monitor the early onset of Axis concern about their exposed position in this crucial strategic cockpit. So, another great achievement in the British secret war against Nazism and fascism—the systematic decryption of enemy radio messages—now greatly enhanced their chances of deceiving the enemy on the strategic plane. Ultra decrypts, in September 1942, revealed the beginning of what British intelligence analysts called Hitler's 'great Crete scare'—an 'anxiety that was to beset him at intervals for years'.[37] Since Crete lies athwart or adjacent to the main maritime approaches from the southern Mediterranean to the Peloponnese, Hitler's obsession with transforming it into a 'fortified bulwark' (as disclosed by an Ultra decrypt of 18 November 1942) becomes comprehensible.[38] Ultra also revealed that Axis commanders had fretted over an apparent Allied menace to Crete and Greece throughout the winter of 1942–3.[39] Nor did the coming of spring alleviate their apprehensions. Italo–German staff discussions held in Rome, in February 1943, produced agreement that Greece would be the spot most liable to Allied attack, once Anglo–American forces had conquered Tunisia.[40] However, in the aftermath of *Torch*, Stalingrad, and El Alamein, the German High Command well knew that their forces were already too overstretched to allow for easy reinforcement of the Balkans. So they, too, had to turn to deception in a desperate bid to conceal their vulnerability in the Eastern Mediterranean. Ultra, however, betrayed their covert purpose to British eavesdroppers, as Guy Liddell noted in his diary entry for 30 January 1943:

> A study of ISOS [Abwehr decrypts] and MSS [German Army and Air Force decrypts] material shows that the enemy's defensive preparations in the Near and Mid East are weak. They are putting over deception which is intended to show that they're fortifying Crete, the Aegean Islands and Salonica.[41]

Naturally, this abortive Nazi endeavour to present a more formidable façade to would-be attackers in the Eastern Mediterranean only compounded the British deception planners' conclusion (also based on their privileged access to Ultra information) that here was a happy hunting ground for those seeking to distract the Germans from the main Allied plot in the Central Mediterranean. The British were able to draw up a credible cover plan for *Operation Husky* because they could attune it exactly to pre-existing German anxieties about the precariousness of their position in the Balkans and the Eastern Mediterranean.

Of course, however persuasive *Barclay*'s misleading message might be i
its content, British deception planners were well aware, also, that they ha
to communicate it to the enemy High Command in a manner that woul
not undermine its credibility or obscure its purpose. Yet, it was over th
most plausible way to convey their deceptive message to their mortal fo
that a sharp difference of opinion emerged between Montagu, on the on
side, and Dudley Clarke, on the other, in March 1943. By March of th
previous year, the Commander of 'A' Force had come to enumerate certai
fundamental principles, drawn from his attempts to hoodwink Romm
during the Desert War, which he believed to be applicable 'to every kin
of Deception Plan throughout the rest of the war'. Prominent among
these golden rules was the prescription that a deception plan 'must neve
rely upon implementation by one method alone'. Instead, it should emplo
a variety of 'intelligence' means to plant a fabricated story on the enemy, an
use a medley of 'physical' methods to corroborate it for his eyes and ears.
True to his 'deceptioneering creed', Clarke sought to plant *Barclay*'s 'stor
in piecemeal fashion upon the enemy's Secret Service' by means of doubl
agents, and to back it up in the following ways: by real military actions an
movements, such as aerial photo-reconnaissance over the Peloponnese an
Western Crete, and the 'special training of Greek troops for BALKAN
operations'; by overt administrative preparations, such as 'the earmarking c
Greek interpreters' and the purchase of substantial sums of Greek currency
by 'the display of dummy landing craft and aircraft in CYRENAIC/
and EGYPT'; by the systematic spreading of rumours throughout Egyp
Palestine, Syria, and North Africa 'to support appropriate items of informa
tion in the STORY'; and an 'extensive Wireless Plan' (which ultimatel
managed, inter alia, 'to put on air the entire network of signals of the bogu
"Twelfth Army" ').[43]

However, unless the secret agents at 'A' Force's disposal did their jol
in foisting *Barclay*'s story upon the Axis intelligence services in the firs
place, then the whole elaborate set of supporting measures would be o
no avail. Yet, Clarke was optimistic on this score, judging 'A' Force to
be 'well placed' by the close of 1942 'for feeding the enemy with a larg
and regular flow of deceptive information'.[44] Indeed, enough succes
had been gained in the running of double agents against the enem
in the Mediterranean and Middle East to warrant the foundation, i
March 1943, of 'Thirty Committees' (made up of members of the loca
security, espionage and deception organizations) to establish and exploi

these channels of disinformation to the enemy.[45] The star turn in this Mediterranean double-cross system was an agent code-named *Cheese*. The *Cheese* case had started with the apparent recruitment by the Abwehr of an Italian Jew, Renato Levi, in December 1939. In fact, Levi had only agreed to work as a Nazi spy after getting the go-ahead from MI6, with whom he had had prior contact. However, it appeared that his potential as a double agent might be wasted, when he arrived in Cairo—at the behest of his new espionage employers, the *Servizio de Informazione Militare* (SIM), the Italian military intelligence service—in February 1941, minus his Axis-provided radio operator, who had taken fright and bolted for home. Still, all turned out not to be lost, thanks to some imaginative British security officers. They managed to provide Levi with a new radio set and operator. Ostensibly, this latter individual was a Syrian, called Paul Nicossof, who had been enterprising enough, allegedly, to make his own wireless telegraphy (W/T) set from parts on open sale in Cairo. In reality, 'Nicossof' was an NCO in the British Army signals corps, by the name of Sergeant Shears. His false persona was devised to allow him to function in the role of *Cheese*'s personal radio assistant—a vital support if the notional Axis agent was to have a means of transmitting his 'secret' reports back to his Axis spymasters. But this humble radio operator was destined for greater things. For, when the British attempted to re-establish Levi's bona fides with the suspicious SIM by sending him to Rome, in April 1941, his wary handlers were not convinced and eventually threw him into prison. There, he had to endure many hours of interrogation but Levi never admitted his true colours, or betrayed the existence of the British double-cross.[46] Of course, Levi's protracted silence must have alerted the British double-cross authorities to the fact that something was amiss with the *Cheese* case, even if they were unaware of their agent's precise fate. Still, they decided to see if they could maintain *Cheese*'s radio channel to the enemy via Nicossof's radio messages. This was not the most convincing ploy and it failed to persuade the professional sceptics of the SIM.[47] Matters turned out differently with the Germans, against whom the British could exploit the Abwehr's 'amazing childishness and inefficiency' (to quote Dudley Clarke's damning description).[48] Remarkably, the Nazi spy service came to rate this reincarnation of *Cheese* very highly. Thus, by July 1942, decrypted Abwehr messages were referring to 'Nicossof' (to whom Shears' handlers now transferred their codename

Cheese) as 'credible' and 'trustworthy'.[49] The British made sure to take full advantage of the reincarnated *Cheese*'s good standing with the Germans in the tactical deception operation to cover the British attack at El Alamein. He bore 'the main burden' of misleading the Germans about the timing of the Eighth Army's offensive in Egypt in late 1942, with his daily radio transmissions to the Abwehr station in Nazi-occupied Athens.[50]

Careful management of such delicate double-cross cases meant that agents might even contrive to retain reputations as loyal servants of the Third Reich, even after actively deceiving the Germans, as '*Cheese*' had done in the run-up to El Alamein. However, crises could also develop suddenly, and at the most inconvenient times for the Allies, even in the careers of such stellar double-agents as *Cheese*. Hardly was the ink dry on 'A' Force's cover plan, *Barclay*, for the invasion of Sicily, on 22 March 1943, when the Abwehr delivered a veritable 'bombshell' to *Cheese* and his British controllers. Having displayed unusual edginess over a number of weeks, *Cheese*'s Abwehr contacts abruptly admonished him as follows, on that day:

> We regard it as our duty to counsel you to exercise the very greatest prudence. Good luck.[51]

Moreover, when *Cheese* made repeated inquiries, via radio, as to the source of his Nazi controllers' apprehension, he encountered either protracted bouts of silence or replies full of evasions. At the same time, British security authorities in Cairo alerted 'A' Force to 'the puzzling movements of suspect characters' in the Egyptian capital. This combination of unfortunate circumstances persuaded British deception planners that they would have to adopt 'a somewhat cautious approach to the way' they 'passed over "Barclay" items through the [*Cheese*] channel'. True, the Germans—without ever offering any satisfactory explanation for their temporary aloofness—did resume normal radio contact with *Cheese* in later May but, by then, *Barclay*'s main story had been delivered to the Nazi High Command by other hands.[52]

Another case of espionage bluff and counterbluff, in which British deception planners became embroiled in the Mediterranean in the spring of 1943, also exposed the dangers of over-reliance upon double agents as the primary means of communicating deception to the enemy in such a complicated theatre of war. On 6 February 1943, a genuine British agent, reporting by radio from Sicily to his British controller in Malta, startled them with the following transmission:

> Colonel, I have been a prisoner of the Italians from the beginning. By violence and under threats of reprisals against my family I have had to work, but with the hopes of vengeance. The moment came. At AGRI-GENTO the supervision is less strict and I am able to substitute this message. Here is my plan which will enable you to deceive the enemy, because I am at a counter-espionage centre . . . Any message signed 'LILOU' is genuine.[53]

Initially, this sensational communication provoked more excitement than consternation within the ranks of Britain's shadow warriors. After all, as Dudley Clarke acknowledged, 'at first sight (it) seemed to "A" Force to promise splendid opportunities for deceiving the enemy regarding our intentions against Sicily'.[54] Clarke had to admit that 'closer examination', however, 'soon showed a multitude of possible snares and traps', not the least of which was this one:

> But, if the Italians suspected that we had learned of the fate of the original agent, they would appreciate that the questions (posed by 'A' Force) were deceptive, would read them in the reverse sense, and almost certainly deduce from them our genuine intention of attacking SICILY.[55]

Thus, the awkward issue of *Lilou*'s allegiance would have to be confronted. How could questions—put to him by radio—be so framed by his British contacts as to allow, simultaneously, for either his loyalty or treachery to the Allies? Again, how could such queries be made compatible with the inquiries addressed to *Mischief* (British code name of his blown alter ego) and, all the while, not give the game away over *Operation Husky*?[56] No wonder that Dudley Clarke should conclude that ' "ifs" stuck out all over the case like the quills on a porcupine'.[57] Yet, despite the obvious dangers inherent in such a risky triple-cross exercise, 'A' Force's leaders felt they had no choice but to take the plunge into such troubled waters—for overriding reasons of grand strategy: 'But SICILY was of such importance in the Spring of 1943 that we were equally afraid of losing what might be a unique medium for passing high-grade deception.'[58]

So, on 10 March 1943, the following question was posed in a British radio message to *Lilou*: 'are there any troops or aircraft going from SICILY to the BALKANS?'. When this direct inquiry received an evasive response, British double-cross specialists proceeded to bombard both *Mischief* and *Lilou* with a series of cognate queries, which embodied 'every conceivable trick to discover how far "LILOU" was genuine'. The rapid British deduction that *Lilou*, in fact, was a mouthpiece for the SIM was confirmed by the all-too-pointed inquiries the agent now began to make of his Malta-based contacts about future Allied offensive intentions. As Clarke noted, 'as early as 3rd April "LILOU" himself, began to ask, almost in so many words, as to the next stage after Tunisia'.[59]

Although the British deftly sidestepped their notional agent's pressing inquiries, they did not sever the *Lilou* link altogether. Instead, they kept it alive until the eve of *Husky*'s launch, in the apparent hope that it might serve their security and counter-intelligence purposes in the run-up to the invasion of Sicily. However, Clarke and his colleagues discovered later that their efforts had largely been wasted on this 'intensely complicated case'. For, in February 1944 a former Italian counter-intelligence officer, who was involved in both the *Mischief* and *Lilou* cases, came into the hands of the Allied counter-espionage service. He was able to confirm that *Lilou*'s radio signal, informing Malta of his forced recruitment by the SIM, had been authentic. However, he also reported that the Italians had monitored the latter transmission and that *Mischief* had been shot dead shortly afterwards, allegedly 'while trying to escape'. Thus, all the subsequent radio traffic sent from Sicily in *Lilou*'s name had been false, as the British had concluded. However, it transpired that the Italians, too, could never quite convince themselves that the British had not tumbled their attempted triple-cross. So, the SIM, also, had come to regard the *Mischief-Lilou* channel as entirely untrustworthy.[60] Clarke, himself, came to accept that mutual Anglo–Italian suspicions had prevented the *Lilou* case from 'playing an effective part in the deception over the SICILY landings'. Still, the 'skill and ingenuity' with which the Italians matched British bluff and counterbluff left 'A' Force with a healthy respect for these heirs of Machiavelli. Indeed, Dudley Clarke reckoned that the British were extremely fortunate that the majority of their double agents within the Mediterranean theatre of war 'worked for the ingenuous and frequently dishonest representatives of the Third Reich'.[61]

Nor were the changing fortunes of individual agents the only problems encountered by British deception planners in the spring of 1943 in the Mediterranean, as they sought to utilize the double-cross system to transmit their misleading design to the Axis. Indeed, several other circumstances made the execution of such a mission there, via such 'special means', well-nigh impossible. The difficulty of double-crossing the highly sophisticated Italian military intelligence service has just been mentioned. Yet, British strategic deception planners in the region might have learned to cope better with the sobering realization that 'the Italian was a more difficult man to deceive than his German Ally', but for some other local conditions.[62] First, there was the additional problem that the Mediterranean theatre represented a much more diverse political environment within which to run double-agents than the almost hermetically sealed British Isles. Section B1A of MI5 and the Twenty Committee were able to manage their double-cross system, secure in the knowledge (at least by July 1942) that there were no uncontrolled Nazi spies active inside Britain who might contradict the reports of the controlled agents.[63] Next, while 'A' Force did command the services of a sizeable number of double-cross agents right across the Mediterranean basin, they could never hope to control all enemy espionage activity throughout the belligerent, colonial, and neutral territories comprising the region's political map. Finally, even the advance of Allied forces from east and west towards Tunisia could not guarantee any clean sweep of Axis spies throughout North Africa. Indeed, the very slow progress of the Allied drive into Tunisia, during the spring of 1943, meant that the Axis spymasters had ample opportunity to organize 'stay behind' networks of agents in the most sensitive staging areas for *Husky*.[64] Even if such spies did not succeed in uncovering the Allies' plan to invade Sicily, they could confuse the issue sufficiently to weaken the impact of the deceptive reports being sent—on *Barclay*'s behalf—by Allied-controlled double agents to their notional Axis spymasters. With so much 'background noise' emanating from sources outside the control of Mediterranean double-cross, Britain's deception planners found it impossible to get their strategic disinformation through, loud and clear, to their intended target. As Sir Michael Howard notes, ' "A" Force was never quite able to convince the enemy of the unambiguous truth of the notional stories with which it so assiduously fed him.'[65] Letting individual items of pseudo-information penetrate into the collective consciousness of enemy intelligence and staff officers, unquestionably, did have the crucial, cumulative effect of inflating the Allied order of battle in *Wehrmacht* estimates. However, to convince the Germans to redeploy their forces across Europe and the Mediterranean, in a pattern conducive to the Anglo–American invasion of Sicily, would require much more dependable and much more direct access to their High Command than that afforded by 'A' Force's network of double agents. Of course, *Operation Mincemeat* appeared to offer just such a hot-line into Hitler's headquarters.

5

Loud and Clear

*M*incemeat's most ardent champion fully understood that the deception plan's misleading message would have to be pitched at an appropriately elevated level if it was to have any chance of catching the eye, let alone seizing the imagination, of Nazi Germany's warlords. Ewen Montagu grasped that only if the forged document to be delivered by Glyndwr Michael's cold hands appeared to come from 'a really high level' of the British military hierarchy, would it be likely to engage the enemy's attention at an equally commanding height: 'no indiscretion or "leak" from an officer of normal rank would do'.[1] In reaching for the sky, however, Montagu also knew that he risked attracting too much attention from his superiors; for they would feel, naturally, that they knew best how to draft a letter ostensibly written by one of their number.[2] Indeed, one early intervention by the military bureaucrats in this delicate exercise in literary composition promised to dash Montagu's hopes of getting the kind of epistle he wanted. When Colonel John Bevan managed to obtain the approval of the Directors of Plans for *Operation Mincemeat* in early February 1943, he also found that they had definite views on the form its central element should take:

> the document or documents should consist of a ... letter from an officer in one of the Service Ministries to his opposite number in Algiers ... the contents of such a letter should be of the nuts and bolts variety and not on a high level.[3]

Not content with attempting to control the tenor of the key *Mincemeat* letter, the Directors also tried to hijack its composition. They 'earmarked' two officers from the Joint Planning Staff (JPS) to write the letter 'when the time came' for its composition.[4]

When Montagu learned of this effort to dilute the character and dictate the actual text of *Mincemeat*'s central message on the part of the Directors of

Plans he voiced his emphatic disagreement with their conception to
Tar' Robertson on 16 February:

> I feel that it would be a very great pity if we used a letter on a low-level. I do
> not feel that such a letter would impress either the Abwehr or the operational
> authorities anything like as much as would one on a high level.[5]

So, he 'strongly' urged, instead, that the vital *Mincemeat* document be cast in
the form of a 'personal and "off the record" ' letter from the Vice-Chief of
the Imperial General Staff, General Sir Archibald Nye to General Sir Harold
Alexander, commander of the newly established Anglo–American Eighteenth Army Group in North Africa. That letter, he also suggested, should
convey its disinformation in a convincingly indirect and informal manner.
The notional target for the forthcoming offensive—Sardinia in Montagu's
draft, as he had not yet got wind of the official decision to include Greece on
the Allies' apparent 'hit list'—might be revealed through a mention of
General Sir Alan Brooke's alleged dissatisfaction with the existing arrangements to house the prisoners of war the invaders expected to capture on that
island. Again, Montagu—with his incorrigible irreverence for his military
superiors—also recommended ending the letter with the following jibe at
the well-known egotism of the Eighth Army's Commander: 'Is Alexander
taking as big a size in hats as Montgomery yet?' To incorporate such a piece
of personal backbiting into the deceptive letter, Montagu clearly felt, should
lend verisimilitude to the whole document.[6]

Bevan, however, preferred not to commit LCS on the contents of the
main *Mincemeat* document until he had the chance to consult the Allies'
deception supremo in the theatre of war targeted by the deception plan.[7]
This Bevan did in person, when he met Colonel Dudley Clarke in Algiers
on 15 March 1943, having flown out from London four days earlier, to
ensure proper coordination between the deception efforts of LCS and 'A'
Force. On being informed by Bevan about *Operation Mincemeat*, Clarke
clearly viewed the audacious scheme as a minor adjunct to the main cover
plan for *Husky* being drafted by 'A' Force. Indeed, his initial contention was
that 'it would be a mistake to play for high deception stakes', via *Mincemeat*,
and that 'perhaps the best contribution to his cover plans would be for the
[*Mincemeat*] letter to give definite false indication regarding the HUSKY
date'.[8] Moreover, during the following week, while Bevan continued to
liaise with Clarke in Algiers, 'A' Force produced the *Barclay* deception plan
which made no mention at all of *Mincemeat* and which—as already noted in

the previous chapter—envisaged selling the deception to the Axis largely
through the medium of double agents.[9] Finally, when Bevan returned from
North Africa to London in late March, he was bearing a version of the main
Mincemeat letter personally drafted by Dudley Clarke to conform to his own
philosophy of deception. As a disgusted Montagu noted, Clarke's draft
merely contained 'a lowish grade innuendo at the (deceptive) target, of
the type that has often been, and could always be, put over by a double
agent'.[10]

All in all, Bevan's trip seemed to have done much more harm than good
as far as Montagu's conception of *Operation Mincemeat* was concerned. It had
uncovered a coincidence of views between the Directors of Plans and the
commanding officer of 'A' Force on the desirability of pitching its central
message to the enemy in a low-level document. Moreover, it had also
afforded Clarke the opportunity to relegate *Mincemeat* to an ancillary role
at best, in the Allied deception scheme for the spring and summer of 1943.
Bevan's performance can only have convinced Montagu of the correctness
of his earlier indictment of LCS's Controlling Officer: his congenital def
erence to authority and inveterate tendency towards consultation with
others seemed to have combined to rob *Mincemeat* of any real chance of
deceiving the German High Command on the critical strategic plane.
However, if his superiors could act according to type, then so could
Montagu, by refusing to acknowledge that they knew better. So, he
summoned all his considerable powers of advocacy to remake the case for
staging *Mincemeat* as a deception on the grand scale.

Moreover, LCS's controlling officer soon confounded Montagu's low
opinion of his character and capacity. For, within forty-eight hours of
returning to London from Algiers, Bevan allowed himself to be persuaded
that 'provided a letter on a very high level could be drafted with sufficient
plausibility, it would be likely to create a greater effect on the enemy' than
one on a lower level.[11] Accordingly, Bevan personally authorized the
dispatch of a telegram to Clarke, on 30 March 1943, defining his funda
mental reason for abandoning 'A' Force's limited vision of *Mincemeat*'s role
in the Allies' grand stratagem for the Mediterranean in mid 1943: 'We feel
MINCEMEAT gives unrivalled opportunity for providing definite infor
mation and consequently we can go further than your preliminary draft.'[1]
Even more impressively, Bevan proceeded to take up the cudgels on
Montagu's behalf with the Directors of Plans. Not only did he manage
to persuade them, too, to drop their objections to the vital *Mincemea*

documents being drafted as an apparent item of correspondence between high-ranking officers, but he also got them 'to reverse their previous decision that MINCEMEAT could not be undertaken later than HUSKY D-2 months' (i.e., not before 30 April, 1943).[13] So, when bureaucratic push came to shove, Bevan was quicker of mind and stouter of heart than an exasperated Montagu had been able to recognize only a month previously. In fact, Bevan now proved perceptive enough to grasp that *Mincemeat* could deliver dividends of truly strategic proportions, if conducted along the lines advocated by Montagu. Again, when convinced on this crucial point, he had demonstrated sufficient strength of character not only to query the decisions of his own immediate superiors, the Directors of Plans, but, also, to question the judgement of such an eminent authority on deception as Dudley Clarke. No wonder then that, with time, Montagu came to have a more favourable view of LCS's Chief—although, typically, he attributed the improvement in his relations with Colonel Bevan as due to a change of attitude on the latter's part: 'the Controlling Officer soon appreciated that he and his staff could benefit by advice and that the criticers were really anxious to help: he lost much of his original touchiness'.[14]

Yet, Bevan did not change his mind over one vital issue affecting *Mincemeat*'s implementation process. He continued to insist that 'A' Force's commanding officer should have the last word about the level on which the deception plan's message would be pitched. As he affirmed, before the dispatch of the 30 March telegram from LCS on that very subject, 'I think we must get Dudley Clarke's approval as it is his theatre.'[15] Bevan's ultimate willingness to bow to Clarke's opinion on this matter probably sprang more from a realistic appreciation that 'A' Force's willing collaboration was essential if *Mincemeat* was to receive the in-theatre corroboration it required than from any innate deference. Either way, however, the practical result was still the same: Dudley Clarke was being conceded a veto over the implementation of *Mincemeat* as a high-level, strategic deception. Doubtless, many of 'A' Force's senior staff fully expected their commander to reject out of hand an effort to cast them in a supporting role for London's flashy deception scheme. Resentment at the prospect of becoming bit players on their own stage was natural, and some of 'A' Force's personnel never forgave the outsiders for trying to steal their limelight. One of their number, Captain David Mure, later dismissed the Twenty Committee and LCS as fellow members of 'the London Debating Society' who 'never seemed to learn how much safer and better it was to pass deceptions by mundane and unspectacular means allowing the enemy to put together the picture'.[16] The original fault, in the view of Clarke's self-satisfied deputy, Colonel Noël Wild, lay with the authorities' 'bad mistake' in 'considering that the intellectually minded (especially the legal) was the best civilian material for recruitment' to Britain's secret war effort. What he preferred were 'men of sound judgment, character and background', working for bodies firmly integrated into 'the military chain of command'.[17] Administrative and imaginative mavericks like a barrister turned deception planner were outside his kith and beyond his ken: he would refer to Montagu, in later private correspondence, as 'a Semitic recorder'.[18]

However, fortunately for the course of Allied strategic deception in the Mediterranean in 1943, the commanding officer of 'A' Force turned out to be a bigger man than his subordinates. He was less obsessed with bureaucratic parochialism, less eaten up by professional jealousy and personal prejudice and, perhaps, above all, more genuinely fascinated by the dark art of deception. Of course, he may also have become increasingly aware of the fallibility of double-cross agents as a means of transmitting deceptive messages to the enemy, during the spring of 1943, in the Mediterranean theatre. Equally, he may have been enough of a realist to understand that 'A' Force had to sink or swim, in partnership with LCS—anointed as the latter had been by the Chiefs of Staff (COS)—for the rest of the war. Yet, what appears to have been even more decisive in persuading him to agree to *Mincemeat*'s being pitched on a high level was that the lofty end justified the elevated means. As Clarke came to accept, *Operation Mincemeat*, although perhaps a risky project, was also 'nevertheless an all-important one of far-reaching possibilities of Strategic Deception on the grand scale'. For, as he also came to understand, if it worked, if the corpse-courier did the job, then 'the major part of the "BARCLAY" Story would have been carried in one bound right to the inmost circles of the German war machine at BERLIN'.[19] As a true connoisseur of the arcane art of deception, Dudley Clarke seems to have recognized a masterpiece of the genre in the making, even if it defied his professional norms. In the end, he could not bring himself to look this (Trojan) gift horse in the mouth. Having assented to the implementation of *Operation Mincemeat* as a strategic-level deception, Clarke now lent it critical, practical assistance. He provided Montagu with 'certain locations and (military) units' for identification in the text of the central *Mincemeat* document.[20] With the joint imprimatur of both LCS and 'A' Force, Montagu and his close collaborators on the project were able to

overcome the opposition of the Directors of Plans to the essaying of deception
on such a rarified plane. In retrospect, Montagu concluded that the deception
planners' success in convincing their superiors that *Mincemeat* represented a
unique opportunity, which could be seized only by aiming high, was 'the
greatest single achievement of the operation'. As bureaucratic battles go, it had
been hectic enough. Indeed, Montagu would also recollect that it had proven
a far more difficult task to persuade the British High Command to believe
in *Operation Mincemeat*'s deceptive possibilities, than it was to induce their
German counterparts to fall for them.[21]

Yet, even with agreement on the notionally top-level nature of the
document to be passed to the enemy via *Mincemeat*, the question of that
letter's precise contents still had to be settled. Once again, Montagu knew
that he was in for a tough fight. Admittedly the 'hush hush' character of the
project meant that the document at issue did not have to run the full
gauntlet of bureaucratic sub-editors.[22] However, even moving up the
command hierarchy on its 'fast track', the letter would still be open to
amendment by 'everyone who felt himself to be an expert, and to know the
German mind'. Doubtless, Montagu feared that, in this process of bureaucratic review and revision, vital points could be obscured and false notes
struck. So, he strongly urged that the final text of this key document should
reflect his own ideas about its contents and character. He recommended that
the deceptive target for the Allies' summer offensive in the Mediterranean
theatre 'be casually but definitely identified', in the body of the letter.
He also wanted the missive to mention two separate cover targets for the
alleged 'real' point of attack. Sicily, he conceded, would have to be one of
these latter, since it was too logical a target for the Allies, credibly, to be seen
to be ignoring it. However, the inclusion of another cover target would
insure against the Germans automatically inferring that Sicily was the actual
Allied point of attack, if they detected that the *Mincemeat* documents were
fakes. Finally, Montagu suggested that 'the letter should be off the record
and of the type that would go by the hand of an officer but not in an official
bag'. To reinforce this impression, the latter should contain 'personal
remarks and evidence of a personal discussion or arrangement which
would prevent the message being sent by a signal'.[23]

Perhaps, inevitably, more than one pair of hands helped draft the text of
the letter, notionally written by General Nye for dispatch to General
Alexander and submitted by Colonel Bevan—with the full endorsement
of Colonel Dudley Clarke and the Directors of Plans—for approval by the

COS, in early April 1943.[24] Yet, when Bevan listed the reasons, in his accompanying memorandum on 'Operation "Mincemeat"' why the Germans would be likely to consider the letter in question to be a genuine article, Montagu's authorial influence was evident:

(a) It is passing between persons who are not only 'in the know' but also on a high enough level to exclude the possibility of mistake.

(b) The tenor and tone of the letter are such that the Germans are likely to accept it as an 'off the record' negotiation between two officers who are personal friends and working in harmony.

(c) The purported real objective is not blatantly mentioned although very clearly indicated.

(d) The Germans will on this occasion be looking for a cover or deception objective and this is given to them.

(e) The purported cover or deception objectives include SICILY which they are already appreciating as one of the most probable of our real objectives, and will also explain our later preparations which may point more clearly to that island.[25]

However, despite Bevan's cogent defence of the draft text, and the impressive show of support it received from all of Britain's senior deception planners and strategic planners, there was no guarantee that *Mincemeat*'s primary document would emerge intact from review by Britain's top brass. For all proposals to the COS were closely scrutinized by the staffs of the Admiralty, Air Ministry, and War Office. Only they could brief their specific Chief of Staff on the advisability of accepting, amending, or rejecting a particular plan at the committee meetings with his fellow heads of the armed services. Predictably, the staff officers in all three armed forces' ministries had their own ideas about the appropriate style and substance of the main *Mincemeat* letter. The Admiralty, for example, suggested that the 'code name HUSKY' be mentioned in the letter and, also, that the tone and contents of the communication be more informal and intimate. The Air Ministry agreed that the letter 'should be of a more personal nature', but it also saw a deceptive opportunity which had eluded Montagu, Bevan, and company: the heavy, pre-invasion aerial bombardment of Sicily might be represented as intended to neutralize the capacity of enemy air forces stationed there to interfere with the notional amphibious assault on the Greek mainland.[26] Apart from some constructive advice on the need to get military details exactly right in the document, the War Office's main suggestion was that General Nye himself be asked to write the actual letter, since that seemed the best way of ensuring that it had the right personal touch.[27] So, contrary to Montagu's fears—and somewhat at odds with his recollections—the 'bright ideas', as he termed them, emanating from the armed services ministries (and seconded by the COS), were all calculated to improve the fabricated finished product.[28]

Unfortunately, it fell to 'Johnny' Bevan to redraft the *Mincemeat* letter in the light of this counsel and he appears, conspicuously, to have failed to rise to the occasion.[29] True, he conscientiously tried to integrate the various substantive amendments proposed by the armed forces' experts. He was careful to cite the code name *Husky* in the text of the document and, also, to make mention of the planned air attacks on Sicily in a manner that deftly identified that island as a plausible cover target for a main assault directed elsewhere:

> The heavy bombing of Sicily which will take place in order to neutralise the airfields and thereby assist the approach to the real objective, will give the enemy an additional indication that we are going to attack Sicily.[30]

However, such subtleties were more than offset in Bevan's draft text by his manifest failure to respond to the universal exhortation from the services' staffs on the need to inject a more personal tone and touch into the letter. Instead of heeding the War Office's studied advice that 'the style of writing' be 'in keeping with that to be expected between military friends in high positions', his version reeked of bureaucratic formality.[31] Stickler that he was for drafting memoranda in the regulation manner he had learned at Staff College, Bevan laid out the letter in an unconvincingly stereotypical style.[32] He not only numbered its constituent paragraphs but also divided it into sub-paragraphs and sub-sub-paragraphs. The inclusion of such bureaucratic terminology as 'Reference Wilson's plans for HUSKY M.E.O/1147/5/G. Plans dated 26 March, 1943', in Bevan's draft, also belied the notion that the letter could be a personal communication between senior military commanders. Moreover, one of the few personal notes struck in Bevan's draft did not ring true. This was in the very last paragraph where a somewhat stilted attempt at informality jarred with the formal tone of what went before:

> If it isn't too much trouble I wonder whether you could ask one of your A.D.C.'s to send me a case of oranges or lemons. One misses fresh fruit

terribly, especially this time of year when there is really nothing one can buy. They would be a great luxury.[33]

To be fair, Bevan did forward his draft to General Nye, on 8 April, so that the Vice-Chief of the Imperial General Staff (VCIGS) might have the opportunity 'of giving it an authentic touch', as the War Office had recommended.[34] Montagu, however, was so appalled by Bevan's ham-fisted version of the crucial *Mincemeat* letter that he felt he could not stand idly by, hoping that Nye might retrieve the situation. Instead, Montagu hastened to harangue the Twenty Committee, at a meeting on the afternoon of the very same day, about the shortcomings of the current draft of the main *Mincemeat* message. At this gathering, he voiced the earnest opinion that the letter was 'not nearly as good a document as before'.[35] Montagu's vehement criticism of a draft produced by LCS's controlling officer, at the prompting of the COS, placed the other members of the Twenty Committee (who included Bevan's deputy, Wingate) in an awkward position. On the one hand, they knew their naval colleague well enough to respect his views on how best to dupe the Nazis. On the other hand, they were well aware that it was not in their own bureaucratic interest to be seen to be spurning the Controller's draft, or to be questioning the authority of the COS. In the end, the most they were prepared to do to respond to Montagu's concerns was to allow him make 'some unofficial efforts to have the document put back into a better form'. However, they also stipulated that if Montagu's attempts to badger his superiors into making the desired changes failed, then the *Mincemeat* letter 'should be accepted as it now stands'.[36]

Such an unappealing prospect guaranteed that Montagu would join the bureaucratic fray once more on behalf of *Mincemeat*. He descended on 'Johnny' Bevan, all over again, to insist that the Operation's deceptive message be reshaped in substance and style. Yet again, too, the head of LCS reacted with notable open-mindedness to criticism—even when it came from this all-too-familiar quarter. Not only did Bevan accept Montagu's urgent pleadings that the vital document as it now stood required significant amendment; he also allowed his NID critic to join him in the process of revision. Over the next forty-eight hours, they devoted much of their time to 'numerous' efforts at redrafting the crucial letter.[37] The result—officially, the third draft of the notional letter between Nye and Alexander—did show marked improvement on Bevan's immediately preceding version. It certainly conveyed the two principal misleading points common to all the drafts, namely that Greece was a major target for forthcoming Allied attack and that Sicily was only a cover target for other real operations, in a compelling fashion.[38] However, in relaying this 'Third Draft' of the *Mincemeat* message to General Nye on 10 April, so that the VCIGS could incorporate its essentials into his own final composition of the letter's text, Bevan did confess to having one major reservation about even this revised version:

> As it stands at the moment the letter is, I think, rather too official and the Germans might wonder why it was not sent by cable. The addition of some personal and confidential information would rectify this.[39]

This very misgiving had already been expressed by all three of the service ministries about an earlier draft, whilst Montagu, of course, had long preached the importance of this same point. So, on Nye's ability to invest the main *Mincemeat* communication to the enemy with an appropriate note of intimacy, now rested the whole credibility of the Operation. It was a challenge the VCIGS did not shirk.

In fact, Sir Archibald Nye had become thoroughly intrigued with this intricate attempt to deceive the enemy by this stage of its preparation.[40] Moreover, with his elevated place in Britain's military command, he naturally understood the grand strategic issues at stake in its success. In addition, the VCIGS was exceptionally well equipped by education and inclination for his designated role in implementing *Operation Mincemeat*. For a start, he had managed to qualify as a barrister in 1932, even while pursuing his full-time military career as a junior staff officer. His legal training honed what were clearly natural talents of comprehension and exposition. The latter capacity won him the admiration and affection of his charges when he was on the Directing Staff at the British Army's Staff College at Camberley. They referred to him as 'that old so-and-so who thinks in paragraphs'. Indeed, Nye's ability to explain complicated military matters to often obtuse and/or sceptical politicians was of immense benefit to British strategic decision-making during the Second World War.[41] Now with his attention definitely engaged, Nye applied his considerable powers of exposition to provide *Operation Mincemeat* with a persuasive text. The deception planners had Nye's version of the letter back in their hands by 12 April and they were greatly impressed with the work he had done upon it.[42] Montagu, in particular, heartily welcomed the sea-changes the VCIGS had made in the Third Draft, laden as that text still had been with bureaucratic ballast.

Indeed, Montagu pronounced Nye's own version of the vital letter to b
'ideally suited' for *Mincemeat*'s deceptive purpose.[43] He would later acclaim
it as 'truly magnificent'.[44] Dudley Clarke was even more captivated by
Nye's subtle and seductive text. He admired how the VCIGS had 'artfully
contrived to convey crucially misleading information 'amid a welter o
indirect references' but, also, in a manner that should ensure that the
German Intelligence Staff had 'no difficulty in piecing them together'.[45]

    The British COS were no less impressed by Nye's literary contribution to
Mincemeat and, on 13 April 1943, they formally approved his version (with a
couple of minor amendments) as the authorized text of the letter to be used
in the deception operation.[46] That letter now read as follows:

Telephone, Whitehall 9400.
Chief of the Imperial General Staff   War Office,
                                                  Whitehall,
                                                  London, S.W.I.
General the Hon. Sir Harold R.L.G. Alexander,   23rd April, 1943
G.C.B., C.S.I., D.S.O., M.C.,
Headquarters,
18th Army Group

                      PERSONAL AND MOST SECRET.

My dear Alex—
    I am taking advantage of sending you a personal letter by hand of one of
Mountbatten's officers, to give you the inside history of our recent exchange
of cables about Mediterranean operations and their attendant cover plans.
You may have felt our decisions were somewhat arbitrary, but I can assure
you in fact that the C.O.S. Committee gave the most careful consideration
both to your recommendation and also to Jumbo's.
    We have had recent information that the Bosche have been reinforcing
and strengthening their defences in Greece and Crete and C.I.G.S. felt that
our forces for the assault were insufficient. It was agreed by the Chiefs of Staff
that the 5th Division should be reinforced by one Brigade Group for the
assault on the beach south of CAPE ARAXOS and that a similar reinforcement should be made for the 56th Division at KALAMATA. We are earmarking the necessary forces and shipping.
    Jumbo Wilson had proposed to select SICILY as cover target for
"HUSKY"; but we have already chosen it as cover for operations "BRIM-
STONE". The C.O.S. Committee went into the whole question exhaust-
ively again and came to the conclusion that in view of the preparations in
Algeria, the amphibious training which will be taking place on the Tunisian
coast and the heavy air bombardment which will be put down to neutralise

the Sicilian airfields, we should stick to our plan of making it cover for "BRIMSTONE"—indeed we stand a very good chance of making him think we will go for Sicily—it is an obvious objective and one about which he must be nervous. On the other hand, they felt there wasn't much hope of persuading the Bosche that the extensive preparations in the Eastern Mediterranean were also directed at SICILY. For this reason they have told Wilson his cover plan should be something nearer the spot, e.g. the Dodecanese. Since our relations with Turkey are now so obviously closer the Italians must be pretty apprehensive about these islands.

I imagine you will agree with these arguments. I know you will have your hands more than full at the moment and you haven't much chance of discussing future operations with Eisenhower. But if by any chance you do want to support Wilson's proposal, I hope you will let us know soon, because we can't delay much longer.

I am very sorry we weren't able to meet your wishes about the new commander of the Guards Brigade. Your own nominee was down with a bad attack of 'flu and not likely to be really fit for another few weeks. No doubt, however, you know Forster personally; he has done extremely well in command of a brigade at home, and is, I think, the best fellow available.

You must be about as fed up as we are with the whole question of war medals and 'Purple Hearts'. We all agree with you that we don't want to offend our American friends, but there is a good deal more to it than that. If our troops who happen to be serving in one particular theatre are to get extra decorations merely because the Americans happen to be serving there too, we will be faced with a good deal of discontent among those troops fighting elsewhere perhaps just as bitterly—or more so. My own feeling is that we should thank the Americans for their kind offer but say firmly it would cause too many anomalies and we are sorry we can't accept. But it is on the agenda for the next Military Members meeting and I hope you will have a decision very soon.

Best of luck
Yours ever
Archie Nye[47]

Perhaps the first point worthy of comment in this final, approved version of the *Mincemeat* letter is contained in its second paragraph. There, the main deceptive message of the operation, i.e., to alert the enemy to the imminent Allied invasion of Greece is revealed in language almost identical to that used in the corresponding paragraph—1 (a)—of the 'Third Draft' of the letter jointly written by Bevan and Montagu. So, the convincingly indirect identification of the Allies' notional landing sites in the Peloponnese, at Cape Araxos and Kalamata, by way of stating the need to amplify the Allied forces assaulting those two spots, represented a major creative contribution by the professional deception planners to the cogency of Nye's final text. Again, Nye also borrows significantly from the wording of the Bevan–Montagu 'Third Draft', both by exact reproduction and paraphrasing, in making the deceptive letter's second main point, namely that Sicily is a cover rather than an actual target for Anglo–American attack. However, in the third paragraph of his letter, Nye does make one issue less explicit than Bevan and Montagu did in paragraph 1 (b) of their 'Third Draft'. In their version, Bevan and Montagu had taken the opportunity to underscore the apparent fact that '*Husky*' was the code name of the forthcoming offensive operation against Axis-occupied Greece. They did so by noting the COS's alleged conclusion that it would be more plausible 'if the cover chosen for HUSKY were an objective in the Eastern Mediterranean such as the DODECANESE'. Nye, however, clearly felt that it might be unwise to present the Germans with so obvious a connection between *Operation Husky* and the projected landings in Greece. Therefore, in his draft of the *Mincemeat* letter, the Dodecanese are mentioned as a more plausible alternative than Sicily to serve as a cover target for the extensive military preparations being undertaken by the Allies in the Eastern Mediterranean—for an unspecified and un-code-named operation. In taking this tack, of course, Nye was showing the same shrewd insight as veteran deception planners, like Dudley Clarke, into the mindset of intelligence officers. Their innate inclination was to value information in proportion to the mental effort they had to make in deducing it.

Still, Nye's distinctive contribution to transforming the central *Mincemeat* document into a potent instrument of strategic deception had less to do with its core content than with its well-crafted character. Right from the very first sentence of his composition, Nye succeeds in hitting the right note and setting the correct tone for such a confidential communication between senior British commanders. Within the span of a single sentence, he simultaneously conveys the importance of the letter and explains why it is being sent by personal courier: it promised to disclose precious details 'about Mediterranean operations and their attendant cover plans', by providing the 'insider history' of recent secret cable communications between London and Mediterranean headquarters concerning these highly sensitive strategic issues. Then, having seized the attention of his hostile readership, Nye proceeds to sustain their illusion of privileged access to an intimate item of correspondence from one of Britain's top brass by a number of devices. For example, he is careful to employ the somewhat derogatory colloquialism of 'Bosche' (*sic*), when twice referring to the German foe, in the course of the letter. The use of this term certainly lent verisimilitude to his text, since it was a common usage amongst veterans of the Western Front during the First World War, like Alexander and Nye, himself. Admittedly, the desired effect might seem to have been vitiated by the fact that Nye misspells the word—as 'Bosche'—at both the points in his text, where he uses it. However, such seeming slips of the pen were meant to have the exactly opposite result, as Nye explained to Bevan on 14 April 1943. He was responding, then, to a suggestion from the Controller that the references to Britain's Commander-in-Chief Middle East, General Sir Henry Maitland Wilson (whose imposing height and girth had earned him the nickname of 'Jumbo' within military circles) be made in a more consistent manner.[48] In reply, Nye had to impress upon Bevan's all-too-tidy mind that the references to the C.-in-C. Middle East in his version of the *Mincemeat* letter as 'Jumbo', then as 'Jumbo Wilson' and, finally, as 'Wilson' were deliberate:

> About the expressions 'Jumbo' & 'Wilson', I referred to him variously intentionally (& committed a couple of—almost—grammatical errors) so as not to be guilty of too meticulous a letter—or sequence. In fact, in dictating letters, which one usually does—these slips occur & I think to leave them in makes it more realistic.[49]

Again, the final paragraph—which is a totally original contribution by Nye to the *Mincemeat* letter—both appears to confirm the overall authenticity of the document and furnishes another reason why it had to be dispatched by confidential courier. For, in addressing the thorny question of how best to deal with an unwelcome offer of American military decorations for British troops, it should strike a chord of credibility among German commanders struggling to cope with the sensibilities of their own Italian allies. Moreover, the Germans should appreciate, too, that such a sensitive inter-Allied issue was best broached outside the normal channels of military communication.[50]

All in all, it is easy to see why Montagu was so pleased with Nye's act of literary composition on behalf of *Operation Mincemeat*. Yet, even as he affirmed that 'nothing could have been better', he did confess to having two regrets about the text finally approved by the COS.[51] The first was the failure, at the Chiefs' insistence, to identify the actual target of the putative operations comprising *Brimstone*, for which Sicily was—according to Nye's letter—the cover. Sardinia was actually meant to be the target for *Brimstone* but the COS vetoed any explicit mention of that island's name as even a notional object of Allied offensive designs in the *Mincemeat* letter. They feared that if the Axis secret services did detect what was afoot, they would read the attempted Central Mediterranean deception in reverse from its notional target, Sardinia, to its real point of Allied assault, Sicily.[52] However, as Bevan and Montagu both appreciated, this cautionary ruling from the top brass strengthened neither the security nor the credibility of the proposed deception plan. First, as the Controller warned the COS, the studied omission of *Brimstone*'s target from the main *Mincemeat* document did not in fact provide any additional security for the Allied Mediterranean offensive plan, real or notional: 'if anything miscarries and the Germans appreciate that the letter is a plant they would no doubt realise that we intended to attack Sicily and possibly the Dodecanese'.[53] Secondly, the absence of any mention of Sardinia as the focus of *Brimstone* did ring rather false in the letter, especially when that operation's notional staging areas in Algeria and Tunisia were specified in Nye's draft. Of course, the COS intended the Germans to deduce the 'fact' that Sardinia was *Brimstone*'s target from such clues. Still, they did not make clear how leaving that conclusion to 'the enemy's imagination' improved *Mincemeat*'s chances of not being read in reverse.[54]

Montagu, however, refused to accept what he saw as a definite weakening of the clarity and precision of *Mincemeat*'s deceptive message. Still, he had learned enough about bureaucratic politics by this stage of the war, not to challenge the authority of the COS directly on the issue. Instead of demanding yet another amendment to the approved text of Nye's letter, he tried a more oblique approach. He managed to persuade his superiors to agree to the insertion of a somewhat leaden joke into another letter being confided to Glyndwr Michael's care. This was written by Montagu and some colleagues under the name of Lord Louis Mountbatten, the Chief of Combined Operations, by way of introduction for the courier and, also, to underline the importance of the 'very urgent and very "hot" ' letter that he was carrying for General Alexander. However, the fact that this letter would be read by German intelligence analysts, in juxtaposition with the Nye–Alexander missive, gave the British deception planners the opportunity to provide a cross-reference to unravel the mystery of *Brimstone*'s target. They asked, in Mountbatten's name, not only for the return of the officer-courier, once his Mediterranean duties were done, but also that 'he might bring some sardines with him'—ostensibly because they were rationed in wartime Britain. Even the stolid officers of the German Military Intelligence Service were expected to be able to work out this punning reference to Sardinia.[55]

Montagu's second regret about the COS-approved version of the Nye letter was, on his own admission, 'less serious'. Reasoning the Germans would be more likely to accept as authentic a document which seemed to confirm their existing knowledge, Montagu had sought to end the letter with his joke at the expense of Montgomery's style of generalship—well known to friend and foe alike as tending towards the self-promotional. So, his suggested final paragraph for Nye's letter read as follows:

> Things seem to be going very well with you. But what is wrong with Monty? He hasn't issued an 'order of the day' for at least 48 hours.

However, the COS directed that this passage be deleted from the approved version of Nye's letter. They may have insisted on the excision out of due deference to Montgomery's military stature—if not from admiration for his abrasive style. However, perhaps more likely, they feared that some un-foreseen setback in Tunisia, or Montgomery's actual issuance of an 'order of the day' during the two days preceding the letter's date (of 23 April 1943) might undermine the credibility not only of the paragraph in question, but of the whole document. Anyway, whatever their rationale, the COS 'firmly banned' Montagu's jest which, however 'poor', he still felt would have appealed to what he called 'the rather heavy-footed German humour'.[56]

Yet, even without this lighter note, the final, approved version of Nye's letter to Alexander was an impressively coherent and convincing central script for *Operation Mincemeat*. Since its transmission to the enemy was the essential purpose of this ambitious strategic deception, a less persuasive text would have rendered the whole exercise futile. It was Montagu's last-minute and last-ditch interventions, Bevan's receptivity to these importun-ings, and Nye's talent for compelling exposition which had rescued the vital document from being fatally imprinted with the dead hand of bureaucracy. Now all that remained to be done, to ensure that its contents were com-municated loud and clear to the enemy, was to pass the document to them 'in such circumstances that they would implicitly accept it as genuine', as Montagu put it.[57] Of course, every care was taken to produce and present the finished version of the letter in ways compatible with its notional provenance. An officer on the staff of the VCIGS typed the text of the letter on the official notepaper of the Chief of the Imperial General Staff. Nye, himself, handwrote the letter's salutation and valedictions in ink and also personally signed it. Then the letter, according to usual practice, was placed in an inner envelope, which was marked 'Personal and Most Secret'. At Montagu's behest, Patricia Trehearne of NID 12 addressed this envelope, which also bore the impress of the VCIG's official stamp, by hand. The latter envelope was then inserted into an outer envelope, which was minutely examined by British postal censorship experts. These 'special examiners' also marked the wax seal on the envelope in a manner which they hoped would make it possible to determine whether that envelope had been opened, if and when they got it back from the Francoist authorities.[58]

Finally, Montagu and company even made sure that the document and its envelopes bore consistent and credible sets of fingerprints. For the letter itself, the typist's own fingerprints were used, but they were supplemented by 'dabs' from two other members of staff, to represent Nye and his Personal Assistant. Since the VCIGS could hardly be expected to mail his own correspondence, only the prints of the typist and PA were discernible on the inner envelope. The same two sets of prints were placed on the outer envelope, but another person's 'dabs' had to appear on its surface, too: for the courier would be bound to handle the letter he was carrying and this requirement posed a real practical problem. Unfortunately, Glyndwr Michael was in no fit state to have his prints impressed on the outer envelope, as well as other articles being employed in the scheme. This was because applying Glyndwr Michael's prints to the quite large number of physical objects placed on his person would have required the—probably repeated—thawing and refreezing of his hands. Such a process would have hastened their decomposition. So, Ewen Montagu left his own personal mark upon *Operation Mincemeat*. His fingerprints were substituted for Michael's on the outer envelope, the case into which it was put and other items placed on the body. The British deception planners knew that they were running the risk that a really thorough examination of the corpse and its personal effects would reveal a highly suspicious absence of the deceased's fingerprints on all these objects. However, they reckoned that the Germans would not get an opportunity to check the dead man's prints against the various 'dabs' detectable on the outer envelope.[59]

Of course, not only the material appearance of the deceptive letter at the core of *Mincemeat*, but all of the operation's physical trappings would have to seem convincing if the plan were to succeed. In fact, the staff of the War

Office had advised the CIGS, on 6 April 1943, that 'the selection, "doctoring" and planting of the body' were the real 'key to the success of the operation'.[60] Naturally, this was not news to the *Mincemeat* team. Not only had they earmarked a medically suitable candidate for the job, a couple of months previously, but had also preserved him on ice for use at the strategic moment. Moreover, during the long weeks while the bureaucratic battles were being fought to provide Glyndwr Michael with a text persuasive enough to dupe the enemy High Command, Montagu and his colleagues had been busy on other fronts, as well. They had been working night and day to equip their unwitting partner with an identity and an itinerary which would help drive his deceptive message home.

6

Tailor-Made

Since Glyndwr Michael was an irremediably mute witness to the notional plans for the forthcoming Allied offensive in the Mediterranean, it was vital that he looked the part. Only if persuaded that they had a genuine British courier on their hands would Francoist officials and their Nazi contacts accept the documents he was carrying as authentic. So, from the very earliest stages of their preparations for the deception, the *Mincemeat* team set about providing the corpse with a credible professional persona. Their first instinct, as already noted in Chapter 3, had been to make the courier an army officer—presumably en route to the Mediterranean to take up new duties in that theatre of war.[1] This seemed a sound choice for a number of reasons. First it would seem plausible that a personal and confidential letter addressed by the VCIGS to the commander of Eighteenth Army should be carried by a courier who belonged to the same armed service as the correspondents. Next, a sensitive letter dispatched from such an elevated military quarter, inevitably, would be confined to the safe keeping of a reasonably senior officer. Again, there were several practical advantages to inducting the corpse-courier into the army. For a start, a military courier could wear battledress whilst on mission. Such relatively loose-fitting garb would ease the lot of those implementing *Mincemeat* when they came to tackle one unavoidable task. The job of dressing a recently frozen, and only partially thawed cadaver in the requisite military attire would be much more manageable if the deceased did not have to be kitted up too snugly.[2] Moreover, army officers, when travelling abroad, had to leave their official identity cards behind them, unlike personnel in the other branches of the armed forces. This would prove a real boon to the deception planners, for it absolved them of the need to produce a photograph of the bearer—which it was standard practice to affix to such documents—for

Glyndwr Michael's ID.[3] Clearly, Montagu and company had found no suitable recent snapshot of the dead man among his few personal effects. Again, given his long estrangement from his relatives, it was unlikely that they possessed a photo of the deceased contemporary enough to be of use for current identification purposes, even if Montagu and Cholmondeley had approached them to try and obtain one. So, not the least advantage of transforming Glyndwr Michael into an army officer was that it would avoid the potentially insuperable problem of having to provide him with credible photo ID.

However, just when all seemed settled in favour of a military make-over for the corpse, bureaucratic complications once more undermined Montagu's best-laid plans. To his consternation he found, in discussing the administrative arrangements for reporting Michael's notional (second) death by drowning off the Spanish coast with the Director of Military Intelligence, General Francis Davidson, that it would be impossible to keep the news within a very limited and secure circle of bureaucrats. Indeed, not only would the Military Attaché at the British Embassy in Madrid, Brigadier Wyndham Torr, have 'to be added to those in the picture' about *Mincemeat*, but the mandarins and minions of the War Office, who would learn, routinely, of the corpse's arrival in Spain, would be legion.[4] Montagu later summarized the alarming vista revealed to him by the DMI, thus:

> The War Office system of signal distribution was such that, if the body of an officer was reported as having been washed ashore in Spain, the signals would be distributed to anyone in the War Office or elsewhere who might even be remotely concerned and it would soon be discovered that no such officer really existed.[5]

Moreover, the DMI also impressed upon Montagu that any attempt to curtail the circulation of such a signal would inevitably provoke even more awkward questions. Here, at last, was a bureaucratic hurdle Montagu could find no way to negotiate. However inconvenient the alternatives might prove, a soldier's afterlife was not for Glyndwr Michael.[6]

Of course, Montagu knew that he would encounter no such administrative inflexibility within his own service ministry, the Admiralty. Under its procedures, he would be able—by citing the authority of the Director of Naval Intelligence, Commodore Rushbrooke—to circumvent the normal distribution channels for any messages occasioned by the arrival of

Glyndwr Michael, in the guise of a dead officer, on Spanish soil. In fact
from his position inside the NID, Montagu was so well placed within the
Admiralty system that he could reserve for his own exclusive attention all
the messages generated by *Operation Mincemeat*—and do so without awa-
kening undue inquisitiveness on the part of his fellow naval administrators.[7] However, apart from the incongruity of a naval officer delivering
a highly sensitive piece of correspondence from one high-level army
officer to another, there was another severe drawback to putting Glyndwr
Michael in naval uniform, i.e., the sheer difficulty of getting him into it.
This problem arose because a naval officer undertaking such a journey as
that planned for the corpse-courier—by air from London to Algiers—
would wear a 'proper', close-fitting uniform. Not only would that
requirement present obvious difficulties when the time came to dress
the corpse for his travels, it also raised the even more intractable problem
of how the suitable garment would be made to measure for the customer
in question. Montagu and his colleagues now confronted the truly night-
marish prospect of having to summon a cutter, from Gieves' bespoke
military tailors in Piccadilly to St Pancras Mortuary, to take the frozen
corpse's measurements and, even worse, to revisit the cadaver for fittings
of the uniform.[8]

Nothing in Gieves' long and illustrious history—their past clients
included Lord Horatio Nelson and the Duke of Wellington—could
have equipped even their most skilful employee to do the necessary
without repeated thawing and refreezing of Glyndwr Michael's remains,
a procedure guaranteed to accelerate his rate of bodily decay. Security
considerations also told against the involvement of a civilian outsider in
this delicate stage of the physical preparations for *Operation Mincemeat*.
Thus, it seems that Glyndwr Michael could neither a soldier nor a sailor
be, without risking exposure as a fraud through bureaucratic indiscretion
or sartorial impropriety.

Clearly, what the dead man needed to conceal his real identity at home
and project his assumed identity abroad was to join a hybrid force—one
whose warriors looked like soldiers but operated under naval authority.
So, Montagu and his partners in deception concluded that where the
corpse really belonged was in the Royal Marines, a corps of naval infantry
who had evolved over the centuries into specialists in amphibious
warfare.[9] At a stroke, this decision solved two serious problems encountered
to date in the efforts to confer a credible military persona on *Mincemeat's*

moribund messenger. What Montagu described as the 'horrid mental picture of Gieves' cutter being brought down to measure and fit our corpse for its uniform' dissolved instantly, with the deceased's transfer to the corps of Royal Marines; for its members could also wear battledress on the types of service envisaged in *Mincemeat*.[10] This meant that Michael could be outfitted for his mission with a minimum of fuss and formality. Thus, the khaki blouse and trousers of the standard battledress uniform were obtained from Lieutenant Colonel Brian E. S. Mountain of GHQ Home Forces, who also supplied the necessary webbing gaiters. As a member of the Twenty Committee, Mountain was already in on the secret of *Operation Mincemeat*. All those garments, admittedly, did have to be adjusted to fit the deceased's physique. However, since these articles of clothing no longer needed to be an exact fit, a live stand-in presented himself at Gieves' premises, 80 Piccadilly, with an official chit requesting that the tailors adjust the battledress to his measurements. In fact, it was Charles Cholmondeley (although he stood six feet four inches tall and took size eleven shoes), whose build was similar enough to the dead man's, to play the part of mannequin for *Mincemeat*. He also bought a khaki-coloured shirt at Gieves for the sum of seventeen shillings and three pence, paying an additional six shillings for cuffs. Finally, Cholmondeley passed on the official request to Gieves that the appropriate corps and unit 'flashes', and badges of rank be sewn on to the uniform, and also on an old trench-coat which he had brought along with him.[11]

Indeed, Cholmondeley had had to act rather like a rag-and-bone man during the spring of 1943, scrounging from official sources and private donors items of clothing for the dead messenger. In this manner, he managed to acquire a coat, braces, boots and handkerchiefs.[12] However, one indispensable part of the courier's outfit proved more difficult to track down, namely, his underwear. This was primarily due to the fact that such essential articles of clothing were only available through the wartime system of coupon rationing.[13] This meant that many people were reluctant to part with their 'smalls', since they could not be replaced at will. On the other hand, Cholmondeley did not want to attract the administrative attention that obtaining a ration card and clothing coupons for the newly minted, but entirely moribund, Royal Marine officer would involve. So, he appears to have sought the advice of the Twenty Committee's Chairman on how to get round the problem of providing the corpse-courier with the necessary underclothing. Dudley Clarke's acerbic

deputy in 'A' Force, Noël Wild, was moved to wonder, after the war
how a man 'so bereft of all military knowledge' as John C. Masterman—
whom he also disparaged as 'gaunt' and 'humourless'—could have been
appointed as head of the Twenty Committee. What made Masterman'
elevation to this key post still more incomprehensible to Wild was 'J.C.'s
status as an 'intellectual' who, *ipso facto*, was bound to be lacking in
'commonsense [*sic*]' and 'a general knowledge of the world'. Yet, Wild
also had to admit that Masterman had managed, somehow, to mesmerize
'most of his wartime colleagues', both regular military and civilians-in-
uniform.[14] The powerful influence Masterman exerted over his Twenty
Committee collaborators was no mystery to Ewen Montagu. When he
came in his turn to reflect, after the war, on the strong impression 'J.C.
had made on his partners in double-cross, he ascribed it to precisely the
quality that Wild had charged was conspicuous by its absence in the
Chairman of the Twenty Committee. For Montagu, 'Masterman was
not only a wise man', but also 'full of common sense'.[15] Indeed, it was
those mental traits often associated with that branch of the academic
profession to which Masterman belonged which now helped solve the
problem of how to procure both vest and underpants for Glyndwr
Michael's person, without undue bureaucratic process.

Like many a jobbing historian, Masterman possessed a keen eye for
detail, a thorough acquaintance with his own academic world, and an
ability to press both into practical service as the occasion demanded. So,
when Charles Cholmondeley reported the difficulty of locating a set of
underclothes for *Mincemeat*'s designated corpse, 'J.C.' instantly realized
where they might be found. As it happened, a very distinguished Oxford
historian, H. A. L. Fisher, had died, aged seventy-five, on 18 April 1940
in St Thomas's Hospital, London, as a result of injuries received when
he had been knocked down by a lorry in the streets of the capital city a
week earlier.[16] As an historical scholar, Fisher had unusually wide-
ranging interests, spanning various ages and different countries. The
breadth of his historical investigations, and the immense energy with
which he pursued them, eventually enabled him to produce his masterpiece in 1938—a three-volume *History of Europe*, covering the continent's evolution from the classical to contemporary periods. It became an
immediate best-seller and remained a standard work for school pupils and
university students, as well as a broad, popular readership for the next
three decades.[17]

Yet, even these substantial scholarly accomplishments would have been insufficient to earn Fisher not only a lengthy obituary, but also a leading article, devoted to celebrating his life and works, in *The Times* newspaper for 19 April 1940. It was H. A. L. Fisher's second career—in politics—which had transformed the historian into a national public figure. Invited by the then Prime Minister, David Lloyd George, to join Britain's government in the middle of the First World War, he became president of the Board of Education. Although decidedly lukewarm on prosecuting the war against the Central Powers (his anti-war instincts also later made him an ardent supporter of the Chamberlain Government's effort to appease Nazi Germany, even though he abhorred its regime), the new minister used his executive position to push through far-reaching reform of Britain's educational system.[18] Particularly through the Education Act of 1918, which as *The Times* leader of 19 April 1940 noted was 'seldom mentioned apart from the name of its architect', Fisher sought to endow Britain with 'a national system of public education available for all persons capable of profiting thereby'.[19] Sadly, Glyndwr Michael seems not to have profited from such well-intentioned provisions of the Fisher Act as compulsory attendance at school until the age of fourteen. However, he would benefit, indirectly and posthumously, from another of the scholar-turned-politician's legacies. For, with the fall of Lloyd George from prime ministerial office in 1922, Fisher's active political career was all but over. Therefore, he chose to return to Oxford in 1925 as 'perhaps intellectually the most distinguished warden that New College has elected in its six centuries of existence'.[20] He continued to serve as Warden of New College, without interruption, until his death in 1940.

Doubtless, the passing of such a distinguished Oxford colleague and fellow historian was fresh enough for Masterman to bring it to mind, even amidst the tumult of another World War in the spring of 1943. Masterman would have recalled, also, that Fisher's lean and frail physique made him a good enough match for the semi-emaciated cadaver of Glyndwr Michael to make his underclothes a reasonable fit for the dead messenger. Masterman would have understood, too, that Fisher's surviving next-of-kin, his widow Lettice and his daughter Mary, were likely to have retained his wardrobe intact, in the prevailing climate of wartime shortages. Again, since Lettice Fisher—a distinguished economist and historian in her own right—remained in residence in the Warden's Lodgings at New College, to manage them until a new Warden could be elected, she was easily contacted by Masterman with an entreaty that she sacrifice a set of her late husband's underwear in the national interest.[21] 'J.C.' recorded the outcome of his unorthodox request in these words:

> The difficulty of obtaining underclothes, owing to the system of coupon rationing, was overcome by the acceptance of a gift of thick underwear from the wardrobe of the late warden of New College, Oxford.[22]

The Times leader on the occasion of H. A. L. Fisher's death had noted that his extensive historical researches had left him with no clear sense of any 'set pattern in human affairs'. Accordingly, in his writings, he made sure to leave 'a margin for the workings of the contingent and the unforeseen'.[23] He surely would have found vindication for this view in the extraordinary twist of fate that saw a virtual outcast from British society being dispatched to conduct (however passively) a military mission of the highest importance for his country, clad in the underwear of a former Cabinet minister and Oxford don. Still, it was important to remove the slightest trace of such august provenance from the undergarments. So, all existing laundry marks on the vest and underpants were expunged—as were those on the donated handkerchiefs. Then all those articles of clothing were put through the wash together, so they emerged with uniform laundry marks.[24] Again, care was taken to plant Montagu's 'dabs'—doubling, of course, for Michael's fingerprints—on all 'good' surfaces (such as metal buckles and buttons) which formed part of the latter's new outfit.[25]

When the problem of dressing the corpse-courier for his mission was on the way to solution, the *Mincemeat* team could turn their minds to determining the particular rank and specific identity to give him as a member of the Royal Marines. Their freedom of choice regarding his rank was limited by two considerations. First, it was obvious that a sensitive, secret letter being dispatched by one of Britain's most senior army commanders to another of almost coequal status would not be entrusted to a very junior officer. On the other hand, Glyndwr Michael's relative youth at the time of his death meant that he could not be awarded too high a rank, since anyone who had won exceptionally elevated promotion by the age of thirty-four would be well known amongst his brother officers—a complication the deception planners could do without, as they tried to hush up the courier's notional demise off the coast of Spain. Caught between these contradictory requirements, Montagu came up with a neat solution. The dead messenger would be appointed a temporary captain, but with the acting rank of major. The rank of major surely qualified the courier to ferry the top-level letter between Nye and Alexander, but its provisional character did not mark him as someone who should have already stood out in his crowd.[26]

Selecting a professional identity for Glyndwr Michael's alter-ego was also a complicated matter. Montagu confidently informed his superiors at the time that 'the name of William Martin' had been chosen for the corpse because there was 'a real Major W. H. G. Martin' in the Royal Marines.[27] The courier had to have a real, living officer's identity stolen for him, in case the Germans checked up to see if his name and rank were included in the Navy List (a periodical publication containing the roster of current serving officers, including those in the Royal Marines). Endowing the corpse with the persona of an actual serving Royal Marine officer would ensure that 'a reference by the Germans to a Navy List would not necessarily explode the story'.[28] Not that Montagu was disposed to make it easy for the Germans to carry out such verification of the courier's identity, as is proven by his careful selection of a cover name for the dead messenger beginning with the letter 'M'. He made that choice because he knew—courtesy of Bletchley Park—that the Germans apparently only had a copy of the first volume of the Navy List in their possession.[29] This tome contained just the names of those officers falling within the 'A' to 'L' alphabetical range. So, in opting for a name listed in the 'M–Z' volume, Montagu was doing all he could to hinder future German inquiries into the precise professional identity of the courier who was destined to wash up on the Spanish coast.

Still, there was an additional reason why Glyndwr Michael's true identity had been concealed behind that of a particular living being. One disadvantage of assigning the dead messenger to the corps of Royal Marines—however imperative that might be on sartorial and administrative grounds—was that its officer class was a compact one, whose members tended to know one another, often by sight or, at least, by name. So, simply to invent a name and rank for Michael within the 'Royals' would be bound to provoke very awkward questions about this stranger who had died in their uniform. Yet, Montagu also had to avoid choosing, as living cover for the deceased courier, an RM officer in such regular contact with his peers that his apparent return from the grave would cause even greater talk amongst them.[30] These were the considerations that prompted Montagu to pick William Hynd Norrie Martin, entirely unbeknownst to the man himself, as the best available candidate for the job. Norrie Martin was a captain (with the acting rank of major) with an unusual career path. For, having learned to fly in the early 1930s and served as a pilot in the Fleet Air

Arm for much of that decade, he was formally posted to that naval air servic
in 1940—although he still retained his status as a Royal Marine office
Moreover, at the time *Mincemeat* was being implemented, Norrie Marti
had been posted (in February 1943)—whether by accident or design—t
the United States to serve as Assistant Superintendent British Air Trainin
instructing Fleet Air Arm pilots in how to handle the new powerful Vougl
F40 'Corsair' carrier-based fighter plane.[31]

So, here was a Royal Marine officer of appropriate rank and nam
(The change in the initial of Martin's third Christian name, from 'N' t
'G', made in Montagu's official record, dated 27 April 1943, of *Operatic
Mincemeat* may have been due to either clerical error, or meant as a cove
gesture of respect to the deceased, whose first name began with th
letter: either way the alteration was immaterial to the deception since th
courier's middle initials did not appear on any of its documents or h
identity papers.)[32] W. H. N. Martin was also of the right age, being onl
a couple of months older than Glyndwr Michael when the latter diec
Above all, he was known to, but not in constant or current contact witl
his brother officers. Moreover, his transatlantic transfer meant that h
would not suddenly reappear in their midst soon after newspaper repor
of the death of a 'Major William Martin, RM' and cause such conster
nation as to jeopardize *Operation Mincemeat*. Indeed, when Norrie Marti
did eventually return from the United States to England in January 194
he was greeted with considerable surprise by several of his friends wh
could not keep themselves from exclaiming, 'But we thought yo
were dead!'[33]

Having selected the cover identity for the dead messenger with such car
Montagu was equally deliberate in equipping him with the necessary offici
documentation to 'confirm' its authenticity. The courier's official identit
card, which as a Royal Marine he would have to carry on his person whil
journeying abroad, contained the following information:

Navy Form S. 1511
Naval Identity Card   No. 148228
Surname   Martin
Other Names   William
Rank (at time of issue)   Captain R.M.
(Acting Major)
Ship (at time of issue)   H.Q.
Combined Operations

Place of Birth	Cardiff
Year of Birth	1907.
Issued by	C.C. Couzens
At	ADMIRALTY
Signature of Bearer	W. Martin [signed in ink with initial and surname]

Visible distinguishing marks   NIL [34]

All this information was consistent with the public persona in whose image Glyndwr Michael was being remade. However, two aspects of that document's physical appearance now threatened to spoil the deception planners' deft handiwork.

The first of these problems was caused by the very look of the identity card forged for Major Martin. All such cards tended to develop a surface sheen over time, through constant handling by their owners and those inspecting the documents. Of course, Major Martin's brand new card lacked the gloss that should have been acquired during years of use, even if it had been carried round in a leather wallet. Therefore, this ID was hardly likely to convince those, into whose hands it was intended to fall, that its bearer was a long-serving British officer. Admittedly, Ewen Montagu was well aware of this flaw in the fabrication of the courier's official personality, so he sought to repair it by artificially ageing the document in question. He spent hours, when seated at work or home, buffing blank ID cards (three in all, for reasons explained below) back and forth against his trouser legs, in the hope of giving them the necessary burnish. However, despite his best efforts, the results were not wholly satisfactory. The cards certainly showed some signs of 'weathering' but even Montagu himself had to acknowledge that had not really taken on an adequately antique hue.[35] Still, as ever, Montagu was not going to let a single detail—however critical—sabotage the entire *Mincemeat* project. So, he thought of an ingenious way round the difficulty. He decided to account for the newish appearance of Major Martin's ID by having the following endorsement inscribed on the top of its second page: 'Issued in lieu of No. 09650 lost'. Of course, the fact that this card purported to be a recent replacement (issued only on the '2nd February 1943', as was specified at the bottom of its second page) should 'explain the lack of the polish given by years of use', on its surface.[36] Yet, Montagu did not neglect to subject the three copies of the identity cards so endorsed to 'the trouser-rubbing process', so as to make them look like they had been in use for the previous few months.[37] Once again, then, the naval Lieutenant Commander's fertile brain had settled a thorny detail of *Mincemeat*'s implementation in a way that maintained the deception's credibility. In doing so, he also made sure that his particular solution of the problem did not attract excessive bureaucratic attention to yet another of the administrative anomalies necessitated by *Operation Mincemeat*. That is why he used his own identity card's number for the one allegedly lost by Major Martin. Since any inquiries about the ostensible loss of an ID bearing his card's number would be bound to be addressed to Montagu, himself, in the first instance, he could employ the authority of the DNI to stop those investigations in their tracks.[38]

If Montagu's supple brain had come up with a way to remedy one of the defects in Major Martin's ID card, mental agility alone could not make up the other deficiency in the appearance of that document: the lack of a current or credible photograph of its bearer on its third page. In their great relief at circumventing the problem of dressing the corpse and, also, at circumscribing the official reporting of the courier's 'death', Montagu and his colleagues had been inclined to underestimate the difficulties of producing a convincing photographic likeness of the deceased.[39] However, when they tried to photograph Glyndwr Michael for his official 'portrait', they rapidly realized that they had run up against a really major obstacle in the practical implementation of their deception plan. No matter how they strove to give their subject a lifelike pose, or adjusted the background lighting to conceal the fact that he was all too lifeless, he still looked 'utterly and hopelessly dead'. Of course, as Montagu commented later, people often complain that they are made to look more dead than alive when they have their picture taken—especially for official purposes. However, as Montagu also noted, the camera could not be made to lie to the opposite effect. No amount of skilled retouching of his photographic image could resurrect Glyndwr Michael for the eye of the beholder. The technology of the day was simply not up to the task of lifting the shadow of death from his features.[40]

Frustrated in their attempt to use the deceased's own image for his official photo, the *Mincemeat* team concluded that they would have to try and locate a living person with a sufficient resemblance to Glyndwr Michael to pose credibly for his portrait. There ensued a frantic hunt for a not-so-dead ringer for the deceased. For several weeks, as they went about their daily lives, Montagu and company constantly scanned their professional and social contacts for any man of the right age and build to qualify as a possible stand-in for Major Martin's photograph. Anybody who seemed at first glance to fit the bill was then subjected to unnervingly close scrutiny. Yet, this collective manhunt produced meagre results. Two individuals who bore a passing resemblance to Glyndwr Michael—including a young officer working in the NID—were persuaded to pose in Royal Marine officer's battledress blouse, without being told the real reason for doing so.[41] However, Montagu was not too happy with the end products and could only hope that the generally low-grade quality of such ID snapshots would allow the deception planners to get away, literally, with blurring the picture in question. In any case, he decided to postpone making a final choice between the two available portraits until 'the body was removed from the refrigerator for final packing for its journey'. Then, the dead man's visage could be compared with the photos of the two different sitters to determine which was the better match.[42] This was a far from ideal outcome to all the *Mincemeat* team's best efforts to equip their courier with an apparently authentic identity card. After all, the whole purpose of such a document was to vouch for the identity of its holder. However, now Major Martin's card would lack the most incontrovertible proof of identity provided by an ID card, namely a true photographic likeness of its bearer. It was far from certain that Francoist and Nazi security officials would be taken in by either of the substitutes' photographs. Yet, it seemed that all Montagu and his partners in deception could do was hope for the best.

Then fate took a hand. Ewen Montagu continued to have to deal with many other matters, while he pursued the implementation of *Operation Mincemeat*. In the course of these duties, he went to a meeting concerned with the running of agents in the double-cross system. As he took his place at this gathering, Montagu found himself staring into the face of a man who looked, for all the world, as if he might be Glyndwr Michael's twin brother.[43] The object of Montagu's rapt attention turned out to be Captain Ronnie Reed. A former radio ham and radio engineer at the BBC, Reed had been recruited into the double-cross system on account of his technical expertise. He proceeded to do invaluable work for 'Tar' Robertson, monitoring and even simulating the radio transmissions made by double agents to their notional German spymasters. Reed would be required to take over the transmissions of some of the allegedly 'turned' German agents, when they proved to be untrustworthy, and B1A wanted to keep their cases alive. He was able to fill in for them, without the Abwehr catching on, because of his extraordinary skill in imitating the 'fist' (the seemingly unique W/T 'fingerprint' made by each operator of a morse transmission) of individual Nazi spies. However, the head of B.1.A was impressed by more than Reed's technical proficiency. 'Tar' Robertson discerned that this self-effacing 'sparks' might be just as adroit in handling people as he was at operating machines.[44]

True, the human instruments employed in double-crossing Germany's spymasters often were even more delicate and less durable than the fragile radio components with which Reed had to work. Still, the steady hand and sensitive ear, which he had developed as a radio ham, combined with his composed manner to mark him as a likely prospect to act as a case officer for important double agents. As Masterman noted at the end of the Second World War, the most successful double-cross cases 'were those in which the case officer had introduced himself most completely into the skin of the agent'.[45] Reed proceeded to prove that he was capable of this kind of deep empathy with his designated charge in one of the most sensational of all the double-cross cases. Its principal was Eddie Chapman, a convicted safe-cracker and con man, whose unsavoury past initially repelled Reed.[46] However, the radio expert soon succumbed to Chapman's personal charm on being appointed his case officer by 'Tar' Robertson in December 1942. In that role, Reed acquitted himself well, as a quietly effective coun-sellor and chaperone to this flamboyant rogue.[47] Actually, Chapman had been in prison in Jersey when the Germans had occupied the Channel Islands in June 1940. He had managed to talk himself out of custody then and out of a subsequent incarceration by the Nazis in France—the second time by offering to spy on his native country. After a thorough training, by Abwehr standards, he was parachuted into England mainly to conduct a sabotage mission. However, he surrendered to the British authorities on his arrival, offering to undertake any covert mission (including even the assas-sination of Hitler) that they cared to assign to him. In the event, the British decided to use the agent, whom they code-named *Zigzag* (apparently after his natural talent for switching sides), for counter-intelligence purposes, sending him back (over Montagu's objections) to penetrate the Abwehr inside Nazi-occupied Europe.[48]

Still, section B1A appreciated that Chapman would have to provide a practical demonstration of loyalty to the German secret war effort, by carrying out his sabotage mission, if he were to stand a chance of keeping in with the Abwehr. So it was that, on the night of 29 to 30 January 1943, the De Haviland works at Hatfield, which manufactured the Mosquito light bomber, apparently suffered serious damage in a sabotage attack. To Ronnie Reed, the whole place seemed 'surrounded by chaos'. Two of the plant's electric main sub-transformers seemed to have blown on to their sides, amidst a sea of rubble, twisted metal, and scorched masonry. Yet, as Reed well knew, the scene was a completely contrived one. It had been carefully conjured into existence by the British magician Jasper Maskelyne, who had already rendered sterling service to the British war effort with his visual deception of the Axis forces in the Western Desert, including during the run-up to Montgomery's offensive at El Alamein. At Maskelyne's direction, wood and papier-mâché replicas of the sub-transformers were constructed by camouflage technicians, whilst preparations were made also to use netting, corrugated iron, and paint to hide the real transformers under what would appear—especially to any German reconnaissance aircraft flying over the spot—to be a large hole in the ground. On the night selected for the mock attack, Reed had accompanied Maskelyne and a group of Royal Engineers (including some former stage designers at the Old Vic theatre) to the chosen target site. There they transformed this particular industrial landscape with their scenic effects and visual props in the space of a few hours. Once the scene of seeming destruction had been set, the pseudo-saboteurs staged an explosion loud enough to warrant reporting in the *Daily Express* for Monday, 1 February 1943.[49] 'Tar' Robertson and Ronnie Reed visited the 'sabotage' site on the morrow of the bogus explosion and were suitably impressed by what they saw. Reed reported, as follows, on his own impressions:

> The whole picture was very convincing. Aerial photography from any height above 2,000 feet would show considerable devastation without creating any suspicion.[50]

Captain Ronnie Reed, therefore, was already deeply immersed in double-cross work by the time he crossed Montagu's path. Moreover, their meeting in the spring of 1943 probably occurred not too long after Reed's personal involvement in the effort to fool the Germans with a false visual display at the De Haviland factory in Hatfield. So, here was an individual already alive to the need to pull the wool over the enemy's eyes. Moreover, as someone working for 'Tar' Robertson, he could be made available immediately, but discreetly, for a photo session shoot on behalf of *Mincemeat*. Again, Reed would constitute no security risk in posing for the *Mincemeat* courier's ID photo, since he was already a trusted insider within B1A and a reliable participant in the double-cross system. Finally, Ronnie Reed not only bore an uncanny resemblance to Glyndwr Michael, but also cultivated the conventional appearance of an average middle-ranking army officer.[51] This orthodox 'look' could be of considerable assistance to the effort to palm off the notional subject of the photo ID as a genuine serving officer. Naturally, Montagu acted promptly to recruit such an ideal candidate as photographic double for *Mincemeat*'s dead messenger—although it is unlikely that he put Reed fully in the picture about the planned deception. Still, Ronnie Reed readily agreed to let himself be photographed for unspecified deception purposes.[52] The resultant portrait was fixed to, and sealed on, Major Martin's identity card. However, the other two photo IDs, (bearing snapshots of the other 'sitters') already to hand were also retained, so that a final selection—as also previously planned—could be made from the three available just prior to Major Martin's departure for Spanish waters. This fact also explains why Montagu had to age and amend no less than three separate ID cards, as mentioned above. When the moment came, however, for Montagu to make that final choice, there was no contest. Ronnie Reed's picture proved to be 'an extremely close likeness' (to use Montagu's own description at the time) of the deceased, as the latter emerged from refrigeration.[53]

Yet, as is evident from a comparison of the picture on the identity card actually used in *Operation Mincemeat* in 1943 with a relatively contemporary photograph of Captain Reed, there are some significant differences of visual detail between the faces on display in the two photos (see illustrations of Ronnie Reed and Major Martin's photo ID). Even allowing for what Montagu termed the generally 'poor quality' of official ID mugshots as against a picture taken by a professional photographer, some of the contrasts seem deliberately drawn.[54] Most noticeable is the one relating to the subject's moustache. In Reed's studio portrait, this is shown to consist of a fairly luxuriant growth of hair, whereas in the Major Martin ID photo it has all but vanished from between the sitter's upper lip and nostrils. Admittedly, apparently careless lighting of the official ID photo has thrown much of the area of the face into such shadow as to obscure its details. However, the fact that Reed's moustache had all but disappeared from Major Martin's left upper lip—which is in plain view in the ID snapshot—indicates the wholesale 'trimming' of this item was carefully contrived to ensure a closer match between the photographic likeness of the Royal Marine courier and Glyndwr Michael's more closely shaven visage. Again, Reed's relatively thick eyebrows have also largely disappeared from the ID picture, thanks again to careful shading and some airbrushing, too. Similar techniques have clearly been employed to obscure other possible discrepancies between Major Martin's official picture and his apparent physical remains: the upper eyelids, and even the upper parts of both eyes (including half the pupils) are cast in dark shadow, whilst the wave in Reed's hair so obvious in his studio portrait has been 'ironed out' in the identity-card's picture (see, also, illustration of Glyndwr Michael's corpse). Finally, perhaps in an effort to reflect the gauntness of Glyndwr Michael's visage—which was exacerbated, doubtless, by his moribund condition and long-frozen state—the British photo fakers have also given a much more definite line to Major Martin's left cheekbone in the ID picture than is discernible in Reed's own picture. So, Montagu and his colleagues seem to have taken considerable pains to improve even on the photogenic 'twin brother' they had managed to locate for Glyndwr Michael. With this photographic facelift, Major Martin's identity card seemed to stand every chance of vouching for his bona fides.

Yet, the implementation team centred on the Twenty Committee had to do more than equip their courier with official proof of his identity; they also had to account for his being singled out to carry the *Mincemeat* letter from England to North Africa. Of course, the sensitive nature of that document would explain why it was preferable not to dispatch this message via normal channels, be they electronic or the routine military courier service. It would seem perfectly sensible to entrust this highly confidential document to the personal care of a trustworthy senior officer, who just happened to be undertaking a journey from England to North Africa. However, as Montagu realized, the Germans, inevitably, would wonder why Major Martin was so conveniently available to discharge this one-off courier duty. That is to say, the British deception planners would have to find a means of justifying to the German intelligence service the Royal Marine Major's trip to North Africa and also explaining how his travel plans had come to the attention of as senior an officer as the VCIGS.[55]

As Montagu pondered this problem, he remembered the precise character of the real offensive for which *Mincemeat* was to supply the cover.

Operation Husky was to be a massive amphibious assault—or 'combined operation' in British military parlance—a form of warfare in which marines were especially experienced and at which some had managed to become increasingly expert. So, as a warrior with 'one foot in the sea and one on the shore', it would seem plausible for Major Martin to have developed professional expertise on some aspect of amphibious warfare—say, in relation to the landing craft which carried troops and equipment right on to the invasion beaches. With such a valuable specialization, it would be natural also for Major Martin to be posted to Combined Operations Headquarters (as his ID card testified), where he could assist in the efforts to improve the techniques and technology of Allied amphibious assaults.[56]

The Chief of Combined Operations (CCO) was no less a person than Vice Admiral Lord Louis Mountbatten, a close relative of the British Royal family and a favourite of Churchill's. Mountbatten was immensely ambitious and hugely vain but also implacable in his will to clear all obstacles in the way of an Allied seaborne thrust into Hitler's 'Fortress Europe'. Mountbatten's responsibilities as CCO included not only organizing commando raids against selected targets on the coastline of the Nazi-occupied continent, but also preparing for the full-scale invasion of Europe.[57] Sometimes, these separate briefs could get dangerously confused (admittedly, due to political and strategic pressures outside the CCO's control) as in the ill-conceived, ill-planned, and ill-executed large-scale raid on the port of Dieppe in August 1942. However, Lord Louis survived this setback, even if many of the Canadian troops who attacked the French port did not. It is true that the CCO was not alone in making the critical blunders which led to this debacle.[58] Moreover, he managed initially, to put such a bold face on this sorry affair that it was a while before Britain's warlords grasped how truly disastrous the failure at Dieppe had actually been.[59] Still, Lord Louis retained Churchill's patronage, the Prime Minister having elevated him already to membership of the Chiefs of Staff Committee in March 1942. Admittedly, Mountbatten only attended the COS meetings on those two days of the week when they considered the broadest issues of grand strategy.[60] Yet, that limited participation was sufficient to cause immense irritation to General Alan Brooke. Thus, at a COS meeting on 6 January 1943, the CIGS found Mountbatten to be 'confused, as usual in his facts and figures'. At another COS meeting forty-eight hours later, the COS impressed the CIGS even less favourably. Alan Brooke was driven 'completely to desperation' on that occasion by Mountbatten, inter alia, and came to the conclusion that Lord Louis was a 'quite irresponsible' individual with 'the most desperate illogical brain'.[61]

However, for Ewen Montagu and *Mincemeat* what mattered was not the actual impression Mountbatten was making upon the other members of the COS Committee. What was important was his regular contact with them and their deputies. Such frequent encounters meant that it would be quite conceivable for Mountbatten to have mentioned, in casual conversation, to Alan Brooke and/or Nye that one of his amphibious warfare experts was about to take off for North Africa. It was equally plausible that the VCIGS should have seized the opportunity to get his sensitive letter to General Alexander, by such seemingly discreet and disinterested hands. Having envisaged this credible scenario, Montagu proceeded to draft a letter consistent with its assumptions—a missive that would both account for Major Martin's official trip to North Africa and, also, explain how he had come to act as courier for the other, top-secret letter in his possession. Montagu composed his letter in the name of the CCO and addressed it to the Royal Navy's Commander-in-Chief for the Mediterranean, the daring and decisive Admiral Sir Andrew Cunningham (who was also overall Allied naval commander for *Operation Husky*). Having completed his draft of the Mountbatten–Cunningham letter, Montagu submitted it to Lord Louis for his consideration. The CCO then signed Montagu's draft, without demur.[62] The approved text read as follows:

> In reply, quote: S.R. 1924/43
>
> Combined Operations Headquarters,
> 1a Richmond Terrace,
> Whitehall S.W.1.
>
> 21st April, 1943.
>
> Dear Admiral of the Fleet,
>
> I promised V.C.I.G.S. that Major Martin would arrange with you for the onward transmission of a letter he has with him for General Alexander. It is very urgent and very "hot" and as there are some remarks in it that could not be seen by others in the War Office, it could not go by signal. I feel sure that you will see that it goes on safely and without delay.
>
> I think you will find Martin the man you want. He is quiet and shy at first, but he really knows his stuff. He was more accurate than some of us about the probable run of events at Dieppe and he has been well in on the experiments with the latest barges and equipment which took place up in Scotland.

Let me have him back, please, as soon as the assault is over. He might bring
some sardines with him—they are "on points" here!

Yours sincerely
Louis Mountbatten

Admiral of the Fleet Sir A.B. Cunningham, C.C.B., D.S.O.,
Commander in Chief Mediterranean,
Allied Force H.Q.,
Algiers.[63]

Of course, this was the letter which allowed Montagu to make his 'frightfully
laboured' joke (as he described it) about 'sardines' to the enemy, in order to
drop them a broad hint about the Allies' notional offensive target in the
Central Mediterranean.[64] Since Montagu was particularly anxious that this
carefully planted clue should be communicated, verbatim, to Germany's
warlords in Berlin, he deliberately inserted the reference to the Allied reverse
at Dieppe in the second paragraph of the Mountbatten–Cunningham letter.
He guessed that Nazi intelligence agents would not be able to resist relaying
this apparent acknowledgement by a member of the British top brass, of the
defeat they had suffered at the French port, to the German High Command.
If Montagu had taken the psychological measure of the enemy, then this
additional missive should complement the main *Mincemeat* letter, from Nye
to Alexander, perfectly. A simple juxtaposing of the two documents should
allow German intelligence and staff officers to deduce the apparently complete Allied offensive plan of campaign for the Mediterranean, during the
forthcoming summer.[65]

Apart from rounding off that deceptive grand design, Mountbatten's letter
also accomplished two less elevated, but equally crucial purposes. Thus, in the
letter's second paragraph, it is revealed that an officer of Major Martin's
considerable expertise in amphibious warfare has been requested by Allied
naval headquarters in Algiers—obviously to assist with technical aspects of the
forthcoming seaborne assaults in that theatre of war. So, the reason for the
Royal Marine's journey to North Africa is elucidated in a manner unlikely to
provoke undue suspicion. Again, his employment as a courier, while en route
to Algiers, is explained in the opening paragraph of Lord Louis' letter. There,
the CCO mentions his promise to the VCIGS to let Major Martin carry a
letter intended for 'onward transmission' to General Alexander, because the
communication was too 'hot' to handle by other means such as cable signal.
The urgency and sensitivity of Nye's letter (again justifying recourse to

Martin's good offices) are underlined by the hope, which Mountbatten expresses at the end of that paragraph, that Admiral Cunningham relay the item 'safely and without delay' on to General Alexander's headquarters—at Constantine in Eastern Algeria (and, thence, doubtless, to the mobile tented camp, from which 'Alex' wielded his authority as Commander of Eighteenth Army Group and Allied Deputy Commander-in-Chief for North Africa, in overall charge of all Allied ground forces in the region).[66] Thus did Montagu's skillfully drafted text for the Mountbatten–Cunningham letter neatly fulfil its two principal goals: the logic of Major Martin's temporary service as a courier was made plain, at the same time as the deceptive message which he was bearing was amplified for its intended audience.

Still, before the enemy could digest those vital documents conveying *Mincemeat*'s deceptive message in its entirety, they had to find them. Mindful, from their experience with the Catalina crash of the previous September, 'that documents in a pocket might not be abstracted', Montagu and his colleagues stuck to their resolution of 10 February 1943 to place the key documents 'in a dispatch or brief case', rather than inside the courier's uniform.[67] They had concluded that it was 'essential to have a bag to encourage the likelihood of the documents being stolen'.[68] The bag they chose to contain the crucial letters was 'an ordinary black Government brief case with the Royal Cypher' on its exterior. However inviting such a receptacle might seem to inquisitive Francoist officials and acquisitive Nazi spies, its unavoidable use posed a whole new set of difficulties for the deception planners, as they strove to maintain a balance between fidelity and feasibility in the presentation of their deception. One such problem was the need to justify to the enemy the use of a capacious case of this kind to carry the two slim letters in Major Martin's possession. Some documentary 'ballast' was clearly needed to warrant Major Martin's taking the case with him. In fact, this point had already occurred to those present at the meeting between Colonel Bevan and representatives from the Twenty Committee on 10 February. They had agreed then that 'other official documents of a non-operational nature might also be included'.[69] Indeed, when the Directors of Plans had been informed, in their turn, about *Operation Mincemeat* a couple of days later, they not only had no objections to padding the bag with such superfluous papers, but even 'felt that the brief case might also include genuine documents', which the British 'would not mind reaching enemy hands'.[70] It was Colonel Robert Neville of the Royal Marines—a senior aide to Lord Louis Mountbatten and the CCO's representative on the Twenty Committee—who came up with an inspired suggestion for the additional materials to fill up Major Martin's briefcase.

Neville had already lent practical assistance to the preparations for *Mincemeat*, from his berth at Combined Operations Headquarters, by providing the clothing chit which Cholmondeley had submitted to Gieves, asking them to fit the battledress he brought with him to his person 'as he would require it for a special duty'.[71] Now Neville came to the rescue of the *Mincemeat* implementation team once more by suggesting that the proofs and photographic illustrations for a particular impending publication should fit the bill, both in terms of the necessary bulk (as long as the printers' proofs were included in duplicate) and requisite relevance to Major Martin's specific military vocation.[72] The work in question was a substantial pamphlet (amounting to a book-length 155 pages on publication) entitled *Combined Operations—The Official Story of the Commandos*, written by Hilary St George Saunders, a prolific author and former assistant librarian (and future librarian) of the House of Commons. Actually, Saunders was no stranger to Montagu.[73] His wife, Dr Joan Saunders, was a professional researcher who had acted as the latter's main assistant within the NID in the handling of Ultra intelligence of a non-operational nature since December 1940.[74] Moreover, Hilary Saunders also worked for Naval Intelligence during the Second World War. As a civilian employee of Section 19, the NID's information agency, he co-edited its 'Weekly Intelligence Report'. This confidential newsletter managed to disseminate—in the words of one of the DNI's personal staff—'a great deal of useful and important, if not highly secret intelligence' about Britain's naval war effort, amongst the officers of the senior service, as well as other interested parties like the BBC and government departments.[75] Neither the British edition (published by HMSO for the Ministry of Information in 1943) nor the American edition (published by the Macmillan Company the same year) identified the author of *Combined Operations* on its title page. However, Macmillan in New York did reprint an article entitled 'About the "Anonymous" Author', from the *Book-of-the-Month Club News* on the rear of the book jacket of Saunders' work which named him as its writer. That article had been written in its turn by the sardonic novelist Evelyn Waugh, who was serving in the Commandos himself and was posted on attachment to Combined Operations Headquarters in the spring of 1943. In fact, Waugh did not take too kindly to being ordered to write 'a "personality handout" for the USA about Hilary

Saunders', considering it to be 'a most singular request'—and obviously beneath him. Still, on being assured by Colonel Neville that this charge came from Mountbatten himself, he dutifully 'wrote (his) praise of Saunders' on 27 March 1943—even though he judged the latter's *Combined Operations* work to be a 'very flat pamphlet'.[76] Yet, it was not the literary merits of Saunders' latest propaganda work (an earlier one on the Battle of Britain had been a best-seller) that made it suitable material as wadding for the courier's bag.

Indeed, Saunders' book-proofs were calculated to add weight, in more ways than one, to Major Martin's mission. For a start, its subject matter was precisely pertinent to that man-at-war's calling. This was made all the more patent because, yet again, some rationale had to be presented to the Germans for the dispatch of this publication's proofs to North Africa. Neville himself—perhaps after consultation with Montagu—came up with the answer to this problem. The Royal Marine Colonel proceeded to draft yet another letter for inclusion in the courier's bag. This missive purported to come from the pen of the Chief of Combined Operations but this time it was addressed to the Supreme Allied Commander in the Mediterranean theatre. In this letter, Lord Mountbatten apparently endorses the request of the British Information Service in Washington that General Eisenhower 'should write a message praising and recommending the (enclosed) pamphlet', which could be used for publicity purposes on the release of its US edition. Mountbatten again raised no objection to signing another letter for use in *Operation Mincemeat*.[77] Montagu for his part had every reason to be delighted with Neville's text; for not only did it furnish a plausible reason for including Saunders' work in the official briefcase, but it also exploited this further opportunity to confirm Major Martin's professional identity and official standing, as is evident from the full text of the letter:

In reply, quote: S.R. 1989/43
Combined Operations Headquarters,
1a Richmond Terrace,
Whitehall S.W.1.

22nd April, 1943.

Dear General,

I am sending you herewith two copies of the pamphlet which has been prepared describing the activities of my Command; I have also enclosed copies of the photographs which are to be included in the pamphlet.

The book has been written by Hilary St. George Saunders, the English author of 'Battle of Britain', 'Bomber Command' and other pamphlets which have had a great success both in this country and yours.

The edition which is to be published in the States has already enjoyed pre-publication sales of nearly a million and a half and I understand the American authorities will distribute the book widely throughout the U.S. Army.

I understand from the British Information Service in Washington that they would like a "message" from you for use in the advertising for the pamphlet and that they have asked you direct, through Washington, for such a message.

I am sending the proofs by hand of my Staff Officer, Major W. Martin of the Royal Marines. I need not say how hounoured we shall all be if you will give such a message. I fully realise what a lot is being asked of you at a time when you are so fully occupied with infinitely more important matters. But I hope you may find a few minutes time to provide the pamphlet with an expression of your invaluable approval so that it will be read widely and given every chance to bring its message of co-operation to our two peoples.

We are watching your splendid progress with admiration and pleasure and all wish we could be with you.

You may speak freely to Major Martin in this as well as any other matters since he has my entire confidence.

Yours sincerely,
Louis Mountbatten

General Dwight Eisenhower,
  Allied Forces H.Q.,
    Algiers.[78]

Of course, the two letters notionally composed by Lord Louis Mountbatten to Admiral Cunningham and General Eisenhower, respectively, were handled with the same close attention to bureaucratic detail and physical appearance that had marked the production of the Nye–Alexander missives. Both the Mountbatten letters were typed on the same machine within the NID, but on the notepaper of Combined Operations Headquarters. To ensure that the two documents looked appropriately official, Montagu gave each of them a 'bogus but plausible' reference number. However, when it came to their packaging, they were treated differently. The letter purporting to be addressed by Lord Mountbatten to Admiral Cunningham was placed in an envelope marked 'Personal', then sealed and inserted inside another envelope. On the other hand, the letter allegedly addressed to General Eisenhower—although also placed in an inner envelope marked 'Personal'—was put subsequently into a much larger envelope lready containing the duplicate proofs and photo illustrations for Hilary ▸aunders' pamphlet on the Commandos. Again, every care was taken to ▸nsure that only credible and consistent sets of fingerprints were detectable ▸n these letters and their wrappings. So, Major Martin had a veritable ▸agful of tricks with which to bamboozle the enemy about his identity ▸nd the Allies' offensive plans in the Mediterranean.[79]

However, there remained still one more practical problem that had to be ▸olved before *Mincemeat*'s deceptive documents could be conveyed to the ▸nemy via a courier's briefcase, namely how to ensure that the case would ▸e discovered alongside the corpse. As Montagu understood, 'it was essen-▸ial that this (brief case) should not sink'. One possible means was to prise ▸pen Glyndwr Michael's fingers as his body was being thawed, then place ▸he handle of the bag in one of his palms and, finally, attempt to close his ▸and around that handle in as firm a grip as could be imposed by downward ▸ressure from a third party. Accordingly, Montagu turned to the Oper-▸tion's medical advisers (doubtless Spilsbury and/or Bentley Purchase) for ▸n expert opinion on the feasibility of fastening the briefcase to the courier ▸y way of the dead man's grip. Unfortunately, the medical experts were ▸nable to give Montagu and his colleagues an assurance that the dead ▸nessenger would be able to maintain a sure hold on the briefcase, as he ▸obbed about in the ocean, supported by his life jacket. Calculating the ▸xact effects of *rigor mortis*, in first stiffening and then relaxing a body's ▸nuscles and joints is difficult enough when a person had died and nature has ▸een allowed to take its course. However, in the case of Glyndwr Michael, ▸he prompt and protracted refrigeration of the corpse, and the subsequent ▸eed to thaw it sufficiently to allow it to be dressed and then dispatched on ▸ts journey to Spanish waters, meant that there were just too many impon-▸erables involved in trying to determine its capacity to keep a hold on the ▸riefcase.[80]

With that solution to their problem ruled out because of the medical ▸ncertainty, the deception planners had to find some other means of 'ensuring the case going ashore with the body', to use Montagu's own ▸words. Members of section B1A of MI5 had conducted experiments into ▸he possibility of using a 'special' bag, similar to that used by military ▸ispatch riders 'with a strap over the shoulder', but it seems that proved to ▸e unreliable when tested in sea water.[81] So, the deception planners decided ▸o resort to a method they had excluded early on in their deliberations, on ▸he grounds that it was so 'doubtful' that it might 'endanger the whole

operation'.[82] Now, in their desperation to overcome this snag in their
scheme, the *Mincemeat* team felt they had no choice but to revive ever
that most dubious option. They resolved to attach the briefcase, with it.
crucial cache of deceptive documents, to Glyndwr Michael's person by
means of a leather-covered chain, such as were widely employed by bank
messengers in Britain to prevent thieves snatching bags filled with money
or other valuables, from their custody.[83] Montagu described the article in
question for the commander of the submarine who was to be charged with
transporting Major Martin to the south-west coast of Spain, as follows:

> The chain is of the type worn under the coat, round the chest and out
> through the sleeve. At the end is a 'dog-lead' type of clip for attaching to the
> handle of the brief case and a similar clip for forming the loop round the
> chest.[84]

Although shackling Major Martin to his briefcase by such a chain should
guarantee their joint arrival in the hands of the Spaniards, it was a solution to
this practical problem that Montagu and his colleagues adopted with the
utmost reluctance. Since British military couriers never fastened bags to
their persons with these leather-covered fetters, Montagu feared that this
'horribly phoney' arrangement might blow the whole deception. After all
the painstaking effort to display the courier down to the last detail in the
most convincing guise possible, it was galling now to have to strike a
deliberately false note. Of course, the British deception planners took it
for granted that the Francoist authorities would inform their Nazi contact
about the exact circumstances in which these ostensibly top-secret documents had reached Spanish soil. All the British covert warriors could do wa.
hope that their enemies would be so fascinated by the contents of the
Mincemeat letters and so persuaded by the other, more plausible aspects o
their dead messenger's appearance and notional identity that they would
overlook this potentially fatal flaw in his outfit.[85]

Still, Montagu and his assistants did their level best to lessen the artificiality of the arrangement for binding body and bag together, which they had
been forced to accept. They attached the chain to the corpse in a way that
should appear more natural, and less contrived, for an officer unused to
being harnessed in this fashion. Reasoning that such an individual would be
unlikely 'to submit to the inconvenience of having the bag attached to his
arm' for the entire duration of a lengthy flight, they decided to place the
chain on Major Martin's person in the following manner: it would be

draped around his shoulder on the outside of his trench-coat and trailed down under his Mae West life jacket to his waist, where it could be looped through the coat's belt. This placement of the chain on the corpse would make it seem that the Royal Marine officer had 'slipped the chain for comfort in the aircraft' but 'nevertheless kept it attached to him so that the bag should not either be forgotten or slide away from him', during his flight.[86] Moreover, as Montagu pointed out to his superiors and colleagues at the time, there was an additional advantage to tying the briefcase to the body of the courier in this loose fashion: it would make it 'as easy as possible for the Spaniards or the Germans to remove the bag and chain without trace'.[87]

Still, the disquiet that the deception planners felt over having to employ an unconventional device like the chain to fasten the bag to the body of the courier testified to their acute awareness that a single incongruous detail in Major Martin's apparel or accoutrements could subvert the entire *Mincemeat* operation. As Montagu later acknowledged, he was 'quite sure that in a matter of this importance every little detail would be studied by the Germans in an effort to find a flaw in Major Martin's make-up, so as to be sure that the whole thing was genuine and not a plant'.[88] Yet, Montagu and his collaborators also realized that the effort they had to invest in this 'war of detail' could not be confined to fabricating a professional persona for Glyndwr Michael; he also had to impress foreign investigators as having a private personality, compatible with and complementary to his official status. On the degree to which the dead body could be made to possess a dead soul also, the ultimate success of *Operation Mincemeat* might depend.

7

Brief Encounter

Inevitably, as Ewen Montagu, Charles Cholmondeley, and the other members of the *Mincemeat* team set about the task of inventing a professional identity for their deceased courier, that individual tended to assume a palpable presence in their midst. Indeed, some of them soon comprehended that this sensation of Major Martin as a live—or, at least, very recently dead—personality was precisely the impression they wished to cultivate amongst future scrutineers of his mortal remains and personal effects in Spain. The less anonymous the courier appeared to be, the more he could authenticate the whole *Mincemeat* enterprise. So, Montagu and his colleagues spent hours analysing the character they were in the process of creating, all the better to endow him with a set of consistent personal traits and a circle of convincing social relationships. Major Martin remained an entirely cooperative participant in the exercise: he was their creature and could be reshaped to meet their needs.[1] For example, the decision was taken to make the Royal Marine officer a Roman Catholic. This 'fact' was stated on the two identity discs attached to his braces and it was confirmed by two religious tokens in his possession: a silver cross attached to a silver chain placed around his neck and a St Christopher's medal carried in his wallet. Since Catholics venerate St Christopher as the patron saint of travellers, this was a natural religious artefact for one of their number to be taking with him on a trip as a military courier. Of course, the purpose of making Major Martin a follower of the Church of Rome was to discourage the holding of any post-mortem examination of his corpse. The British clearly still believed that the Francoist authorities—who were uniformly Catholic in their religious profession—would be averse to violating the 'temple of the Holy Ghost', particularly when it belonged to a co-religionist.[2]

Yet, making Major Martin a member of a specific church did not do much to fill out his personality as a distinct individual. What more could be done to transform him from an archetypical staff officer into a recently living and breathing human being? The first fruit of the deliberations on this critical issue was the conclusion that this Royal Marine officer was likely to have the vice of his virtues. After all, as a relatively young warrior who had already made such a favourable impression upon his commanding officers he was sure to be somebody who devoted himself heart and soul to his military vocation. Indeed, it was entirely plausible that an individual who was utterly absorbed in his labour to improve the Allies' ability to wage amphibious warfare should have been less attentive to his own affairs—even to the point of neglecting his personal finances. Distracted as he might be by the demands of his crucial war work, and also possibly possessed of what Montagu termed a 'reasonably extravagant streak', he could have easily run up an overdraft, instead of living within his means. Since the group of people implementing *Operation Mincemeat* contained more than a few unfortunates who had cultivated a similar talent for incurring overdrafts, they naturally felt that recruiting Major Martin to the ranks of the indebted could help their effort to represent him as a real-life character, with his quota of human failings. Deciding that their Royal Marine officer might well have run up an overdraft of £79 19s. 2d., they made sure that 'fact' would become known to all who searched his personal effects, by planting on his person a dunning letter from a bank manager over this outstanding debt.[3]

Again, most of the *Mincemeat* team were so familiar with the peremptory tone and pointed text of these menacing missives from financial institutions that they could have replicated them with ease. However, Montagu decided the best way of ensuring that the demand that Major Martin settle his overdraft forthwith had an absolutely authentic aspect was to get a real-life banker to write it. Here he encountered yet another of the many practical problems afflicting the implementation of a scheme as sensitive as *Mincemeat*. Operational security, as ever, required that the circle of those 'in the know' about the deception plan's secrets should be as limited as possible, and certainly consist of only the most trustworthy individuals. One of the team implementing *Operation Mincemeat* did have an utterly reliable contact in London's financial community, but he was a rather senior figure, a Joint General Manager at Lloyds Bank's Head Office. Now Montagu knew from 'bitter' personal experience that it usually fell to ordinary branch managers to sign the minatory letters dispatched to spendthrift clients. So, he naturally wondered whether obtaining the dunning letter to be addressed to *Mincemeat*'s courier from higher up the banking hierarchy might not be just the kind of infelicity that could undermine the whole operation's credibility. Discreet inquiries, however, relieved his worry on that score. Montagu was informed that it was not uncommon for the letters sent to overdraft dodgers to come from the head office of a bank. A repeat offender, or a member of a prominent family who had fallen into bad financial habits, might merit such a stricture from on high.[4]

So, Montagu was persuaded to let Ernest Whitley Jones of Lloyds Bank draft the necessary financial demand for dispatch to the fictional Major Martin. Whitley Jones not only composed the text of the letter; he also had it typed up on bank notepaper in his own office at Lloyds, and personally signed the communication.[5] No wonder, then, that it looked and sounded like the real thing:

Telegraphic Address	Lloyds Bank Limited,	Postal Address,
"Branchage, Stock, London".	Head Office,	G.P.O. Box 215,
Telephone No	London, E.C.3.	71, Lombard Street,
		E.C.3.

Mansion House 1500.

In replying please address   14th April, 1943.
The Joint General Managers.

PRIVATE.

Major W. Martin, R.M.,
   Army and Navy Club,
      Pall Mall,
         LONDON, S.W.1.
Dear Sir,

I am given to understand that in spite of repeated application your overdraft amounting to £79.19s.2d. still outstands.

In the circumstances, I am now writing to inform you that unless this amount, plus interest at 4% to date of payment, is received forthwith we shall have no alternative but to take the necessary steps to protect our interests.

Yours faithfully,
Ernest Whitley Jones,
Joint General Manger[6]

To make this letter appear all the more like a genuine article, Montagu and company deliberately had it misaddressed to the Army and Navy Club on Pall Mall. In fact the *Mincemeat* team had decided—for reasons explained in Chapter 9—to make their Royal Marine officer a temporary member of the

Naval and Military Club in Piccadilly. This allowed them to give 'a most convincing indication' that the Lloyds Bank Manager's letter was legitimate by having the porter at the Army and Navy Club inscribe the phrase 'Not known at this address' and 'Try Navy and Military Club, 99 Piccadilly' on its envelope. They also provided proof that the letter had been sent through the Royal Mail twice over, by ensuring that it carried a double set of postmarks with different dates and times. Such confusion between two similarly named clubs and over Major Martin's exact whereabouts was just the kind of mix up that might be expected to occur in the real world, especially a world immersed in the flux of total war. So, the team were careful to place the Lloyds letter inside one of the dead messenger's pockets whilst still in the envelope, whose markings seemed to authenticate not only its particular contents but also its addressee—and, by extension, his whole mission to North Africa. Doubtless, the financially feckless members of the *Mincemeat* team derived some satisfaction from demonstrating that bank managers were fallible human beings too, quite capable of misdirecting one of their reprimands with a slip of the pen.[7]

Actually, the team were guilty of a slip up of their own, as they sought to depict Major Martin as a real person, warts and all, to the Germans. Indeed, it was only after the body had been packed off to Spain that Ewen Montagu realized that they had committed a real blunder in regard to one of the incidental items they had placed in one of the pockets of the trench coat worn by the dead messenger. This was the receipt, or 'sale note', from Gieves for the khaki shirt and cuffs which Charles Cholmondeley had bought, on the occasion of his visit to that firm of tailors, to have the battledress adjusted for the corpse-courier. Montagu and his helpers had thought that it would make their creation look like a very recent inhabitant of the lands of the living, if he were to be found with such a quotidian item as a scrunched-up Gieves' receipt on his person. However, they had neglected to notice how their RAF colleague had settled this particular bill. Of course, the fictitious Major Martin was unable to open an account in person with the tailors' firm, to which such a purchase might be charged. So, it must have seemed to Flight Lieutenant Cholmondeley that the only course left to him to ensure that his own name did not end up on the 'sale note' was to pay it in cash. It was only when their courier was 'winging' his way to Spain that it dawned on Ewen Montagu that this prompt settlement of account was neither in keeping with the general practice of naval officers, nor in character for their impecunious invention. A Royal Marine officer being hounded by his bank manager for repayment of his overdraft would be unlikely to pay cash where credit might be forthcoming from such 'a long-suffering firm' as Gieves. Montagu could only hope that the Germans would imagine that a 'Temporary Captain' in the Royal Marines like William Martin, with the 'Acting Rank of Major', would not enjoy the same automatic access to credit at Gieves as a regular officer. Still, what seems to have concerned Montagu most about this faux pas was less the fact that, in itself, it really risked blowing the whole deception plan, but rather that it was 'inartistic'. It was a blemish on what was shaping up to be a masterpiece of the counterfeiter's art.[8]

There was yet another mistake on one of the documents to be carried by Major Martin on his person which was bound to be noticed during any future inspection of his personal effects. This time, however, the lapse was a carefully contrived one. Inside his wallet was placed a cellophane container which held both his photo ID card and a separate pass, authorizing its bearer to enter Combined Operations Headquarters, while on 'official duty'. At the foot of the front of this pass (which bore Major Martin's signature but not his photograph), there was printed the following stipulation: 'Not valid after 31st March, 1943'. In short, Major Martin would be seen to be carrying an official pass to Mountbatten's headquarters which had expired. This apparent failure to renew the pass on the Royal Marine officer's part served to bolster his own credibility and to boost Operation Mincemeat's chances of success in a number of ways. For a start, it prevented his identity papers from looking just too pat. Again, it lent verisimilitude to the whole attempt to palm Glyndwr Michael's alter ego off as a genuine serving officer, since his real-life counterparts were prone to similar sins of omission. It was consonant, too, with the deception planner's attempt to demonstrate that the courier had been—until very recently—a living, breathing human being with his fair share of foibles and failings. Montagu and his colleagues had tried, already, to temper the necessarily glowing estimate of Major Martin's professional prowess conveyed in Mountbatten's letters to Admiral Cunningham and General Eisenhower by portraying him—as revealed in the communication from Lloyds Bank—as somewhat irresponsible in money matters. A similar inattentiveness to administrative detail would appear both in character and in accord with the endeavour to represent the courier's personality as a credible combination of vices and virtues. Finally, the team intended to supply their Royal Marine major with another excuse or neglecting to renew his pass for Combined Operations Headquarters: William Martin, it would seem, was in love.[9]

In fact, the deception planners' decision to make their courier the subject of a typically whirlwind wartime romance sprang from a fundamental difficulty encountered in the elaboration of his fictitious personality. How could the members of the *Mincemeat* team convey the individual character of their dead messenger in a sufficiently vivid manner with the limited means at their disposal? After all Montagu and company could only build up Major Martin's private personality with those materials that could be placed credibly in his pockets. Since most people carry about a number of impersonal articles in their clothing, the actual number of personal memorabilia that could be placed alongside them was not great. Indeed, the need to include such staples as a box of matches, a packet of cigarettes, a bunch of keys, a book of stamps and money (one five-pound and two one-pound notes, whose serial numbers were recorded, were placed inside the officer's wallet, whilst a half-crown, two shillings, two sixpenny pieces and four pennies were inserted into his pockets) left little enough room for items of a more biographical nature. True, a couple more articles of a quotidian nature—a pencil stub and two used London Transport bus tickets—were added to the courier's modest stash of personal possessions. However, although such commonplace articles might strengthen the general aura of authenticity the deception planners sought to bestow on their messenger, they did not help tell his life story. Of course, the Lloyds bank manager's dunning letter did reveal Major Martin's apparent affection for the good life, an impression reinforced by two other documents placed on his person. These were a receipted bill from the Naval and Military Club for a six-night stay from 18 to 23 April 1943, costing one pound ten shillings, and a personal letter of invitation to join the Cabaret Club in London. Still, Montagu and company realized that much more was needed to conjure Major Martin into existence as a real person. On the other hand, to increase the amount of personal documentation in the dead messenger's pockets, in an obviously artificial effort to achieve that effect, would jeopardize the whole deception scheme. For, as the *Mincemeat* team appreciated, normally people do not carry about comprehensive documentation on their private lives. So, it seemed inevitable that Nazi suspicions would be aroused by any attempt to furnish the future scrutineers of Major Martin's mortal remains and personal effects with the narrative tools to construct his biography. Yet, unless the messenger's persona was persuasive, his message was unlikely to convince.[10]

It was one of the more self-effacing members of the Twenty Committee'
personnel—from which the group implementing *Operation Mincemeat* wa
essentially drawn—who rescued his colleagues from this impasse. John H
Marriott was a solicitor by profession, who had been recruited into MI5 o
the outbreak of the Second World War. Once taken on by the Securit'
Service, he not only served along with 'J.C.' Masterman and 'Tar' Robert
son in B1A's Directorate (which decided that subdivision's basic policie
and handled relations with other branches of the military and civil services
but also acted as secretary to the Twenty Committee.[11] Although the ver
model of a discreet bureaucrat, Marriott was adept at composing the comi
form of verse known as clerihews. Indeed, the head of MI5's B Division wa
so impressed by the amateur versifier's effort to capture his own personalit'
that he recorded it in his diary:

> They can't diddle
> Guy Liddell.
> He is sufficiently deep
> To look asleep.[12]

During the festive season in late 1942 however, another form of literar
inventiveness engaged Marriott's mind when he remembered reading a
article in a weekly newspaper. He reported the chain of thought tha
this holiday musing had set in motion, in a letter to the Deputy Chief c
the London Controlling Section, Major Ronald Wingate, early in th
New Year:

6th January, 1943.

Dear Wingate,
   I read in "The Field" an account of a deception which was practised in the
last war on the Turks by an officer on Allenby's staff. The deception consisted
in "losing", near the Turkish lines, a notebook belonging to a staff officer,
and containing some suitably doctored notes. Whether or not the deception
worked I do not know, but the interesting feature of the scheme was the fact
that in addition to the military material the notebook also contained a
selection of purely private letters, including one announcing the birth of
the officer's son (together with, for all I know, a photograph of the infant),
the argument being that the Turks would conclude that nobody would ever
part with such virtually irreplaceable documents except as the result of a
genuine accident.
   I do not think that this sort of technique is likely to be used by us in
connection with any of our agents, but it occurs to me that something of the

sort may well one day be practised by Bevan, in which case I think that you will agree that this is a valuable illustration of the necessity for including a suitable amount of irrelevant material solely for the purpose of making a "plant" appear genuine.

Yours sincerely,
J.H. Marriott[13]

The Field was an unlikely source of inspiration for military covert operations, since it mainly catered to the rural community as a whole and the devotees of hunting, shooting, and fishing in particular. However, its interest in this particular hoax could be explained by the fact that its principal perpetrator was the flamboyant outdoorsman and reputed ornithologist, Richard Meinertzhagen.[14] The latter had also won considerable fame as an intrepid warrior while serving in the British Army before and during the First World War.[15] Yet, his most sensational exploit during that war was an attempt to outfox rather than outfight the enemy. This plan was the one mentioned in the article read by John Marriott. The trick had been employed during the British campaign against Ottoman Turkish forces (which had been reinforced by German contingents and commanders) in Palestine. Having been rebuffed twice during the period April–May 1917 in their efforts to breach the primary Turkish defensive perimeter in southern Palestine, the Gaza–Beersheba line, the British decided to change the target for their assault next time around. The new head of the Egyptian Expeditionary Force (EEF), General Sir Edward Allenby (who took up his post on 28 June 1917), readily accepted the advice of his senior staff officers that the Turkish defensive line could be turned more easily, if the British shifted the weight of their attack to its left, i.e., against Beersheba.[16] However, Allenby also understood that operational deception measures could facilitate his actual assault on Beersheba by maintaining an apparent threat to Gaza. Allenby's resolve to mount a feint against Gaza was strengthened by the accurate appraisal he had received from his intelligence officers of the focus of Turkish fears on that front: 'It is there [Gaza]', he reported home to London on 21 August 1917, 'that the Turks at present expect us to attack and I hope to keep their attention so fixed'.[17]

The British strove to confirm the erroneous Turkish assumption—that their hammer-blow was to be directed mainly against Gaza, and not Beersheba—by a variety of means. One was deceptive signals intelligence. A carefully orchestrated campaign of clues, dropped in apparently casual radio conversations or contained in secret messages encrypted in a cipher whose key had been divulged deliberately to the Turks, seemed to highlight the imminent danger to Gaza.[18] False visual display of military encampment and misleading manoeuvres of forces on land and at sea compounded this inaccurate impression of British offensive intentions. However, in addition to these incremental efforts to pull the wool over the enemy's eyes, the British also attempted an audacious stratagem. This action was meant to deliver into the foe's hands, at one fell swoop—just like *Operation Mincemeat* during the Second World War—a clear outline of the overall British plan of attack. No less an authority on the First World War in the Middle East than Colonel T. E. Lawrence was certain as to the unique character responsible for the inception and implementation of this daring deception. 'Lawrence of Arabia' identified Meinertzhagen as the prime mover behind the scheme in his post-war account of the revolt by the Desert Arabs against Turkish rule:

> Meiner thought out false Army papers, elaborate and confidential, which to a trained staff officer would indicate wrong positions for Allenby's main formation, a wrong direction of the coming attack, and a date some days too late . . . Meinertzhagen rode out with his note books, on reconnaissance. He pushed forward until the enemy saw him. In the ensuing gallop he lost all his loose equipment and very nearly himself, but was rewarded by seeing the enemy's reserves held behind Gaza and their whole preparations swung towards the coast and made less urgent.[19]

Admittedly, Lawrence did add a note of caution to his recounting of what was really Meinertzhagen's own version of these events, noting that the 'Galloping Major' took great pleasure in deceiving his enemy and friend, alike.[20] In fact, in his retelling of this episode, Meinertzhagen seems to have indulged in the same self-promotion through falsification which, recent revelations have shown, taint his real achievements as a soldier, adventurer, and ornithologist.[21] Indeed, the 'haversack ruse', in which a satchel containing misleading British military documents was abandoned in the desert for the enemy to find, was not Meinertzhagen's brainchild, but that of Lieutenant Colonel James Belgrave, who held a much more senior staff post as principal intelligence officer in the EEF.[22] Nor did 'Meiner' personally abandon the haversack under fire from a Turkish mounted patrol, as he later claimed. The truth was more pedestrian, as the diary of Acting Major Arthur Neate, the intelligence officer in the Desert Mounted Corps, who actually deposited the satchel in a spot where the foe would be likely to stumble upon it, reveals:

11th September [1917]

I went over with car to Yeomanry Div with the precious bag for Major Meinertzhagen . . .

12th September

Left early with a horse . . . & joined myself to a Yeomanry regt of the 9th Mounted Brigade commanded by a Col. Salt . . . We hacked laboriously over the dry sandy burning country—till El Girheir. Saw many Turks moving about but none came near. Dropped the bag near Pt. 730 & returned, trusting all will be well. Returned quite tired.[23]

So, although Meinertzhagen was centrally involved in the implementation of the 'haversack ruse', he felt compelled to exaggerate his role in this operational deception. The false gospel about the Gaza feint was publicly proclaimed as early as ten years after the event, in an account of Allenby's assault which appeared in *The Times* newspaper. That article, which acclaimed the capture of Beersheba as 'a triumph of surprise', included a version of the 'haversack ruse', apparently dictated by Meinertzhagen (probably through the good offices of his old friend, Geoffrey Dawson, the paper's editor):[24]

Among the ruses adopted by the British to mislead the enemy as to their intentions in the days before the action there was one which deserves special mention. On October 10 Major R. Meinertzhagen . . . set forth into the open areas of the enemy front, accompanied only by a few men that his mission might appear to be one of reconnaissance. Near Bir el Girheir, on the Wadi Hanafieh, he drew the fire of a Turkish cavalry patrol. He simulated injury and reeled in the saddle. Then, dropping his haversack (stained with fresh blood) and glasses, as though by accident, he fled to safety, chased by the Turks. His haversack was taken by the Turks. In it was a faked agenda of a G.H.Q. conference suggesting that the main attack would be against Gaza, accompanied by a landing on the Turkish side of Gaza. There were also draft keys of a cipher in which, later, false wireless messages were to be issued. The Turks, according to their own admission, accepted the papers as genuine and were misled by their contents. The haversack, that the Turks might be convinced that its dropping was no matter of design, also contained £E.20 in notes.[25]

It was fortunate for Meinertzhagen's public credibility that, when Arthur Neate wrote to dispute this account of the deception practised against the Turks in the run-up to Allenby's attack on the Gaza-Beersheba line, he did not address himself to the letter pages of *The Times*. Instead, as an officer still serving in intelligence in the post-First World War period, Neate opted for

the more discreet route of writing to 'the Galloping Major' in person wit
a polite request that Meinertzhagen himself get *The Times* to publis
a correction to their story. This could specify the actual date (12 Septemb
1917) when the 'haversack ruse' was carried out, and mention the tru
identity of the man who had really risked life and limb to execute it in th
field. Meinertzhagen failed to comply with Neate's request and even wer
on to claim the credit for thinking up the haversack ruse in the first place—
claim that he could make with some impunity in view of the fact that its re
author, the precociously brilliant Lieutenant Colonel James Belgrave, ha
been killed during the last year of the First World War while still onl
twenty-one years old.[26]

There was one of Major Meinertzhagen's claims about the 'haversac
ruse', however, which even those intimately involved in this operation
deception were not inclined to challenge too vigorously. This was h
contention that the Turks and their German commander on the Palestinia
front had fallen for the ploy and adjusted their dispositions and defences in
way that facilitated Allenby's main attack against Beersheba. Certainly, th
sequence of military events, which began with the British assault on 3
October 1917, appears to justify the most inflated assertions of the succe
of the documentary deception in question. Beersheba itself fell on the ver
first day of the offensive, a victory that allowed Allenby to reinforce h
secondary front against Gaza. Menaced by potential envelopment on bot
flanks, Turkish forces quit their entire defensive line. The way was the
open for the EEF to drive deep into the Holy Land and Jerusalem surren
dered to the British on 9 December 1917.[27] Yet, the extent to which th
sweeping operational success was due to deception measures in general, an
the 'bloody haversack ruse' in particular, has to be considered carefully. Th
commander of the Turkish Eighth Army occupying the Gaza–Beersheb
front, the German General Friedrich Kress von Kressenstein, did admit afte
the war that he had been taken in at first by the contents of the plante
satchel. However, he also maintained that later he came to discount thos
fabricated documents, when the British build-up opposite Beersheb
became too obvious to ignore.[28]

In fact, Turkish aerial and ground reconnaissance units had performe
exceptionally well in pinpointing the redeployment of British force
from Gaza to Beersheba during the week before the main attack wa
launched against the latter town. In spite of this remarkably accurat
order-of-battle intelligence, however, von Kressenstein did not heavil

reinforce the southern sector of the Turkish line. He argued, again after the event, that what persuaded him to assign continuing priority to defence against the threat to Gaza was his realization that a British breakthrough there could spell disaster for the whole army.[29] It is also true that, by the autumn of 1917, British forces were so numerically superior to their Turkish opponents in southern Palestine that Allenby could afford to mount not just a feint but an actual full-scale secondary attack on Gaza, with an entire army corps (the XXI).[30] The menace to Gaza, then, was no mere desert mirage, but rather a proximate and palpable one. However, the critical factor in persuading the German–Turkish command to remain focused on the secondary threat being posed by British deception planners in Palestine at the time was its coincidence with their preconceptions and preoccupations. By battening on to pre-existing enemy fears about Gaza, they were able to exploit an ingrained insecurity, which mounting evidence that the real danger lay elsewhere could not overbear in the time available for reconsideration. Yet, even then, the Turks failed to act in accordance with the British expectation that they would increase greatly the number of troops defending the Gaza sector.[31]

Of course, this earlier effort to pass deceptive documents to the enemy via a lost bag served as a precedent for similar schemes during the Second World War. Indeed, one such scheme was clearly modelled on Meinertzhagen's apparent example. This was the attempt to foist on Rommel, in late August 1942, a misleading map designed to lure the *Panzerarmee Afrika* into difficult terrain when it launched its expected attack against the British in Egypt at Alam Halfa. This document—which was spattered with tea stains for authenticity's sake, but still perfectly legible—was contained in a haversack, left behind with other kit by the crew of a scout car, who had apparently bailed out of their vehicle when it struck a German landmine. Still, after the event, British military intelligence could not be absolutely sure that it was this 'false-going' map which had persuaded Rommel to send his troops across soft sandy terrain where they consumed fuel at three times the normal rate.[32] Whatever his reasons for choosing a line of attack which his limited stocks of fuel could not sustain, Rommel thereby fluffed his last chance at breaking through to the Suez Canal before Montgomery felt strong enough to counterattack at El Alamein. In any case, ingenious as these haversack ruses staged in the deserts of the Middle East during both world wars were, they were deceptions confined to the tactical and/or operational plane of warfare. They were devised to achieve local, if important, battlefield advantage. *Operation Mincemeat* was of an altogether different order. Its purpose was to enable the Allies to seize, irrevocably, the grand strategic heights of the entire Mediterranean theatre of the Second World War. Again, even if the more remote and more recent haversack ruses stood as precedents for *Mincemeat*, the immediate inspiration of that particular plan was the crash of the Catalina aircraft off the coast of Spain in late September, 1942. It was this accident which prompted Charles Cholmondeley to propose that a dead body, apparently lost in the sea, might be used to convey strategic misinformation right into the heart of the enemy High Command. *Operation Mincemeat* was a truly original deception project in the reach of its ambition and in the depth of difficulty involved in its execution.

However, when it came to the implementation of that deception plan, Richard Meinertzhagen's inflated reputation as an outdoorsman and sometime covert warrior proved to be of definite service. It earned him the attention of the press and John Marriott remembered the coverage of the adventurer's alleged exploits at a most opportune time—just before British deception planners began mulling over the best way to present *Mincemeat*'s misleading papers to the enemy. At that strategic moment, Marriott was able to remind them how documents of an 'irrelevant' personal nature had been used to authenticate the 'official' papers inside Meinertzhagen's haversack in 1917.[33] Certainly, Montagu and his colleagues readily appreciated that 'a selection of purely private letters' would convey a vivid impression of their courier as a real-life character and not just an anonymous abstraction thought up to promote a deception plan.[34] Still, they also remained aware that packing too much biographical material into their dead messenger's pockets might arouse suspicions rather than assuage them. Yet, the precedent from the Palestine campaign of the First World War suggested how the *Mincemeat* team might justify their courier's carrying more than the normal quota of private papers on his person. If a recent 'happy event' could help explain why Meinertzhagen's haversack contained some revealing personal documents, which also made that whole bag of tricks look genuine, then why should an impending marriage, say, not do the same for *Mincemeat*'s courier and his cache of papers? Indeed, that refinement on the original ruse was a stroke of genius. For, by arranging an engagement between Major Martin and a young lady named 'Pam', whom he had

et apparently only a few weeks before his air trip from Britain, Mon-
gu and company had come up with the perfect excuse to fill their
essenger's pockets with an array of private documents. The presence of
ese intimate items on the deceased courier would be accounted for,
lly, by the recent emotional epiphany he had experienced in his
ersonal life.[35] Again, these articles could be designed carefully so as to
elong to the category defined by Marriott as 'virtually irreplaceable
ocuments' that 'nobody would ever part with', other than 'as the result
f a genuine accident'.[36] So, in entering the matchmaking business, the
anners were able to breathe new life—or at least a vital sense of one
idely interrupted—into their creation, making his mission as a courier
f top-secret documents seem all the more genuine.

Accordingly, the *Mincemeat* team set about the task of providing Major
1artin with a set of tokens of his recent betrothal. For a start, such a smitten
ul would be likely to carry a picture of his fiancée inside his wallet, next to
is heart. To obtain the necessary snapshots of Pam, Montagu and his
olleagues evidently decided that it would be best to use an existing photo-
raph of a suitable subject. Staging their own photo session with an amateur
r professional model might produce a portrait that looked too good to be
ue. So, the deception planners approached a number of the female em-
loyees in the offices of MI5 and the armed services' intelligence branches
ith a request that they donate snapshots of themselves for a photographic
dentity parade'.[37] Since the object of William Martin's affection was meant
o have captivated him virtually at first sight, inevitably it was the more
hotogenic young women working inside these departments, who were
ivited to join in the exercise—with no explanation given to them as to its
eal purpose. However, the 'very attractive girl'—to cite Montagu's judge-
nent at the time—whose likeness was chosen to serve as that of Major
1artin's fiancée, did gradually divine the covert purpose for which her
ortrait was required.[38] However, as a clerk working within MI5, Jean Leslie
illy appreciated the importance of deception operations in the war against
ie Axis. She did not hesitate to hand over her own photograph for inclusion
1 the materials being assembled for this particular plan. In doing so, she
1ade a vital contribution to the credibility of *Operation Mincemeat*, for her
icture had a convincingly natural look. It depicts its subject as windswept
nd shivering, apparently after having had a 'dip' in typically frigid English
aters. Mrs Jean Gerard Leigh (née Leslie) confirmed the veracity of her

pose—with the goose pimples all but discernible—many years afterwards, a newspaper interview:

> The picture was taken by a friend just after I had been swimming in the Thames near Oxford. I can tell you that it was a very cold day.[39]

Undoubtedly, the selected snapshot met the deception planners' aesthe criteria: it was 'charming', as Montagu later acknowledged.[40] Still, its ou standing merit for the *Mincemeat* team was its obvious naturalness. There w not a hint of staginess or artificiality about it.

It was equally important that the same sense of genuine spontaneity infor the other main personal items placed inside Major Martin's wallet to confir his recent engagement and to corroborate his real existence. These were tv love letters from Pam, which it would be perfectly natural for him treasure and, therefore, to carry about on his person. However, the writi of love letters from a young woman's perspective was one form of litera composition that Montagu and his partners in deception knew was beyo their experience and expertise.[41] So, according to Montagu's later testimon they sought the help of a female office worker inside MI5 in locating colleague capable of writing 'a first-rate paean of love' from the femini perspective. However, Lady Victoire 'Paddy' Ridsdale remembered that was she who composed these love letters to the non-existent Major Marti with a feigned ardour that made her recently wedded husband, Julian, fe 'rather jealous'. Victoire 'Paddy' Ridsdale was Commander Ian Fleming sometime assistant in the NID, and she is recognized to be one of the real-li models for James Bond's 'Miss Moneypenny'.[42] Certainly, the authoress Pam's billets-doux achieved a literary effect that Bond's creator might ha envied. As an impressed Ewen Montagu observed, these love letters—writte without the benefit of even the briefest of encounters with the object of the affection—managed to convey a real sense of 'the thrill and pathos of a w (time) engagement'.[43] Still, Montagu did contribute one critical detail Pam's primary love letter, courtesy of his own brother-in-law, Oliv Harry Frost. The latter had married the Hon. Joyce Ida Jesse Montagu ar served in the British Army during the Second World War, winning tl Military Cross for gallantry in action. However, it was the irresistibly Engli resonance of the couple's home address, in rural Wiltshire, which Monta now exploited to confer an additional aura of authenticity on Pam's ma text, which contrived to be at once passionate and poignant.[44] It read, missir apostrophes and all, as follows:

The Manor House,
Ogbourne St. George,
Marlborough, Wiltshire,
Telephone: Ogbourne St. George 242.
Sunday, 18th.

I do think dearest that seeing people like you off at railway stations is one of the poorest forms of sport. A train going out can leave a howling great gap in ones life & one has to try madly—& quite in vain—to fill it with all the things one used to enjoy a whole five weeks ago. That lovely golden day we spent together—oh! I know it's been said before, but if <u>only</u> time could sometimes stand still for a <u>minute</u>—But that line of thought is too pointless. Pull your socks up Pam & don't be a silly little fool.

Your letter made me feel slightly better—but I shall get horribly conceited if you go on saying things like that about me—they're utterly unlike ME, as I'm afraid you'll soon find out. Here I am for the week-end in this divine place with Mummy & Jane being too sweet & understanding the whole time, bored beyond words & panting for Monday so that I can get back to the old grindstone again. What an idiotic waste!

Bill darling, do let me know as soon as you get fixed & can make some more plans, & don't <u>please</u> let them send you off into the blue the horrible way they do nowadays—now that we've found each other out of the whole world, dont think I could bear it—

All my love,
Pam.[45]

Pam's plea, at the end of this letter to her 'darling' Bill that he should not allow himself to be whisked away from her, on some new military assignment is taken up as the dominant theme of the second love letter to be placed on Major Martin's person. Apparently written at his fiancée's place of wartime work and under the nose of her vigilant supervisor ('the Bloodhound'), this missive continued to convey both the vitality of a romance in first flood and some specific information intended to bolster *Mincemeat*'s credibility. The second love letter read as follows:

Office.
Wednesday, 21st.

The Bloodhound has left his kennel for half an hour so here I am scribbling nonsense to you again. Your letter came this morning just as I was dashing out—madly late as usual! You do write such heavenly ones. But what are these horrible dark hints you're throwing out about being sent off some-where—<u>of course</u> I wont say a word to anyone—I never do when you tell me things, but it's not abroad is it? Because I wont have it, I <u>wont</u>, tell them so from me. Darling, why did we go and meet in the middle of a war, such a silly thing for anybody to do—if it weren't for the war we might have been nearly married by now, going around together choosing curtains etc. And I wouldn't be sitting in a dreary Government office typing idiotic minutes all day long—I <u>know</u> the futile sort of work I do doesn't make the war one minute shorter—

Dearest Bill, I'm so thrilled with my ring—scandalously extravagant—you know how I adore diamonds—I simply can't stop looking at it.

I'm going to a rather dreary dance tonight with Jock & Hazel, I think they've got some other man coming. You know what their friends always turn out to be like, he'll have the sweetest little Adam's apple & the shiniest bald head! How beastly & ungrateful of me, but it isn't really that—you know—don't you?

Look darling, I've got next Sunday & Monday off for Easter. I shall go home for it of course, <u>do</u> come too if you possibly can, or even if you can't get away from London I'll dash up and we'll have an evening of gaiety—(By the way Aunt Marian said to bring you to dinner next time I was up, but I think that might wait?)

Here comes the Bloodhound, masses of love & a kiss

from
Pam.[46]

Of course, the 'dark hints' allegedly let drop by Major Martin to his fiancée about his impending departure on a military mission, as mentioned in this second of Pam's letters, would reinforce the 'official story' that his life had ended tragically while he was acting as a courier of top-secret documents. However, that letter also contained information designed to reinforce the credibility of *Operation Mincemeat* in more specific and material ways. Thus, the prospect that Pam holds out to Bill of their meeting in London 'for an evening of gaiety' would allow the deception planners to include documentary evidence of that night on the town among Major Martin's personal effects. As is explained in the next chapter, that 'proof'—in the form of dated theatre ticket stubs—would permit the communication to the enemy of a date for the courier's departure from England by aeroplane consistent with *Operation Mincemeat*'s schedule for the discovery of his body in Spanish waters.[47] Naturally, the fact that Pam had mentioned first the possibility and, then, the actual prospect, of William Martin's dispatch on a military mission in her successive letters, also reveals that their actual writer was not left entirely without guidance in composing them. Clearly, she received official direction on the need to suggest that Major Martin was about to be 'sent off somewhere' and on the lovers' plan for a night out in London, before they were separated by the exigencies of military service. So, for all their seeming spontaneity, Pam's love letters were written very carefully. They were drafted so as to reinforce the credibility of their recipient and, even more important, of the official documents he was apparently attempting to courier to senior Allied commanders in North Africa.

As always, *Mincemeat*'s implementation team paid meticulous attention to the physical appearance and condition of these seemingly intimate communications. For example, Montagu obtained some sheets of his brother-in-law's headed notepaper to confirm that Pam's letter of 'Sunday 18th' April 1943 had been written at, and sent from, her family's notional rural residence in Wiltshire.[48] On the other hand, the letter Pam apparently dashed off at work, on 'Wednesday 21st' April, was written on much inferior unheaded paper of the kind which civil servants used at the time for making carbon copies of typewritten documents. The letters themselves were handwritten by yet another unidentified member of MI5's female clerical staff.[49] Doubtless, her 'calligraphy' was judged stylish enough to be consonant with Pam's vivacious personality, whilst crucially remaining sufficiently legible for the Germans to be able to read it without real difficulty. However, in another realistic touch, Pam's handwriting apparently deteriorated into a scrawl in the last sentence-cum-paragraph of the letter allegedly composed at her place of work, as her 'Bloodhound' of a supervisor hove into view.[50]

Yet, there was an additional obstacle which the planners had to surmount in ensuring that Pam's manuscript letters were in a readable state. After all, the plan was to have the corpse-courier bobbing around in the ocean for some time—kept afloat by his Mae West—before he was taken ashore. During the time he was all but immersed, sea water would saturate his uniform, the contents of his pockets and wallet, and even the briefcase chained to his person. Was it not inevitable, then, that the ink on all Major Martin's handwritten correspondence, as well as the signatures on the official letters from Nye and Mountbatten, would run in these circumstances, making them completely illegible?[51] Yet, any obvious measure they took to preserve the manuscript letters and signatures in the courier's mixed collection of official and private documents against the elements might prove counterproductive. For instance, the substitution of a watertight bag for the standard government briefcase or of a similarly sealed pouch for Major Martin's conventional type of wallet, could well cause enemy investigators to suspect that there had been some prior design to plant the messenger and his papers in the ocean—otherwise why 'waterproof' his documents in this fashion? Again, any attempt to have the manuscript items written in a special indelible ink (not generally in use) could only arouse identical doubts amongst the Abwehr's technical experts about the genuineness of the courier and all his papers.

To tackle this problem, Montagu and his colleagues consulted MI5's scientists. They conducted a whole series of tests to determine the rates of solubility amongst various proprietary inks then commonly used by correspondents in Britain. These experiments did demonstrate that many of the inks in widespread use at the time would dissolve, almost instantly, on contact with water. However, some of the popular brands of ink proved fairly resistant to running, even when wet through, as long as they had been allowed to dry thoroughly after being initially applied by pen to paper. This was extremely good news for *Mincemeat*'s implementation team. It meant that Major Martin's official documents, duly inserted in envelopes and then placed inside his briefcase, could survive quite a time at sea with their manuscript signatures still legible. Similarly, even wholly handwritten letters carried inside a wallet, or just put directly into the pocket of a battle dress uniform should remain readable also, even after prolonged exposure to water—certainly for long enough to serve *Mincemeat*'s purposes.[52] So, all the deception planners needed to do to get the manuscript components of their misleading message through to the enemy was to have them written in one of the less soluble brands of ink, and also make sure that they were allowed to dry thoroughly.

Montagu and his associates took these precautions both with regard to the crucial deceptive documents, ostensibly signed by General Nye and Lord Mountbatten, and Pam's handwritten love letters. They also subjected a number of additional manuscript items included among Major Martin's bogus batch of personal papers to the same careful treatment. Once more, these documents were meant to impress their intended audience with persuasive evidence of a real life, tragically terminated by accident or act of war. Of course, the presence of such extra material relating to the courier's personal affairs had to appear natural. This effect was achieved, yet again, by exploiting Major Martin's recent engagement to be married. This major event in their messenger's private life allowed them to place what Montagu termed 'a pompously Victorian letter written by his father', on the dead body.[53] This bleak epistle and its even more austere enclosure (a copy of a letter of instruction to the Martin's family solicitor about the marriage settlement he was proposing to make on the young couple) clearly conveyed their notional author's sense of self-importance. More importantly, however, these items also confirmed the 'fact' of the marital arrangement between Bill and Pam and, therefore, also explained why the Royal Marine Major was carrying so much of his life story around with him.[54] As already noted, these additional literary contributions to the courier's personal biography were handwritten and read, respectively, as follows:

Tel. No. 98

> Black Lion Hotel,
> Mold,
> N. Wales.
> 13th April, 1943.

My Dear William,

I cannot say that this Hotel is any longer as comfortable as I remember it to have been in pre war days. I am, however, staying here as the only alternative to imposing myself once more upon your aunt whose depleted staff & strict regard for fuel economy (which I agree to be necessary in war time) has made the house almost uninhabitable to a guest, at least one of my age. I propose to be in Town for the nights of the 20th and 21st of April when no doubt we shall have an opportunity to meet. I enclose the copy of a letter which I have written to Gwatkin of McKenna's about your affairs. You will see that I have asked him to lunch with me at the Carlton Grill (which I understand still to be open) at a quarter to one on Wednesday the 21st. I should be glad if you would make it possible to join us. We shall not however wait luncheon for you, so I trust that, if you are able to come, you will make a point of being punctual.

Your cousin Priscilla has asked to be remembered to you. She has grown into a sensible girl though I cannot say that her work for the Land Army has done much to improve her looks. In that respect I am afraid that she will take after her father's side of the family.

> Your affectionate
> Father.[55]

Copy.
Tel. No. 98.

> Black Lion Hotel,
> Mold, N. Wales,
> 10th April.

My Dear Gwatkin,

I have considered your recent letter concerning the Settlement which I intend to make on the occasion of William's marriage. The provisions which you outline appear to me reasonable except in one particular. Since in this case the wife's family will not be contributing to the settlement I do not think it proper that they should necessarily preserve, after William's death, a life interest in the funds which I am providing. I should agree to this course only were there children of the marriage. Will you therefore so redraft the Settlement as to provide that if there are children the income is paid to the wife only until such time as she remarries or the children come of age. After that date the children alone should benefit.

I intend to be in London for the two nights of the 20th & 21st of April. I should be glad if you could make it convenient to take luncheon with me at the Carlton Grill at a quarter to one on Wednesday 21st. If you will bring the new draft with you we shall have leisure to examine it afterwards. I have written to William & hope he will be able to join us.

> Yrs. sincerely,
> (Signed) J. G. Martin.

F.A.S. Gwatkin, Esq.,
McKenna & Co.,
14 Waterloo Place, London, S.W.I.[56]

As Montagu commented later, these letters rang so true that it seemed inconceivable that anybody could have concocted them for a secret purpose.[57] The impression given in the letter William received from his father was that the old man regarded his son's forthcoming nuptials as yet another inconvenience inflicted upon him by the Second World War. Such self-absorption certainly befitted a paterfamilias of the old school. Again, J. G. Martin's intention, as stated in his letter to the family's solicitor, of barring his future daughter-in-law from benefiting from the marriage settlement, if his own son died before their union produced any children, was also in keeping with his curmudgeonly character. Remarkably, these convincing evocations of the apparently forbidding figure of Major Martin's father came not from the pen of another old codger. They were composed, instead, by a young serving officer.[58] Although the precise identity of that officer is unclear, he surely had encountered enough parental pomposity in life, or literature, to conjure up the spirit of pater Martin through these skilfully crafted letters. Naturally, the more real the patriarch of the Martins could be made to seem, the more vivid would be the impression made by his son and heir on *Operation Mincemeat*'s target audience.

One other document placed inside the courier's pockets also bore handwriting done in less readily soluble ink. This item, too, had been let dry completely before being handled again by the deception planners. This was a partly manuscript bill for the purchase of an engagement ring from

S. J. Phillips of 113, New Bond Street, a firm of jewellers with an active trade abroad, as well as at home. This fact explains why Montagu chose that particular jewellery store as the one where Bill Martin bought the 'scandalously extravagant' diamond engagement ring for his fiancée. After all, it was possible that the Nazi secret services might be conscientious enough to check on the genuineness of the courier's jeweller's bill by comparing it to another such document in the possession, say, of a pre-war German customer of Phillips.[59] Of course, the jeweller's bill also served to confirm the other aspect of the yarn the deception planners were spinning about Major Martin: *ipso facto*, it corroborated the recent betrothal between Bill and Pam. Again, the fact that the bill was unpaid was consistent with the future bridegroom's impecunious lifestyle (and his habit of living on credit where possible).[60] Finally, the jeweller's bill recorded that the purchase of the single-diamond ring from S. J. Phillips had been made on 15 April 1943 (although the invoice itself was dated 19 April).[61] This was apparently incontrovertible proof, along with Pam's letters of 18 and 21 April, that William Martin was definitely present in London during the middle weeks of that month. Again, as is explained in the following chapter, the deception planners reinforced that impression of Major Martin's whereabouts by planting other dated documents on his person. Taken together, they seemed to establish beyond all reasonable doubt that the deceased messenger could have reached Spanish waters, by the date his corpse turned up there, only by aircraft.

The last personal letter inserted by the *Mincemeat* team into William Martin's uniform also confirmed this alleged schedule of events. This document purported to be a letter from the Martin's family solicitors, McKenna & Co., about the major's testamentary intentions. The team had nominated that particular firm for the role of legal advisers to the Martins, senior and junior, because Ewen Montagu was friendly with one of their partners. At Montagu's request, that individual drafted the following letter on the firm's headed notepaper:

McKenna & Co.
Solicitors.

14, Waterloo Place,
London, S.W.I.

Our ref.: McL/EG

19th April, 1943.

Dear Sir,

Re your affairs

We thank you for your letter of yesterday's date returning the draft of your will approved. We will insert the legacy of £50 to your batman and our

Mr. Gwatkin will bring the fair copy with him when he meets you at lunch on the 21st inst. so that you can sign it there.

The inspector of taxes has asked us for particulars of your service pay and allowances during 1941/2 before he will finally agree to the amount of reliefs due to you for that year. We cannot find that we have ever had these particulars and shall, therefore, be grateful if you will let us have them.

Yours faithfully,
McKenna & Co.

Major W. Martin, R.M.,
Naval & Military Club,
94, Piccadilly, London, W.I.[62]

This letter, once more, served the deception planners' covert purpose in a number of ways. Addressed to Major Martin at the Naval and Military Club on 19 April, and acknowledging receipt of a communication sent only the day before, it pinpointed his location in London at that time. Moreover, in stating that their colleague, Mr Gwatkin, would be meeting William Martin for lunch on 21 April, this letter both confirms the arrangement made by J. G. Martin in his letter of 13 April to his son, and specifies the latter's whereabouts on that day. Last but not least, this item of correspondence, yet again verified the impending change in Major Martin's marital status. In view of his forthcoming marriage, it would appear quite natural for Bill Martin to feel that he should make a will in his future wife's favour, before returning to front-line military service.

As always, the *Mincemeat* team paid the utmost attention to ensuring that these additions to Major Martin's store of biographical papers looked absolutely authentic. Montagu explained how this effect was achieved in his post-war record of the deception plan:

> All these documents were on the appropriate genuine letter paper, bill-heads, etc., which had been obtained by various excuses; so that the typing, language, etc. was absolutely correct, frequently the letters or bills were made out by the purported senders, who were persuaded to do so by various excuses.[63]

One contribution to the miscellaneous documentation for Major Martin' 'biography' was acquired not by misrepresentation but by outright theft, if of a very minor order. The deception planners had decided to have their courier's father seek shelter from the rigours of the war in a small-town hotel. This was a plausible move, for many elderly people of means had been driven from hearth and home by a dearth of servants and official requisitioning of their dwellings. More to the point, the 'fact' that J. G. Martin was residing in a hotel meant that there was no need to specify a home address for the Martin family on his letters. This studied act of omission would frustrate any German efforts to check up on such an address. Not that Britain's secret warriors felt that they had much to fear from Nazi espionage inside Britain by early 1943. They knew that MI5 had virtually all the enemy's agents in the bag—either in custody or under control as double agents However, the simple consultation of a relevant telephone, commercial/trade or county directory—copies of which might well be accessible in enemy-occupied territory (such as the Channel Islands) or neutral countries—could expose the deception planners' invention or adoption of an address. True, *Mincemeat*'s makers had included a home address for Pam's family—the one they had borrowed from Montagu's brother-in-law—but they managed to pre-empt any German efforts to verify its genuineness by another conscious omission: nowhere in the personal correspondence that Major Martin carried off to war was mention made of Pam's surname. Thus, any check on the identity of the inhabitants of the Manor House at Ogbourne St George, in a local phone book or the county directory for Wiltshire, could not have easily proven that Pam had no family link there, even though her second initial was given as 'L' on the bill for her engagement ring.[64]

On the other hand, Montagu and company could be confident that the enemy could have no access to a hotel's current register of guests—especially if it was a relatively remote rural establishment. That is why it was necessary to locate Martin senior as a paying guest in a rural refuge and the Black Lion Hotel at Mold in the county of Flintshire in Wales fitted the bill perfectly. Its location in Wales (even if Mold lies at the opposite end of that country from William Martin's ostensible birthplace of Cardiff) made it a natural retreat for the Welsh father of a Welsh son. Again, Mold's distance from the larger British cities and towns, which still might be subject to enemy air raids, made it an obviously attractive sanctuary for an elderly person in those tumultuous times. The Black Lion's quintessentially British name, also, should help authenticate the letters notionally written by J. G. Martin to his son and solicitor, while allegedly staying there. Accordingly, a member of the *Mincemeat* team travelled to North Wales for the express purpose of pinching some of that hotel's notepaper. The success of this criminal enterprise seems to have troubled the conscience of the King's

Counsel (and future judge) in charge of implementing *Operation Mincemeat* less than the fact that he found it necessary to besmirch the Black Lion's well-deserved reputation for hospitality. Of course, it was perfectly in character for the cantankerous Martin *père* to find fault with his hotel's standard of service in the letter he wrote on 13 April 1943 to his son. Indeed, it was a particularly persuasive touch to have the old man complain about his own lack of physical comfort—while yet well-removed from the full blast of war—in the very first sentence of this letter to a son on active service in the global conflict. So, Montagu had to allow false witness be given by its crotchety guest against the Black Lion in front of *Operation Mincemeat*'s target audience of German spies and Nazi warlords. However, when it became possible for Ewen Montagu to publish his own version of the *Mincemeat* story after the war, he made public amends. He not only apologized for pilfering the hotel's notepaper but also, and particularly, for calling its high standards of accommodation and service into question.[65]

Of course, when Major Martin's personal letters and other biographical documents were to hand, the deception planners had to apply the appropriate finishing touches to their surfaces. No fewer than nine people—with Ewen Montagu, one more, standing in for the main character of *Operation Mincemeat*—impressed their fingerprints on the envelope containing the misaddressed letter from Lloyds Bank, demanding that the Royal Marine officer repay his overdraft forthwith. This was a reasonable number of separate sets of fingerprints to appear on an envelope which had been handled by the hall porters of two service clubs in London, in addition to bank staff, postal workers and its ultimate recipient.[66] The letters from Pam required more intimate treatment, however. Those highly personal epistles bore only the 'dabs' of Ewen Montagu (again in lieu of Glyndwr Michael's) and an unidentified set of female fingerprints doubling for Pam's.[67] Still, the number of Montagu's fingerprints to be found on these love letters had to outnumber Pam's, for only then would they provide tangible proof of the strength and, therefore, the reality of their romantic relationship. What was more natural for a lover than to have read his betrothed's precious words, over and over again?

Yet, this need to make sure that Pam's letters should show every sign of having been pored over, presented the *Mincemeat* implementation team with yet one more cosmetic challenge. While most of Major Martin's personal papers and other effects only needed to be carried round in their own pockets for a few days to assume an adequately 'aged' appearance,

Pam's letters posed more of a problem: they had to appear treasured and so had to look as if Bill had opened and refolded them repeatedly, as he read and reread them. On the other hand, the letters had to remain legible and the one which Pam had written on the flimsy government-issue notepaper, in particular, required careful handling if it were to survive this artificially induced 'wear and tear'. So, Montagu had to reject, outright, the suggestion made by one of his colleagues on how best to achieve the desired patina on the paper. This well-meaning individual, who clearly had little experience of how lovers might treat their billets-doux actually proposed scrunching up the letters and, then, uncrumpling them, in an attempt to make them appear suitably cherished by their recipient. However, since paper once crumpled up in this fashion can never be smoothed out properly again, such rough treatment might have rendered some of the letter's contents unreadable. What was even worse, for Major Martin to appear to handle Pam's declarations of affection so rudely would belie the sense of mutual infatuation the team were trying to confer on these star-crossed lovers. Instead of proceeding in so ham-fisted a fashion, they employed the patient approach already adopted to give Major Martin's photo ID its appropriate sheen. It seems that Montagu and Cholmondeley shared the labours involved in suitably 'ageing' these key personal documents for their dead messenger. They repeatedly unfolded and refolded Pam's two letters, so as to make it seem that Bill could not resist reading them over and over again. Occasionally, also, they buffed the letters against the fabric of their own uniforms so as to give their pages the shine that paper develops from constant handling. Throughout this process, the letter written on the flimsier official notepaper had to be treated with special care to make sure that it remained intact.[68]

Having made these cosmetic adjustments to the appearance of Pam's love letters, Montagu and his colleagues could rest content with their act of creation. They had managed to paint a remarkably vivid picture of their deceased courier, despite being strictly limited in the materials they could use to compose his portrait. Employing only the few personal papers they could place on his person so as not to arouse undue suspicion, they had contrived to impart a convincing impression of the love life, lifestyle, and family life of a man apparently cut down in his prime. They had produced this effect not by broad and bold strokes but by scrupulous attention to particulars, as one of their most formidable critics came to realize. Although he had taken some persuading to go along with *Mincemeat* as an effort at truly strategic deception, Colonel Dudley Clarke was unstinting in the post-war praise that he lavished on the Operation's implementation team:

> Preparation of the body had called for infinite pains and untold ingenuity: not the smallest detail had been overlooked and every conceivable contingency had been provided for. It was a masterpiece of planning and stage-management.[69]

Perhaps, however, the greatest tribute to the team's powers of invention was the fact that they came to believe in their own creation. Montagu acknowledged, after the war, that the personality they had manufactured for Major Martin 'became completely real' for those intimately involved in the project.[70] Charles Cholmondeley's widow, Alison, received exactly the same impression from her husband, despite his reluctance to talk about his wartime work: 'I think the fake identity of the body became much more alive for them all than the actual (dead) man.'[71] Yet, unless Glyndwr Michael's mortal remains could be got to Spanish waters in a presentable condition, then neither Major Martin's winning personality nor his beguiling message could seduce the enemy.

8

Travel Arrangements

Right from the very inception of *Operation Mincemeat*, its sponsors had little doubt about where their moribund messenger should fetch up. The same meeting of the Twenty Committee, which had adopted the deception plan on 4 February 1943, directed Montagu, as the Admiralty's representative, to 'find out a suitable position off the Spanish coast' where the corpse could be dropped into the sea.[1] Indeed, even earlier, in late November 1942, when Montagu had consulted Sir Bernard Spilsbury concerning the medical feasibility of the scheme, the scenario he delineated for the pathologist was one that envisaged a body being 'washed ashore in Spain'.[2] Again, at that same first meeting, Spilsbury had pointed out to Montagu the apparent advantages of depositing *Mincemeat*'s predeceased courier in that country's coastal waters: 'Spaniards were bad pathologists; as Roman Catholics they had a dislike for post mortems'.[3] Undoubtedly, such medical considerations had a major influence in determining the shortlist of countries which might serve as a suitable destination for Major Martin. This point was made clear in the report on *Operation Mincemeat* that Montagu and Cholmondeley submitted to their superiors in late April 1943:

> It would have been dangerous for the body to have been washed ashore in enemy or enemy-occupied territory in view of the undesirability of a full and capable post mortem. This left a choice, on a plausible route for the suppositious aircraft, of Portugal or Spain.[4]

The only realistic alternative shore to Iberia's, upon which a military courier en route from Britain to North Africa might wash up after an aviation accident over the sea, was the Atlantic coast of France. That littoral had been occupied by Nazi forces since the fall of France in June 1940. So any medical examination of the dead messenger's remains there would be conducted— or at least supervised—by German official experts, who would ensure that it met the latest scientific standards. In any case, engineering the arrival of Major Martin on or near the French coast without arousing enemy suspicions that the cadaver had been planted in those waters could prove impossible. This was because Allied military transport aircraft naturally gave the hostile shore of Nazi-occupied France a wide berth, but were able to fly much nearer the coastlines of neutral Portugal and Spain in relative safety. So, either Salazar's Portugal or Franco's Spain might do as a destination for Major Martin's mortal remains. However, Ewen Montagu was sure as to which of these right-wing dictatorships was the more likely to pass on *Mincemeat*'s message to its intended audience: 'of these, Spain was clearly the country where the probability of the document being handed, or at the very least, shown, to the Germans was greater'.[5] Indeed, by later 1942, the British were well aware of the lengths to which the Franco regime seemed prepared to go to cooperate with Nazi Germany's secret war effort on Spanish soil against Allied interests. Certainly, British code-breakers' ability to read the encrypted radio traffic generated by the various Abwehr stations within Spain—including that between the Germans' spy centre in Madrid and their headquarters back home—revealed the growing scale of Nazi–Francoist collusion in both anti-Allied espionage and sabotage over the course of 1941 and 1942. However, British success in recruiting Spaniards willing to spy on, or counterspy against, the Abwehr and its collaborators within the Francoist state also helped London monitor the manifold abuses of its 'non-belligerency' that regime was prepared to tolerate, in favour of the Axis.[6] Thus, from one of their diligent agents (a lieutenant in the Spanish army's reserve) British security agents in Gibraltar learned of the deep complicity of Spanish officials in the Abwehr's acts of sabotage against the Rock's airfield and its dockyards, and on ships at anchor in its harbour.[7] The individual who had first established, and then given general directions to the ring of saboteurs responsible for these attacks, was Colonel Eleuterio Sánchez Rubio. The latter was based in the town of La Linea, right on Spain's frontier with the British Crown Colony, but was attached, formally, to the office of the Spanish Army's General Staff located in Algeçiras.[8]

Algeçiras, which lies directly across the bay of the same name from Gibraltar, also afforded a grandstand view of the movement of Allied naval and merchant ships in to and out of this British capital-ship base during the Second World War, particularly from a terrace of seaside villas known as 'spy row'.[9] The city of Algeçiras, however, was only one site (although admittedly the most important) of a series of observation posts the Abwehr established at eleven different locations within Spanish territory, on both sides of the Strait of Gibraltar, to monitor maritime traffic through the western mouth of the Mediterranean. The scale of official Francoist connivance in this German surveillance scheme is indicated by the facts that Spanish personnel manned two of these posts and that the remainder were staffed by Germans and Italians wearing Spanish Army uniforms. The teams operating these spy stations also proved to be highly productive. By the autumn of 1941, the Algeçiras post, alone, was transmitting an average of twenty radio messages daily about the movement of ships in and around Gibraltar.[10] Thanks to the successes of Bletchley Park's code-breakers, the British were able to read these radio reports and often even do so in real time. One of Dilly Knox's former assistants had made a particularly critical contribution to opening up this enemy reportage on Allied maritime activities in the Gibraltar area. In February 1942, Mavis Lever solved a unique form of the Enigma machine exclusively employed by the Abwehr in the environs of Gibraltar (where such encryption devices were vulnerable to capture by British operatives and, consequently, the risk of the standard Abwehr Engima machine falling into enemy hands had to be avoided).[11] Access to the radio reports produced by this agent-based surveillance effort (augmented in 1942 by a scientific system using infra-red technology) alerted the British security and counter-intelligence authorities to the unusually serious menace arising from Axis ship watchers in the Pillars of Hercules.[12] As the official history of British intelligence in the Second World War notes, most Nazi espionage efforts against Allied shipping posed little real threat:

> The Allies know from their decryption of the communications of the German secret services, primarily the Abwehr, that most of these agents constituted no danger; either they invented their material, which was a common practice in places like Lisbon and Madrid, or, like those installed in distant ports or Spanish merchant ships, they could not report in time to be useful.[13]

One cluster of enemy agents, however, was not so innocuous:

> But those who exploited Spain's position astride the Straits of Gibraltar were an exception. They could for most of the time observe shipping movements with the naked eye or collect information locally, and report without delay. Of the various forms of war-time assistance the Axis received from Spain, its freedom to maintain a reporting organisation at the Western entrance to the Mediterranean was operationally the most important.[14]

Yet, the position of entrenched German spies in and around Gibraltar did
not prompt Britain's deception planners to regard that stretch of Spain's
coast as the ideal destination for Major Martin. Even if the Nazi agents at
work in the immediate vicinity of Gibraltar might be granted easy access to
the courier's papers by the complaisant Spanish authorities in the area, there
was one insuperable problem involved in depositing Major Martin in the
shadow of the Rock. Like Paymaster-Lieutenant Turner before him, he
could be handed over to British officials in Gibraltar for burial there. This
was an event that Montagu and his colleagues wanted to avoid at all costs,
since the bureaucratic processing of the putative Royal Marine's remains in
Gibraltar would be sure to reveal irregularities in his military record. These
would provoke further unwelcome inquiries and undesirable speculations,
which might well reach enemy ears through the Axis agents operating
under cover of the many Spanish workers commuting daily back and
forth between the Crown Colony and Franco's state.[15] So, the deception
planners had to find another location, at some distance from Gibraltar,
suitable for receiving their 'special delivery'. Once more, the British ability
to eavesdrop on the Germans' spy service came to their rescue. Intelligence,
Illicit Services Oliver Strachey (ISOS), and Intelligence Services Knox
(ISK) radio decrypts revealed that the Abwehr had sufficiently active nests
of spies in both Cadiz and the other main city in the Gulf of Cadiz, Huelva,
to suggest that *Mincemeat*'s message might fall into the intended 'wrong'
hands, in either place.[16]

Montagu decided to call on local knowledge to help the team choose
between these two possible destinations for their dead messenger. At his
prompting, the Director of Naval Intelligence, Commander Rushbrooke,
summoned one of the two Assistant Naval Attachés in Britain's embassy in
Madrid home to the Admiralty for consultation. Lieutenant Commander
Salvador Gomez-Beare, RNVR, was a native Gibraltarian with a natural penchant for clandestine activities.[17] Indeed, on one formal occasion, his immediate superior, Captain Alan Hillgarth (the British Naval Attaché in Spain)
had been startled to discover his subordinate mounting a surreptitious
chemical warfare attack. At a levee where General Franco was extending
formal New Year's greetings to the assembled diplomatic corps, Gomez-
Beare contrived to linger in the *Caudillo*'s immediate vicinity. From that
vantage ground he proceeded to wave a handkerchief—liberally laced with
sneezing powder—at enemy envoys as they filed past Franco. Once Hillgarth,
alerted by the sneezing fits amongst the Axis and Japanese representatives,

realized what was afoot, he ordered Gomez-Beare to 'stop that bloody nonsense!' However, he could not but admire his assistant's gumption.[18] Indeed, Hillgarth had long appreciated what an asset Gomez-Beare was in the waging of Britain's naval intelligence and counter-intelligence campaign right across Spain. The prank which the Gibraltarian had staged at the diplomatic levee was in keeping with a puckishly attractive personality that won him friends all over Madrid and throughout the country as a whole, and in Hillgarth's estimate 'it was this popularity with all Spaniards that paid the richest dividend' for Britain's war effort in Spain.[19] Britain's Assistant Naval Attaché used these many social contacts to good effect in helping Hillgarth organize a network of British ship watchers inside Spain's ports. These British agents monitored maritime movements and reported any unneutral behaviour on the part of Axis nationals and Francoist officials. Gomez-Beare personally visited many of the Spanish ports, keeping the British spies on their toes, and himself gathering valuable information on clandestine Axis activities such as the resupply and refuelling of German U-boats in Spanish harbours.[20]

Gomez-Beare's thorough familiarity with Spain's dockside demi-monde meant that he was well qualified to advise Montagu as to where the dead courier's documents were most likely to be passed on to enemy agents. He persuaded the NID man that Cadiz would not be a suitable site for such a transfer, presumably because of the strong Spanish naval presence in that city and the surrounding province of the same name.[21] Indeed, the Spanish Navy's local headquarters and base (which was situated in the town of San Fernando, not very far from Cadiz itself) had ensured that the remains of another deceased courier—those of Lieutenant Turner—were returned so promptly to British custody the previous September that Nazi spies had no chance of getting a hold of the secret papers he was carrying on his person.[22] Britain's deception planners would want to avoid any repeat performance of such honourable conduct by the Spanish naval administration in the Cadiz area. Yet they knew that, if anything, the chances were that elements within the Armada might be even more inclined to be seen to be doing the right thing by the British, by the spring of 1943. For many Spanish naval officers knew enough about their profession to have a healthy respect for Allied maritime power in general, and for the Royal Navy in particular, especially when the fortunes of world war appeared to be swinging in favour of the anti-Nazi bloc. So, Spain's sailors might not be quite as ready as members of that country's other armed services to do the Germans' secret bidding.[23] Certainly, in places like Cadiz which lay almost in the shadow of the Rock of Gibraltar, it was all too possible that Spanish naval commanders might be prepared to show some deference to the 'White Ensign', when it came to dealing with Major Martin's body and briefcase. Again, even if *Mincemeat*'s key deceptive documents did end up in the 'wrong' hands via Cadiz, that city's proximity to the Rock meant that the local authorities still might send the courier's corpse to Gibraltar for interment there, with consequent risks to the security of the whole deception operation, as already explained above.[24]

With Cadiz ruled out as a possible reception point for Major Martin's misleading message, Huelva remained his only possible port of call. Yet, Gomez-Beare argued that Huelva had more to recommend it as a destination for the corpse-courier than the fact that there was nowhere else for him to go. For a start, the Assistant Naval Attaché was able to convince Montagu and his colleagues that in Huelva 'the danger of the body being recovered and/or dealt with by the Spanish Navy (who might not have cooperated with the Germans) was much less than at Cadiz'.[25] Huelva, both city and province, were also Germanophile in the main, despite the prominence of the huge British mining concern of Rio Tinto in the region's economy.[26] True, Rio Tinto's Spanish operations were no longer as important by 1943 as they had been before the First World War when the company's Huelvan mines were the largest producers of sulphur in the world, while also yielding significant amounts of copper and pyrites.[27] Yet, Rio Tinto still rankled Spanish nationalists as an 'economic Gibraltar' and it still riled local leftists as a symbol of foreign capitalist exploitation.[28] Resentment at a state of affairs in which British businesses, including Rio Tinto, seemed to lord it over Huelva's economy and society helped foster a 'very strong' pro-German sentiment in the area, as Gomez-Beare again impressed upon the Naval Intelligence officers in London.[29]

Clearly, such an Anglophobic atmosphere proved conducive to the recruitment of collaborators with Nazi Germany's clandestine war effort against the British in South-Western Spain. That covert campaign of espionage, counter-espionage and sabotage was spearheaded by the local Abwehr spy chief, Adolfo Clauss Kindt. Gomez-Beare was preaching to the converted when he highlighted the contribution this very 'active and influential German agent' could make to ensuring that the *Mincemeat* papers ended up in Nazi hands.[30] Thanks to the ISOS and ISK decrypts, British Naval Intelligence officers and their partners in deception from the other services were already well aware of the scale of this enemy agent's activities.[31] Residing just outside Huelva, he operated out of an office inside the German consulate (at number 51, Avenida de Italia) with the help of his brother, Luis, and under the cover supplied by his father, Ludwig Clauss Röder, Germany's honorary consul in the city. More of a Nazi true believer than either his brother or his father, Adolfo Clauss worked to damage British and Allied interests in a number of ways. He organized a group of spies to report on Allied ships in Huelva harbour. These agents kept the Germans informed about the names of these merchant vessels, the cargoes they were carrying, and the ships' dates and times of arrival and departure. The local Abwehr chief also helped establish a network of German military coast watchers in the region who were equipped with radios so they could relay the movement of Allied ships off the province's shores to the Germany Navy and Air Force. Finally, Adolfo Clauss Kindt was especially active in mounting sabotage attacks on consignments of British goods entering Spain, and on Spanish exports destined for the Allies, not only in Huelva but also in Seville, where his immediate Abwehr superior, Patricio Gustav Draeger, was stationed.[32] With such a track record, Adolfo Clauss Kindt seemed the ideal candidate for the job of willing, if unwitting, accomplice in *Operation Mincemeat*: he should be assertive enough to demand access to the contents of Major Martin's brief-case and well connected enough to succeed in his importunings.[33]

Yet, it was not only the German personnel based in Huelva who should prove cooperative; for, once more, Gomez-Beare was able to give *Mincemeat*'s planners the benefit of his knowledge of the region's personalities. He pointed out to them that Huelva possessed another useful asset for their scheme, in the person of the British Vice-Consul in that city. Francis Kinnaird Haselden was a mining engineer by profession, but his superior intellect and refined manners had won over many local hearts and minds to the Allied cause, despite the general antipathy of the area's populace towards Britain.[34] Indeed, Haselden had already proven himself to be 'a reliable and helpful man' in the conduct of counter-intelligence and counter-espionage operations in south-western Spain since the outbreak of the war.[35] So, here was a British official, strategic-ally placed on Spanish soil, who could be relied upon to deal with one of the most delicate problems associated with Major Martin's posthumous presence there. This was the very issue which was worrying Colonel John Bevan, at the beginning of March 1943, as he informed Ewen Montagu:

> I think we all agree that there are quite a number of things that might go wrong, and in any case there will be a number of details to be arranged to

ensure that everything in fact goes right. I was thinking in particular of the funeral arrangements which the Consul will have to make, and numerous small matters which will have to be tied up.[36]

Of course, as Gomez-Beare did not fail to remind his colleagues, Huelva was situated 'far enough from Gibraltar to make it probable that the body would be handed to the Consul for burial'.[37] Moreover, with such a competent representative as Francis Haselden to take change of the dead messenger's local interment, Bevan's doubts about that phase of *Operation Mincemeat*'s practical implementation could be dispelled. Their man in Huelva clearly impressed Britain's deception planners as having the discretion and deftness to handle this tricky task without arousing undue suspicions in any official quarter—Spanish, German, or even British. Yet, the Vice-Consul should be sufficiently quick-witted, if properly briefed, to fend off any premature attempt by sympathetic Spaniards to deliver the courier's top-secret papers into his custody, before German agents had a sporting chance to get a look at them.

So, Huelva's geography—physical, political, and human—made it an ideal locale to receive Britain's dead messenger and his deceptive message. However, Montagu had to make one final inquiry before that city would be fixed as the terminus of Major Martin's first and final journey. This query he addressed, in person, to the Hydrographic Department at the Admiralty and it concerned 'the prospects of a floating object being washed ashore at the desired point' near Huelva.[38] The initial response of the Royal Navy's Superintendent of Tides was not too positive. He did not hold out much hope that the local tides, tidal streams, and/or currents would help an object cast into those Spanish coastal waters to drift shorewards. However, he did concede that 'winds between S[outh] and W[est] might set it toward the head of the bight near P. Huelva'. Since the tides in that stretch of sea ran 'mainly up and down the coast', it would be necessary to launch the object into the ocean during a period when the prevailing wind was an onshore southerly one. Fortunately, for the deception planners, the prevailing wind off Huelva during springtime was an onshore, South-Westerly breeze. Montagu concluded that this favourable wind should waft Major Martin towards the Huelvan coastline, not least because a body wearing a Mae West life jacket was 'likely to be more affected by the wind', than the inanimate object the hydrographers had been led to believe was the subject of the NID's inquiry.[39]

Huelva, in short, seemed to meet *Operation Mincemeat*'s need for a destination for the dead messenger from every point of view, as Montagu explained to Bevan, on 26 March 1943:

> On the advice of the Assistant Naval Attaché the body is to be dropped just off Huelva as it is there that the Germans are at their strongest vis a vis the Spanish police and the chances are regarded as very high that anything that washes ashore there will be made available to the Germans. The currents on the coast are unhelpful at any point but the prevailing south west wind will bring the body ashore if... [we] ... can ditch it near enough to the coast.[40]

The precise dropping-off point for the body was also settled, more or less, by the end of March. It was to be 'put into the water as close inshore as prudently possible and as near to HUELVA as possible, preferably to the North West of the river mouth'.[41] Actually, some subsequent personal reconnaissance of the area by Gomez-Beare allowed him to recommend an even more specific target point for *Operation Mincemeat*, by signal to London on 9 April 1943. He now advised the NID that the best spot at which to lower Major Martin's body into the sea was 'between Portil Pillar and Punta Umbria just West of the mouth of the Rio Tinto river'.[42]

Refining the 'target point' for the placement of the messenger's mortal remains was only one of the many practical contributions made by Britain's Assistant Naval Attaché in Spain to the implementation of *Operation Mincemeat*. Once he had persuaded the Admiralty to accept Huelva as the launching site for the deception scheme in Spain, Gomez-Beare was ordered to travel by air to Gibraltar with a whole set of verbal instructions for local British officers and officials in the Crown Colony or inside southern Spain. First of all, he had to brief both the senior British naval commander on the Rock and his intelligence staff officer about the intended strategic deception plan. They would need to know what was afoot, because they would have to be informed—in accordance with normal procedure—of the route followed by the vessel transporting the body. Giving the naval officers fair warning about this clandestine scheme ensured that they would be alert to the need to handle the body of the courier and/or the contents of his briefcase with the utmost discretion, should they turn up on their doorstep.[43] Indeed, to make sure that Britain's covert warriors inside Spain and on the Rock did not make any unwitting, false move that could blow the deception plan, the chief MI6 representatives in Madrid and Gibraltar and the senior MI5 operative in the Crown Colony were inducted into the *Mincemeat* secret through their own secure channels. MI5's man in Gibraltar was directed, also, 'to inform the Governor and C.-in-C. for his personal information, in case the body was sent there by the Spaniards'. This limited briefing should mean that General Mason–MacFarlane had enough prior knowledge of the plan to avoid compromising it inadvertently, but no authority to intervene clumsily in its implementation, as he had in the cover plan for *Operation Torch*.[44]

A similar concern to tell people only exactly as much as they needed to know to play their own parts in *Mincemeat* was evident in the oral instructions Gomez-Beare conveyed from London to the British Consul in Seville, and Vice-Consuls in Cadiz and Huelva. In Seville and Cadiz, Britain's representatives were told that they had to report 'the washing ashore of any body in their area' exclusively to the Naval Attaché at their embassy in Madrid, Captain Alan Hillgarth. No other British authority was to be informed of such an incident. Gomez-Beare was not given leave to explain the real reason for the change in the procedure for reporting fatalities of this type from Seville and Cadiz. Instead, he spun them a yarn—which had been fabricated for them back in London—about the need to avoid the kind of mistakes in the identification of these unfortunates, and in the notification of their relatives, which had caused misinformed family members unnecessary distress on previous occasions.[45]

When it came to briefing the British vice-consul in Huelva on his allotted role in *Operation Mincemeat*, however, Gomez-Beare was directed to reveal the covert intent behind the new procedure. Accordingly, he proceeded to give Francis Haselden a broad outline of the deception scheme, without disclosing its specific strategic purpose or the precise content of the misleading documents contained in the predeceased courier's bag. Montagu justified Haselden's admission to the select circle of those at least partially privy to *Operation Mincemeat*, on the following grounds:

> This was necessary as he [Haselden] had to be instructed to make such enquiries as he would normally make to learn whether anything else had been found with the body, but not to make them energetically enough to learn of the bag of documents if it had not been given to him.[46]

Haselden was told, also, that 'it was considered highly probable that the documents would be given, or at least shown, to the Germans', in Huelva. However, if 'unfortunately', this did not happen and the papers were handed right over to him for safekeeping, then he was directed to give

he courier's briefcase to Gomez-Beare who, in turn, would arrange for
ts return to London.[47] To try and avoid such a frustrating outcome to all
he deception planners' best efforts, Gomez-Beare also relayed to Haselden
detailed instructions on how the Vice-Consul was to handle the affair at his
nd. His first step should be to make a telephone call to the Assistant Naval
Attaché in Madrid, reporting the discovery of the courier's body and such
particulars as he might have gathered from Spanish officials about the case.
Gomez-Beare, in reply, would ask whether Haselden had learned of any other
rticle coming ashore with the body. Of course, if the Francoist officials
n Huelva acted true to pro-Nazi form, then the vice-consul would be able
o answer in the negative. Gomez-Beare would reply by saying that he
ntended to relay Haselden's report to London. Then, he would close the
irst phone conversation with Haselden, in the immediate aftermath of
Major Martin's arrival on *terra Hispanica*, by requesting that he arrange for
he burial of the Royal Marine major locally, with the funeral bill to be
orwarded to Captain Hillgarth for settlement. After a lapse of forty-eight
ours or so, during which Gomez-Beare, reasonably, might be expected to
ave received a signal from London concerning the fate of such an import-
nt courier, the assistant naval attaché would call Haselden by phone,
stensibly to inquire again if any other items had turned up in the wake
f the dead messenger. Once more, Haselden was to reply that he was
naware of any such objects being found. This reply would prompt a
eemingly worried Gomez-Beare to cut their conversation short, with a
promise to visit Huelva in person to pursue the matter further. When he
rrived post-haste in Huelva, Gomez-Beare would 'make discreet inquiries
whether any bag or paper had been washed ashore'.[48]

The whole point of these deliberately uncoded, but studiously scripted,
phone calls, would be to communicate to the enemy the apparently gen-
ine alarm of the British authorities at the loss of their courier's top-
ecret documents. The British considered that 'the telephone conversations
would possibly be reported to the Germans'.[49] In fact, the chances of these
nscrambled verbal exchanges being picked up by Nazi agents were very
reat. This was because the Franco regime systematically tapped the telephone lines of all major non-Axis embassies in Madrid, with the active
ssistance of German technicians. Indeed, without this help from the Nazis,
he counter-espionage section of the Spanish Army's general staff would
ever have been able to mount such a comprehensive campaign of elec-
ronic eavesdropping on the telephone calls made to, and from, many of the

embassies in Madrid. Naturally, the Franco regime had to pay a price i
return for the Germans' technical and technological assistance in intercep
ing foreign diplomats' phone calls—which were routed through the switch
board of the telephone exchange located on Madrid's Gran Vía, for precise
that purpose: the Nazis hardly could be denied access to the intelligenc
product made available by their own expertise.[50] So, just as Montagu an
company suspected, the carefully pre-scripted conversations, which the
included in the plot of their deception drama should have a very attentiv
audience.

  Mincemeat's planners, however, understood that they could not confin
the flurry of official British communications occasioned by the loss of suc
sensitive papers as Major Martin was apparently carrying to a few phon
calls. They realized that they would have to arrange, also, for an adequat
volume of telegrams to be sent between the British embassy in Madrid an
London to demonstrate how seriously British officials were taking th
apparent loss of their top-secret documents. In any case, Gomez-Bear
had also advised the deception planners, during his visit to London, that
number of such messages should be sent in his name. This was because h
reckoned that he might well learn from other sources about the fate of th
documents, possibly during his promised personal visitation to Huelva, afte
Major Martin had come ashore.[51] He would have to be seen to be urgentl
relaying this information back to the British government so as to reinforc
the impression of high-level disquiet over the episode. Not that the Britis
expected the enemy to be able to decipher the text, and learn the conten
of, these communications. Indeed, British confidence in the security c
their main diplomatic cipher and the 'naval shore code' used for commu
nication between the Admiralty and the naval attachés abroad was well
founded, and foreign code-breakers had little success against them.[52] Thu
although the cryptographic sub-section of the Spanish Army's general sta
again called on German technical assistance to crack the encoded commu
nications of the American, Portuguese, and even Japanese embassies durin
the Second World War, it had no success against those of the Britis
embassy in Madrid.[53] Still, intelligence inferences can be made from an
variations in the patterns of even unreadable signal traffic. So, an appropriat
increase in the volume of telegrams/airmail signals between the apparentl
concerned British representatives in Spain and their agitated masters i
London, in the aftermath of the disappearance of Major Martin's offici
papers, should serve to authenticate the latter documents still further.[54]

The *Mincemeat* team also accepted that another member of the British embassy's roster in Madrid might have to communicate with London over the affair. This individual was the Naval Attaché, Captain Alan Hillgarth, whose own staff would find it distinctly odd if he failed to report the arrival of a dead Royal Marine major on Spanish soil to London. Montagu, therefore, had to take administrative precautions to try to prevent such a signal from Hillgarth being circulated widely within the Admiralty.[55] Yet, it was clear that most of the fancy footwork required to ease the passage of the deceptive documents into enemy hands would have to be executed on the spot, in Spain. Moreover, no one was better placed, or more qualified, than Alan Hillgarth to accomplish a task whose ostensible purpose—to regain prompt possession of the top-secret documents Major Martin was couriering—was the exact opposite of what his diplomatic interventions were intended to achieve. At the best of times, as one informed commentator has noted, the lot of a British Naval Attaché is not a simple one, since he is expected to serve two different superiors simultaneously: his Ambassador who expects him to behave with due diplomatic decorum as a member of the embassy team, and the Director of Naval Intelligence, who expects the Attaché to cultivate contacts and gather intelligence in a less hidebound manner. As the same commentator has observed, 'what looks at first sight like a straightforward representative post can become the centre of a complex and delicate web of diplomatic, intelligence and commercial relationships'.[56] Managing that tangled web in a geo-strategically significant neutral country, in the midst of a world war, was an even greater challenge.

Alan Hillgarth, however, rose to that challenge with considerable aplomb. Hillgarth was a born adventurer who had led an eventful life in and out of uniform. When only sixteen years of age, he had been seriously wounded, as a midshipman in the Royal Navy, during the Dardanelles campaign.[57] In Bolivia in 1928, he had saved the life of a fellow gold prospector by amputating the latter's gangrenous limb with a knife.[58] Hillgarth drew on his own escapades to write a number of adventure novels. Perhaps the most successful of these was a story inspired by his Bolivian experiences, entitled *The Black Mountain*, which earned a favourable review from Graham Greene. By the time this novel was published in 1933, Hillgarth had been appointed British Vice-Consul in Palma on the Spanish island of Majorca, where he had come to reside. As Britain's official diplomatic representative on the largest of the Balearic Islands, he was able to help British warships navigate the troubled waters between the archipelago and mainland Spain, during the Civil War there from 1936 to 1939. The commander of one British warship, Captain J. H. Godfrey of HMS *Repulse*, was especially impressed when His Majesty's Consul—to which higher position Hillgarth had been promoted in 1937—was able to negotiate safe passage from the Francoists and their German Allies, for his battle cruiser to Republican-held Barcelona in 1938.[59] Consequently, on becoming Director of Naval Intelligence in 1939, Godfrey engineered Hillgarth's appointment, first as Assistant Naval Attaché and then, in January 1940, as Naval Attaché in Madrid, where he could use his 'many contacts in high places, political and social', inside post-Civil War Spain to Britain's advantage. The DNI never had cause to regret his selection of Alan Hillgarth for this key position. On the contrary, Godfrey came to regard him as 'rather a super-Attaché', on account of the many sterling services he rendered the British cause in Spain during the Second World War.[60] These included the recruitment and running (along with the able assistance of Don Gomez-Beare) of a network of agents among Spanish dockers, port officials, and even local police to monitor Axis exploitation of Spain's maritime facilities and any unneutral Francoist collusion with the Germans or Italians. These vigilant port watchers, for example, restricted the instances of German U-boats being resupplied in Spanish harbours to not many more than two dozen.[61] Again, Hillgarth was eventually able to prove to an embarrassed Franco government that Italian human torpedo attacks on Allied warships and merchant vessels at Gibraltar, between July 1942 and August 1943, had been launched from a modified Italian oil tanker inside Algeçiras harbour.[62]

Yet, remarkably, this swashbuckling sailor also turned out to be a deft diplomat, giving as much satisfaction to his Ambassador in Madrid as he did to the DNI back in London. For most of his time as Naval Attaché in Spain, from 1939 to 1943, Hillgarth worked under the ambassadorship of Sir Samuel Hoare. Hoare was a former Cabinet minister who had fallen foul of Winston Churchill, not least over the prudence of appeasing Hitler's Germany during the pre-war years.[63] Arriving in Spain, on 1 June 1940, to conduct a diplomatic rearguard action for Britain as German forces overran the Low Countries and Northern France, the new British Ambassador found himself immersed 'in a bewildering turmoil of futility, intrigue and .. risk'.[64] Hillgarth had acted promptly to steady Hoare's nerves and also to propose a plan to rescue Britain's waning influence within Franco's Spain.[65] The idea was to offer financial incentives to senior Spanish army officers to restrain any ambition on Franco's part to join the Axis at war. Hillgarth convinced not only Hoare, but also Churchill, of the merits of this effort to practise bribery and corruption inside Francoist Spain. His success in this regard was helped, undoubtedly, by his own acquaintance with Churchill, who considered Hillgarth to be a 'good man' and one who was 'equipped with a profound knowledge of Spanish affairs'.[66] With such authoritative approval, Hillgarth was able to distribute millions of dollars over the next few years among thirty senior Spanish Army officers. The British deposited most of this money in foreign bank accounts, to which the individuals involved would have access only after the war was over and Spain had been seen not to intervene on the Axis side. Whilst Churchill, Hoare, and Hillgarth believed they had struck a good bargain with these peculant members of the Spanish military hierarchy, other British policymakers were not so sure. Thus, as early as April 1941, the Foreign Secretary, Anthony Eden, admitted to wondering whether his country's representatives in Spain were 'being fooled' in this covert transaction, which seemed to produce no obvious diplomatic returns for all the money invested.[67] Still, however limited the leverage Britain was able to purchase, ultimately, over Spanish foreign policy during the Second World War, Hillgarth's achievement in mounting such an ambitious clandestine operation cannot be denied. It stands as impressive testimony to the extent of his personal influence inside both Spain's and Britain's ruling circles.

Naturally, Hillgarth had to manage this shady venture with the utmost discretion. Certainly, Sir Samuel Hoare was impressed by Hillgarth's adroit handling of such sensitive operations. Indeed, averse as the British Ambassador was to upsetting the Franco regime, he insisted his Naval Attaché be granted authority by the British Government, in early 1941, to direct the clandestine activities undertaken inside Spain, not only by the NID, but also by the Special Operations Executive (SOE)—the British organization for conducting irregular warfare. By then also Hillgarth had had to create 'a sort of substitute S.I.S.' (Secret Intelligence Service—namely MI6) in Spain, to replace the work of French spies on behalf of the Allies, which had come to an abrupt end with their country's defeat in June 1940. However, as MI6 built up their own organization inside Franco's Spain, Hillgarth gradually returned to them control over much of the British espionage effort there.[68] Yet, the Naval Attaché continued to maintain, into 1943, his own high-level sources within the Francoist state and even received special funds from, and privileged access to, 'C', the head of Britain's spy service, Sir Stewart Menzies, to facilitate his top-level intelligence gathering inside Spain.[69]

However, the preferential treatment enjoyed by Alan Hillgarth did not g
down well with some of Britain's spies. For example, when MI6's Kir
Philby came to publish his memoirs over twenty years later—after h
defection to the Soviet Union—he could not resist giving voice to h
professional resentment at the sailor's favoured status:

> There was an arrangement, prompted by Hillgarth's personal acquaintance
> with Churchill, by which secret funds were made available to him for
> undercover activity. A condition of this arrangement was that Hillgarth's
> only contact with SIS should be with the Chief himself. The ostensible
> reason for this was security; Hillgarth's sources were to be particularly
> sacrosanct. But the condition also helped to feed the gallant officer's illusions
> of grandeur. As pseudonym for correspondence with the Chief, he chose
> Armada—natch![70]

Yet, Hillgarth for all his easy access to the high and mighty was also quit
prepared to get involved in the seamier side of Britain's secret war in Spair
On one occasion, he even did so with the express approval of his Ambas
sador, who normally frowned upon cloak-and-dagger activities. Howeve
Hoare clearly felt that he had no choice but to resort to skulduggery whe
confronted, in July 1943, with the case of a Free French naval officer wh
was found to be betraying secrets about British espionage efforts to th
Vichy French. 'Faced with the dilemma' of kidnapping or killing the enem
agent and, thereby, 'running the risk of irrevocably compromising' th
British Mission in Madrid, or letting him abscond to Vichy France witl
secret information that would 'destroy' the existing British 'intelligenc
organisation in Spain and do even greater harm elsewhere', Hoare obtaine
London's sanction for direct and drastic action. Accordingly, around mid
night on the 24th July, Hillgarth and MI6's Head of Station in Madrid lure
the disloyal Frenchman to the British Embassy where they plied him witl
drugged drinks. The plan was to spirit the traitor (who admitted his guilt t
Alan Hillgarth) by embassy car to Gibraltar, where he would be arrested
formally charged with treason and returned to Britain for trial. So, Hillgartl
and his MI6 colleagues set out for the Rock, on the evening of 25th July
with a passenger sedated by morphine. Initially, the snatch squad, includin;
Hillgarth himself, journeyed south without let or hindrance. However, a
they drove through a small village in Andalusia, their captive regaine
full consciousness and began shouting for help from startled bystanders
His abductors promptly quietened him by hitting him on the head with :

revolver but soon discovered that they had silenced their prisoner perman-
ently. This awkward fact took some explaining away when the car reached
the Rock and its occupants were vetted by British border guards.[71]

However, this sorry affair did not end there, thanks to the incorrigible
officiousness of the British border agents. Now, they refused to admit
Hillgarth and his party into the Crown Colony, on the grounds that they
lacked the proper documentation to permit them to bring a dead body into
Gibraltar. The ensuing row between the two sets of British officials grew so
heated that it attracted increasing attention from the guards on the Spanish
side of no-man's land between La Linea and the Rock. It took a supreme
assertion of personal and professional authority by Hillgarth to prevent the
diplomatic hearse and crew—dead and alive—being sent back to the jurisdiction of the now all-too-interested Francoist border guards, where a
major international incident might well have erupted.[72] Yet, even if this
counter-espionage action had nearly backfired, it did provide further confirmation for the deception planners back in London that Britain's senior
mariner in Madrid had the nerve and the nous to play his planned part in
Operation Mincemeat. Indeed, not the least advantage of choosing Spain as
the terminus for Major Martin's intentionally ill-fated journey was that
Britain had such a trustworthy trio of representatives already in place—in
the persons of Francis Haselden, Don Gomez-Beare, and Alan Hillgarth—
to handle this sensitive affair on the ground.

Yet, if these individuals were to perform their supporting roles in Major
Martin's dumbshow, the main character had to appear on the Spanish stage
at the right moment and in one piece. At the first meeting between Colonel
Bevan and the *Mincemeat* team from the Twenty Committee, on 10 February
1943, both parties had agreed that the former, as chief of LCS, should seek
approval from the appropriate authorities to drop the corpse-courier 'either
from an aircraft or submarine'.[73] It took only two days for Bevan to get the
Directors of Plans to agree that 'the necessary aircraft or naval unit would be
made available' to transport the body to its destination. However, the
Directors also suggested that, if the dead messenger were to travel by sea,
then 'an escort vessel from a convoy might easily undertake the job, rather
than a submarine'.[74] Montagu, however, soon scotched that suggestion.
The inquiries he made in the Admiralty's Hydrographic Department
revealed that it would be 'necessary to place the body in the water close
inshore somewhere in the neighbourhood of Cadiz at a time' when an
'onshore wind' was blowing. These preconditions for floating Major Martin

successfully shoreward in the Gulf of Cadiz ruled out the use of a surface vessel as his possible means of transport, as Montagu authoritatively informed the Admiralty's Director of Plans, Captain Charles Lambe, on 12 March 1943.[75] A convoy escort would have too deep a draught to deposit the body in the shallow waters close to shore, whilst it would also be too easy to spot from the coast if it had to hang around waiting for the wind to start blowing in the right direction. Using a land-based aircraft might have circumvented these difficulties, as it could drop the body from above, into the shallow water, and quickly fly in to do so at a time when meteorological reports indicated that local wind conditions were favourable. However, as Montagu also advised Lambe, the drawback with placing the corpse in the sea in this manner was that 'it might be smashed to pieces on landing'.[76]

This left only two ways of carrying the body to its designated destination: by flying boat or by submarine. Of course, a flying boat could also wait upon favourable weather, before taking off for southern Spain. Moreover, unlike a conventional aeroplane, a flying boat could land on the sea's surface which meant that its crew could lower the messenger into the ocean without much risk of inflicting physical damage, let alone dismemberment, upon his remains. Indeed, Montagu presented quite a detailed scenario to the naval staff for this method of delivering the cadaver:

> The most convincing procedure would be for the aircraft to come in from out at the sea simulating engine trouble, drop a bomb to simulate the crash, go out to sea as quickly as possible, return (as if it were a second flying boat) and drop a flare as if searching for the first aircraft, land, and then, while ostensibly searching for survivors, drop the body, etc. and then take off again.[77]

For all the advantages of employing a flying boat in the manner described, Montagu did not recommend it as the surest way of getting *Mincemeat*'s messenger on to dry land. Perhaps, he even had doubts as to whether a flying boat could execute the devious manoeuvres he had outlined, without somebody on shore noting its suspicious flight path.

However, it was not the possible disadvantages of ferrying the body by flying boat but the inherent superiority of sending Major Martin by submarine which prompted Montagu to conclude that it would be the 'ideal method' of conveying the courier to his rendezvous. This was because this mode of transport should ensure that the dead messenger would be put over

ie side only when the wind conditions were just right to waft him towards
ie Spanish coast.[78] A submarine, loitering submerged and unseen in the
icinity of the appointed dropping-off point, could wait until the wind was
lowing in exactly the direction required to propel the floating cadaver
iorewards. A flying boat, on the other hand, would not be able to linger for
ong in the Gulf of Cadiz, awaiting a favourable shift in the wind, for fear of
eing caught in the act. In fact, an airborne delivery of Major Martin would
ave to be undertaken on the basis of a weather forecast made several hours
efore and from over a thousand miles away. Yet, as Montagu also noted, a
ibmarine's crew could stage an air crash just as effectively as, and doubtless
vith less risk of discovery than, a flying boat:

> After the body had been planted it would help the illusion if a 'set piece'
> giving a flare and explosion with delay action fuse could be left to give the
> impression of an aircraft crash.[79]

ver the conscientious counsellor, Montagu, however, had also to warn
Captain Lambe that there were also drawbacks to relying upon carriage by
ibmarine for *Mincemeat*'s 'special delivery'. The first of these actually
orang from Montagu's own limited knowledge of the capacity of modern
British submarines to operate in shallow waters. This caused him to advise
ambe that a rubber dinghy would have to be launched from the submarine
o take the body etc. close enough inshore'.[80] The other problem posed by
ishore submarine transport for Major Martin seemed much more serious:
ow was the dead body of the courier to be kept reasonably fresh during its
naritime passage? Preserving the corpse in a presentable state would not be
oo difficult if it were to travel by plane because of the relatively short
uration of an air trip between Britain and Gibraltar. A similar journey by
ibmarine, however, would last around ten days, ample time for Glyndwr
Michael's thawed remains to decompose to a degree incompatible with
heir notional status as those of a recent drowning victim.[81] Montagu,
owever, did not accept second best, and settle on a flying boat as the
nly practical means of ferrying *Mincemeat*'s messenger to his rendezvous.
nstead, he urged Captain Lambe to recognize the superiority of sending the
ourier by submarine, if only the problem of 'the necessary preservation of
ie body' could be solved.[82]

   In highlighting this practical difficulty with *Mincemeat*'s implementation
o his colleague in the Directorate of Plans, Montagu was not simply passing
he buck. Indeed, as the brief he submitted for Lambe's consideration on

12 March revealed, he had taken expert advice, already, on this problem. As before, when the medical feasibility of *Operation Mincemeat* seemed in question, Montagu turned to Sir Bernard Spilsbury for professional advice. Once more, Sir Bernard was prepared to draw upon his considerable experience in the field of human pathology to assist the covert scheme. He counselled Montagu against being overly concerned about the ambient temperature that Major Martin would experience in his travels. If Glyndwr Michael's remains, once removed from their refrigerator, were placed in a container while still very cold, they should not deteriorate noticeably, even over the course of a sea journey to Spain according to the pathologist. However, Spilsbury also impressed upon the deception planners that it was vital to exclude oxygen—the main accelerant of bodily decay—as much as possible from the corpse's container. The medium he proposed to protect the body was dry ice, i.e. carbon dioxide in the form of frozen blocks. As they melted, these blocks of dry ice would turn back into CO_2 gas and shield the body from contact with the surrounding air.[83] Montagu, clearly, had received this advice from Spilsbury in time for his consultation with Captain Lambe on 12 March. This is so because he informed the latter, on that occasion, that keeping the body in a container with dry ice might be one way of addressing the technical difficulties involved in keeping the body fresh during the passage by sea. However, as Montagu also commented, although a dry-ice container might be a suitable means for carrying the corpse-courier on board a surface vessel, it could prove positively lethal inside a submarine. There, he contended, the apparently inevitable leak of carbon dioxide from the canister containing the corpse could poison some, or even all, members of a submerged submarine's crew, dependent as they were on the limited air supply available within their boat's pressure hull. Of course, Montagu had already ruled out delivering the body to its destination by surface ship, for the reasons given above. So, all he could do, to keep open his preferred mode of maritime transportation for Major Martin, was to suggest—without great hope—that 'it might be possible to arrange some form of suitable storage outside the pressure hull' of a submarine, to carry the dead messenger and his noxious insulation. Montagu pressed Lambe to make sure that this possibility be investigated, if the Royal Navy did decide to try and shift *Mincemeat*'s courier by sea.[84]

Of course, as we have seen, while Montagu was seeking the practical assistance of his colleagues in the senior service to transport the dead body and its misleading documents to Spain, he was battling simultaneously with other elements of Britain's military bureaucracy to maintain *Mincemeat* as an attempt at strategic deception. If the naval staff had joined the chorus of naysayers, particularly by raising allegedly insuperable technical objections to its implementation, they might have killed it off altogether. However, amongst his fellow sailors, Montagu encountered only encouragement and a willingness to help in the execution of the deception plan. He was particularly fortunate in being able to make his primary plea for naval assistance in conveying Major Martin to Spanish waters to one of the most imaginative individuals to serve within the upper echelons of the Admiralty during the Second World War. The naval Director of Plans, Captain Charles Lambe— with whom, as already noted, Montagu had raised the issue on 12 March 1943—had the kind of versatile intellect likely to be fascinated by a scheme as unconventional as *Operation Mincemeat*. An accomplished pilot, pianist, and painter, Lambe impressed contemporaries as able to 'apply a clear-sighted and original mind to difficult problems where the stereotyped would frequently have failed'. Yet, for all 'his catholic tastes and widespread interests beyond the Navy', Lambe was also an exceptionally expert sailor, who excelled in the role of naval staff officer, in which he served for most of the Second World War. Indeed, so persuaded were Lambe's peers and superiors of his virtues as a naval planner that he rose to the very pinnacle of his profession-at-arms after the war. In May 1959 he became First Sea Lord and Chief of Naval Staff, although mortal illness would curtail his tenure of Britain's most senior naval command to a solitary year.[85] Even during the Second World War, he enjoyed such favourable report as to carry considerable weight with his fellow military planners and among the Chiefs of Staff.[86] So, here was one individual imaginative enough to grasp the strategic potential of *Operation Mincemeat* and influential enough to protect that potential for high-level deception from sceptics within the armed forces' bureaucracy. Having been briefed personally about the deception plan by Ewen Montagu in March, he seems to have played a key role in winning his fellow Directors of Plans (from the Army and Air Force) to the view that *Mincemeat*'s misleading message should be pitched at the highest level, if it were to have any chance of yielding strategic consequences. Lambe, doubtless, also played his part in getting the Directors of Plans to agree to an earlier launch date for the deception plan than they had envisaged originally.[87] He also helped ensure that *Operation Mincemeat* was fast-tracked for approval by the COS.[88] Still, even before rendering these vital services to the deception plan, from late March to early April 1943,

Captain Lambe acted as a crucial intermediary between Montagu and the naval staff over the intractable issue of Major Martin's mode of travel to his appointed destination.

In fact, Montagu had specifically asked Lambe, at their meeting on 12 March, to obtain a decision 'from the appropriate authority', on the method to be used for transporting the body. Lambe approached the Assistant Chief of Naval Staff, Admiral Wilfrid Patterson, with the sugges-tion that the corpse-courier be carried by submarine, if at all possible, to Spain's coastal waters. Admiral Patterson readily accepted the proposal coming as it did from such a respected colleague. Accordingly, he directed that 'a submarine should be used if arrangements could be made'.[89] To determine whether it was at all practical to transport Mincemeat's unique cargo in such a boat, Lambe also got permission for Montagu to confer with the Flag Officer in command of the Royal Navy's submarine force, Rear Admiral Claud Barry. Barry certainly had no objections in principle to conveying the dead messenger in one of his craft and he made his senior officers available to Montagu to tackle the practical difficulties involved in doing so. Moreover, the seeming snags with this mode of transport turned out to be more apparent than real. Thus, the submarine's staff assured Montagu that one of their vessels should be able to 'bring the body close enough inshore to obviate the need to use a rubber dinghy to transport it'. The fact that Major Martin could be placed in the sea so near to the Spanish coast as to make it under his own steam, ruled out the burning of flares, or the staging of other visual and sound effects, to simulate a plane crash.[90] Their phoniness would be all too evident to any onlookers on the nearby shore. Captain S. M. Raw, who was Rear Admiral Barry's Chief of Staff, also saw no reason why the body should not be carried within the pressure hull of a submarine, as long as it was placed inside 'an air-tight but not pressure proof container'.[91] This expert opinion was a major boost to the feasibility of transporting Mincemeat's dead messenger by submarine, for if the cadaver had to be carried on the external casing of a submarine it would have to be made pressure-proof to withstand the weight of sea water when the boat was submerged. Constructing the container, with a sufficiently thick skin to cope with that water pressure meant that it would also have to be so heavy an object as to make it difficult to control the trim of the submarine bearing its load.[92]

However, in view of Captain Raw's assurance that the corpse-courier could be accommodated within the pressure hull of a submarine, the practicality of transporting Major Martin in such a vessel now depended on one technical question: 'whether a container could be provided which would be suitable for the submarine and also keep the body fresh'.[93] That problem Raw and his colleagues passed back to Ewen Montagu to solve. However, all concerned were agreed on what was needed: a container that was sufficiently airtight to protect both its corporeal contents from oxygen-induced decay and the submarine's crew against any leakage of poisonous carbon-dioxide vapour. The container also had to be capacious enough to hold the dead body and, yet, of a suitable size and shape to fit through the hatches of a Royal Navy submarine. Such containers were hardly standard items of military equipment, and no suitable container would be found lying around in any Army, Navy, or Air Force supply depot. It would have to be custom-designed and manufactured to meet *Operation Mincemeat*'s precise requirements. Since aircraft manufacturing was the most techno-logically advanced branch of wartime industrial production, it made sense for Montagu to turn to his Air Force partner in deception, Flight Lieutenant Charles Cholmondeley, to mobilize the plane makers' skill for this task. In doing so, he provided his RAF colleague with a precise set of specifica-tions for the container-coffin. These 'specs' had been worked out, not only in consultation with the expert submariners but, also, after taking further advice from Sir Bernard Spilsbury regarding the requirements from a medical viewpoint. Armed with this detailed mandate, Cholmondeley approached officials of the Ministry of Aircraft Production to commission the construction of a container suitable for *Mincemeat*'s very specific needs. The main priority was to ensure that the receptacle was so hermetically sealed as to prevent the entry of fresh air inside it, or the escape of poisonous gas from it. Accordingly, the container was manufactured of inner and outer skins of 22-gauge steel, welded together but separated by a lining of asbestos wool. To the same end, the container's 'flush fitting lid' (also consisting of two skins of 22-gauge steel with a layer of asbestos wool between them) was 'bedded down onto rubber washers by means of a number of bolts and nuts'.[94] Sir Bernard Spilsbury was so impressed by the airtight features of the container Cholmondeley had had built, that he gave it his unqualified approval as a medical man. He assured Montagu that the courier's remains 'ought to keep perfectly satisfactorily in this [receptacle] until required for duty'.[95]

However, the laden container would also have to be portable enough to be manhandled on board a standard Royal Naval submarine, and to be hoisted back up onto the casing of such a vessel, at journey's end.

The container would also have to be opened on deck (immediately before the body was to be lowered into the sea), both to avoid the prying eyes of the submarine's crew and to prevent its members being overcome by a sudden release of carbon dioxide in the confined space inside the boat. So, the canister was made in the shape of a cylinder one foot, ten and one-eighth inches in diameter and six feet, six inches in length, which allowed it to be lowered and raised through the selected submarine's torpedo hatch and also to be stowed for the duration of the voyage on one of that vessel's torpedo-reloading racks.[96] To make carting it about easier, lifting handles (which folded down flat) were attached to each end of the container, while a box-spanner (clipped when not in use) was chained to its lid to aid its opening, at the appropriate moment.[97] Although fabricated from light-gauge steel, 'to keep the weight as low as possible', its loaded and (literally) dead weight would be 400 lbs.[98] Since the ratings who stowed this unusual receptacle on board the submarine, and those who also sailed with it, might be tempted to speculate about what was inside it, the following misleading description of its contents was painted along its upper sides: 'HANDLE WITH CARE—OPTICAL INSTRUMENTS—FOR SPECIAL F.O.S. [i.e. Flag Officer Submarines] SHIPMENT'.[99]

Security concerns also played a part in the decision to reduce to a minimum the other items Montagu and company saw fit to cast into the sea along with their dead messenger. This was because the Mincemeat team had been informed by experts that 'little or no wreckage floated from a modern aircraft in normal circumstances'.[100] This news certainly suited the planners' aim of keeping the operation, throughout its execution, a strict secret from all but the chosen submarine's officers who would be charged with actually launching Major Martin on the maritime phase of his mission. Having to load a lot of aircraft debris onto a submarine before it sailed, would inevitably raise eyebrows among its crew and, worse still, likely loosen their lips once they were back on shore. Montagu must have been relieved to hear that he could limit the additional items to be set afloat with the dead messenger to just a couple: a rubber dinghy equipped with only one out of a normal set of two paddles (both craft and paddles were standard issue for Catalina aircraft). Of course, Mincemeat's implementers now under-stood that there was no need to place the body in this inflated craft, but they clearly reasoned that a capsized dinghy adrift 'near the body but not too near' might help account for the corpse's presence in the sea off Huelva. Again, to prevent the crew guessing what was afoot, the submarine's

ommander was to be handed the rubber dinghy as a covered parcel, at the
ime time as the container-coffin was being loaded on to his vessel. Charles
Cholmondeley was able to get hold of the right sort of dinghy from his RAF
contacts to help consolidate the image of Major Martin as the victim of a
Catalina crash.[101]

Thus, it was resolved, Major Martin would journey in a sealed container
n board a submarine to execute his posthumous mission. All that now
emained, by way of finalizing his travel arrangements, was to select the boat
1 which he could sail and to schedule its departure. In arranging these
matters, Mincemeat's planners had a real stroke of luck. They learned from
Admiral Barry's staff that HMS Seraph (P. 219) was due to set sail for Gibraltar
rom Britain 'at a suitable time' (i.e., 'probably on the 10th April' 1943) under
he command of Lieutenant N. L. A. Jewell, RN.[102] A delighted Montagu
eported to Colonel Bevan how fortunate Mincemeat's planners were to be
ble to employ this particular submarine captain in their top-secret decep-
ion scheme:

> The Commanding Officer happens to be Jewell who fortunately enough is
> experienced in such undertakings having already dropped Giraud into the sea
> twice (!) and landed General Clarke [sic] in North Africa.[103]

Both the risky ventures which Montagu mentioned had occurred during the
un-up to Operation Torch and both had been launched in the hope of
orestalling, or at least minimizing, French resistance to the Anglo–American
nvasion of their North African Empire.[104] The first of these cloak-and-dagger
nterprises was a truly madcap affair which had been authorized by the
ormally ultra-cautious Eisenhower in an attempt to resolve what he saw as
he unfavorable potentialities' inherent in 'sailing a dangerous political sea'.[105]
t involved the dispatch of 'Ike's' deputy, General Mark Clark, to a secret
endezvous with General Charles Mast (who was deputy-commander of the
Vichy French Army in North Africa) in a seaside villa, on the coast just west
f Algiers. This was a breathtakingly reckless endeavour, since as Eisen-
ower's Naval Aide, Harry Butcher, noted in his diary at the time, General
Clark was 'thoroughly familiar with the whole operation' (Torch) and had
olanned most of the detail under policies and decisions laid down' by the
Commander-in-Chief.[106] To deposit such a well-informed, high-ranking
ndividual on a potentially hostile shore, along with a few staff officers and
aree British commandos to protect him, was to endanger not only his
erson, but also the security of the entire forthcoming invasion. Indeed, the

foolhardy enterprise nearly ended in disaster, when Vichyite police interrupted Clark's discussions with Mast and other anti-Axis French officers during the night of 22 October 1942. Clark and his companions had to hide in a cellar while the villa's owner reassured his police visitors that nothing was amiss. Then they tried to regain the safety of the submarine, HMS *Seraph*, which had ferried them to their tryst with Mast and his colleagues. However, Clark's party found that relaunching the flimsy canvas boats—or folbots—in which they had paddled ashore to be no easy task. Their fragile craft capsized in the high waves and dumped their occupants into the Mediterranean. Although all the Allied personnel managed to swim back to the Algerian beach, other members of the General's entourage beheld a singular sight, once they dragged themselves from the heavily rolling surf: 'there stood Clark, naked as God made him, except for his overseas cap, and shivering'. Upon returning to the villa the American General did manage to intimidate the now badly frightened owner into providing him with an eclectic outfit: a pair of trousers and 'a fancy silk French tablecloth' which Clark wrapped 'about himself like a sheik'. Then the Allied party hid in nearby woods until dawn, when the sea calmed somewhat, and they tried again to paddle out to HMS *Seraph*. This time, thanks to Jewell's skill in sailing his boat dangerously close, actually within only a quarter of a mile of the shore, they all made it back on board the submarine.[107]

Lieutenant Jewell's feat of seamanship had avoided a potentially fatal security lapse for *Operation Torch*. It had prevented the all-too-well informed General Clark from falling into the hands of the Vichy regime's police and their Axis cronies. Moreover, Clark was able to return to Eisenhower with valuable intelligence for the *Torch* invaders about French North Africa' defences.[108] Admittedly, Clark failed in his broader purpose of blunting the French will to resist the forthcoming Anglo–American landings, not least because of the conflicting loyalties and competing ambitions rife within their North African command.[109] However, he did draw one conclusion of strategic importance from his Algerian adventure, as he informed Captain G. B. H. ('Barney') Fawkes—the commander of the Royal Navy's Eighth Submarine Flotilla based at Gibraltar—once he was back on the Rock: 'by golly, I'm going to tell Ike that if we have to fight alongside people like yourself, Bill Jewell and the boys of *Seraph* and those Commando cut-throats, then this war is about to be won'.[110] He was as good as his word. When he returned to England and briefed Eisenhower in person on 21 October 1942 about his secret mission Clark was loud in his praise of

Lieutenant Jewell and the *Seraph*'s submariners, as Captain Butcher recorded, once more:

> The submarine commander had manoeuvred his craft so skilfully and had been such a fine officer throughout that Clark is recommending him for an appropriate American decoration... Clark couldn't speak too highly of the quality and bravery of the skipper and his crew.[111]

Indeed, Jewell's service was deemed so meritorious that he was promptly given another high-level secret mission designed to ease the entry of Anglo–American forces into the French North African Empire. This was a commission to rescue General Henri Honoré Giraud from Vichy France, and to transport him to Allied headquarters on the Rock of Gibraltar in time to employ his apparent prestige in favour of cooperation with the *Torch* troops. Giraud was a hero to many French people, especially after his audacious escape from German captivity in April 1942. The Vichy authorities, however, were none too pleased to have Giraud back within their jurisdiction and they subjected him to increasing pressure to return to Nazi imprisonment. So when General Mast consulted him secretly about lending a hand with Allied landings in North Africa, he eventually agreed—under the illusion that the Americans would be happy to serve there under his own supreme command.[112] The US authorities did have high hopes of the French General, although they were not as inflated as Giraud's own ego. Still, Eisenhower was persuaded that an appeal, made in Giraud's name to French forces in North Africa on the eve of *Operation Torch* to refrain from firing on the Allied forces, might secure a bloodless victory for the invaders. President Roosevelt even came to regard Giraud as a more acceptable leader for the 'Free France' movement than Charles de Gaulle, whose personal ambition and political agenda he found suspect.[113] Of course, these prospects could be fulfilled only if Giraud could be plucked from virtual house arrest in Lyon and spirited away to Eisenhower's headquarters on the Rock of Gibraltar. The French Resistance could be relied upon to smuggle the General down to France's Mediterranean coast, but an Allied vessel would have to lift him from that less than friendly shore.[114]

Given the favourable impression Jewell and his crew had made on Mark Clark, *Seraph* was his obvious choice to pick up another VIP in a new clandestine operation in potentially hostile waters. However, Giraud's pronouncedly anti-British sentiments meant that he might refuse to make good his escape from Vichy France in a boat sailing under 'the White

Ensign'. Indeed, General Mast insisted that an American craft would have to be used for the rescue mission. The problem with this proposal was that the nearest US submarine was over 3,000 miles away and could not reach France's Mediterranean coast in time to do the job before *Torch*. Again, such American submariners would not have the necessary experience to navigate the dangerous shallows of the Mediterranean Sea successfully. The solution was to induct HMS *Seraph*, and all its officers and men, into the United States Navy on a temporary basis and place both the boat and crew under the nominal command of an American officer.[115] So, it was as the USS *Seraph*, under the formal command of the United States Navy Captain Jerauld Wright (a future Admiral and NATO Supreme Commander, Atlantic), that the submarine left Gibraltar on 27 October 1942, heading for the Golfe de Lion. Although the *Seraph* was flying the Stars and Stripes, Bill Jewell remained in de facto control of the submarine. He it was who worked the boat and guided it to a precise rendezvous with a small fishing craft, carrying Giraud and fellow escapees, around 1.00 a.m. on Friday 6 November, near the small southern French seaside resort of Le Lavandou. Although Giraud did fall into the gap between the rowing boat and the submarine's casing, when trying to clamber on board the *Seraph*, sturdy hands lifted him on deck before he was crushed between the two vessels. Once on board the *Seraph*, Giraud soon saw through the fiction that he was being rescued by a US boat, despite the best efforts of Lieutenant Jewell and his crew to imitate American mannerisms in speech and behaviour. However, Giraud must have realized also that it was too late by then to turn back to the Vichy regime's unwelcoming embrace. Moreover, despite losing the ability to send messages, due to the fact that his radio's aerial had become disconnected from the transmitter, Jewell managed to rendez-vous, on the morning of 7 November, with a Catalina which had been sent from Gibraltar to search for the silent submarine. The successful transfer of the *Seraph*'s VIP passenger to the amphibian aircraft meant that the French General should arrive at Eisenhower's headquarters, on the Rock, just in the nick of time to make the eve-of-invasion broadcast to France's North African garrison that *Torch*'s planners envisaged.[116] However, although his aircraft did reach Gibraltar around 4.00 p.m. that same afternoon, Giraud declined to play his part in the Allies' grand design. When Eisenhower refused to surrender supreme command of all the *Torch* forces to him, Giraud flatly turned down the request that he broadcast a pre-invasion appeal to the French forces in North Africa to side with the Allied intruders.[117] Although the Americans would persist for some months to come in trying to foist Giraud's leadership on French North Africa and the forces of 'Free France', he turned out to be a sore disappointment to them. Eisenhower came to realize that he was a military reactionary with no political talents, while Roosevelt eventually had to accept that his protégé had been completely outsmarted by General Charles de Gaulle in the struggle for control of 'Fighting France'.[118]

Of course, the captain and crew of the Seraph could not be held responsible for the fact that the VIP they had snatched from the clutches of the Vichy regime's security services turned out to be such a dud. Indeed, both the British and American top brass were much more inclined to praise rather than blame Jewell and his men for their sterling work on special operations for Torch. Thus, Britain's naval supremo in the Mediterranean, Admiral Cunningham, complimented Jewell for accomplishing his 'delicate and important mission' in rescuing Giraud 'with judgment and efficiency'.[119] The initial American appreciation of gratitude came from an equally elevated level of their military command. In mid December 1942, Generals Eisenhower and Clark invited Jewell, along with Barney Fawkes, to dine with them in Algiers (where both the Allied Commanders' headquarters and the Royal Navy's Eighth Submarine Flotilla were now based), to thank the Seraph's captain for his invaluable assistance on clandestine missions in the countdown to Operation Torch.[120] These fine words were then followed by more formal recognition. In February 1943, the London Gazette (the British government's official journal of record) announced that Jewell had been awarded an MBE 'for skill, daring and cool judgment while executing special operations for the Supreme Allied Commander in North Africa'. Ironically, the receipt of this British honour rendered Jewell ineligible to receive an American medal for the same special operations, under Anglo–American rules to eliminate duplication in the conferral of military decorations.[121] However, the US senior commanders in the Mediterranean did not forget their debt of gratitude to the Seraph's skipper and would find an occasion in the not-too-distant future to reward Lieutenant Jewell's gallant conduct. Perhaps as striking as these official acknowledgements of Jewell's meritorious service was the degree of respect he won amongst his fellow submariners. Thus, Lieutenant David Scott, who joined the Seraph as first officer in April 1943, soon formed the most positive opinion of his new captain, coming to regard him as a 'true professional' who 'knew every facet of the submarine business'. He also found Jewell to be 'quite fearless' and 'invariably very cool and calculating'.[122] This is praise, indeed, particularly from a professional sailor who, himself, ultimately rose to the rank of Rear Admiral in the Royal Navy.

Yet, however qualified Lieutenant Jewell and his crew were to steer Major Martin and his bag of tricks to the spot appointed by *Mincemeat*'s planners, their availability to do so was purely a matter of accident. When not employed on covert assignments, HMS *Seraph* reverted to its primary function as a warship—or to be precise, a long-range patrol submarine searching for, and seeking to destroy, enemy shipping, both merchant and naval. In this role, *Seraph*, as one of Britain's 'S' class of submarines, was 'the most deadly instrument of war of its size yet devised by an offensive-minded Navy', according to one assessment.[123] Equipped with seven torpedo tubes (six in the bow of the boat and one in its stern) and a four-inch deck gun, *Seraph* did pack quite a punch.[124] However, on Christmas Eve night 1942, it was Jewell and his men who saw stars—and not Yuletide ones—when their vessel was involved in an underwater collision with an enemy submarine off the northern coast of Tunisia. Although the officers and ratings of the British submarine suffered no more than abrasions and bruises as they were knocked off their feet by the shock of the impact, their boat did not escape so lightly. It sustained significant damage to its bows, and its starboard torpedo tubes. It was evident, upon the *Seraph*'s return to Algiers, that she required more extensive repairs than could be done locally. So, on 8 January 1943, Jewell and his crew set sail for England in their battle-scarred boat. They took twenty days, in their battered condition, to reach the dry docks at Blyth on the coast of Northumberland. There the submarine received not only new bows and torpedo tubes, but also an additional weapon: an Oerlikon 20 mm anti-aircraft cannon, mounted aft of the boat's conning tower. While his warship was being made fully seaworthy and fighting fit once more, Jewell enjoyed some well-earned leave with his parents at home in Pinner, Middlesex. However, his receipt of the MBE in February provoked such interest from the press that he had to bolt and stay with friends for a few days, until the reporters abandoned their siege of his family home.[125]

Urgent attention from another quarter proved less easy to elude. Once *Mincemeat*'s own press gang got wind of Lieutenant Jewell's presence in England, they were determined to recruit him for their covert project. His proven ability in the conduct of special operations, the fact that he commanded an 'S'-class submarine capable of navigating quite shallow waters and the local availability of his craft and crew for the mission, made Jewell the ideal candidate to take charge of transporting Major Martin and his precious briefcase to the Gulf of Cadiz.[126] Moreover, as already noted above, Admiral Barry's staff also informed Montagu that the refitted HMS *Seraph* was due to set sail for Gibraltar on a date in April compatible with the *Mincemeat* team's schedule of departure for Major Martin.[127] So, Bill Jewell was summoned to the headquarters of the Flag Officer Submarines at Northways, Swiss Cottage, London where, on 31 March 1943, he found not only Captain Raw of the Submarine Staff but also Lieutenant Commander Ewen Montagu of the Naval Intelligence Division waiting to meet him.[128] Montagu proceeded to let Jewell in on the secret of *Operation Mincemeat*, defining its 'object' with pithiness and precision in operation orders (approved in advance by Captain Raw) which he gave to the submarine commander, on that occasion:

> To cause a brief-case containing documents to drift ashore as near as possible to HUELVA in Spain in such circumstances that it will be thought to have washed ashore from an aircraft which crashed at sea when the case was being taken by an officer from the U.K. to Allied Force H.Q. in North Africa.

Montagu's operation orders also specified the singular means by which this operational object was to be achieved:

> A dead body dressed in the battle-dress uniform of a Major, Royal Marines, and wearing a 'Mae West' will be taken out in a submarine, together with the brief case and a rubber dinghy.
> The body will be packed fully clothed and ready (and wrapped in a blanket to prevent friction) in a tubular air-tight container (which will be labelled as 'Optical Instruments').[129]

Jewell, for all his previous experience of top-secret, special operations must have been taken aback by the macabre nature of the mission he was being assigned. However, since his father was a surgeon and former colonial medical officer, the sight of a dead body would not be new to him.[130] So, he seems to have regained his native composure quickly and was soon deep in conversation with Montagu over the practical details of ferrying *Mincemeat*'s unique cargo by submarine to the waters off Huelva. Montagu's orders addressed many of these issues, including the following: the place where the dead messenger was to be deposited in the sea; how the briefcase containing the all-important documents was to be attached to the body, once it had been removed from its container; what cover stories might be used to keep the deception secret; and what cancellation plans should be followed, if the need arose to abort the mission, while *Seraph* was sailing to execute it.[131]

Bill Jewell had volunteered for the service in 1936, qualifying as a commanding officer in May 1941 and had taken charge of the newly commissioned *Seraph* in May 1942.[132] However, he already knew enough about handling such a boat in the open ocean to identify, immediately, the trickiest part of the mission he was being given. This was the need to lift the container—with its irretrievably dead weight—through the submarine's torpedo hatch and up on to its casing, while the vessel pitched and rolled in the sea's swell. So, Lieutenant Jewell apparently suggested, then and there, to Montagu and Raw that his boat be fitted with 'specially prepared slides', on which the coffin-container could be moved through the torpedo hatch with greater ease and speed. Even then, Jewell also proposed to accomplish the awkward maneouvre of hoisting the cylinder through the submarine's torpedo hatch at some distance from the shore—and, therefore, out of range of easy observation from the Spanish coast. This precaution would also minimize the time *Seraph* had to linger on the actual spot where Major Martin was to be lowered into the sea. On the other hand, it would be necessary to take additional steps to ensure that the container was not lost overboard, as the submarine steamed towards the appointed position. To avoid such a last-minute accident wrecking all the elaborate plans and painstaking preparations of the *Mincemeat* team, Jewell intended to have the container securely lashed to the rail round the submarine's gun platform, after it had been brought up on deck.[133] Jewell's instant attention to such a critical detail, and the general aura of professional competence which the *Seraph*'s skipper displayed in these exchanges with Montagu and Raw, can only have reassured them that their 'special delivery' would be in very capable hands. However, in view of the supreme strategic stakes riding on the success of the subterfuge, Montagu also impressed upon Jewell the heavy responsibility he was assuming. The deceptive documents had to be communicated to the enemy in absolute secrecy and with the utmost security:

> It is in fact most important that the Germans and Spaniards should accept these papers... If they should suspect that these papers are a 'plant' it might have far-reaching consequences of great magnitude.[134]

The fact that HMS *Seraph* was scheduled to depart for Gibraltar during the second week of April and, essentially, along the route already designated for

Major Martin, initially provided convenient cover for his covert trip.[135] However, at Captain Raw's insistence, the submarine's date of departure from the UK was delayed for another week, until 17 April 1943 and then, again, changed to 19 April.[136] Raw made these amendments to the courier's travel schedule so that *Operation Mincemeat* could be executed at a time of the month ('approximately 28th–29th April') when the moon was waning. This should permit Jewell and members of his crew to extract Major Martin from his container, and lower his body in to sea, during 'a reasonably dark period'. Raw also assured his colleagues that such a postponement of *Seraph*'s departure date need not look suspicious, since the extra week would be devoted to 'normal training' of the boat's crew.[137] As it turned out, this deferral of the date for launching *Operation Mincemeat* was a godsend to Montagu and his fellow planners. This was because the process of obtaining final official approval from the Allied High Command for the deception scheme's implementation proved to be fraught with more difficulties and delays than they had expected. Thus, although the COS had agreed, in principle, on 7 April 1943, to the mounting of *Operation Mincemeat*, it took them almost another week, until 13 April, to accept the revised version of General Nye's letter to General Alexander, which was the central document in the set of deceptive papers being palmed off on the Germans.[138] This protraction of the process of COS ratification inevitably left Montagu and his assistants with a tight schedule for preparing the corpse for its journey and delivering it to HMS *Seraph*, which would be waiting in Holy Loch, on the river Clyde in Scotland, in time for that vessel's departure date of 19 April.

However, the COS did more than delay matters with their own deliberations. They now made another intervention in the implementation of *Operation Mincemeat* which almost threatened to postpone its execution beyond the time when it could serve as an effective cover plan for the invasion of Sicily. The deception planners realized that, unless they could get their misleading papers in Spanish hands by the start of May, it was unlikely the Germans would have sufficient time to digest their deceptive contents and respond to the danger they apparently revealed, of an imminent Allied offensive against Greece. The Abwehr had to be given a sporting chance to get hold of the *Mincemeat* letters, and a breathing-space within which to authenticate and assess them, before passing them to the German High Command. Again, the OKW had to be given time, too, to absorb the operational and strategic significance of this documentary windfall and, most critical of all, to retain their forces in southern Europe, and perhaps even redeploy their troops from other fronts to meet the notional Anglo–American threats to Greece and Sardinia. With the D-Day for *Operation Husky* set for 10 July 1943, any postponement of Major Martin's mission to Spain beyond the third week of April almost certainly meant that he would arrive too late to inspire any decisive misdeployment of German forces. Again, the planners could not afford to forget their medical experts' advice that the body they had chosen to play the part of their dead messenger would be unusable beyond the end of April. Presumably, this was because, for most of the period he was kept on ice, Glyndwr Michael's remains were refrigerated rather than deeply frozen. A corpse preserved in this state could be dressed for its mission in several stages without the need of such repeated thawing and refreezing as would accelerate its rate of decomposition. So, for both military and medical reasons, it was imperative that Major Martin be on his way by late April. Given the immutability of this deadline, Montagu's consternation can be well imagined when the COS, on 14 April 1943, abruptly suspended the implementation of *Operation Mincemeat*, pending a further round of consultation. Now the COS insisted that the daring strategic deception would have to receive a seal of approval from the topmost level of Britain's wartime leadership:

> The COMMITTEE discussed the procedure to be adopted for informing the Prime Minister of the proposed plan for MINCEMEAT and invited Lieut.-General Ismay to take action as proposed.[139]

Montagu deplored this decision, which he regarded as a classic instance of buck-passing by the Chiefs.[140] However, he had no choice but to wait upon the Prime Minister's pleasure, while the time limit on using Glyndwr Michael's all too mortal remains inexorably approached.

The economical minute-taking style of Britain's War Cabinet secretariat does not permit certain identification of the member of the Chiefs of Staff Committee who urged his colleagues to refer *Operation Mincemeat* to the Prime Minister for ultimate endorsement. However, the likely culprit—as Montagu doubtless would have regarded him—was General 'Pug' Ismay. The latter served upon the COS Committee as the representative of the Minister of Defence, namely, Winston Churchill, who held that government portfolio along with the leadership of the British Government. As Churchill's chief military staff officer, 'Pug' unquestionably acted well within his rights, and in due discharge of his responsibilities, in insisting that such a risky strategic deception scheme required prime ministerial authorization before it could be set in motion. Still, Ismay also seems to have been prompted by personal reservations about the unorthodox nature of the *Mincemeat* venture. When informing Churchill, later on 14 April, of the reason why Colonel Bevan would be calling on him at 10.15 a.m. the following morning, Ismay could not conceal his scepticism about the suggested scheme: 'The Chiefs of Staff have approved, subject to your consent, a somewhat startling cover plan in connection with HUSKY.'[141] Ismay's characteristic efficiency in arranging an early appointment for the chief of LCS to brief the Prime Minister about *Mincemeat* meant that Major Martin still might be able to make his scheduled departure date of 19 April, as long as Churchill raised no objection to its immediate implementation. That seemed unlikely, for—as insiders like Ismay well knew—the British warlord had a natural penchant for covert actions and clandestine activities.[142]

Sure enough, when Bevan was ushered into Churchill's bedroom, located in the Government's Annexe building in Whitehall, at the set time on Thursday, 15 April, he found it easy to engage the Prime Minister's interest in the macabre project. Churchill lay in bed, 'surrounded with (official) papers and black and red Cabinet boxes', but gave his full attention to his visitor once Bevan embarked upon his explanation of *Operation Mincemeat*. The LCS chief handed over a single sheet of foolscap to the Prime Minister, containing an outline of the deception plan, and waited until Churchill—all the while puffing away on one of his trademark cigars—had read it through.[143] Then, honest and true counsellor that he was, Bevan pointed out the main ways in which *Operation Mincemeat* might miscarry. The Spaniards might ascertain that the dead man was not in fact a drowned military courier but 'a gardener in Wales [*sic*] who'd killed himself with weed killer'. Although also noting Sir Bernard Spilsbury's opinion that such a medical discovery by the Spaniards was very unlikely 'because it was a very difficult technical job to find out the cause of death', Bevan cautioned that there was a chance that the deception would be 'found out'.[144] Of course, such a turn of events might enable the Germans to read the attempted deception backwards and identify Sicily as the real target for the forthcoming Allied summer offensive in the Mediterranean theatre. Churchill, however, was not daunted by that prospect, as his response to Bevan's warning made clear: 'Everyone but a bloody fool would *know* that it's Shishily.'[145] Churchill was equally dismissive when Bevan pointed out that the 'body might never get washed up or that if it did, the Spaniards might hand it over to the local British Authority without having taken the crucial papers'. 'In that case', Churchill retorted, 'we shall have to get the body back and give it another swim'.[146] That would hardly have been a practical proposition, given the rapidly declining shelf-life of Glyndwr Michael's remains and the narrowing window of opportunity to influence German troop deployments in the run-up to *Husky*. However, the crucial point to emerge from Churchill's exchanges with Bevan was that the Prime Minister had become a convert to *Mincemeat*'s cause, and was undismayed by the Controlling Officer's devil's advocacy about the ways in which the Operation might misfire. Indeed, Churchill proceeded to given Bevan his own formal assent to the deception plan.[147]

Then, however, Churchill dropped a bombshell. He concluded his meeting with Bevan by directing that final authority for the execution of *Operation Mincemeat* must be obtained from General Eisenhower, the overall Allied Commander in the Mediterranean.[148] Of course, this additional round of consultation threatened to delay the start of Major Martin's journey to Spain beyond 19 April, thereby calling in question *Mincemeat*'s medical credibility and, perhaps even, its strategic significance. Yet, Bevan and Montagu had to accept the Prime Minister's conditional approval for their long-developed plan, since contesting it might delay matters still further and, conceivably, produce an even less satisfactory outcome. Churchill, for his part, did not make clear why he was insisting that Eisenhower be given the ultimate say over *Operation Mincemeat*'s imple-mentation. However, the deference he accorded the American General over this matter may have been a form of Churchillian compensation for the rough treatment he had meted out to 'Ike', the week before. At that time, in early April 1943, General Eisenhower was struggling to maintain pressure on the slowly yielding Axis forces in Tunisia, while keeping the national rivalries amongst his coalition commanders within bounds.[149] He was doubtless aware that his own military career rested upon the results of his efforts there. This uncomfortable fact of life had been made clear to one of Eisenhower's aides by the US Army's Chief of Staff, George C. Marshall, a few weeks before: 'The General said that Ike's rise or fall depended on the outcome of the Tunisian battle.'[150] In fact, total victory in North Africa was hardly over a month away, and a series of coordinated Allied attacks, launched from later April on would overwhelm every resistance in Tunisia by 13 May.[151]

Ironically, however, on the very day which saw American troops from the *Torch* forces at last link up with soldiers from the British Eighth Army to form a single battle line around the doomed Axis army in Tunisia, Eisenhower gave voice to his inner concerns about the Allies' future prospects.[152] In a message sent to his superiors on that date, he reported the pessimistic appreciation shared by Anglo–American staff planners, senior British theatre commanders, and himself. They were in apparent agreement that if the Germans were to station more than two 'well-armed and fully-organised' divisions in Sicily, then *Operation Husky* would have 'scant prospect of success'.[153] This assessment provoked an angry riposte from the British Prime Minister. The notion that a couple of Nazi divisions should suffice to outface the vast array of military manpower, air power, and sea power now massed by the Western Allies in the Mediterranean theatre of war was one that Churchill would not countenance. He immediately called on the British COS to repudiate 'these pusillanimous and defeatist doctrines, from whoever they came'. The COS did as they were told, but more from conviction than any habit of compliance with the Prime Ministerial will. Their response to Eisenhower (which won full endorsement from the US Joint Chiefs of Staff) concluded on a note of simultaneous reproof and resolution:

> We feel bound to record our view that the abandonment of the Operation at any stage solely because the number of Germans in Huskyland had reached a small predetermined fraction of our own strength would be unthinkable.[154]

Yet, the British COS also assured Eisenhower and fellow pessimists that there was no reason to be so gloomy about the prospects for the Allied landings in Sicily. In particular, they questioned the assertion in Eisenhower's message of 7 April 1943 that the invaders could not hope to spring a strategic surprise on the enemy. This contention they queried on the grounds that it assumed 'the complete failure of all our cover and deception plans'.[155]

Duly chastized and suitably chastened, Eisenhower hastened to assure the Anglo–American combined COS that he fully intended to follow their orders in launching *Operation Husky*.[156] However, now that 'Ike' realized that the invasion of Sicily was going ahead, come hell or high water, he became as concerned to reduce the risks and minimize the casualties involved in this massive amphibious assault as he had been in the previous case of *Operation Torch*. He gave voice to his disquiet, in a letter written to General Marshall, on the day Axis forces in Tunisia finally capitulated:

Just as I suffered, almost physically, all during January, February and March while the enemy was fortifying his positions in Tunisia, so now I resent every day we have got to give him to perfect and strengthen HUSKY defences. I have gotten so that my chief ambition in this war is finally to get to a place where the next operation does not have to be amphibious, with all the inflexibility and delay that are characteristic of such operations.[157]

The same normally cautious commander who could sanction as madcap a venture as General Mark Clark's *liaison dangereuse* in French North Africa, to try and ease the way for *Torch* was hardly likely to look a Trojan gift horse in the mouth, especially when it promised to divert potential German reinforcements away from *Operation Husky*'s target.

Again, Colonel John Bevan had become adept at framing requests to his superiors in ways that made it difficult for them to refuse, as his telegram of 15 April 1943 to the senior American deception officer at Eisenhower's headquarters in Algiers (which was repeated to Colonel Dudley Clarke) reveals:

1. Prime Minister and Chiefs of Staff have approved operation MINCE-MEAT but have decided that General Eisenhower must be informed of project immediately.
2. MINCEMEAT sails 19th April and operation probably takes place on 28th April but could if necessary be cancelled on any day up to and including 26th April.
3. Kindly inform General Eisenhower accordingly and cable his approval urgently.[158]

The phraseology of this communication did not leave Eisenhower much opportunity to withhold his consent to *Mincemeat*'s implementation, even if he had been so inclined. However, having gone on record so recently with his concern about the size of the Nazi component in the Axis garrison on Sicily, he could not now object to a deception scheme precisely designed to keep the German military presence on the island within tolerable proportions.

Still, conscious as Montagu and *Mincemeat*'s other makers were of the deadline they had to meet, for both strategic and medical reasons, they must have been on tenterhooks throughout the rest of Thursday 15 April and Friday 16 April as they waited for word from Algiers about the fate of their long-nurtured deception plan. As Bevan's telegram to Eisenhower's headquarters indicated, the planners in London were contemplating sending Major Martin on his way on 19 April, even if nothing had been heard

1. Ewen Montagu, holding a copy of the book (*The Man Who Never Was*) which he wrote about *Operation Mincemeat*, after the war.

2. Sir Bernard Spilsbury, the celebrated and self-assured pathologist who acted as chief medical adviser to *Operation Mincemeat*.

3. William Bentley Purchase, the Coroner who provided the corpse for *Operation Mincemeat*.

4. The deceased Glyndwr Michael, having been transformed into Major William Martin, R.M.

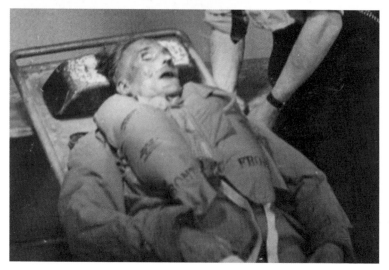

Page 2.
Issued in lieu of N° 09650 lost.

Surname MARTIN

Other Names WILLIAM

Rank (at time of issue) CAPTAIN, R.M.
(ACTING MAJOR)

Ship (at time of issue) H Q
COMBINED OPERATIONS

Place of Birth
CARDIFF

Year of Birth 1907.

Issued by *[signature]*

At ADMIRALTY

Date 2nd February 1943.

Page 3.
Navy Form S.1511

**NAVAL
IDENTITY CARD No. 148228**

Signature of Bearer
W. Martin

Visible distinguishing marks
NIL.

5. Naval Photo Identity
Card of Major William
Martin, R.M.

6. Major Ronnie Reed,
M.I.5. double-agent case
officer who posed for
the photograph on Major
Martin's Identity Card.

7. Lieutenant General Sir Archibald Nye, Vice-Chief of the Imperial General Staff and author of the main deceptive letter in the *Mincemeat* plan.

8. A snapshot of M.I.5's Jean Leslie, which was used to depict Major Martin's fictional fiancée, Pam.

9. An extract from the second of the manuscript letters allegedly written by Pam to her fiancé, Bill Martin, before he took off for foreign parts, never to return.

10. Major Martin's belongings.

11. Flight Lieutenant Charles Cholmondeley and Lieutenant Commander Ewen Montagu sample the morning air in Scotland, shortly before delivering their corpse-courier to the submarine depot on the Clyde.

12. Lieutenant N.L.A. Jewell, R.N. (second from the right) standing with fellow submariners in front of the gun platform on board H.M.S. *Seraph*.

THE ROLL OF HONOUR

ROYAL NAVY

The Board of Admiralty regrets to announce the following casualties which have been sustained in meeting the general hazards of war. Next-of-kin have been notified:—

OFFICERS

KILLED

A/Capt. Sir T. L. Beevor, Bt., R.N.; T/Lt. D. A. Burgass, R.N.V.R.; Lt. J. L. Fraser, R.N.V.R.; Lt. P. F. S. Gould, D.S.C., R.N.; T/Sub-Lt. (A) J. H. Hodgson, R.N.V.R.; T/Sub-Lt. (A) K. R. Joll, R.N.V.R.; Rear-Admiral P. J. Mack, D.S.O.; T/Lt. (A) G. Muttrie, R.N.V.R.; T/Lt. (A) G. Raynor, R.N.V.R.; T/Sub-Lt. J. N. Wishart, R.N.V.R.; ROYAL MARINES.—T/Capt. (A/Major) W. Martin.

DIED FROM WOUNDS OR INJURIES

T/Sub-Lt. (A) J. Hall, R.N.V.R.; T/Lt. A. G. D. Heybyrne, R.N.V.R.

MISSING, PRESUMED KILLED

T/Lt. (A) H. V. Donald, R.N.V.R.; T/Lt. R. A. Edmunds, R.N.V.R.; T/Lt. D. H. Goldsmith, R.N.V.R.; T/Sub-Lt. (A) F. W. Leng, R.N.V.R.; T/Sub-Lt. B. C. W. Milns, R.N.V.R.; T/A/Sub-Lt. D. J. B. Mitchell, R.N.V.R.; T/Lt. G. L. Russell, R.N.V.R.; T/Lt. C. H. Sanders, R.N.V.R.; T/Sub-Lt. (A) T N. Shinkfield, R.N.V.R.; T/Lt. P. A. Walter, R.A.N.V.R.; Lt. (A) D. D. White, R.N.; ROYAL MARINES.—T/Sec. Lt. (A/T/Lt.) A. Roxburgh.

PRISONER OF WAR

ROYAL MARINES.—Capt. C. D. L. Aylwyn; Py/Lt. C. J. Verdon.
T/Sub-Lt. C. E. Crawley, R.N.R.

WOUNDED OR INJURED

T/Lt. T. J. Bligh, R.N.V.R.; T/Lt. J. M. Caniley, R.N.V.R.; Sub-Lt. A. E. Henderson, R.N.; Lt. D. D. Knight, D.S.C., R.N.; T/Lt. G. D. K. McCormick, R.N.V.R.; T/Sub-Lt. (A) L. H. Nichols, R.N.V.R.; T/Surg. Lt. R. B. Stark, R.N.V.R.; T/Mid. A. Youati, R.N.V.R.

13. Official casualty list published in *The Times* on the 4th June 1943, which includes the name of Major W. Martin, R.M., amongst the fallen. © *The Times* and 4 June 1943/nisyndication.com

14. Allied political and military leaders meeting in strategic conference at Algiers on the 3rd June 1943: General Sir Alan Brooke is seated second from the left; Admiral Sir Andrew Cunningham is standing behind a seated Prime Minister Churchill; General Sir Harold Alexander is standing immediately to the right of the Admiral; and General Dwight D. Eisenhower is seated on the right of the group.

15. The beneficiaries of *Operation Mincemeat*: British troops find the going easy as they land on the South-Eastern coast of Sicily, on the 10th July 1943.

16. Major William Martin's tombstone in Huelva, Spain.

ck in time. In that case, if a later message was received from Algiers
toing the project, then Lieutenant Jewell would be ordered by radio to
ncel *Mincemeat*, according to prearranged instructions. In such an even-
ality, the canister containing the corpse-courier was to be 'sunk in deep
ater', while the documentary contents of the briefcase were to be
rned.[159] As it turned out, Major Martin did not have to set sail under a
oud of uncertainty. Just in the nick of time, a message came through from
eneral Eisenhower in North Africa which allowed *Operation Mincemeat* to
set in motion, on the scheduled date, without any fear of its being counter-
anded while HMS *Seraph* was en route to the Gulf of Cadiz. At 4.20 p.m. on
turday 17 April, Colonel Bevan received from Allied Force Headquarters
Mediterranean Theatre) (AFHQ), Algiers, a 'most secret cypher telegram'
forming him that Eisenhower's formidable Chief of Staff, General Walter
edell ('Beetle') Smith had given 'full approval MINCEMEAT', on 'Ike's'
ehalf.[160]

Bevan hastened to give the good news to those in the know about the
peration, including the COS.[161] Predictably, however, it was Ewen Mon-
gu who seems to have reacted fastest to the green light from Algiers. By
oo p.m. the same day, he had arrived at Hackney Mortuary (to which
lyndwr Michael's body had been removed on 1 April), in the company of
harles Cholmondeley and one of MI5's specialist drivers, the racing car
ampion, 'Jock' Horsfall. The trio had driven to Hackney together in a
cwt Ford military van, which was to be Major Martin's mode of con-
eyance to Holy Loch in Scotland. Once they entered the mortuary, they
und the coroner, Bentley Purchase, already waiting to help them put the
nishing touches to their creation. As throughout the entire development of
Operation Mincemeat, they set about their task methodically and according to
redetermined design.[162] After all, as Montagu later acknowledged, *Operation
Mincemeat* was 'really 90 per cent planning' and a careless move, at even this
te stage, could subvert the entire master plan.[163] However, it was also clear
those intimately involved in developing *Mincemeat* that, unless the remain-
g 10 per cent—consisting of the Operation's execution by HMS *Seraph*'s
rew and the transmission of its misleading message through Spanish good
ffices to the German High Command—also went more or less according to
lan, then all their immense labours would have been in vain.

9

Mincemeat Digested

It was not long after midnight on 1 April 1943 when Ivor Leverton, wh[o] worked as a funeral director in his family's firm of undertakers, drew up [at] a vehicle outside their head office. He then entered the premises as quietly [as] he could and picked up a 'removal coffin' to carry back out to his van. H[e] managed to accomplish this task—which normally required more than on[e] pair of hands—without waking any of the staff who lived above 'the shop[.] With his coffin safely loaded, Leverton drove to St Pancras Mortuary, whic[h] he reached about 1.00 a.m. There, the man responsible for his nocturn[al] excursion was waiting for him. Police Constable Glyndon May was a[n] officer of the Coroner's Court presided over by William Bentley Purchas[e.] Acting on his superior's orders, PC May had commissioned Ivor Leverton [to] transport a body from St Pancras to Hackney Mortuary on Mare Street [in] North-East London. May, however, had impressed on the young unde[r-] taker that this was no routine transfer of a corpse, since those involved woul[d] be bound by the Official Secrets Act. Accordingly, the Policeman caution[ed] Leverton not to mention the removal to anyone else (not even oth[er] members of his own family) and also not to keep any written record of th[e] service—for which his firm could expect no payment. Security concerns als[o] meant that Leverton could not ask any of his co-workers for assistance [in] transporting the human remains in question from one place to the othe[r.] Only the Coroner's officer himself would be allowed to lend a helping han[d.] Leverton's doubts that such inexperienced help would be enough to enab[le] him to do the job increased when he saw the size of the body to be carrie[d] from St Pancras to Hackney. Glyndwr Michael's physique may have been o[n] the gaunt side, but he was lanky, with long legs and unusually big feet. Sinc[e] the Leverton's removal coffin only measured 6 ft 2 ins. long, it was quite [a] task for Ivor and his neophyte assistant to place the cadaver inside it. Only b[y] adjusting the body's knees and 'setting the very large feet' at an angle, di[d]

:y succeed in inserting it into the coffin. Then they had to carry the coffin
:tween them to the waiting van and hoist it inside. Next, they drove off to
ackney Mortuary, where they managed, once more, to carry the coffin
side that building and remove its corporeal contents 'quite unbelieveably,
thout causing any alarm'.[1]

The main reason for Glyndwr Michael's midnight ramble seems to have
en the conclusion of the *Mincemeat* team that they needed a more secure
ting than a busy hospital morgue within which to outfit their dead
essenger for his covert mission. Hackney Mortuary, located as it was
hind the gates of St John's Churchyard, offered secluded surroundings
r such clandestine preparations. So, the very same day that the remains
re transferred to Hackney, Ewen Montagu and Charles Cholmondeley
sited the mortuary there to place the silken underwear, which had been
nated by H. A. L. Fisher's relatives, on the corpse. They came back two
ys later, in the company of Bentley Purchase, and proceeded with the
lp of the mortuary keeper—George Grayling who was a discreet
-member of the Royal Army Medical Corps—to dress the body in its
ilitary uniform. Of course, this dressing of the dead messenger in readiness
r his mission meant that he would be ready for a quick getaway if
cessary. This had turned out to be a sound precaution, in the light of
e last-minute departure imposed upon *Mincemeat*'s courier by the delib-
ations of Britain's warlords over the deception plan. When the body was
lly clothed, on 3 April—save for the Mae West life jacket, military boots,
d webbing gaiters—it was placed inside Hackney Mortuary's 'extra-cold
frigerator'.[2] There, as Montagu recorded, shortly afterwards, it was per-
ctly safe from prying eyes:

Mr. Bentley Purchase made arrangements to prevent the body thus dressed
being seen by anyone other than the mortuary keeper who is regarded as
completely reliable, and who does not, in any event, know the purpose for
which it was to be used.[3]

he placement of the body in the 'extra-cold refrigerator' at Hackney
ortuary would arrest the accelerated rate of decomposition in the decea-
d's remains consequent upon their removal from St. Pancras to Hackney,
d during the period they were being dressed in the latter mortuary. For
e two months Glyndwr Michael's body had lain in a normal morgue
frigerator at St Pancras, his body would have kept well at a temperature of
us four degrees Celsius. However, once exposed to the air, on the journey

between the two mortuaries and while being outfitted at Hackney, t
corpse would have experienced the onset of rapid decomposition which
unchecked, would have rendered it unusable for the deception plan. Y
Mincemeat's medical advisers knew that freezing the body would halt t
process of decay, without leaving any obvious signs that the body had be
so treated. It is true that modern forensic scientists can detect stigmata
freezing in a cadaver by examining sections of its liver for 'ice clefts'. The
are formed when the fluid in a liver freezes and they are indicative
previously frozen tissue. Yet, such artefacts of freezing would hardly
likely to have been the focus of any possible post-mortem examination
the remains of an individual plucked from warm waters off the southe
coast of Spain in the later spring of 1943. Any Spanish post-mortem co
ducted on Major Martin's remains would concentrate, most probably, up
the exterior of the body in looking for the apparent causes of its demis
This likelihood explains why the British deception planners took such pai
to make their corpse-courier appear to be the victim of a recent death at s

The demands of the living world did not intrude upon Glynd
Michael's glacial repose until Saturday 17 April, when Montagu and I
colleagues raced to Hackney, with authority at long last, to launch *Operat*
Mincemeat. Apparently, they brought the custom-made container for t
body, as well as a supply of dry ice, with them. Once they had entered t
mortuary, they set the container upright and packed it with 21 lbs of dry i
to expel decay-inducing oxygen from its innards. While that dry ice w
melting, the corpse's attendants—Montagu, Cholmondeley, Bentl
Purchase, and Grayling—could concentrate on making Major Martin hir
self as fully presentable as possible for his public debut. They removed t
body from the 'extra-cold refrigerator' and proceeded to insert the carefu
selected personal items and papers into the pockets of its military uniforn
However, when the group attempted to add the finishing touches to the
courier's outerwear they ran into an unexpected snag. None of them h
foreseen the impossibility of pulling military boots on to the more or l
frozen corpse, especially when the feet were sticking out at rigid right angl
to its legs. Obviously, allowing the entire body to thaw would have ma
the feet pliable enough to be fitted with the regulation footware. Yet th
solution to their problem would have entailed other serious difficultie
Waiting for Glyndwr Michael to defrost thoroughly and, then having
give him additional time to refreeze completely again for his journey
Spain, would have made it unlikely that he could be got to Holy Loch c

chedule for his departure in HMS *Seraph*. Worse, as an expert in forensic medicine like Bentley Purchase would have been sure to point out, repeated thawing and freezing of the cadaver was bound to accelerate its rate of decomposition. Yet, it was almost certainly the Coroner, with his medical knowledge, who proposed a way out of this dilemma. Members of the group literally held Glyndwr Michael's feet (and ankles) to the fire—a compact electric one—which expedited their thawing to the degree where the boots could be laced on.[6] This procedure saved precious time, while confining any acceleration of the body's decay to its lower extremities. The webbing gaiters and Mae West were also placed on the body without undue difficulty.[7]

Of course, as a coroner, William Bentley Purchase and, as a mortuary keeper, George Grayling were accustomed to examining and/or handling corpses as part of their stock-in-trade. Consequently, they would have taken the potentially distressing measures required to outfit the predeceased messenger for his mission in their stride. Ewen Montagu and Charles Cholmondeley, however, had not made a professional habit of mixing with the dead. Understandably, then, Montagu later acknowledged that the three visitations that he and Cholmondeley had made to dress the corpse—on 1, 3, and 17 April—were 'the least pleasant' of their many labours on behalf of *Operation Mincemeat*. Not only were they conscious of violating Glyndwr Michael's right to rest in peace, but they also deeply regretted having to subject his mortal remains to such indignities as the roasting of his frozen feet and ankles. Their unease was compounded by the feeling that in handling the Welshman's cadaver so rudely they were simultaneously mistreating their own mental offspring, Major William Martin. Still, the cause which the dead civilian and the invented officer were being drafted to serve was a mighty one: nothing less than opening up a breach into Hitler's 'Fortress Europe' and possibly knocking one of the fascist powers—Mussolini's Italy—out of the war altogether. So, they suppressed their misgivings and soldiered on.[8]

Happily, the rest of their ministrations to the dead body could be more decorous. Now that Major Martin was fully attired in his trench coat, uniform and boots, he was photographed 'for purposes of record', while reclining upon a mortuary stretcher. One snapshot was taken of the full length of his recumbent figure, and another—closer up—of just the upper half of his body.[9] Then, Montagu and his helpers wrapped the body in an army blanket which they tied loosely with tape. This covering should

preserve the body from suffering abrasions during its travels by road and sea
At his stage of their preparations, the deception planners had a lucky break
they discovered that their custom-built container was capacious enough to
accommodate not only the dead messenger, but also the briefcase with its set
of misleading documents. This meant that the case could be fastened, by
bank messenger's chain, to the courier's person in Hackney Mortuary
rather than on the rolling deck of a surfaced submarine immediately prior
to the launching of the body into the sea off Huelva.[10] Having attended to
that critical detail, the team in the mortuary then lifted Glyndwr Michael'
body, with due delicacy, and placed it inside the canister. They then filled
that container with another load of dry ice, before tightly screwing down
its lid.[11]

After two and a half months of intensive grooming, Major Martin was
ready to embark upon his potentially momentous mission. However, the
enemy would have to be kept in the dark about the true time of his
departure from England. This was because both the condition of his body
and the date of its arrival in southern Spain must be made to seem compatible with a notional air journey which had come to a sudden end there. That
is why the ever-imaginative Charles Cholmondeley had suggested a last-
minute addition to the courier's stash of personal documents, namely, two
counterfoil ticket stubs, dated 22 April 1943, for an evening performance at
London's Prince of Wales Theatre of George Black's variety show, 'Strike a
New Note' (notable for the belated West End debut of one of Britain'
greatest comic talents, Sid Field). These items, apparently stuffed casually
into the courier's coat pocket, should prove to any inquisitive Spanish
officials and their Nazi intelligence contacts that Major Martin could not
have reached Spanish coastal waters 'by the 28 April [HMS *Seraph*'s scheduled date of arrival off Huelva] by any other means of transport than
aircraft'; for the ticket stubs would reveal him to have been out on the
town only days before he turned up dead in the Atlantic Ocean.[12] In fact
this additional documentation corroborated the apparent departure date for
Major Martin already supplied by one of the original items placed on his
person. This was the bill from the Naval and Military Club, which specified
that the Royal Marine Officer had stayed there for six nights from 18 April
until 23 April, and had apparently quit the premises on the morning of 24
April.[13] A notional departure date of 24 April, on a flight which came to
grief later that day, or the next one, would make it look like the deceased
had been floating about for five or six days, when plucked from the sea near

uelva on 29 or 30 April. *Operation Mincemeat*'s medical advisers reckoned at the rate of bodily decay Glyndwr Michael's thawing remains would undergo during their actual ten-day journey in the sealed container on board the submarine, would be approximately equivalent to that suffered by someone who had perished at sea, after an air crash, and then drifted slowly towards the Spanish coast for five or six days.[14] Right to the very last moment then, the *Mincemeat* team made adjustments to their implementation plan to try and improve its chances of success.

Having attended to these final details, Montagu and his helpers carried the coffin-container (with Michael Glyndwr firmly sealed inside) out of Hackney Mortuary on the evening of 17 April, and placed it inside their Fordson BBE van. Major Martin's escort to the submarine waiting in Scotland to ferry him to southern Spain was to consist of *Operation Mincemeat*'s two main champions, Lieutenant Commander Montagu and Flight Lieutenant Cholmondeley, as well as MI5's 'top chauffeur', Jock Horsfall.[15] The trio had a marathon all-night drive ahead of them because the *Seraph*'s skipper had requested that they reach his berth in Holy Loch before noon the following day, Sunday. This would allow time to deal with any problems that might arise when the container was being taken on board the submarine and, thereby, ensure that it could set sail at the appointed time, on Monday, 19 April.[16] Faced with this all-night dash to western Scotland, the party first drove to Cholmondeley's flat in Queen's Gate Place Mews (off the Cromwell Road in South Kensington), where they prepared and ate a meal. Then, after further stocking up with sandwiches and hot drinks in thermos flasks, they started their journey north.[17] As a professional driver, Horsfall probably spent most time at the wheel, but he was relieved by Montagu for a few spells. Driving at some speed at night, with masked headlamps, through a country still maintaining its wartime blackout against enemy air raids, was not for the faint of heart. There was one alarming moment when the van ploughed straight across a traffic roundabout, which its driver had failed to make out in his dimmed headlights. Luckily, the roundabout had no elevated central island. So, *Mincemeat*'s 'hearse' was able to continue on its way without sustaining damage to the vehicle or its passengers, dead and alive.[18] With the shortest of stops to answer nature's calls, the party made such good time that they arrived at Greenock on the Clyde in the early hours of Sunday morning—long before the time when the Captain commanding the Second Submarine Flotilla (from his headquarters in the depot ship, HMS *Forth*) had been led to expect them.

The Naval Intelligence Division had informed the Flotilla Captain that 'L
Cdr. Montagu RNVR' would 'arrive Albert Harbour approximately 16c
on 18th April with package weighing 400 lbs to be taken to H.M.!
FORTH for H.M.S. SERAPH for F.O.S. shipment'.[19]

However, it was not the early arrival of the *Mincemeat* party at the
destination, but the weight of the consignment they brought with thei
that proved awkward when they reached there. Unfortunately, the com
munication informing the local submarine command of the imminen
arrival of an NID officer with a 400 lb package had been taken to mea
that Montagu would be accompanied by several items of baggage, collect
ively weighing that amount. So, to their dismay the van's occupants found
launch bobbing up and down beneath the dock, with only a single sailor o
board. Montagu rapidly realized that more hands would be needed to lowe
the container with its precious contents safely into the pitching launch. H
was not happy about turning to the area's shore-based naval headquarters fc
assistance, since it was likely to entail administrative delay and maybe eve
endanger the top-secret operation's security. Still, with no alternative, h
braced himself to do battle with a service bureaucracy, once more, on beha
of *Operation Mincemeat*. Yet again, however, Montagu's naval colleague
lent him every assistance in executing the deception plan. What certainl
helped, on this occasion, was the fact that the duty officer for the harbou
turned out to be a former colleague of Montagu's, from the time of his earl
wartime service in naval intelligence at Hull. This individual, who was
member of the Women's Royal Naval Service had been an ordinary nav;
rating in those days but, now, she was an officer with the authority to len
more than one hand to her former superior. Indeed, she provided a group c
six sailors to lower the container by rope into the launch in Albert Harbou
When it was safely stowed on board, Montagu clambered down into th
vessel himself, and it set out for HMS *Forth* which was anchored out in Ho!
Loch, with the *Seraph* alongside.[20] Once back in London, Montag
reported on the secure transfer of *Mincemeat*'s unique cargo to these vessel:

> No comment was caused in H.M.S. FORTH, or in the submarine, the
> container being accepted as merely being a more than usually urgent and
> breakable F.O.S. shipment. Only four officers in H.M.S. FORTH were 'in
> the know' and they only partially.[21]

However, before motoring back to London, Montagu also made sure t
confer with Lieutenant Jewell on a couple of occasions before the *Seraph* se

ut to deliver Major Martin to his destination. The wardroom of HMS
ORTH was a renowned gathering-place, where officers from returned
oats exchanged tales of underwater adventures and submariners' lore.[22]
However, the visitor from the NID sought out a quieter corner of the depot
ship, on Sunday 18 April, to hand over to the *Seraph*'s skipper the parcel
ontaining the rubber dinghy and single aluminium oar which were to be
thrown into the sea, once the dead courier had been set afloat.[23] On
Monday 19 April—the actual date of the submarine's departure for Spanish
waters—Montagu waited until the coffin-container had been passed carefully through the boat's torpedo hatch and safely secured within its pressure
hull before giving its captain final advice. Yet again he urged Jewell to
exercise all discretion possible in the discharge of his unorthodox mission,
since the more of his crew who learned its true nature the greater was the
risk that somebody would blab.[24] Doubtless he also reminded Bill Jewell
that matters of the utmost strategic importance depended upon the submariner's ability to deliver Major Martin to his rendezvous with punctuality
and precision, and in absolute secrecy. Having delivered this last 'pep' talk,
Ewen Montagu left Lieutenant Jewell to deal with the business of getting his
boat ready to sail. However, the NID man took heart from the fact that the
mortal remains of *Mincemeat*'s messenger (whose soul had already departed
for another world) would be sailing away from an inlet called the Holy
Loch, in a submarine named *Seraph*—signs, perhaps, that Heaven itself was
blessing the enterprise.[25]

Lieutenant Jewell, for his part, had to attend to more mundane concerns,
his submarine was to get under way on time. He checked that the boat's
fuel and freshwater tanks were full and that the *Seraph* had taken on board its
allocated stores of food, beverages, ammunition, and lubricating oil. There
was only one shortfall: the submarine was to carry only twelve of its usual
supply of thirteen torpedoes. This was because one of the boat's reload tubes
had to be left vacant to accommodate the 'F.O.S.' container.[26] All was ready
and waiting by 4.00 p.m. of that Monday and exactly two hours later—at
6.00 p.m. Double Summer Time on 19 April 1943—HMS *Seraph* 'let go' its
moorings with HMS *Forth* and sailed out into the Clyde estuary.[27]

Although spring should have sprung by the date of *Seraph*'s departure to
execute *Operation Mincemeat*, there was little evidence of it among the
vegetation visible from the boat's port side. The view on the starboard
side was almost as dispiriting: the town of Dunoon was blanketed in a mist
somewhat thickened by the smoke curling from the chimneys of its austere,

grey-coloured houses.[28] Soon, however, the submariners were diverte
from this cheerless prospect by the arrival of some good company. The
rendezvoused in the Firth of Forth with the Flower class corvette which wa
to escort them through the Irish Sea, the St George's Channel, and th
Celtic Sea to a point off the Scilly Isles. This corvette, HMS *Acanthus*, ha
actually been loaned to the Royal Norwegian Navy, and its crew consiste
of exiled Norwegian sailors fighting for the liberation of their German
occupied homeland.[29] Still, their main purpose on this voyage was to dete
'friendly' fire rather than to defend against Nazi attack. The problem wa
that British aircraft, in particular, tended to regard any submarine the
espied as an enemy boat, in the absence of clear proof to the contrary
Hence arose the need for HMS *Acanthus* to accompany HMS *Serap*
through these notionally friendly waters in order to vouch for the subma
ine's British bona fides.[30] The escort vessel did its job well and by the late
morning of Wednesday 21 April, the *Seraph* was in position to sail out int
the Atlantic proper.

At 11.00 a.m. on that day, south of the Bishop Rock Lighthouse (whic
stands on a rock ledge four miles west of the Scilly Isles), Lieutenant Jewe
exchanged 'Good Luck' signals by lamp with the skipper of the departin
Norwegian corvette.[31] Then he set course for Huelva, soon giving th
order for his craft to dive beneath the surface of the ocean. This was
necessary precaution as *Seraph* was now entering waters constantly patrolle
by enemy warships and aircraft.[32] Instead, until she reached Gibraltar (afte
executing her phase of *Operation Mincemeat*), HMS *Seraph* would trave
submerged for safety by day (at a rate of up to 9 knots) and on the sea
surface for greater speed (up to 14.5 knots) by night.[33] Overall, the sub
marine managed to maintain an average rate of progress of 130 miles pe
day, during the ten-day voyage from Holy Loch to Gibraltar.[34] As the
entered the Bay of Biscay, the next day, the *Seraph*'s crew received a rud
reminder that they remained in peril, even under the sea. Gliding beneat
the surface of the Atlantic south-west of the French port of Brest, their boa
was rocked by shock waves from salvos of depth charges being dropped—i
three separate attacks from the late afternoon to early evening—on anothe
British submarine in the area.[35] Another pair of distant explosions in th
early evening of Sunday 25 April, as the *Seraph* was sailing off the north
western coast of Spain, and the need to crash dive on a couple of occasion
to avoid contact with patrolling aircraft—be they hostile or trigger-happ
friendly ones—also kept the submarine's crew on their toes. Shortly afte

o a.m. on the morning of Wednesday 28 April they were off Cape
Vincent, at the extreme south-western tip of Portugal, and they dived
neath the waves less than two hours later, to press on towards Major
artin's rendezvous point in safety, during the daylight hours.[36]
However, when the British submarine crept into position off Huelva, in
: early hours of Thursday 29 April, Lieutenant Jewell soon realized that the
rather conditions were not favourable for the successful completion of his
ssion. As already noted, Montagu had impressed upon *Seraph*'s skipper
w imperative it was to lower the corpse-courier into the sea only when
ere was an onshore wind blowing that would carry him towards the
anish coast. As luck would have it, there was a brisk offshore wind
owing as the HMS *Seraph* reached the *Mincemeat* drop-zone, although it
d abated to 'light airs' by 4.00 a.m.[37] By then, however, Jewell had decided
wait around for another day, in the hope that the wind would veer in a
ore favourable direction.[38] Certainly, the fact that it proved impossible to
unch Major Martin into the sea on his immediate arrival near Huelva
idicated the decision of *Mincemeat's* planners to opt for a submarine as the
urier's mode of transport. The *Seraph* could loiter off the Spanish port for
other twenty-four hours, without much risk of detection—as long as it
yed out of sight during the daytime. Accordingly, the British submarine
bmerged at 6.31 a.m., in a position about twenty miles south-west of
uelva. Lieutenant Jewell and his lookouts spent the rest of the day survey-
g the shore through their boat's periscope and pinpointing landmarks
nich could assist in the accurate delivery of their consignment on target
e following day.[39]
When that day—Friday 30 April—dawned, 'the wind conditions', as
ven Montagu recorded a month later, 'were not ideal at the moment of
unching [the body] but Lt. Jewell had wisely judged them to be favour-
le, and he had also virtually assured success by approaching as close in
ore as he did'.[40] In fact, although the wind had changed into a more
vourable southerly one ('altering between SW and SE'), it was not really
ong enough at 'Force 2' to propel Major Martin, in his Mae West, on to
e Huelvan coast.[41] So, Jewell proceeded to follow Montagu's other
struction—that the body should 'be put into the water as close inshore
prudently possible and as near to HUELVA as possible', so exactly that he
inerved his fellow officers.[42] First, he postponed having the container
isted through the *Seraph*'s torpedo hatch, until she had less than two
thoms of sea water beneath her keel—as the boat's alarmed First Lieutenant,

David Scott, established by running its echo-sounder for a short time. Wh
Jewell and his two assistants extracted the body from its container a
checked its condition and appearance, the submarine sailed still closer
the coastline and into ever shallower water.[43] By the time Jewell h
conducted the impromptu burial service for the dead messenger and t
corpse had been lowered into the sea at 4.30 a.m. 'in a position 148 degr
Portil Pilar 1.3 miles approximately eight cables from the beach', Scott w
seriously concerned that the submarine might run aground.[44] Havi
watched with growing anxiety from Seraph's bridge as his skipper methc
ically prepared Major Martin for his dip, he was delighted, finally, to recei
a thumbs-up sign from Jewell. Lieutenant Scott immediately 'went f
astern', doing so 'with some relief', as their boat 'seemed to be practica
on the beach'.[45] He later recalled that the wash from the submarine's tw
screw propellers helped push the deceased courier towards the beach
point which Lieutenant Jewell also made in the report about the launchi
of Mincemeat's messenger which he drew up, on the very day it happen
for Ewen Montagu.[46]

   As it transpired, however, the Royal Marine Major did not have to ma
it to the shore under his own steam. At around 9.30 a.m., after HMS Sera
was long gone from the waters off Huelva and was well on its way
Gibraltar, a local man by the name of José Buceta Flores was out fishing
his small boat, the Ana, at Playa del Portil close to Aljaraque, which l
within the maritime jurisdiction of the Isla Cristina. As the fisherm
surveyed the surrounding sea for a potential catch he saw an object sor
distance away, bobbing up and down in the water. Since a small launc
La Calina, was sailing by the spot, he hailed the crew and drew th
attention to the floating object, which turned out to be a dead body dress
in a khaki uniform and overcoat. The crew of the launch managed to g
hold of the body and tow it the short distance to the shore. They landed t
body on the beach at La Bota, where a unit of the Spanish Army—
detachment from the 72nd Infantry Regiment—happened to be in positio
The launch's crew reported their grisly discovery to the officer in charge
the infantry unit and he immediately placed the body under armed guar
Two Civil Guards from Isla Cristina soon reinforced the party of infantr
men keeping watch over the corpse of this foreign warrior. By then, t
infantry officer had phoned the military commandant of Huelva to put hi
in the picture. The infantry unit was apparently ordered to maintain
guard over the dead body and await the arrival of a naval judge.[47]

So, in the space of a few hours on the morning of Friday 30 April 1943, *Operation Mincemeat* had been well and truly launched, largely thanks to the seamanship of Lieutenant Bill Jewell and the professional competence of his officers and men. Major Martin had been placed in the sea so close to the coast that, even though he was still floating about five hours later he was inevitably spotted by local fishermen and brought ashore. Moreover, he was now not only on terra firma but also in official Spanish custody, just as the British had intended. The British deception planners were also gratified to learn some weeks later, from a British spy working inside the Franco regime, that one of their most critical, practical arrangements for *Operation Mincemeat* had withstood the elements. This was evident from the British agent's description of the first actions taken by the magistrate who arrived to take charge of the corpse and its personal effects, on the morning after it had been carried ashore (1 May 1943):

> The naval judge searched the body and found that it had a metal chain round its neck which had penetrated the muscles of the neck as the result of swelling. This had a leather document case attached to it about 30 × 20 cms. with the initials G.VI.R and the English royal crown . . . it also . . . was locked.[48]

Crucially, the courier's briefcase, still securely fastened to the corpse, had survived Major Martin's passage to Spain. Its notionally top-secret contents now lay within easy reach of the local German espionage nest, as long as their Spanish collaborators could deliver the goods into their hands. So far, all seemed to be going according to plan.

Yet, as the British knew very well, appearances can be deceptive. In fact, their carefully laid plans were already going awry. For a start, the magistrate who now had formal charge of the case was a naval judge, by the name of Lieutenant Mariano Pascual del Pobil Bensusan.[49] This development, of course, was one of the circumstances *Mincemeat*'s planners had sought sedulously to avoid, in view of the distinct possibility that officers of the Armada might not prove amenable to approaches from German agents seeking access to the contents of the courier's briefcase. Indeed, they had selected Huelva as a destination for Major Martin precisely because they had assumed that the Spanish Navy would be less likely to recover and/or deal with the dead messenger there, than in Cadiz.[50] Yet, not only had a naval judge now assumed jurisdiction over the case, but his next action was even more potentially detrimental to the deception's success. Judge Mariano Pascual del Pobil directed that the corpse be removed to the morgue located in Huelva's Catholic cemetery of *Nuestra Señora de la Soledad*. So, Sir Bernard Spilsbury's confident assertion that Catholic officials of the Franco regime would be averse to holding a post-mortem—especially on the remains of an individual whose identity discs seemed to mark him as a fellow believer, turned out to be wrong. In accordance with the judge's instructions, Major Martin's body was carried by military bearers through Macete to the banks of the Río Tinto where it was transferred to a motor boat supplied by the local naval commandant's office. That craft transported him to the Catholic cemetery's morgue which had an autopsy room equipped with dissection tables.[51]

When the body was examined in that setting, it seemed that another aspect of Spilsbury's medical counsel to the *Mincemeat* team was also exposed as flawed. He had categorically assured them that the courier's corpse 'ought to keep perfectly satisfactorily' inside a container packed with dry ice, 'until required for duty'.[52] Yet, as Ewen Montagu had to acknowledge after reading Lieutenant Jewell's graphic testimony (contained in his report of 30 April 1943 to the DNI) on the visible signs of decay displayed by the corpse upon its extraction from the container on the deck of HMS *Seraph*, 'the body had suffered rather more change than had been expected'.[53] As already noted above, the naval magistrate had found the neck of the corpse to be swollen when he first inspected it, over a day later, on 1 May. It is, then, no surprise that the official post-mortem conducted by the forensic pathologist of Huelva's Town Council, Dr Eduardo Fernández del Torno and his son, Dr Eduardo Fernández Contioso, later the same day, should conclude that the British officer's remains were 'in an advanced state of decomposition'.[54]

Thus, not only had Spanish doctors performed a post-mortem examination on the corpse of *Operation Mincemeat*'s messenger, but they had also discerned that its degree of putrefaction was considerable. This finding inevitably raises two questions concerning the *Mincemeat* deception. How could the Operation's main medical adviser, Sir Bernard Spilsbury, have got his sums so apparently wrong, and what were the consequences of his seeming error to be for the outcome of the hoax? It is tempting, in answer to the first question, to assume that Sir Bernard was simply losing his legendary touch as age and a heavy work load took their toll. He was sixty-six years old when Montagu first consulted him, in late 1942, on the feasibility of a *ruse de guerre* using a dead body. Perhaps, even more to the point, the pathologist had suffered a stroke while performing an autopsy in

May 1940. Although he made a partial recovery from that apoplectic attack, he suffered another slight stroke over the Easter weekend in April 1943, while Major Martin was en route to Huelva, on board HMS *Seraph*.[55] Yet, the eclipse which Spilsbury had experienced by the time he got involved in the planning of *Operation Mincemeat*, was more pronounced in his professional reputation, than in personal health.

Once described by a colleague as 'an astral figure in orbit, beyond all challenges', his dogmatic refusal to countenance alternative expert opinions to his own, or to admit the possibility of error in his own forensic findings, eventually alienated many fellow doctors, numerous lawyers, and even some judges and juries.[56] Indeed, his own instinctive inclination to come up with such pathological judgements as would make the prosecution's case, is now regarded as having led to a number of unsound verdicts in murder cases, and even some 'terrible miscarriages of justice'.[57] However, although Spilsbury had sustained some significant court-room setbacks by the time he was approached to give medical counsel to *Mincemeat*'s makers, requesting his opinion was still a clever move on their part.[58] For, just as he had tended to bolster the case for the prosecution in most of the many murder trials in which he had appeared as an expert witness, so he seemed equally inclined to tell those prosecuting the deception plan what they wanted to hear—that the Spaniards, as Catholics, would be averse to holding any post-mortem on the corpse; that they had no competent pathologists if they did hold one on the dead messenger; and that the latter's remains would keep 'perfectly satisfactorily' in a sealed container, laden with dry ice, while being transported to Spain. Of course, such unconditional opinions—emanating from a source still held in high esteem by the British establishment—had been a real asset to Montagu and his partners in deception, as they did battle with the bureaucratic naysayers within British governmental and military circles. However, now that Glyndwr Michael's body was seen to have turned up on Spanish territory in 'an advanced stage of decomposition', were the deception planners about to pay a heavy price for recruiting a medical adviser for their project who was both overconfident in his pronouncements and overanxious to please them?

Yet, it also has to be recognized that synchronizing Glyndwr Michael's rate of bodily decomposition to accord with the apparent death of *Mincemeat*'s courier after a recent plane crash was never going to be easy. Montagu sought to account for the seeming underestimation of the corpse's pace of putrefaction by noting the number of variables involved in the

calculations (when he submitted an addendum to the official record of
Operation Mincemeat at the end of May 1943):

> It must be borne in mind when assessing the condition of the body that it
> would only take a comparatively few hours to reach the shore, and might
> indeed have been picked up by a fishing boat shortly after it had been
> launched, yet it had to present the appearance of having been in the water
> since an aeroplane crash about six or seven days before.[59]

This complex calculation was made more difficult by the singular treatment
which Glyndwr Michael's mortal remains had received since his death in
London. As Bentley Purchase also noted in later May 1943, the courier's
cadaver had been 'frozen, then partly thawed so that he could be dressed,
then frozen again, then again thawed in the container', in a manner bound
to accelerate the process of decomposition.[60] In view of these considerations, Spilsbury had warned Montagu and his colleagues that 'an ample
margin of safety' had to be factored into the estimation of the predeceased's
corporeal condition, as and when he was expected to fetch up in Spain.[61]

In fact, for all his personal frailties and professional predilections, Sir
Bernard Spilsbury managed to arrive at the remarkably accurate appreciation that a body treated as Glyndwr Michael's had been in the travel
arrangements for *Operation Mincemeat*, should end up looking like one that
had been adrift for 'six or seven days'. Of course, the body had spent an
extra day, sealed inside its coffin-container on board HMS *Seraph*, while
Lieutenant Jewell waited for the wind to change, and an additional day and a
half on land, before being transported to the morgue in Huelva. These
unscheduled delays, before the holding of the Spanish post-mortem, doubtless explain why the doctors who conducted it not only found that the body
was in 'a state of advanced decomposition' but also concluded that it 'had
been in the water for from five to eight days'.[62] So, Spilsbury had clearly
allowed a sufficient margin of error in his calculations to be able to foist a
false chronology of Major Martin's death and decay upon the Spanish
pathologists—one entirely compatible with the *Mincemeat* plan's version of
events.

However, even the most meticulously made plans and precisely measured
calculations can be upset by the unpredictable human capacity for getting
the wrong end of the stick. Ironically, it was the very effort of the British to
make it crystal clear to the Spanish authorities when Major Martin had
apparently left England to travel by air to Spain, which now threatened to

reck the whole carefully wrought strategic deception plan. The problem
rose because the Spanish officials who examined the British courier's
ersonal papers, managed to confuse the dates and even the character of
ome of them. They reported finding a 'London night-club bill dated 27
April' among these items. This led the Francoist officials to conclude that
Major Martin left London on the afternoon of 28th April and during the
forenoon of the same day the aircraft met with an accident in the neighbourhood of Huelva'.[63] This deduction, of course, contradicted the opinion
of the Spanish pathologists that the body had been floating about in the
Atlantic for between five and eight days and, therefore, suggested a significant discrepancy between the courier's physical state and the documents on
his person. Of course, *Mincemeat*'s planners had taken great pains to avoid
any such inconsistency between the condition of the messenger's body
when he reached Spain and the dates of the various documents, both official
and personal, which he carried. In fact, they may have even tried too hard,
for the documents whose date the Spanish investigators misread appear to
have been the very items which were included among the courier's personal
effects, at Charles Cholmondeley's last-minute suggestion, to clinch the
impression that their bearer had left England on 24 April. These were the
counterfoil ticket stubs for Bill and Pam's evening at the Prince of Wales
Theatre on 22 April. Since the invitation to an actual nightclub (*The
Cabaret*), which Major Martin had in his possession, was undated, it might
have been an erroneous reading of the date on the theatre-ticket stubs (or
possibly on the invoice-receipt from the Naval and Military Club for 24
April) which caused the chronological confusion that now threatened to
discredit *Mincemeat*'s messenger—and, therefore, his message.[64]

For if Major Martin had only died in the sea off Huelva on 28 April, how
could his body have suffered such substantial decomposition between then
and its being brought ashore on 30 April and its post-mortem on the
following day? Inevitably, the Spanish doctors pointed out this seeming
contradiction between their medical findings and the documentary evidence
recovered on the body to the Francoist authorities. Moreover, Francoist
officials eventually drew the attention of their German espionage contacts to
these conflicting data in the case of the 'drowned English courier picked up
at Huelva' (as the Abwehr came to call it). However, Doctor Fernández del
Torno and his son did not simply highlight the inconsistencies between the
case's medical and documentary evidence. They also suggested a possible
way to reconcile them. They gave it as their considered opinion that it was

'possible that the effect of the sun's rays on the floating corpse accelerated th
rate of decomposition'.[65] Certainly, the fact that Major Martin's Mae We:
kept his head and shoulders above water, and exposed to the air in the warr
temperatures round about, might have helped hasten the process of bodil
decay. However, the Spanish pathologists were probably persuaded less b
that possibility than by the success of the British deception planners' effort t
present the dead courier as so obviously a victim of death at sea.

For such was the formal verdict of the Spanish autopsy (which found th:
the corpse's 'inside had deteriorated badly') performed on the remains c
Major William Martin, RM. The Abwehr's Madrid station recorded th:
verdict, as follows:

> A medical examination of the corpse showed that there were no apparent
> wounds or marks which could have resulted from a blow or stab. According
> to medical evidence, death was due to drowning (lit.: the swallowing of sea
> water).[66]

Of course, this was the type of verdict that *Operation Mincemeat*'s medic:
advisers had also expected all along, if any post-mortem exam were conducte
on their dead messenger. Bentley Purchase, therefore, expressed no surpris
when Montagu informed him of the Spanish pathologists' conclusions, a fev
weeks later (as the NID man reported to Colonel Bevan of the LCS):

> The coroner is not surprised that the verdict was death by drowning even if
> there had been a reasonably competent post mortem examination. There
> would have been a good deal of water in the body through the open mouth,
> and such checks as to whether there is water in the lungs or whether the lungs
> have burst through trying to breathe under water would be impossible to
> carry out as the lungs would probably have been liquefied by then.[67]

Indeed, as Sydney Smith noted in the 1943 edition of his text book o:
Forensic Medicine, 'the typical signs of death from drowning are found only i:
the bodies which are recovered from the water soon after death, for whe:
putrefaction advances the signs are masked or entirely obliterated'.[68] Sc
although Major Martin's advanced state of bodily decay had raised a doub
over the chronology of his arrival in Spain (especially when coupled with
misreading of the date on a document meant to pinpoint his departure fror:
England), that same physical condition materially contributed to a post
mortem verdict of death by drowning, so conducive to the success o
Operation Mincemeat's deceptive purpose. At the very least, the fact tha
the courier had been 'thoroughly on the way to decomposition' (to quot

entley Purchase again) 'when he reached the (Spanish) shore', made it
irtually impossible to conclude that he had definitely not drowned.[69] Once
rowning could not be excluded as a cause of death for this lost soul, then
ie circumstances in which the body was found—floating in the ocean with
life jacket—predisposed the Spanish medical examiners to reach the
erdict they did. All the painstaking efforts of Montagu and company to
mulate a scenario in which their courier would appear to have perished at
a—whether from exposure, or shock or drowning—now paid huge
ividends. The carefully stage-managed way in which Major Martin had
opped up in the sea near Huelva effectively predetermined the result of the
ost-mortem. Indeed, it even offset the blunder made by Francoist agents in
iisreading the date on Major Martin's theatre-ticket stubs. Presented with
rong circumstantial indications that Major Martin had died at sea, the
panish father-and-son team were naturally inclined to construe other
vailable evidence, be it medical or documentary, in a manner supportive
f their primary judgement on the case. Thus, in coming up with an
xplanation of accelerated decomposition for Major Martin's remains—to
count for any alleged departure from London as late as 28 April—the
octors Fernández were guilty of what pathologists term 'confirmation
ias'. This is the phenomenon whereby subsequently gathered data are
terpreted so as to reinforce an original impression. In this instance,
onfirmation bias' helped save *Operation Mincemeat* from being exposed as
fraud for an entirely mistaken reason.[70]

This same tendency to view later post-mortem findings through the
ism of preliminary impressions was evident in the Spanish doctors' res-
onse to another discrepancy between Major Martin's physical appearance
id his accompanying documentation. Undoubtedly, one of the most vul-
erable parts of the *Mincemeat* plan was the unavoidable necessity to equip its
ead messenger with an identity card bearing someone else's photograph.
or all their technical skills in adjusting Ronnie Reed's features, by selective
rbrushing and shading of his snapshot, to resemble those of the deceased,
e deception planners must have wondered whether their handiwork
ould withstand foreign scrutiny. However, when the doctors Fernández
rned their professional gaze upon the defunct courier's facial features
id compared them with his official photo ID, they were almost comp-
ely convinced, as their Nazi contacts were again informed eventually.
he Germans duly recorded the Spanish pathologists' opinion that the
orpse was identical with the photographs [*sic*] in its military papers'—for

the most part; for the Abwehr also took note of the fact that the Spani
doctors had detected one inconsistency between the visage of the Briti
officer lying on their slab and the face in the photograph of his military I
card. There was 'a bald patch on the temples' of the corpse's head which 'w
more pronounced than in the photographs [sic]'.[71] However, before Frar
coist security agents and Nazi spies became overly suspicious of this discre
ancy, the Spanish pathologists again attempted to explain it away. The
suggested that 'either the photograph of Major Martin had been take
some two or three years ago' or, alternatively, that 'the baldness was due
the action of sea-water'.[72] The first of these explanations should have bee
ruled out of court immediately. For even the most cursory reading of th
details entered on the Royal Marine Officer's identity card would hav
picked up on the 'fact' that it had been issued as recently as 2 Februar
1943, apparently to replace a previously lost card.[73] Of course, Ewen Mor
tagu could never have imagined that his ploy (described in Chapter 6),
counter the newish appearance of Major Martin's ID card, might undermir
the attempt of Spanish pathologists to reconcile a dissimilarity between th
courier's real face and his official photographic image. Nevertheles
the 'confirmation bias' influencing the Spanish pathologists' examinatic
of the corpse-courier induced them to propose an explanation for Majo
Martin's excessive baldness around the temples, which was actually contra
dicted by his own official ID. Even more remarkably, the slapdash inspectic
of that ID by Francoist officials meant that the doctors' suggestion was take
seriously and even forwarded to the Germans.

Moreover, as already noted, the Spanish pathologists also made anoth
contribution to preserving Major Martin's face value. This was the alterna
tive explanation which they tendered to account for the variation in hairlir
between his actual face and its photographic likeness. Their suggestion–
also passed on by Francoist authorities to the Abwehr—was that this mig
have been caused by the action of sea water slapping his temples as his bod
floated in the sea for some days. This idea, again, seems to have derived fror
the Spanish doctors' initial diagnosis of the causes of death in this instanc
If the courier had drowned in the sea, then any apparent anomaly in h
appearance—in comparison with his official I.D. snapshot, for example–
should be explicable in terms of his encounter with that same elemen
Certainly, it is true that, with the advance of decomposition, skin slippage i
the scalp-area can lead to hair loss. However, even if such hair loss as wa
assumed to have occurred in this case was aided by the action of sea wate

more forceful contact with an abrasive surface would seem to have been necessary to produce such an effect. Again, there is no obvious reason to explain why this accelerated hair loss was already discernible on both of the corpse's temples and not on other areas of his scalp.[74] Yet again, mesmerized as they clearly were by the *mise-en-scène* that the deception planners had so carefully staged for their courier's arrival in Spain, the Huelvan pathologists could not resist the conclusion that the man in the ID photo was one and the same as the body given up by the sea. Accordingly, the details of his death, decomposition, and documentation were made to fit into that preset framework. The Spanish medical examiners had done their level—if unwitting—best to confirm the British messenger's bona fides and, thereby, to authenticate the top-secret documents contained in his briefcase. In the end, far from jeopardizing *Operation Mincemeat,* as the British had feared, a Spanish post-mortem examination of the remains of its courier had actually advanced its cause.

With the death of the British officer officially attributed on 1 May 1943 to 'asphyxiation through immersion in the sea', his body could be released for burial.[75] This interment the British Vice-Consul now proceeded to arrange as expeditiously as possible, in accordance with the earlier briefing on the clandestine mission he had been given by Don Gomez-Beare. The sooner Major Martin was six feet under, the less opportunity there would be for second opinions about the actual cause of his demise, and the less occasion there would be for second thoughts about his real identity. Haselden, of course, had followed his prior instructions about reporting the arrival of the body in a telephone call which he had made to the assistant British Naval Attaché in Madrid, on 1 May. He followed that phone call up with a telegram in the evening of the same day informing the British embassy he had managed to arrange for the dead messenger's funeral to be held on the morrow.[76] Captain Alan Hillgarth, in his turn, formally reported (again, as per previous instructions) to the Director of Naval Intelligence, by signals received in the early hours of Sunday 2 May, that a body had come ashore near Huelva and, then, that the corpse in question was a Royal Marine Major, W. Martin, who had drowned near Huelva 'probably 8 to 10 days ago'.[77] Of course in Hillgarth's cable to the DNI the period of time during which Major Martin was floating at sea is reported—presumably as advised by Spanish doctors after a post-mortem—to be up to two days longer than the maximum of eight days recorded in the Abwehr report of 22 May cited above. This difference of forty-eight hours is not great and the shorter estimate may be the result of the pathologists' being queried several weeks after the event and relying on their memories, rather than consulting their notes, to come up with a figure. Anyway, it was fortunate, perhaps, that the shorter estimate was the one passed to the Nazis, since it was easier to reconcile with the error made by Francoist officials (due to their misreading of the date on one of his personal documents), in identifying his notional date of departure by air from England on 28 April. In fact, the British agent, *Andros*, who was an official of either Spain's Navy or Ministry of Marine, reported on 8 June—after making inquiries, at Hillgarth's prompting, into the fate of Major Martin's papers—that the Spanish pathologists' estimation of how long the British courier 'must have been in the sea' was 'at least 15 days'.[78] These differing assessments do not necessarily reflect either inaccuracy on the part of the sources informing the British and the Germans, respectively, or indecisiveness on the part of the Spanish doctors: what they do suggest is the inherent difficulty of reaching firm conclusions about a matter influenced by so many variable factors, a point highlighted by an authoritative, modern textbook, *Knight's Forensic Pathology*:

> the time scale for decomposition may vary greatly in different circumstances and climates, and even in the same corpse: the head and arms may be skeletalized, whilst the legs and trunk, perhaps protected by clothing or other covering, may be moderately intact. All permutations may be found, making it even more difficult to estimate the probable time since death.[79]

Anyway, the Spanish doctors and Huelvan authorities were satisfied enough with the result of their investigations to permit the local British Vice-Consul to proceed with the funeral arrangements for the British officer. So, at noon on Sunday 2 May 1943, Major William Martin, RM, was laid to rest in the Catholic cemetery of *Nuestra Señora de la Soledad* in Huelva. The ceremony was attended by officers of the Spanish Army and Navy—to pay their respects to a fallen warrior—as well as Vice-Consul Haselden and some other members of Huelva's British and Allied countries' communities. After a religious service in the cemetery's chapel, the funeral party proceeded to the designated grave site. There, as shots rang out from the Spanish honour guard, a wooden coffin (stained black), which was draped in a Union Jack, was lowered into the earth.[80] It was appropriate that Glyndwr Michael's coffin should be wrapped in his country's flag, since he had passed the crucial tests of his medical and military credentials with flying colours. Now that, in the guise of Major Martin, he had played his central part in *Operation*

Mincemeat so flawlessly, his supporting cast had a real chance of getting their deceptive message across to the intended audience—Nazi Germany's intelligence service and High Command.

However, this phase of *Mincemeat*'s execution proved to be more troublesome than the deception planners had hoped, and for a reason they had feared: the interference of the Spanish Navy in the smooth passage of the deceptive documents into German hands. Indeed, the natural respect, if not always active sympathy, of many Spanish naval officers for the British was reinforced at that time in Huelva by a bond of individual friendship. As it happened, the very naval magistrate, Mariano Pascual del Pobil, who had taken legal charge of Major Martin's remains and effects, was on close personal terms with Francis Haselden. Understandably, but, doubtless also much to the latter's dismay, the judge handed over the British courier's briefcase to the Vice-Consul for safekeeping, while the post-mortem was being performed. Worse was to come when that examination was completed. Then, according to the recollection of Margaret Haselden (one of the Vice-Consul's daughters), Judge Pascual del Pobil turned to his friend and suggested that Haselden simply take the briefcase and its documentary contents away with him. However, in a document he compiled a decade later, Francis Haselden himself identified the individual who had 'politely suggested (the) B(ritish) V(ice) Consul take (the) dispatch case away with him' as the local naval commander. Captain Francisco Elvira Alvarez might seem an unlikely figure to have made such a chivalrous gesture to the British, since he was known to be a personal friend of the German consul in Huelva, Ludwig Clauss. Yet, presumably Haselden himself should be best able to recall the identity of his would-be benefactor. Still, whichever Spaniard made the offer and whether it was motivated by genuine friendship or a more calculated sense of respect, it placed the British Vice-Consul in an extremely awkward position. To accept it would mean an abrupt end to all hopes of passing strategically misleading documents to the enemy High Command via Major Martin's bag of tricks. On the other hand, to refuse to take the papers back might arouse such deep suspicions about their true nature and purpose as to discredit them as means of deceiving the enemy. Thinking fast on his feet, Haselden tried to avoid both unfortunate possibilities by professing to be worried that the Spaniard's generous offer to hand over the courier's briefcase might get him into trouble with his superior. So, he advised the naval officer to handle the matter through official channels which, in due course, 'would restore the briefcase to British custody in a regular manner'.[81]

Francis Haselden's presence of mind both persuaded the Spanish authoritie
to retain the British courier's briefcase in their possession without, in hi
own judgement, their suspecting 'any "plant"'. True, there was a thire
party present at the exchange between the Vice-Consul and the Spanisl
naval officer in question, who found the British representative's attitude tc
be rather strange. He was a United States Army Air Force pilot, Willian
Wilkins, whose own aircraft had crashed landed in Punta Umbria, durin§
the afternoon of 27 April. The American aviator had been brought tc
identify Major Martin as a possible member of his own air crew. Naturally
Wilkins assured the Spanish authorities that the dead British officer had nc
connection whatever with his aeroplane. Yet, while the young US pilo
seems to have taken his visitation to view Major Martin's decomposin§
remains in his stride, he was unsettled by Haselden's exchange with the
Spanish naval officer. The American was clearly dumbfounded at the Vice-
Consul's refusal to take the important-looking, official briefcase back from
the Spaniard. Of course, Haselden realized that declining to do so made him
look like a complete fool in the young pilot's eyes. Still, that price he wa
more than willing to pay to keep *Mincemeat*'s messages within the Germans
reach.[82] Haselden, however, did prevail upon the generosity of the loca
naval official to allow him to take a look inside the courier's briefcase. B}
doing so, he was able to verify that at least one envelope was still secure
inside the bag, a fact which he later communicated to London.[83] So, Franci
Haselden had managed to save *Operation Mincemeat* from ending in farce anc
Operation Husky from ending in tragedy.

Yet, if Don Gomez-Beare had had his way, the British Vice-Consul ir
Huelva would never have been admitted to the privileged circle of those ir
the know about *Operation Mincemeat*. When he had been recalled to Londor
in the spring of 1943 for consultation about the implementation of the
deception plan, the British Assistant Naval Attaché in Spain had counsellec
against letting Haselden in on Major Martin's secret role as a medium fo»
transmitting misleading information to the Germans' spies. Gomez-Beare
probably doubted the wisdom, on security grounds, of imparting such a
sensitive state secret to a lowly consular official, even if he had proven to be
'reliable and helpful' in the past. Montagu, however, rejected the advice o1
this respected authority on Franco's Spain, in this one instance. The NID
man maintained (as already noted above) that Haselden had to be given ar
'outline of the plan (without, of course, any description of its object or o1
the papers in the bag)', if the Vice-Consul were to play his allocated part in

he Huelvan phase of the stratagem successfully.[84] This was a prescient
provision on Montagu's part. Without his 'outline' briefing, Haselden
would not have known how vital it was to fend off the friendly Spanish
offer to hand the briefcase back. Indeed, to avoid having to turn down
further offers of Spanish help to recover the British Government briefcase,
Haselden had the good sense to make himself scarce for a while after Major
Martin's funeral. He locked up the offices of the British Vice-Consulate in
Huelva, and literally got out of town—hopping on the first bus to Seville.[85]
Francis Haselden's quickness of wit and nimbleness of foot prevented the
impression getting abroad that Britain's representative in Huelva was trying
to foist a bag of British documents on to the Francoist authorities and their
Nazi associates in a highly dubious manner.

Yet, for all that the secrets locked up in the British courier's briefcase
appeared to be the genuine articles, it was another matter for the Abwehr to
get hold of them. The British had assumed that the well-established German
espionage nest in Huelva, headed by the energetic Adolfo Clauss Kindt,
should have little trouble in gaining access to this intelligence windfall.[86]
Certainly, their Huelvan sources quickly informed the local Abwehr ring of
the British official bag and its contents, including the top-secret letters
addressed to Admiral Cunningham and Generals Alexander and Eisenhower. However, despite the fact that these missives promised to divulge
high-level Allied military secrets, Adolfo Clauss made no special or subtle
effort to acquire them. Instead, either he, himself, or his brother Luis (who
generally acted on behalf of their eighty-year-old blind father, Ludwig, in
the role of German consul in Huelva), simply asked one of their closest
collaborators within the Francoist administration to facilitate their access to
the letters in question. The individual whom they approached was Lieutenant Colonel Santiago Garrigos, district commander of the Civil Guard
in Huelva. He was well used to doing the Nazis' bidding, but like any
relatively senior official of Franco's regime, he was acutely sensitive to the
complicated corporate politics which dominated the internal workings of
the regime run by the *Caudillo* ('Chief')—to give Franco his formal political
title. Consequently, when presented with a request from the Clauss brothers
to 'do everything necessary to obtain copies of the documents which were
found in the (British) brief case', he shied away from challenging the
authority of the naval judge, Lieutenant Pascual del Pobil.[87] An even
more senior figure within Huelva's administration, its civil governor, Joaquín
Miranda, who was known to be an 'intimate friend' of the Germans, also

'did not dare to ask the naval judge for copies of the documents', when prompted by his Nazi cronies to do so. The local Abwehr nest even failed to exploit the first official visit by General Franco himself to Huelva, on 4 May 1943, to pull strings on a sufficiently high level to get their hands on the British courier's secret communications, in spite of the fact that Miranda was the *Caudillo*'s main host and escort on that occasion.[88] Indeed, as the British learned a month or so later, Major Martin's 'documents were neither copied nor photographed in Huelva'.

However, when judge Pascual del Pobil forwarded the British messenger's briefcase and documents to the Spanish Navy's headquarters in San Fernando (Cadiz), Adolfo Clauss had another stab at getting a look at them. Lieutenant Colonel Garrigos journeyed to Seville on 7 May to enlist the help of yet another Civil Guard officer in the Nazis' quest for this secret intelligence prize. He was Major Luís Canis who, according to British sources, was 'very pro-German and in German pay' and, unsurprisingly therefore, 'under complete German control'. This individual was a very valuable clandestine asset for the Abwehr, because he was no ordinary Civil Guard officer. In fact, Canis was chief of counter-espionage services 'in the Seville Captain-General's headquarters and therefore of all Andalucia'. Garrigos earnestly entreated Canis to do what he had so abjectly failed to do himself, namely, to intimidate the Armada's authorities into disgorging Major Martin's key documents. However, Canis was too finely attuned to the Franco regime's complex set of internal jurisdictional boundaries to wish to be seen to be crossing them. So, he declined to address a formal written request to the naval staff in San Fernando for access to the British documents. Instead, he dispatched an individual of quite lowly military rank to see what could be found out about these documents from the naval authorities at San Fernando. However, since Canis had warned his emissary to act with 'the utmost discretion', this half-hearted inquiry did not impress the naval staff officers. They rebuffed this démarche with the comment that 'if the Captain General of Seville wanted any information about the documents he should address himself to the Ministry of War in Madrid'.[89]

At least the tentative inquiries made on behalf of Major Canis had revealed the ultimate destination within Spain of Major Martin's itinerant briefcase. Although, as the British also learned some weeks later, most of the documents and photographs inside their courier's bag were copied at San Fernando, their sources reported that the three sealed envelopes (addressed to Alexander, Cunningham, and Eisenhower), containing the essence of

peration Mincemeat's deceptive message, were still inviolate when they
ere sent on to Madrid. This was because the naval staff officers were either
fraid to break the seals lest the Minister of Marine should disapprove or
en more probably because they had no experience in opening them
ithout leaving a trace'.[90] As the Germans, for their part, learned a little
ter too, 'the courier's briefcase, together with all papers found in his breast
)cket, were then taken to Madrid by an official of the Marine Command-
t's Office (in San Fernando) and handed over personally to the Minister
r Marine', Admiral Salvador Moreno Fernández.[91]

So, as it happened, the trust placed by the British deception planners in
e ability of the Abwehr nest in Huelva to learn the contents of the key
)cuments carried by their courier was not justified. Adolfo Clauss had to
form his superiors at the Kriegsorganisation (KO) in Madrid of his failure to
t hold of Major Martin's papers locally.[92] Now the only hope that the
azi High Command might receive the cover plan for Operation Husky
)ud and clear' rested on the capacity of Nazi Germany's senior spies to
ert greater influence over the members of the Franco regime than their
;ents in Huelva had managed to do. Certainly, the large-scale German
pionage enterprise inside Spain operated with the acquiescence and, often
en active, assistance of Franco's fascist-style, authoritarian regime.[93] Its
)ntroller, Wilhelm Leissner (who worked under the nom de guerre of
ustav Lenz) had served the Abwehr's interests inside Franco's Spain
nce 1937, and had won the admiration of both his own subordinates and
any Spanish officials with his quiet courtesy, personal discretion, and
rofessional competence.[94] However, although Leissner's own boss, the
ief of the Abwehr, Admiral Canaris, was well pleased with the position
d power the head of the KO in Madrid had won for their secret service
ithin Spain, not all Germany's senior covert warriors were as satisfied.[95]
hus, when the head of the Nazi Party's foreign intelligence service visited
ladrid in July 1942, he was not impressed by what he found. Admittedly,
S-Brigadeführer Walter Schellenberg, head of Department VI of the
eichssicherheitshauptamt (RSHA)—the Central Office for Reich Security—
as a competitor of Canaris and company in the intra-regime struggle for
verall control of the Third Reich's secret intelligence communities, a
ureaucratic battle the RSHA would eventually win in 1944. Still, however
redisposed Schellenberg was to find fault with all of the Abwehr's efforts,
e does seem to have genuinely concluded that the working methods of,
d results achieved by both the main Abwehr stations in the Iberian

Peninsula left a lot to be desired. Thus, having attended a conference
senior Abwehr operatives (including Leissner) from both KO Madrid ar
KO Lisbon in the Spanish capital, Schellenberg came seriously to dou
their proficiency and performance.[96]

The RSHA observer was prepared to make only one exception to th
general condemnation of the Iberian-based Abwehr organizations. Sche
lenberg formed 'a good opinion of Kühlenthal's capabilities'.[97] Specialis
Captain Karl Erich Kühlenthal recruited and ran the Madrid KO's mc
important spies inside the Western Allies. In that role, he impressed not on
his own side, but even his enemies: the British judged him to be a ve
efficient and energetic opponent.[98] Still, the British also knew—as h
German colleagues did not—that Kühlenthal's apparent achievements
the field of foreign espionage were largely illusory. Thus, his star agent, Ju;
Pujol García, in reality was an ardent anti-Nazi who could not wait to l
taken on board by the British as a double agent. Ironically, Pujol four
it much more difficult to persuade the sceptical British of his genuir
allegiance to the Democracies, than to convince the Germans of his bog
sympathy for Nazism. Yet, after being recruited into the double-cro
system under the code-name *Garbo* in April 1942, Juan Pujol became th
most potent human channel for the transmission of Allied strategic disir
formation. Agent *Garbo* had earned that code name from his British handle
because of his superior acting ability, which would be displayed to greate
effect in his selling of the strategic deception plan for the Norman
invasion in 1944.[99] However, the British double-crossers would attribu
their own success in this critical case, above all, to Kühlenthal's inabili
to see through 'the absurdities of the story' *Garbo*'s handlers were feedir
him.[100] Yet, in May 1943, Kühlenthal's reputation as the most productive
the Third Reich's spymasters was still intact.[101] Surely, this dynamic ind
vidual, in tandem with the greatly respected and well-connected Leissne
should be able to coax their many contacts within the Franco regime int
yielding up Major Martin's secrets.

Experienced as the veteran Nazi spies were in dealing with the comple
make-up of Spain's body politic, they chose their point of pressure carefull
Either Leissner himself, or Kühlenthal, personally raised the matter of th
British courier's documents with officers of the *Alto Estado Mayor* (AEM
the Supreme General Staff of the Spanish Armed Forces.[102] That body w
headed by General Juan Vigón Suerodiaz, who was also Minister for Air i
Franco's government. Vigón was a pro-Axis diehard and a long-time clo

collaborator with the Germans. He was also an old friend of the chief of the Abwehr, Admiral Wilhelm Canaris (who, himself, was an old hand at forging clandestine relations between different German and Spanish regimes).[103] However, the fact that top-level British communications had apparently fallen into Spanish hands was news to the AEM. The Germans (with both Leissner and Kühlenthal certainly being personally involved) addressed further inquiries about the whereabouts of the papers to the Ministry of War and the Directorate General of Security, but again drew a blank. They did not try approaching the Ministry of Marine, despite these disappointments, knowing the cool reception they might receive there in the absence of backing from other quarters of the Franco regime. Yet, neither did they throw in the towel. For all that Kühlenthal and Leissner would prove no match, ultimately, for their British opponents in the great game of wartime double-cross and deception, they had the virtue of persistence, for which *Mincemeat*'s planners would be in their debt.[104]

So, the Madrid KO's leaders now decided to try a new tack. They sought the help of one of their most active agents, a Captain Groizar of the Spanish Air Force. Groizar had already heard about the discovery of the British courier and his briefcase and he was quite prepared to try and track the elusive documents down. The Air Force captain had good contacts within the AEM but the initial queries he posed there and also at the Directorate General of Security once more failed to produce any new information on the contents of these British letters, or even their current location. Still, unlike the Abwehr's timid champions in southern Spain, Groizar kept up the pressure on the AEM and the Ministry of the Interior (of which the Directorate General of Security formed part) to involve themselves in the German effort to procure copies of the British courier's documents.[105] Groizar was certainly targeting the most important nerve centres of intelligence-gathering within the Franco regime. The AEM's Third Section housed a central organization, under the leadership of Colonel Arsenio Martínez de Campos, for the collection, evaluation, and distribution of foreign political and military intelligence. Again, the authority exercised by the Directorate General of Security inside Franco's Spain, primarily derived from one of its subsections, the Commissariat General of Information, which received domestic intelligence from police stations all over Spain.[106] Groizar's importunings in these quarters dedicated to intelligence-gathering and assessment eventually paid off. They caught the attention of one of the topmost officials of the Directorate General of Security: its

Secretary General, Lieutenant Colonel José López Barrón. The latter had served, from late 1941 to mid 1942, as a senior staff officer with the Spanish 'Blue Division', fighting as part of the German Army on the Russian front. Alerted by Groizar, Barrón 'took a personal interest in the matter' (as Britain's agent *Andros* found out, somewhat later).[107]

A combination of prompting from Lieutenant Colonel Barrón and further direct pressure from the Abwehr seems to have persuaded General Vigón and 'the strongly pro-fascist' Minister of War, General Carlos Asensio Cabanillas, to intervene decisively in the affair.[108] Admiral Moreno may have had a more realistic view, by mid 1943, of how the Second World War would turn out than his pro-Axis colleagues.[109] However, he was no match in terms of intra-regime influence for such political heavyweights as Vigón and Asensio. Moreover, it seems they may well have invoked Franco's authority to force the Ministry of Marine to hand over Major Martin's 'whole collection' of papers, official and personal, 'untouched' to a representative of the AEM.[110] The staff officer assigned by that body to take charge of the covert opening and duplication of the official British letters, as well as other aspects of the case of the drowned Royal Marine courier, was Lieutenant Colonel Ramón Pardo de Santayana. He arranged for Spanish technical experts to try and extract the three top-level letters from their envelopes, without leaving any obvious signs of having done so. The Spaniards were aided in this task by the fact that the sea water had washed off all the gum along the three letters' flaps. This meant that only their wax seals kept them closed. Yet, Pardo and his experts must have known that any attempt to loosen, let alone break, these seals would be all too obvious. So, they resorted to the tricky manoeuvre of extracting the letters from the envelopes without touching their seals in any way. With dextrous fingers they managed to roll the letters out from under the flaps of the envelopes, without disturbing the seals that were holding them together. The Spaniards then inspected the letters and found them to be in 'good condition', but wet through. To ensure that they were in a fit state to be photographed, the Spanish technical experts dried them with artificial heat and duly made copies of these seemingly top-secret communications. Before replacing the letters back under the covers, the Spanish technical team re-immersed them in salt water for a full twenty-four hours. The Spaniards hoped that another soaking would eliminate any tell-tale signs of the letters' having been abstracted from their envelopes and artificially dried, so they could be photographed.[111]

So, the Spanish government itself, was now fully apprised of Major
Martin's secrets, and the main one—the letter from General Nye to General
Alexander—was translated into Spanish and forwarded to Spain's autocratic
ruler, General Francisco Franco, himself, for his consideration.[112] One of
the matters the *Caudillo* then had to decide, of course, was whether to pass
on this British state secret to Nazi Germany. The official Spanish inclination
to facilitate German access to the copied documents was indicated, already,
by the appointment of Colonel Pardo as the 'case officer' for the affair.
The Abwehr in Spain regarded the Spanish staff officer as having 'well
established connections'—not least with those closely involved in clandestine cooperation between Franco's Spain and Hitler's Germany during
the Second World War. In July 1940, for example, he attended a meeting
between representatives of both Germany and Spain in Madrid, to discuss a
future joint attack by both countries on Gibraltar. Those present also
included General Vigón, Admiral Canaris, and Wilhelm Leissner. In the
ensuing months, Pardo actively assisted the Abwehr nest in Algeçiras to
conduct an extensive reconnaissance of the Rock for the German military.
He also acted as 'both greeter and escort' to high-level German visitors in
Spain, including Admiral Canaris again, during later 1940 and 1941.[113]
Placing such a practised collaborator with the representatives of the Third
Reich in charge of duplicating the documents Major Martin was couriering,
suggests that there was a prior Francoist intention of passing photostats of
the more important items to the Germans, once they had been copied.
Indeed, it seems that, at some time on 8 May 1943, a Spanish official
(probably Lieutenant Colonel Pardo) briefed an Abwehr contact (almost
certainly Leissner) on the contents of the Nye–Alexander letter and promised also that copies of all the top-level correspondence found in the British
courier's briefcase would be given to the Germans in the near future.
Leissner hastened to dispatch news of this sensational discovery, and of its
apparently priceless revelations about Allied offensive plans, to his superiors
in Berlin. Clearly, however, this ultra-sensitive report, with its assurance
that documentary corroboration would soon follow, had to go via a safe
route.[114] So, Leissner entrusted it to the care of another airborne courier.
The man charged with conveying *Mincemeat*'s misleading message to the
German High Command, on this occasion, was the chief of the counter-
espionage section in the Madrid KO, Kurt von Rohrscheidt. Although von
Rohrscheidt was definitely in the land of the living, he was as oblivious as
Glyndwr Michael to his role in furthering the British deception. So, bearing

a 'Most Secret Letter' from Leissner to Abwehr Headquarters, the German
counter-intelligence officer flew to the Reich's capital on a regular Lufthansa flight from Madrid, on 9 May 1943, and his journey was not interrupted by any aviation accident—real or imaginary.[115] So, in the heel of the
Nazi hunt for Major Martin's papers, the senior officials of the Franco
regime had lived up to the image the British had of them as fascist fellow
travellers—who could be relied upon to relay Operation Mincemeat's misleading message to Hitler's Germany.[116] Yet, there should be no doubt as to
the ultimate authority for this unneutral act on the part of the Spanish
government. Leissner informed Abwehr headquarters on 13 May that it
was General Franco himself who had ordered that copies of the British
courier's documents be forwarded to the Abwehr in Madrid for onward
transmission to Germany.[117] Even at this stage of the war, the Caudillo was
still trying to keep in Hitler's good books by rendering the Führer such non-
belligerent services. The Spanish leader had no inkling—thanks to the
infinite pains Mincemeat's planners had taken in preparing and presenting
their dead messenger and his official briefcase for foreign scrutiny—that he
was actually passing Allied disinformation to the German High Command.

The efforts of British officials in London and their colleagues in Spain to
uphold the fictions of Operation Mincemeat had not flagged while they
waited upon word of its outcome. Indeed, Ewen Montagu, once he had
returned to London from Greenock, made sure that Major Martin still
commanded his colleagues' attention by holding a kind of farewell party
for the courier who was now departed in more ways than one. He had had
the foresight to purchase four tickets to the variety show at the Prince of
Wales theatre on the evening of 22 April. So, Charles Cholmondeley and
he invited the two main female contributors to Operation Mincemeat—Jean
Leslie (who had provided her own photograph to serve as one of 'Pam') and
the unnamed authoress of Pam's love letters—to join them for a night out.
The foursome managed to persuade the theatre manager that a friend had
detached two of the ticket stubs, and made off with them, as a prank, which
neatly explained away the absence of stubs in two of the tickets they were
tendering. Duly admitted to the performance, they were so taken with one
of its comic turns that Montagu would recall the multi-act review a decade
later as the 'Sid Field' show. With their spirits lifted, the four then moved on
to the Gargoyle Club in Meard Street in Soho, for a late dinner. The
Gargoyle Club was a haunt of painters, writers and spies—an appropriate setting in which to raise a glass to one of the greatest creations of

e British covert imagination. Montagu stood in for Bill Martin on this
cial occasion. With his impish sense of humour, he even managed to raise
me eyebrows in the reasonably permissive atmosphere of the Gargoyle
ub, by remarking to his notional fiancée that she would soon find out that
  really knew his stuff (as Lord Mountbatten had vouched for Major
artin in the *Mincemeat* letter to Admiral Cunningham).[118]

Of course, once Montagu and company returned to the office—perhaps
ittle the worse for wear—there were plenty of other secret labours to keep
em occupied. Yet, even during this period of waiting for word from the
raph and Spain, they still had to remain alert to any problems affecting its
iplementation. In fact, one of these had arisen even before HMS *Seraph* set
l. The matter was a routine one which the deception planners had taken
ps to try and settle in advance. On 15 April, Admiral Barry had requested
at the naval authorities in Gibraltar, 'arrange total bombing restrictions' in
e area off Huelva where the *Seraph* was due to execute *Operation Mince-
at* from 12.01 a.m. on 29 April.[119] Since the Royal Navy's Flag Officer,
ibraltar, Vice Admiral Sir (George) Frederick Edward-Collins and his Staff
fficer (Intelligence) (SO (I)) were meant to have been briefed about the
pending deception operation, Barry and Montagu were astonished to
ceive a reply from the Rock claiming not to understand 'the purport of
ie) message' requesting a ban on the bombing of submarines off Huelva
om the date in question.[120] Moreover, when the DNI, Rushbrooke,
minded Edward-Collins that Lieutenant Commander Gomez-Beare had
en 'instructed to explain MINCEMEAT verbally to you and S.O. (I)
ibraltar on his recent visit', the Flag Officer on the Rock flatly denied that
e Assistant Naval Attaché had done so. Gomez-Beare, for his part, equally
amantly insisted that he had 'imparted every detail he knew himself',
out *Operation Mincemeat*, to the SO (I) at Gibraltar, just as he had been
structed by Montagu to do—a version of events which Captain Alan
illgarth endorsed.[121]

Indeed, the fault for this misunderstanding may well have lain with the
oyal Navy's command on the Rock. Certainly, the Flag Officer had made a
egative impression upon Admiral Cunningham's senior staff officers some
onths before. Encountering Vice Admiral Edward-Collins in Gibraltar in
e days immediately before the launching of *Operation Torch*, the gifted
ommander 'Lofty' Power found him to be 'a fat, stupid, pompous man',
d dubbed him 'His Pregnancy the Panda'.[122] To be fair, however, it was
e SO (I) based in Gibraltar to whom Gomez-Beare claimed to have given

a full verbal briefing about *Operation Mincemeat*.[123] Either that staff officer h[...]
neglected to pass the word on to Edward-Collins, or the Flag Officer cou[...]
not remember him doing so. Certainly, 'Fat Fred' (to quote another [...]
Power's terms of disrespect for the Vice Admiral) was not the kind of seni[...]
officer to take kindly to having any lapse in memory pointed out to him b[...]
subordinate. In any case, Montagu and his colleagues realized that they h[...]
no time for recriminations with *Seraph* steaming south towards the dang[...]
zone. So, they ordered Gomez-Beare to revisit the Rock and put the seni[...]
naval staff there in the picture about the deception plan, once and for a[...]
However, to make such a visit from Spanish territory required an ex[...]
visa from the Francoist authorities, and the time required to obtain th[...]
document, meant that he might not get to Gibraltar before 27 April, [...]
Hillgarth's earliest estimate. In the event, Gomez-Beare did not make it [...]
the Rock until the afternoon of 29 April, only hours before Jewell's bo[...]
surfaced to launch the corpse-courier on his posthumous mission.[124] By th[...]
date, however, Edward-Collins had been given authority from London [...]
read a briefing about *Operation Mincemeat*, which had been dispatched [...]
MI5 to their senior officer on the Rock, Major H. G. 'Tito' Medlam (who [...]
formal title was 'Defence Security Officer').[125] Edward-Collins was al[...]
informed, by the same message of 29 April that the *Seraph* was now waiti[...]
in the area designated for bombing restriction 'until the weather was suitabl[...]
to carry out the deception scheme.[126] Thanks to these timely interventio[...]
Montagu and his colleagues were spared the ultimate frustration of seeing the[...]
project literally blown out of the water, along with forty-nine *Seraphim*—a[...]
by friendly fire at that.

   This belated realization that, for whatever reason, the naval staff at Gibralt[...]
had not taken on board their advance warning about *Operation Minceme*[...]
was not the only one of the plan's carefully made arrangements to co[...]
unstuck in late April to early May 1943. Another complication arose—[...]
despite the best efforts of the deception planners to forestall it—in connecti[...]
with the signals that would have to be sent by British officials in Spa[...]
about the arrival of the deceased courier there. Lieutenant Jewell's ow[...]
communications about the dropping of Major Martin's body into the s[...]
off Huelva could be kept within the tightly circumscribed circle of tho[...]
already in the know about the Operation. Anyway, the radio signal whic[...]
the *Seraph*'s skipper sent, at 7.15 a.m. on 30 April, did not give much aw[...]
to the uninitiated: '*Operation MINCEMEAT* completed. Request onwa[...]
route.'[127] Of course, the longer report on the execution of his mission th[...]

/ell completed on the same day, to be forwarded to the DNI, for 'Lt. Cdr.
e Hon. E. E. S. Montagu, R.N.V.R. personal', contained much revealing
l even graphic detail, about the launching of the corpse and the briefcase
) the ocean. However, this highly confidential document was sent from
)raltar by courier straight to the NID in the Admiralty, in London, where
prying eyes could glean its contents.[128] The problem arose, not with
ard to the official reportage of Major Martin's immersion in the sea but his
val on land.

As already noted, Haselden and Hillgarth had carried out their prior
:ructions to report, promptly, the arrival of the British officer's body at
elva. However, it was the follow-up signal that Britain's Naval Attaché sent
w hours after midnight on 2 May 1943, confirming the identity of the body
led from the sea near Huelva as that of 'Major W. Martin R.M. card
mber 148228', that created problems.[129] This was by way of a 'normal signal
the Admiralty, which would be sent in such circumstances' but Montagu
l appreciated, in advance, that this message could attract such unwelcome
ntion from the naval bureaucrats as to jeopardize the absolute secrecy
:essary for the success of Operation Mincemeat.[130] So, he had arranged,
orehand, with Captain Hillgarth for the Naval Attaché to dispatch him,
a secure but speedier channel, a message 'stating that he was about to send
h a signal and giving its code number so that the action for suppressing it
ıld be taken'.[131] This alternative special route was the 'Embassy's W/T
ion operated by S.I.S.' and usually reserved for the considerable quantity of
ionage reports and more urgent diplomatic messages being radioed back to
gland by MI6 agents and British Embassy staff. Encrypted messages, sent in
rse code over the radio, could be virtually guaranteed to reach London
ore an encoded telegram sent through the Spanish Post Office, where such
tish communications were often delayed for more or less nefarious
sons—sometimes for up to six days at a time.[132]

Given these facts, the confidence of Montagu and his colleagues in
uming that a radio message from the British embassy in Madrid would
ch the NID before a telegram formally reporting the 'beaching' of a
yal Marine Major's body near Huelva, seemed justified. However,
cumstances conspired against their pre-emptive plans, as Montagu rue-
ly recorded:

In the event the signal from 'C''s [i.e. MI6's radio] channels was not given a
sufficient start over the normal Naval signal and the latter had already started its

distribution before it could be suppressed; most of the Admiralty distribution
was stopped, but copies had already gone to Bath [where some of the
Admiralty's administrative departments had been relocated] and some other
recipients.[133]

So, Montagu and his NID colleagues had to scramble to contain the secur
leak resulting from this premature arrival of the official notification of t
drowning of Major Martin off Huelva. They phoned and wrote to the he
of the naval departments concerned to arrange for 'the suppression of t
signal on the excuse that the individual in question was not a Naval offic
but had, with the authority of the First Sea Lord, been given the cover
rank in the Royal Marines when he was setting out on a special and ve
secret mission abroad'. Accordingly, they directed the naval bureaucrats
refrain from taking any administrative action in response to the sig
reporting Major Martin's death, on the grounds that the individual involv
was not actually an officer of the Royal Navy. As a clinching argument
the signal's suppression, Montagu pointed out that another person mig
now have to undertake the secret mission which had been assigned
the deceased, so 'the secrecy of his task' must be preserved. Faced w
the high-level authority that Montagu was now able to invoke on *Operat
Mincemeat*'s behalf, the naval administrators did as they were bidden.[134]

Yet, while *Mincemeat*'s main champion had managed to mend this brea
in the deception plan's security, Ewen Montagu must have had a sinki
feeling about the Operation's chances of success at this juncture. T
was because of one of the items of information contained in that sai
signal from Hillgarth of early 2 May confirming the identity of the cor
retrieved from the ocean near Huelva. For reasons already explaine
Montagu would not have been too alarmed at the news contained in th
cable to the effect that a Spanish post-mortem exam had been conducted
the corpse, or that the deceased was reckoned to have died 'probably 8 to
days ago'. After all, the *Mincemeat* team had got what they wanted from a
Spanish post-mortem, namely an official verdict that Major Martin's 'dea
(was) due to drowning'.[135] So, on balance the medical news from Huel
was not unwelcome. What was worrying, however, was the report that t
'Spanish Naval authorities have possession of papers found'.[136] This wa
situation that the British deception planners had striven sedulously to avo
One of the main advantages apparently in dropping the dead messenger in
the ocean off Huelva was that it seemed much less likely that his remai
would come under naval jurisdiction there than in Cadiz. Certainly, t

British fears that Spanish naval officers might not be willing to surrender *Mincemeat*'s deceptive letters to local Abwehr agents, simply upon request, were soon justified by further reports from Spain.[137] On 3 May, Hillgarth repeated his report that the Spanish Navy had all Major Martin's papers and further stated that all these documents would 'have to go to Madrid'.[138] Five days later he modified that report to say that all the courier's 'effects' were now being sent to the naval commander in Cadiz who, 'in due course', would forward them to the Ministry of Marine in Madrid.[139] This information meant the end of the deception planners' hopes that the supposedly energetic Huelvan Abwehr nest would get a look at the courier's top-secret letters in Huelva—and, incidentally, made redundant the carefully choreographed series of communications between Haselden and Gomez-Beare designed to sustain the Huelvan Abwehr's interest in those documents.

Now, the whole burden of conducting a credible, but not too prematurely successful, diplomatic campaign to retrieve the courier's briefcase from official Spanish custody devolved upon Captain Alan Hillgarth. The British naval attaché in Spain was able to draw on a wealth of personal experience in dealing with the locals and had definite views on how best to approach them:

> Handling Spaniards is a special technique, which, once acquired, yields rich dividends... One can offend a Spaniard very easily, but it is equally easy to avoid offence if one is careful. By sticking quietly to your objective and contriving whenever possible to make the Spaniard you are dealing with feel that you like him and appreciate his difficulties, you will eventually gain your point. It seldom pays to quote rules or precedents. Everything in Spain is on a personal basis. One of my best moments in Madrid was when I managed to make the Minister of Marine so sorry for me because he could not do what I wanted that in the end he did it, at considerable hazard to himself, just because he felt he was letting a friend down if he didn't.[140]

Yet, the rapport which Hillgarth had managed to establish with senior officials of the Francoist state might have proven disastrously counterproductive for *Operation Mincemeat* if one of them had become so friendly with the Naval Attaché as to return the courier's briefcase before German agents had a chance to look at its contents. The deception plan's prospects had come to depend on Hillgarth's ability to maintain sufficient pressure on the Ministry of Marine to demonstrate London's apparently genuine concern over the fate of the documents which had been confided to Major Martin's care, without prompting a premature restoration of the key letters

to British possession. It must be said that the advice Hillgarth received from
Montagu, on how best to comport himself in this tricky situation, was no
of great practical value. For example, on 6 May, Montagu sent the following
message to the Naval Attaché via a 'special route' (probably by MI6's W/T
channel), as opposed to the pro forma messages about the missing briefcase
sent by ordinary airmail signal:

> Normally you would be getting frantic messages asking you to get the secret
> documents at once, and to hurry the Spaniards. You must adjust your actions
> to achieve desired results and maintain normal appearances.[141]

Hillgarth reassured the NID officer that he had got the message and was
broaching the topic with Francoist officials in the prescribed manner. In
fact, the British Naval Attaché played his awkward hand skillfully. He did
make a formal request to the Ministry of Marine, on 5 May, for the return o
all the British courier's papers but was careful to present it as an oral, rather
than written one. This made it easier for the Ministry's officials, whilst
registering the official British concern, to claim to 'know nothing of effect
or papers recovered'. However, the Ministry's representatives did assure the
respected British naval officer that the matter would receive their prompt
attention, once they received any news.[142] So, Hillgarth had managed to
avoid putting such pressure on the Francoist officials as to intimidate them
into handing back Major Martin's top-secret letters before they had a
chance to copy them. On the other hand, the fact that someone of his
standing with the Spaniards had made an official request for the return of
these items seemed to indicate that their contents were well worth examining
and recording.

The personal bond that Captain Hillgarth had established with senior
officials of the Ministry of Marine was also of service when it came to
determining whether the Franco regime had actually gained access to the
main deceptive missive inside the courier's briefcase. The embarrassed
behaviour of these individuals, in discussing the transfer of these documents
to Hillgarth's custody, gave their game away. In the absence of Admiral
Moreno (who was out of town on official business), it fell to Vice Admiral
Alfonso Arriaga Adam, Chief of the Spanish Naval Staff, to hand all these
items over to the British Naval Attaché on 11 May 1943. As Hillgarth took
possession of the official briefcase—which was open with the key in its
lock—the Vice Admiral could not resist attempting to assure him that the
official documents were 'all there'. That injudicious remark revealed, at the

ry least, that the Spaniards had made a careful inventory of the items
side the briefcase. Indeed, Hillgarth had no difficulty in deducing from
rriaga's 'manner' that 'it was obvious Chief (of) Naval Staff knew some-
ing (of the) contents' of Major Martin's bag.[143] The same uneasiness at
ving to deal with a respected fellow sailor in less than honest fashion
aracterized the conduct of the Spanish Minister of Marine when he met
e British Naval Attaché to discuss the case, four days later. On that
casion, Admiral Moreno maintained that, once word reached him in
lencia (where he was visiting) that the courier's papers had reached the
anish capital, he had immediately ordered Arriaga to give them back to
illgarth without delay. When the latter wondered 'why he had gone to
ch trouble', the Minister replied that Hillgarth's request for the return of
e courier's documents had highlighted their importance. Accordingly,
oreno said he had become 'anxious no one should have (an) unauthorized
ok at them "which might be a serious matter"'. Hillgarth, however, was
amant that nothing he had said to officials of the Ministry of Marine, even
reported verbatim to Admiral Moreno—which, in itself, was highly
likely—would ever 'alone have led' the Minister 'to say what he did'.
deed, Hillgarth concluded that there was only one possible reason for
dmiral Moreno's behaviour and the Naval Attaché spelt it out for London:
can be taken as a certainty that Spanish Government know contents of
cuments'.[144]

Still, the British deception planners had never intended to rely solely upon
lan Hillgarth's ability to read the body language and interpret the
nguarded utterances of Francoist officials in ascertaining whether Major
artin's high-level documents remained inviolate. In fact, Montagu had
arned Hillgarth, by 'special route', the day before the Naval Attaché rec-
ved the courier's papers back from the Francoist authorities, that it was
iost important' that the 'letters from the black bag' not be 'tested or tam-
red with' in Madrid. Instead, they should be sent by the 'quickest route'
ck to London where 'secret checks' had been arranged to determine
hether they had been 'opened illicitly'.[145] What the 'Special Examiners'
om the British postal censorship service had done was to mark the wax seals
1 the flaps of the envelopes, containing the letters to Alexander and
unningham, in such a manner that any attempt to disturb these seals should
e evident, not least because they had photographed them in close-up to
cord their exact shape and pattern before dispatch.[146] When Hillgarth
ceived Major Martin's papers back from Vice Admiral Arriaga on

11 May, he scrupulously followed his instructions not to subject them to an intrusive, physical examination. However, he did report to London his acute first impression of the state of the documents which had just been returned to him:

> Many much damaged by sea water, but many legible. While not tampering with them in any way I can see somebody else has. Envelopes have been opened. Among other [sic] there appear letters addressed [to] General Eisenhower and Alexander and Admiral Cunningham. These look as if drier than other papers.[147]

Hillgarth then dispatched the principal *Mincemeat* letters by diplomatic bag on 14 May. The bag was taken by diplomatic courier to Lisbon and, thence by air to London.[148] Montagu fretted at the time this secure passage of the papers back to London consumed but, when the documents did arrive at last, he rushed them to the special examiners in postal censorship for their expert assessment. These experts produced their verdict on 21 May, but it was not exactly what *Mincemeat*'s planners wanted to hear. For a start, despite Hillgarth's report that the envelopes containing the high-level letters had been opened, the British examiners had found—like their Spanish counterparts—that they were still held shut by their official wax seals. The sea water had dissolved all the gum on the envelopes (which is probably the condition that Hillgarth had meant to convey by informing London that those envelopes had been 'opened') but, as Montagu recorded, the wax seals themselves proved to be 'all intact and untampered with', when minutely compared with the photographs taken of them prior to the courier's journey. That careful conclusion of the British experts raised the practical question of whether the Spaniards might have managed to gain access to the contents of the envelopes in question without breaking the wax seals holding them shut. The British experts guessed that the most likely method employed by an inquisitive agent to read the letters, without interfering with the wax seals, would be to try and roll them out from under the flaps of the envelopes. They conducted their own experiments on the feasibility of this approach and found that it was quite possible to extract the letters from their envelopes in this manner without affecting their wax seals. Moreover, they were able to go further than proving that it was feasible to remove the courier's letters from their envelopes in this surreptitious way. In the case of the letter addressed to Admiral Cunningham they were virtually able to prove that it had been treated in this fashion.[149]

This the British technical experts did by examining the letters with the [...]d of a high-magnification lens for any signs that they had been handled by [...]reign parties. During the exercise, they detected two anomalies in the [...]tter from Lord Mountbatten to Admiral Cunningham. The first of these [...]as the fact that 'the letter had been folded up twice, once symmetrically [...]d secondly', as it now appeared, 'irregularly'. The British experts were [...]re that this second crease in the paper of the letter 'was made while the [...]tter was wet', which proved that it had been rolled out of its envelope and [...]en unfolded and read by the Spaniards, prior to being re-soaked, [...]-folded, and reinserted. The other physical trace of tampering which [...]ught the British postal technicians' attention was the distinctive upward [...]rve of the letter's edge, 'showing it curled after being taken out of the [...]velope'.[150] This was a brilliant set of deductions on the part of the British [...]ostal censorship experts. It perceptively recaptured the process—recorded [...] the Abwehr's report of 15 May 1943 cited above—whereby the Spaniards [...]lled the letters from their envelopes, dried them under artificial heat, re-[...]aked them for 'some twenty-four hours in salt water', re-folded them and, [...]nally, rolled them back inside their envelopes without disturbing the wax [...]als on their flaps.[151] Yet, for all its insightfulness this expert assessment did [...]ot prove conclusively that the key *Mincemeat* message—the one from [...]eneral Nye to General Alexander—had been read by the Francoists, [...]t alone copied and passed on to the Nazis. Montagu had to acknowledge [...]is unpalatable fact in the official report on *Operation Mincemeat*, which he [...]bmitted at the end of May 1943:

It was possible to extract all the letters through the envelopes by twisting them out, but while there were slight indications that this might have been done to the letter to Admiral Cunningham there was no trace whatsoever of this having been done to the crucial letter to General Alexander.[152]

[...] Montagu sounds surprisingly stoical about the failure of this particular [...]ritish effort to discover whether *Operation Mincemeat*'s main deceptive [...]essage was getting through, then that was because the British could afford [...] accept this setback; for, as Montagu put it, they had 'a second string to [...]eir bow'.[153] This consisted of their capacity—thanks to the unflagging [...]forts of the code-breakers at Bletchley Park—to monitor enemy radio [...]ommunications, including those transmitted by all three branches of the [...]erman armed forces, as well as those of the various Nazi intelligence [...]rvices, including the Abwehr. That British ability to decrypt intercepted

radio signals delivered the first definitive proof that, in Montagu's words, 'th
Spaniards handed a copy or photograph of at least the crucial document to th
Germans and that the latter accepted that document as genuine'.[154] The pro
came in the form of a W/T signal addressed by Colonel Freiherr Treusch vc
Buttlar-Brandenfels, First General Staff Officer (Army) in the OKW Staff,
senior German commanders in the Balkans and the Mediterranean, on
May 1943.[155] The text of that decrypted message, as translated by the boffi
of Bletchley Park on 14 May 1943, was the following:

> According to a source which may be regarded as absolutely reliable, an
> enemy landing undertaking on a large scale is projected in the near future
> in both the eastern and western Mediterranean. Namely: Eastern Med: The
> undertaking in the Eastern Med has as its objective the coast near Kalamata
> and the coastal sector south of Cape Araxos (both places on the west coast of
> the Peloponnese). The landing near Kalamata is to be carried out by the 56th
> Infantry Div and that near Cape Araxos by the reinforced 5th Infantry Div. It
> is not yet clear whether both divisions will operate at full strength or only
> with elements. If the former were the case about 2 or 3 weeks would be
> needed before the beginning of the landing. Should only elements of the
> divisions operate the landing could take place at any time. The cover-name
> for the landing is Husky. A feint against the Dodecanese, must be reckoned
> with. Signed: Freiherr von Buttlar, IA. OKW-Armed Forces, OPS Staff. OP
> (Army) no 00268.[156]

The British deception planners understood the moment they received th
'Ultra' decrypt that the Germans—very obligingly, if unwittingly—ha
supplied them with incontrovertible evidence of their audacious plan
first impact. The German radio intercept proved beyond a shadow of
doubt that the Spaniards had managed to gain access to the critical Nye
Alexander letter; that they had passed a copy of that missive to agents of th
Abwehr; and that spy agency had relayed the crucial *Mincemeat* documen
onto the High Command of the German Armed Forces. Moreover, vo
Buttlar's signal seemed to suggest that the OKW was taking the imminer
Allied offensive plans, as indicated by the apparent revelations contained i
General Nye's letter, very seriously.[157] Indeed, not only the deceptio
plan's ardent advocates, like Montagu and Masterman, but even som
amongst senior military bureaucrats, who had tended to look askance ;
this bizarre scheme, were now prepared to acclaim its success. Certainly
one of the most senior of this elite group was immensely impressed by th

:ial effect of *Mincemeat*'s main message upon the German High Command.
on receiving a copy of the OKW signal in question, Brigadier Leslie
llis (secretary to the Chiefs of Staff Committee and senior military
stant to the War Cabinet) immediately dispatched the following tele-
m to Churchill (who was conferring with President Roosevelt in
shington at the time): 'Mincemeat swallowed rod, line and sinker by
ht people and from best information they look like acting on it.'[158]
Yet, even amidst his euphoria at the initial German impulse to gobble
ncemeat up, 'Jo' Hollis, displayed his recognized 'gift for picking out the
portant points from diffuse documents'.[159] The distinction he drew in his
ort communication to the Prime Minister between German attitudes and
ions was a critical one. Clearly, the Germans had been impressed by the
arent Allied threat to Greece indicated in Nye's letter to Alexander, but
w long would that impression last? Above all, would it be translated into
ions—especially the deployment of German forces across the Mediterra-
n and Balkan regions in positions that actually facilitated the Allied assault
Sicily? If British deception planners managed, with Major Martin's help,
retard German reinforcements of Sicily' and 'to reduce the scale of air and
val attacks on (the) HUSKY assault forces', as their overall plan for the
editerranean postulated, then *Operation Mincemeat* could be deemed a
cess—and one on the truly strategic plane, at that.[160]

10

Mincemeat Dissected

On 31 May 1943, Guy Liddell returned to work after weeks of lea spent recovering from a bout of jaundice. The head of M counter-espionage section found that the main excitement he had miss was the final stage of *Operation Mincemeat*'s implementation. By all accoun the deception seemed to have been 'an unqualified success', as was 'reflec in both ISOS and MSS' (i.e., in the decrypted radio messages of both Abwehr and the German armed services). Moreover, these intercepted an decoded messages appeared to confirm that the British deception plan h achieved genuinely strategic results, as Liddell noted in his diary: 'it see that a number of troops have in consequence been sent to Greece'.[1]

This British impression that *Mincemeat*'s message was hitting home w not mistaken. The Abwehr, of course, were rather easily impressed a tended to pass on any information coming its way in an indiscrimin manner. This habit did not endear the espionage service to the evaluati branches of the Army, Navy, and Air Force; they found it virtually impo sible to pick out the grains of truth from the clouds of chaff with which t Abwehr tended to enshroud them.[2] Perhaps the senior intelligence anal with most cause to be exasperated by the Abwehr's uncritical mode reporting, by the spring of 1943, was the head of Foreign Armies W (*Fremde Heere West*), Colonel Alexis von Roenne. Although FHW wa branch of the German Army's High Command, it was the prime provider military intelligence appreciations to the operational staff of the OKW (t *Wehrmachtführungsstab*), about the Anglo–American–Canadian bloc.[3] So, FHW and von Roenne fell the task of determining where the Western All would unleash their next offensive, once they completed the conquest North Africa. Faced with this challenge, von Roenne and his colleagu doubtless would have preferred to treat the reports from the Abwehr which had so spectacularly failed to forecast the correct target for *Operati*

Torch—with their usual mixture of disdain and scepticism. However, with the Allies now in possession of the strategic initiative and their other sources of information, such as signals intelligence (SIGINT) and photo-reconnaissance, all drying up due to Allied countermeasures, they could not afford to be so dismissive of their spies' efforts.[4] That attitude may explain, at least partly, why the documentary windfall from the Huelva shore received more of a welcome from the FHW and the OKW's operational staff than they usually afforded to the Abwehr's intelligence product.

Needless to say, the Abwehr itself also had a vested interest in championing the case for the documents they had managed to obtain through Franco's good offices. As Hugh Trevor-Roper notes in his end-of-war report on the German spy service's performance in the global conflict, 'in the Spring of 1943, the Abwehr sought feverishly to guess the next Allied move aright, and in the months immediately preceding *Husky* (July 1943) the insistence from headquarters on the necessity of accuracy assumed an almost hysterical tone'. This panicky call for accurate information from on high had the opposite effect: an avalanche of gossip, hearsay, rumour, and Allied misinformation engulfed the Abwehr, effectively burying the few nuggets of truth that its agents had stumbled upon.[5] Canaris and company must have known that such imprecise intelligence reporting would not rehabilitate the Abwehr's reputation after the *Torch* debacle, nor help it fight off a takeover bid from Schellenberg and the RHSA. With spring turning into summer, the Abwehr desperately needed to come up with reliable information on the Western Allies' next strategic move, in order to placate their critics and see off their competitors. In such do-or-die circumstances, Canaris and his headquarters staff inevitably looked on Major Martin's messages as heaven-sent in more ways than one. Here it seemed, was a veritable bonanza of high-grade intelligence which could not fail to satisfy their customers and confound their detractors. Hence, also, is explained the unseemly haste with which the Abwehr's leadership sought to spread the news of the documentary discovery in Spain.

In fact, even before they had seen a full photostat of the Nye–Alexander letter, Nazi Germany's military espionage chiefs could not resist reporting its major revelations, as revealed in Leissner's 'most secret letter' of 9 May, which von Rohrscheidt had couriered to Berlin on that same day.[6] Barely having had time to digest the contents of that communication, Abwehr I (the espionage branch proper of that organization) sent a signal to the OKW's operations staff and the evaluation branches of the German Army,

Navy, and Air Force at 4.45 p.m. on 9 May, to advise them of the significance of this apparent intelligence coup. Dispatched under the name of Colonel Georg Hansen (who had taken charge of Abwehr I only recently), this message reported the discovery of 'a personal letter' from the 'Chief of the Imperial General Staff [*sic*] of 23.4 to General Alexander', which disclosed Allied plans to launch two amphibious assaults: one code-named *Husky*, 'apparently' aimed at Greece and the other code-named *Brimstone*, 'apparently' aimed at some objective in the Western Mediterranean. The letter also seemed to reveal the cover targets for the two attacks: the Dodecanese for *Husky* and Sicily for *Brimstone*. Finally, Hansen's signal noted that complete copies of the original documents were being sent on to Berlin by KO Madrid. Although the Abwehr I did not pronounce on the authenticity of the Nye–Alexander letter, or the other documents in the British courier's bag, the very fact that they reported the find so promptly, to such interested and influential parties, shows which way they were leaning on this crucial question.[7]

However, there was a danger in announcing the supposedly good news before the full facts were to hand: the professional sceptics of the three armed services' intelligence evaluations branches might condemn this rush to judgement—however implicit—by the Abwehr. Certainly, the third branch of the German Naval War Command (3 *Seekriegsleitung*) reserved its position after receiving the Abwehr's initial briefing on the discovery of the British documents. It advised the naval staff that 'for the time being' no judgement could be passed on the genuineness of the Nye–Alexander letter. The German Navy's intelligence appraisers preferred to await the outcome of the critical investigation being undertaken by the General Staff of the Army (in effect, FHW) on whether the British Army units mentioned in that letter could be employed, realistically, in the allegedly forthcoming attacks.[8] Remarkably, however, FHW produced that crucial assessment of the compatibility of the Allied order of battle (at least as understood by the German Army's staff) with the leaked operational plans at breakneck speed. It also did so in a spirit of almost total credulity, as a post-war British analysis of this appreciation issued by Foreign Armies West on 9 May 1943, noted:

> The Army Intelligence Directorate, Foreign Armies West, did not apparently feel that it was necessary to await inspection of the actual documents, as this Department issued an appreciation of the 'courier trove' (Kurierfund) that same day. Admittedly it was pointed out that it was still too early to state categorically whether the documents were genuine or not, but their

authenticity was considered 'possible' and indeed the tone of the appreciation as a whole was one of almost eager acceptance.

It stated that the existence of enemy plans for a large-scale operation in the
western Mediterranean, which had been accepted for some considerable
time, received fresh confirmation from the 'courier trove'. It was reckoned
that the enemy had three to four battle-strength infantry divisions and one to
two armoured divisions ready in North Africa, 'at any time', and that once
hostilities in Tunisia had ceased a further 10 to 12 Infantry Divisions plus 3 to
4 Infantry Brigades, and 4 to 5 Armoured Divisions plus the same number of
armoured brigades, would be 'fully available'. There were already in North
African ports enough landing craft to transport 4 to 5 'combined divisions' as
a first wave landing force, to be followed by further waves either brought
over from Africa or through the Straits of Gibraltar. The fact that Sicily had
been named as the target for a diversionary attack meant that German
attention must now be focused on Sardinia and Corsica—it seemed
'altogether likely' that the British would choose the at present weakly-
defended island of Sardinia as their first objective.

Where the other (so-called) Operation Husky was concerned, Foreign
Armies West seemed even readier to believe what it was being told.
Although it had last positively identified 5th Division in India, there was
no boggling at the possibility of this division's transfer to the Eastern Mediterranean, probably Egypt, and the fact that two brigades of 56th Division
were known to be in the front line in Tunisia at that very moment did not
worry them either; it was assumed that a reinforced brigade of this division
was being held in Egypt in readiness to land at Calamata. The landing-points
chosen by the British seemed 'favourable', but they were presumed only to
represent points from which bridgeheads would be established later; large-
scale operations in the Peloponnese were not to be expected while the
fighting in Africa was still going on ... [9]

As noted herein, the verdict delivered by FHW, at this time, on the British
courier's main document of interest was an open one: 'on the basis of a short
report of the contents (of the Nye–Alexander letter) it is not possible yet to
decide whether this is a question of deliberate deception or of genuine
information'. Still, the inclination of the normally sceptical evaluators of
FHW to take the key *Mincemeat* document at face value—just as their
Abwehr counterparts had done—was also evident in this appreciation of
9 May.[10] That disposition would be more obvious in their follow-up
appraisal of the deceased British courier's set of documents. Like its predecessor, this appreciation was issued in the name of FHW's extremely capable
and experienced chief, Colonel Alexis Baron von Roenne. Although relatively new to running Foreign Armies West, von Roenne had demonstrated

his critical faculties when analysing captured Red Army documents i
Foreign Armies East. He also possessed 'a brain as clear as glass', in th
estimate of one eminent historian of secret intelligence.[11] How was it the
that one equipped with such a crystalline intellect failed to see throug
Operation Mincemeat?

Von Roenne supplied the solution to this puzzle, himself, in the first tw
paragraphs of the report on the 'Discovery of the English courier' which h
submitted to the operations staff of the OKW on 11 May. Colonel von Roenn
and his own staff had very limited time to examine, absorb, and assess th
photostats of the three British documents—which may have arrived in Berli
by Lufthansa courier as late as the evening of the same day. Still, the FHW
appraisers admitted to no doubts as to the letters' provenance and purport:

I. On the corpse of an English courier which was found on the Spanish
coast, were three letters from senior British officers to high Allied officers
in North Africa namely:-

   a) A letter from the Deputy Chief of the British General Staff (General
   Nye) to the Deputy Commander-in-Chief North Africa (General
   Alexander).

   b) A letter from the Chief of Combined Operations (General [*sic*] Lord
   Mountbatten) to the Admiral commanding the fleet in the Mediterranean (Admiral Cunningham).

   c) A letter from the above (Lord Mountbatten) to the American Commander-in-Chief in North Africa (General Eisenhower).

II. The circumstances of the discovery, together with the form and contents
of the despatches, are absolutely convincing proof of the reliability of the
letters. They give information concerning the decisions reached on the
23rd April, 1943, regarding Anglo–American strategy for the conduct of
the war in the Mediterranean after the conclusion of the Tunisian
campaign.[12]

The statements made by von Roenne in this evaluation reveal the reason
why he was fooled by these British forgeries, in spite of his normal scepticism towards the Abwehr's reports. First of all, he was clearly captivated by
the idea of having access to top-secret correspondence among such 'high
Allied officers'. This intelligence was simply too good not to be true
Montagu's judgement that *Operation Mincemeat*'s letters had to appear to
emanate from the elevated echelons of the Allied command, so as to engage
the enemy's attention, was vindicated completely by the instant respect

hich the Nye–Alexander letter elicited from this top-level German
telligence analyst. Again, the strong impression made upon von Roenne
d company by the circumstances in which the body of the British courier
d been found proved how right Montagu and his colleagues had been to
ke such pains over their deception plan. All the long hours invested by
ritish deception planners, doctors, submariners, and diplomats in preparing
d presenting Major Martin for foreign inspection turned out to be time
ell spent. The tough bureaucratic battle Ewen Montagu had fought to
sure that the main *Mincemeat* message—the letter from General Nye to
eneral Alexander—was persuasive in both substance and style was also
stified by the German intelligence appraisers' absolute acceptance of their
rm and contents' as authentic. Indeed, the overall assessment made by
n Roenne and FHW—that, taken together, the external evidence of
e courier's posthumous arrival on the Spanish coast and the internal evi-
nce contained in the letters he was carrying, offered 'convincing proof' of
eir genuineness—was an unwitting tribute to the coherence of a deception
heme crafted from many separate parts.

The contributions of two other British parties to making the Nye–
lexander letter such a compelling instrument of deception should be
ted also. It will be recalled that, when drafting the final version of his
tter to 'Alex', Archie Nye had declined the suggestion, made by both
evan and Montagu, that there be an explicit link made in its text between
e projected Allied invasion of Greece and the code name *Husky*. Instead,
stinctively appreciating that intelligence analysts tend to value infor-
ation in proportion to the effort they have to make in order to deduce
Nye deliberately left it up to the Germans to work out the connection
tween the projected British assaults at Kalamata and Cape Araxos
d that operational code name. They did not let him down and FHW's
duction in that regard was unequivocal, in its 11 May evaluation of Major
artin's documents: 'the code-name for the landing on the Peloponnesus is
USKY'.[13]

It will be also recalled that the British Chiefs of Staff had prohibited Nye
om making another overt reference in his letter—that to the island of
rdinia as the target for *Operation Brimstone* (which was to be mounted in
ndem with *Husky*, apparently). Of course, this veto had given Montagu
s own opportunity to exploit the intelligence analysts' susceptibility to be
ore persuaded by what they actively infer, rather than passively ingest.

In the letter the deception planners drafted in the name of Lord Lou
Mountbatten and addressed to Admiral Cunningham to 'introduce' Maj
Martin to his new commanding officer, a rather heavy-handed hint ha
been dropped to *Brimstone*'s notional objective, by a punning mention
'sardines'. The pride the officers of FHW felt in penetrating the inscrutab
British sense of humour to decipher this allusion is palpable in their report
11 May to the OKW:

> The operation to be conducted in the Western Mediterranean by General
> Alexander was mentioned, but without naming any objective. A jocular remark
> in the letter refers to Sardinia. The code-name for this operation is BRIM-
> STONE. The proposed cover operation for BRIMSTONE is SICILY.[14]

No matter that the 'jocular' mention of 'sardines' actually was to be foun
in the Mountbatten–Cunningham letter, rather than Nye's missive t
Alexander: FHW had noticed the planted cross-reference between th
two and was all the more inclined to believe the item of informatio
because the British deception planners had made them work it out fo
themselves, and they were predisposed to do so by the fact that they ha
already come up with Sardinia as the most likely target for *Brimstone*, in the
initial appreciation of the 'Kurierfund' on 9 May.[15] Indeed, so thorough
were the analysts of FHW duped by *Operation Mincemeat* that their re
concern was that the outlined attacks might not now occur, because th
British might revise their offensive plans in the light of the dead messenger
compromised papers. However, von Roenne concluded that, as long as th
fact that the deceased courier's key documents had fallen into German han
was 'treated with the greatest secrecy, and knowledge of it confined to
few as possible', the Allies might fire ahead: 'it is, therefore, to be hoped th
the British General Staff will continue with these projected operations an
thereby make possible a resounding defensive success through correspon
ing acceleration of German precautions'.[16] To encourage the British to stic
to their guns, Roenne even proposed initiating a German 'misleading pla
of action' to 'deceive the enemy by painting a picture of growing Ax
concern regarding Sicily, the Dodecanese and Crete'.[17] So, the Allies we
to be encouraged to press ahead with their ostensibly compromised plans
attack by an Axis display of anxiety over the cover targets included in thos
plans. The web of deception was becoming truly tangled in the Mediterra
nean by May 1943.

That this FHW appreciation of Major Martin's main letters convinced
 OKW of the authenticity and importance of these British documents is
ar from two warnings about the apparent Allied threats which Supreme
mmand issued to the main German headquarters in the Mediterranean
atre on 12 May 1943. One of these communications was the signal of that
e which the British intercepted and decrypted two days later. It was
dressed to the German commanders in the south-east (Löhr) and the
th (Kesselring) to inform them of the assaults about to be unleashed in
th the Eastern and Western Mediterranean.[18] The very same day, the
KW issued a more general order, to all German military authorities
olved in the defence of the Mediterranean against further Allied inva-
ns, to unite in resisting them. Identifying the likely Allied objectives in
 Western Mediterranean as Sardinia, Corsica, and Sicily and, in the
stern Mediterranean as the Peloponnese and the Dodecanese, this direct-
 gave absolute priority to the two places most immediately menaced,
ording to the revelations in the letters being couriered by Major Martin:
e (defensive) measures for Sardinia and the Peloponnese (must) take
cedence over all others'.[19]

The second half of this directive (which followed on 13 May 1943) was
ned by Field Marshal Wilhelm Keitel, Chief of the OKW Staff, who
essed that the Führer had personally assigned priority to certain matters,
luding the following:

More detailed information concerning the state of fortifications, armament
and number of troops in the 'most endangered sectors' must be obtained and
submitted to OKW, Ops Branch. These sectors were—(a) the Italian islands
(Sardinia, Sicily, Corsica) and (b) Rhodes and the Peloponnese, especially the
sectors of Araxos and Calamata.[20]

e inclusion of the Dodecanese and Sicily, in the defensive preparations
w thought necessary to meet the threats apparently disclosed by the Nye–
exander and Mountbatten–Cunningham letters, seems to show that
tler was heeding Roenne's counsel to feign concern about the targets of
 Allied cover plans. That the Führer did not really consider those places
 be immediately menaced by large-scale Anglo–American invasion is
ident from a statement he made at a meeting with the head of the German
vy, Grand Admiral Karl Dönitz, on 14 May 1943. Dönitz came to
tler's headquarters—code-named *Wolfsschanze*, in the Forest of Görlitz

several miles outside Rastenburg in Eastern Prussia—to report on his recen
mission to fascist Italy.[21] Hitler had sent his naval chief to Rome to measu
and mobilize the Italian will to fight on, as their homeland came und
direct threat of invasion from Allied forces.[22] Dönitz duly reported h
none-too-positive impressions of the Italians' resolve but judged that Mu
solini himself might be 'determined to carry on to the end'.[23] Althoug
Hitler may have found some consolation in this estimate of his fello
dictator's continuing commitment to the Axis war effort, he was le
impressed with Il Duce's assessment as to where the next Western Allie
blow would fall. The official record of the conference with the Germa
Navy's C.-in-C. reiterated Hitler's emphatic disagreement with Mussoli
on this score:

> The Führer does not agree with the Duce that the most likely invasion point is
> Sicily. Furthermore, he believes that the discovered Anglo-Saxon order
> confirms the assumption that the planned attacks will be directed mainly
> against Sardinia and the Peloponnesus.[24]

In writing to Mussolini, on 19 May 1943, Hitler corrected his inaccura
description of the Nye–Alexander and Mountbatten–Cunningham lette
as an 'Anglo-Saxon order', but did not change his mind about their meanir
and significance: 'it is also clear from documents which have been fou
that they [the British] also intend to invade the Peloponnese and will in fa
do so'.[25] Faced with this alarming prospect, Hitler did not hesitate to tell tl
Italian leader that the Second Italian Army (based in Croatia) was not stror
enough, in equipment, armament, or training, 'to protect the Peloponne
and Greece in general' from invasion. If the British invaders were to l
repelled—and Hitler insisted that must be done 'at all costs'—then Germa
units would have to do the job. Accordingly, he proposed to reinforce the
numbers in South-Eastern Europe by transferring a whole armoured di
ision to Greece.[26] On the same day that he wrote to Mussolini, the Führ
personally informed some of his most senior assistants at a 'Military Situatio
Conference' of the logic behind his decision to shift a complete panz
division to Greece:

> During the last few days, and especially during the night last night, I reflected
> about what would happen if we were to lose the Balkans. There is no question
> that the consequences would be serious . . . This would result in problems for
> our allies, and also in the loss of the Romanian oil fields and the bauxite and

chrome mines...We would also lose the copper. In view of this situation, I consider it necessary to take precautions against a possible attack on the Peloponnesian Peninsula. We are currently bringing in a division, the Luftwaffe field division, but we don't have any panzer unit there.[27]

Hitler then sought the advice of those present—Field Marshal Keitel, General Walter Warlimont (Deputy Chief of the OKW's Operations Staff) and General Walter Buhle (Chief of the Army Staff attached to the Chief of OKW)—as to which particular panzer formation might be available for this important redeployment. His subordinates accepted the Führer's view that such a division could be spared best from Western Europe, since that region was not immediately threatened by enemy action. Again, a panzer division, being transported along the superior west–east railway networks, should reach Greece much sooner (in fifteen days of its departure, according to Hitler's calculation, as long as it was given an additional week to get ready for its transcontinental journey) than one travelling on the inferior north–south rail links in Eastern Europe.[28] Of the reserve armoured divisions available in the west to come to the defence of Greece, Generals Buhle and Warlimont agreed on which unit was the nearest to combat readiness. As Warlimont put it: 'in the cold light of day, the 1st Panzer Division is the only operational one'. Buhle was more inclined to make a virtue of necessity:

It's by far the best. It has 60 Panzer IVs, 12 flame-thrower tanks and a dozen command tanks. A Panther detachment is being trained now. The personnel are available and the first vehicles are said to have arrived. This division has 60 Panzer IVs today.[29]

Hitler agreed that the addition of a detachment of Panther tanks (each weighing 45 tons and equipped with extra-long 75 mm guns) to the chosen formation should mean that the Germans would have 'a first-class panzer division in the Balkans'.[30] So the order went out from the *Wolfsschanze* to the 1st Panzer Division at the military camp of Coëtquidan in Brittany to prepare for redeployment to Greece.[31] This order, given at Hitler's personal behest was material proof that *Operation Mincemeat* was succeeding as a truly strategic deception. The British deception was not only giving the Führer sleepless nights as he fretted over the threat of attack in the Balkans; it was prompting him to alter the strategic disposition of his forces to counter the notional danger of invasion. Moreover, the British were instantly aware of their success in affecting not just the attitudes but also the actions of their main enemy's High Command.

Indeed, not the least benefit the British enjoyed because of their ability—courtesy of the code-breakers of Bletchley Park—to access enemy radio communications was the opportunity it afforded to monitor German reaction to the deceptions being practised against them. That cryptanalytical capacity soon provided solid evidence to the expectant British deception planners that *Operation Mincemeat* was having the desired effect on German troop movements. Thus, on 21 May, Bletchley Park decoded a German military signal, which had been transmitted the previous day, revealing the enemy's intention to transfer the 1st Panzer Division from France to Greece. This message was in the form of a request from C.-in-C. South-East (Army Group E) to C.-in-C. West for a report from 1st Panzer Division on its composition, war establishment, and condition. Army Group E also asked for a breakdown of the panzer division's 'tracked elements', in terms of the type of vehicles, the number of their crews, and the loaded weight of each kind of vehicle, so as to facilitate proper preparation for the transportation of these elements from Salonica southward in Greece.[32] The British also duly intercepted, and decoded after a two-day delay, 1st Panzer's reply of 23 May 1943 to this request. That signal set out the 'order of battle and strength of the tracked elements' within the division. This detailed inventory revealed that 1st Panzer actually had a complement of over eighty tanks, although a few were the older Panzer Mark IIIs and there were no modern Panther tanks in the divisional establishment, as yet. Although there was no explicit mention in these decrypts of the reason for this military movement, it was eminently reasonable for the British to conclude that it was being undertaken in response to their handiwork.[33] Any doubts about the soundness of their deduction were removed entirely by the receipt of yet another signal about the transfer of 1st Panzer on 7 June. This message had been sent by the headquarters of General Löhr (C.-in-C. Southeast) to OKW's operations staff at 10.00 p.m. on 5 June. It reported the arrival of part of the panzer division in the Balkans on board seventy-one trains (many hundreds of trainloads would be required to transport the entire formation), and detailed their onward journey.[34] As a delighted Montagu informed Bevan on 8 June, this 'Ultra' decrypt seemed to prove, beyond all doubt, the practical impact of *Operation Mincemeat*, upon the actions of the German High Command:

MSS 2693/T42 . . . sets out the arrangements for the passage through Greece to Tripolis, in the Peloponnese, of the 1st German Panzer Division (last identified in Brittany). This is a strategic position well suited to resist our invasion of Kalamata and Cape Araxos.[35]

his intercepted itinerary for the elements of 1st Panzer, for their 'march' om Serbia through Macedonia and down into the Peloponnese, did rovide irrefutable evidence of the influence being exerted by *Mincemeat* pon German troop dispositions; for, as Montagu noted in his end-of-war eport on the deception plan, Tripolis was 'ideally at the centre of commu-ications to cover an invasion of the Peloponnese', since it actually had 'a ›ad leading both to Kalamata and Araxos, which were the landing beaches amed' in the Nye–Alexander letter.[36] This strategic destination could have o other purpose than to protect against the precise threat outlined in the 1ain letter carried by the British courier.

Yet, this military redeployment was not the only one made by Hitler nd his Generals under the spell of the British deception planners during 1e early summer of 1943. Thus, Colonel Dudley Clarke noted—when pdating the overall deception plan for the Mediterranean theatre (*Bar-ay*) on 20 May 1943—that 'the main movement of enemy forces' was ›wards the Balkans and southern France, according to recent SIGINT. qually noteworthy was the fact that there had 'so far been no indication 1at more than individual German units' were being moved into Italy or icily. The Commander of 'A' Force drew the obvious conclusion: 'We 1ay therefore assume that the required threats to the BALKANS (from n invasion of Greece) and Southern FRANCE (from an Allied-occu-ied Sardinia) have already been established and we have only to main-1in them to achieve this primary object'.[37] Dudley Clarke doubtless rould have claimed a substantial share of this success, in distracting the nemy from the actual point of Allied attack, because of the various 1ethods—from disseminating disinformation through double agents, 1rough false radio traffic to misleading visual display—employed by is organization to promote the Mediterranean deception plan. How-ver, he also generously conceded, after the event, that *Operation Mince-eat* had provoked 'the keenest interest' amongst 'the very highest levels f the Wehrmacht', persuading them to adopt 'all sorts of military ounter-measures' in order 'to meet the threatened assaults'. Dudley :larke also noted that, among these military precautions, 'seems to have een the immediate move of at least two German Divisions into the 'ELOPONNESE'.[38]

On 19 May, the day before Dudley Clarke issued his upgrade to *Pla*
Barclay, the Joint Intelligence Sub-Committee (JIC)—Britain's central bod
for strategic intelligence evaluation—advised the Chiefs of Staff on 'th
probable enemy appreciation of Allied intentions in the Mediterranean
Their assessment of the enemy's mindset, in the immediate aftermath c
receiving *Mincemeat*'s deceptive message, was similar to 'A' Force's. Whils
concluding that the Axis powers were still in a 'state of confusion an
uncertainty' as a result of 'the unexpectedly rapid overthrow of their force
in Tunisia', they detected some definite areas of Italo-German concern: i
the Central Mediterranean, where they feared an assault on both Sicily an
Sardinia, and in the Eastern Mediterranean, where the Germans wer
'showing considerable concern about both the land and air defences' c
south-western Greece (i.e., the Peloponnese) because of the 'early threat
they expected the Allies to direct against it.[39] Indeed, although the *Luftwaf*
was seriously overstretched, as it sought to do battle on the Russian an
Mediterranean fronts and, simultaneously, defend the skies over German
itself, it had to follow orders to reinforce both the Greek mainland an
Crete with fighter planes in May 1943. Long-range bombers were als
dispatched to Greek bases, including Salonica.[40] Again, these air forc
redeployments were an open book to British cryptanalysts who continuall
provided the 'cold facts' about the *Luftwaffe's* 'dispositions and deficiencies
to their own armed services.[41]

Not only the code-breakers who attacked the ciphers of the Germa
Army, Navy, and Air Force contributed to the British deception planners
growing certainty that *Mincemeat*'s misleading message had hit home. Th
team built up by Dilly Knox to unravel the complexities of the Abweh
Enigma machine, with its distinctive mode of encryption, also pitched i
with the intelligence product gleaned from Nazi spies' communications
Although their great mentor had died a few months previously (on 2
February 1943), his living legatees in the ISK section—Peter Twinn (th
team's new leader); Margaret Rock; Mavis Batey (née Lever) and her hus
band, the mathematician Keith Batey; as well as a new band of assistants—
continued to tackle the Abwehr's cipher with considerable success. In th
run-up to *Operation Husky* they also set about their daily code-breakin
chores with a renewed sense of responsibility. This was because—just a
during the weeks immediately preceding the launching of *Operation Torch*—
the members of the ISK section (along with their Bletchley Park colleague

ho were working on the ciphers of the German Armed Forces) were
ow subject to a 'JUMBO RUSH' alert. This meant that the lives of
llied troops literally depended upon the promptness and proficiency of
1eir code-breaking. In the fraught weeks before *Torch*, some of the
:male workers in ISK had sought to relieve the strain of those tense
.mes by placing a toy elephant on view in the section's premises, as both
 gentle reminder and a timely talisman. When news was broadcast on the
3BC of the successful Allied landings in North Africa, this mini-tusker, as
1avis Batey recalls, 'was patted on the back and returned to his box for
1e next alert which was the invasion of Sicily'. 'JUMBO' did indeed
1ake another public appearance in the weeks leading up to the assault on
1at Italian island, as the ISK section worked assiduously to steal the
Abwehr's secrets from the airwaves.[42]

   The fruits of the code-breakers' labours were analysed with great insight-
ulness by the Radio Intelligence Service (RIS) under Captain Hugh
revor-Roper. The RIS had escaped the restrictive control of MI6's Section
' on 13 May 1943, and was now free to distribute its analyses more widely
vithin Britain's secret intelligence community.[43] This was just in time to
:nd assistance to the deception planners' effort to measure the impact of
Mincemeat on the enemy. In early June, the RIS produced a report on the
Abwehr's communications which the British had intercepted and decoded
luring the previous month, and what they revealed about the German
spionage service's appreciations of Allied intentions. For monitoring the
Abwehr's radio messages not only produced intelligence of interest to Allied
ecurity officers and counter-espionage agents; such surveillance also
rielded material of considerable significance from the operational and
trategic perspectives. So, after reviewing the monthly haul of Abwehr
lecrypts for May, the RIS reported that 'during the last month, the emphasis
►f the strategic reports passed by the Abwehr has again been on the Eastern
Mediterranean, and particularly on Rhodes and Crete, and the Balkan
1ainland'. Of all the decrypts they had read to reach the conclusion that
he Germans were 'most apprehensive of action in the Balkans and the
Aegean', Trevor-Roper and his colleagues deemed one particular item to be
the most significant' and 'of more importance than any other individual
1essage'.[44] They summarized its contents and circulation, thus:

On 17/5/43, the German Abwehr station in Rhodes reported to Athens, as
from the Italian High Command, Aegean, that the Allied attack would be

directed against Cape Araxos and Kalamata...[and] Athens passed the
information on to...Salonika [which] forwarded it to Belgrade and Sofia.
The Italians gave the report without date or details of source, only calling it
reliable but unproved.[45]

Trevor-Roper initially hoped that this report might represent an independent Italian confirmation of the *Mincemeat* deception from a source other
than Major Martin's papers. However, the RIS analysts soon concluded—
after reviewing further Abwehr radio traffic—that 'Rome received the plans
either from Berlin, or direct from Berlin's source, and transmitted them to
the appropriate operational commands, including the High Command,
Aegean, in Rhodes'.[46] In fact, Mussolini was informed, separately, by the
Franco regime of the contents of the British courier's official letters,
through the good offices of the Italian Ambassador to Spain, Marchese
Paolucci.[47] Still, however the strategic gospel according to *Mincemeat* was
being spread throughout the Axis chain of command in the Eastern Mediterranean, the fact that it was doing the rounds there was extremely good
news both to the British deception planners and the Anglo–American
commanders of *Operation Husky*.

   Again, of course, the Allies wanted proof, in the form of definite actions
on the part of their enemy to show that the Axis commands were being
taken in by the British deception. Once more, the ISK team delivered the
goods. As the RIS review for May noted, it was 'not only the actual
intelligence carried by the Abwehr' which exposed their anxieties; additional 'and perhaps more reliable deductions' could be made from 'the
administrative orders and changes' so 'conspicuous recently' in their radio
traffic. These were noticeable in the Mediterranean theatre as a whole, but
particularly so in the Balkan and Aegean regions. In southern Italy and Sicily
plans had been prepared to engage in sabotage and incite rebellion, in case of
an Axis military withdrawal before invading Allied armies. However, 'more
extensive preparations' to wage such irregular warfare were being 'made in
the Greek than in the Italian Peninsula'. ISK had laid bare a number of
concrete steps being taken by the Abwehr to cope with and counter an
Allied invasion into Greece and its Balkan hinterland. For example,
'important sabotage and insurrections experts' like Major Strojil and
Major Seubert were being employed in the region (the former at Salonica,
the latter at Sofia). Another whole 'sabotage organization', *Abwehrtrupp 250*,
had been ordered into the Balkans, too. Again, the head of the Abwehr
himself, Admiral Canaris, as well as the chief of its foreign espionage section

Abwehr I), Colonel Hansen, visited Vienna, Salonica, and Sofia in late May '43, to review such preparations in person. They were also seen to be calling for 'progress reports from all Balkan stations giving an account of the development of their withdrawal plans', including 'the recruiting of Greek and Armenian guerillas, W/T training of "stay-behind" agents, etc.'[48] These and other German pre-emptive measures to wage irregular and covert warfare against an invading Allied force in South-Eastern Europe, provided yet more concrete evidence that *Operation Mincemeat* had passed the really critical test for a strategic deception: it was causing the enemy to redeploy resources away from the actual target of the impending Anglo–American attack and towards a notional, alternative objective.

Of course, there was a third advantage conferred on the British by their ability to decode the radio signals of the German military intelligence service, namely its usefulness for counter-espionage purposes. Being able to read the enemy agents' encrypted messages meant that British counter-spies could keep tabs on the Abwehr's activities and, when necessary, thwart them. In the case of *Operation Mincemeat*, this counter-intelligence advantage conferred on the Allies by ISK enabled the British to monitor the German efforts to verify the authenticity of the documents found in Major Martin's briefcase, and to check up on the genuineness of the officer who had been carrying them.[49] This window into the Abwehr brought welcome corroboration, on 14 May, in the form of a signal from that organization's headquarters to its man in Madrid, that *Mincemeat*'s deceptive message had got through to the central command of the German war effort. This particular signal (sent on 13 May and decoded by the British the following day), revealed the interest being taken by elements of the Third Reich's High Command in the British courier's documents. Yet, the nature of that curiosity was not altogether wholesome, as far as the British were concerned; for it disclosed a desire, on the part of the senior German staff officers, to make absolutely sure they could trust this intelligence windfall. Accordingly, the chief of KO Madrid, Wilhelm Leissner, was informed of the need to make prompt inquiries about some of their pressing concerns:

The evaluating Stellen [offices] attach special importance to a more detailed statement of the circumstances under which the material was found. Particular points of interest are: when the body was washed ashore, when and where the crash is presumed to have taken place, whether a/c [i.e., the aircraft] and further bodies were discovered, and other details. Urgent reply by W/T necessary.[50]

The British also intercepted Leissner's 'urgent reply' of 14 May to th
demand from Abwehr headquarters, and managed to decode it the ve
same day. Once more, the deception planners surely found some cause f
alarm in its contents. First, they would have noted Leissner's assurances
his superiors that he had already pressed the Spaniards, on his own initiativ
for more facts on the case. Then, they should have been concerned to he
that the ever-cooperative Francoist AEM had agreed to send one of the
officers to investigate the whole affair in Huelva. Finally, they must hav
been dismayed to learn, from the same ISK decrypt, that this on-the-sp
investigation had produced results which 'partly' differed 'in detail from th
facts of the case, as first presented by the (Spanish) General Staff' to th
Madrid-based Abwehr.[51] The British, of course, would have loved to lear
in just what ways the Spaniards were now changing their story, if only
gauge how damaging these revisions might be to *Mincemeat*'s credibilit
However, they were frustrated in that regard, because the chief of K
Madrid chose to send his new 'detailed report' on the matter to Berlin l
airmail courier service, informing his superiors that they should arrange
collect it on arrival in the evening of 15 May, at Templehof airport.
Although Bletchley Park did decipher another Abwehr Enigma sign
dealing with the British courier's case, it merely conveyed the dissati
factions of the German Naval War Command's intelligence-evaluation
branch with Leissner's assurance that a further detailed report was bein
forwarded to Berlin. The naval intelligence appraisers were clearly n
amused by the dilatory ways of KO Madrid and demanded 'more detaile
statements as quickly as possible concerning place and circumstances'
Major Martin's landfall.[53] This display of impatience, on the part of th
German Navy's senior intelligence analysts certainly showed a willingne
to take the British messenger and his official letters seriously. On the othe
hand, it also revealed their suspicion that the deceased courier and his pape
might be frauds.

The London Controlling Section were sufficiently disturbed by th
German probe into Major Martin's bona fides to alert their counterpar
in Cairo, on 16 May, as to what was afoot.[54] Dudley Clarke, in reply
admitted that this news had caused 'slight disquiet at first' amongst th
veterans of 'A' Force. However, 'on second thoughts', they were le
concerned at such understandable German attempts to verify the facts
the case in view of the potential strategic significance of the documen
carried by the deceased courier. Time would tell if there were re

grounds for concern. Yet, if Dudley Clarke and company had calmed the London-based planners' nerves on this issue, they proceeded to agitate them on another count. They wondered whether there was any possibility of Major Martin's remains being exhumed, either by due legal process or by body-snatching, 'with a view to more thorough autopsy'. That seemed to 'A' Force to be the 'only serious danger' still standing in the way of *Mincemeat*'s success as a strategic deception.[55] Colonel Bevan promptly responded to Cairo's concern with the assurance that such a potentially damaging development was not considered likely by 'general opinion' in London.[56] However, *Mincemeat*'s sponsors were rattled enough by the prospect of Major Martin's remains being dug up for further investigation to seek medical advice on how injurious that could prove to the credibility of the Operation. It took Ewen Montagu a week to arrange to consult William Bentley Purchase about this matter. However, the Coroner was able to set the London deception planners' minds at rest on this score with a number of weighty medical arguments, namely that the deceased had taken such 'a minimal dose of rat poison containing phosphorus' that only 'a first rate post mortem' could have identified the actual cause of death at that time, let alone months later; that phosphorus was 'not one of the poisons readily traceable after long periods'; and that by late May 1943 even 'a highly skilled medico-criminal-chemist' would be unable 'to determine the cause of death with sufficient certainty to go through the witness box'. A relieved Montagu conveyed this reassurance to Bevan on the next day, 28 May: 'although no one in this world can be certain of anything it does not seem that the fear that the Germans may learn anything from a disinterment and subsequent autopsy is well founded'.[57]

Still, while waiting to see Bentley Purchase, Montagu had taken practical steps, also, to obstruct any effort by enemy agents to rob Major Martin's grave in Huelva. First of all, he encouraged frequent visits to the grave of the deceased Royal Marine by British representatives and sympathizers, so as to maintain a relatively constant watch over the Royal Marine's resting place during daylight hours. One such visitor was Francis Haselden, bearing a wreath of flowers to place on the grave (supposedly from 'Father and Pam')—in accordance with Montagu's instructions.[58] Doubtless, a discreet vigil was kept also over the plot in the cemetery during the hours of darkness. However, the best barrier against any illicit German attempt to steal the courier's corpse would be a solid tombstone. So, on 21 May

Hillgarth received a request from Montagu to arrange for 'a medium-priced tombstone' to be laid over the dead messenger's grave. It was to bear the following inscription:

William Martin
Born 29th March 1907
Died 24th April 1943
Beloved son of John
Glyndwyr Martin
And the late Antonia Martin of
Cardiff, Wales
Dulce Et Decorum Est Pro Patria Mori
R.I.P.[59]

This tombstone of white marble, once laid horizontally over the length of the deceased's coffin and cadaver (which, fortunately was the fashion in the cemetery of *Nuestra Señora de la Soledad*) would prevent any surreptitious removal of his remains, whilst also seeming to be a perfectly normal mark of respect.[60] However, the tombstone's quotation from the Latin poet Horace— 'Sweet and fitting is it to die for one's country'—should also reinforce the deception plan's fiction that the grave contained the body of a genuine warrior, who had perished while doing his duty for his *patria*. The fact that the officer's date of death was specified on the gravestone as 24 April 1943 was also intended to corroborate the schedule of Major Martin's departure from London, on his doomed flight to the environs of Huelva, that *Mincemeat*'s planners were trying to communicate to the Spaniards and Germans. Once the tombstone was laid—in more or less record time—it was photographed, ostensibly for use as a memento for the fallen warrior's nearest and dearest. However, one purpose behind these snapshots, taken from several angles, must have been to produce a visual record of the monument which could be used to detect any future attempt to shift it in order to gain access to the grave's contents.[61] Although all of these formal tributes to the deceased were paid in the name of Major William Martin, RM, and with a view to preserving or promoting the deception against the Franco and Hitler regimes, Montagu and his colleagues firmly believed that they were also showing proper respect to the remains of Glyndwr Michael. Indeed, so earnest was their desire to give the dead Welshman some personal recognition for the great posthumous service he had done for the Anglo–American cause, that they smuggled his real first name of 'Glyndwr' (misspelled as 'Glyndwyr', by accident or design) on to the tombstone—in the guise of his fictional father's middle name.[62]

Having done what they could to frustrate further enemy inquisitiveness about Major Martin's mission, the British could only scan the airwaves, from late May, for the results of the inquiries the German intelligence services had already instigated. 'Ultra' did yield evidence during that time of the German High Command's continuing belief in the misleading offensive designs planted on them by the courier's official letters—as noted above. However, it was not until after the close of the Second World War, that captured German documents revealed the findings of the additional investigation undertaken by the Abwehr in Spain, at the urging of their military intelligence analysts back in Berlin, into the case of the 'drowned' British courier and his bag of documents. The Germans' extra checks did discover some errors of detail in the original Spanish reportage of the episode. Yet if anything, these corrections of detail—such as that the body was found floating in the sea (rather than on the coast) and that it had been brought ashore by local fishermen—seemed even more consistent with the version of Major Martin's death which the British were trying to convey.[63] Moreover, another of these revisions to the official Spanish account of the case to emerge from the AEM's fact-finding mission to Huelva (undertaken by Cavalry Commandant José Caruana Gómez de Barreda) was one which justified all the care Montagu and company had taken over one particular item of the courier's accoutrement.[64] The Abwehr communicated this rectification to the evaluation branches of the German Army, Navy, and Air Force on 22 May 1943:

> In contrast to the first statement of Oberst Lt. Pardo that the corpse carried the brief case clutched in his hand, it appears that the above mentioned brief case was secured to the corpse by a strap round the waist. The attache case was fastened to this strap by a hook. The strap is at present in the possession of the General Staff. The brief case was locked and the key was found, together with other keys, on a key-ring in one of the corpse's trouser pockets.[65]

Again, far from finding the use of a bank messenger's chain to fasten a government briefcase to the person of an official British military courier to be incongruous, the German intelligence analysts appear to have seen it as providing a plausible explanation for the bag's remaining attached to its deceased bearer in the ocean.

Of course, this Abwehr report of 22 May was also the one that relayed the findings of the Spanish post-mortem on the courier's corpse. That examination—conducted on 1 May—had found the remains of Major

Martin to be in a more advanced state of decomposition than would b
compatible with his being alive as recently as 27 April, as seemed to b
established by a supposed 'night-club bill' of that date found on his person
Yet, as we have seen, this apparent anomaly was the result of a mistaken
reading of the date on the document in question by a Francoist official. Still, i
was an error which might have scuppered *Operation Mincemeat* but for the
predisposition of the Spanish pathologists to explain the seeming inconsist
ency away.[66] Abwehr headquarters—and, it appears, their 'customers' in the
Army, Navy, and Air Force—were satisfied with the Spanish doctors' asser
tion that the allegedly accelerated body decay in this instance was due to sur
and sea. The hard-headed German intelligence analysts also apparentl
accepted the Huelvan medical examiners' explanations for the variation in
hairline visible between his person and the photograph on his identity
card.[67] Leissner told a British journalist after the war that there were no furthe
demands for more information about the case of the British courier after he
submitted the findings incorporated in the Abwehr's report of 22 May.[6]
Certainly, the Abwehr's chief, Admiral Canaris, had become a true believe
in Major Martin's bona fides, to judge from a conversation he had with Naz
Germany's Propaganda Minister, Joseph Goebbels, on 25 May 1943. When
Goebbels questioned whether the 'very revealing' letter from 'the Englisl
General Staff to General Alexander' which had come into the Abwehr'
possession, might 'only be a deception', Canaris 'energetically disputed' the
suggestion. Moreover, the Nazi minister paid an unwitting tribute to the
British deception planners' skill in preying upon pre-existing German fears fo
the Allies' deceptive purposes. Goebbels confessed to this diary that the
offensive plans outlined in the Nye–Alexander letter—for diversionary as
saults on Sicily and the Dodecanese to be followed by more substantial attack
against Sardinia and Greece—confirmed German expectations.[69]

Still, for all their chief's faith in the British courier's letters, the Abweh
did not neglect to use another major intelligence asset, apparently at thei
disposal, to check up on the accuracy of the offensive plans which had faller
into their hands. This resource was the seemingly successful network o
reliable and productive spies which they had established in Britain. So, or
7 June 1943, one of their foremost agents operating inside that country
received the following radio message from his controller:

> Try to find out if Greek troops are stationed in the south of England in the
> area of the First Canadian Army, and if so, which. It is of the greatest

importance to discover the next operation. Keep most careful watch for possible attacks against Spain and the Balearics. Wireless results . . . [70]

The recipient of this message was Juan Pujol who, of course, was a British double-agent, code-named *Garbo*. Far from activating a spy capable of exposing *Operation Mincemeat*, the Abwehr was presenting Britain's covert warriors with a golden opportunity to consolidate its credibility in their enemy's eyes. However, those who managed the double-cross system (including *Garbo*'s gifted case-officer, Tomás Harris), knew that such Abwehr assignments had to be handled in a way that supported the current strategic deception scheme, while preserving their precious double-agents' potential to dupe the foe on a future—and perhaps even more momentous—occasion. So, it was resolved to discharge the mission conveyed in the message of 7 June in the following manner. Since, as far as the Germans knew, *Garbo* had established 'an active and well-distributed team' of real spies across Great Britain, it did not seem odd that one of these fictional sub-agents should try to track down Greek units in England. This individual spy reported to find no trace of Greek troops in the vicinity of the First Canadian Army in southern England. However, he also claimed to have found out that a Canadian infantry division had moved north for extensive training. Another recent Abwehr directive had ordered *Garbo* to 'check up on' reports of 'large troop movements in the north of Scotland', which possibly indicated an Allied intention to invade Norway. So, the Catalan double-agent could legitimately allow some of his sub-agents to focus their efforts in that direction. As a result of their notional investigations, *Garbo* assured the Abwehr that there was no immediate danger of an Allied attack in Norway. However, he also reported that there were extensive preparations being made in Scotland for a major military operation. This reportage was definite enough to keep the Germans apprehensive, as far as the menace to Greece and other potential Allied targets in the Mediterranean was concerned, without being specific enough to discredit the double agents when the real *Operation Husky* was launched. Indeed, several weeks after the invasion of Sicily took place, *Garbo*'s British controllers had the effrontery to send a message of complaint, in his name, to their German counterparts. In that apparent *cri de coeur*, agent *Arabel* (to use Juan Pujol's Abwehr code name) denounced his Nazi spymasters for the way they wasted his network's time on wild-goose chases. In effect, *Garbo* was blaming his Abwehr controllers for failing to concentrate his espionage

efforts in uncovering the real target of *Operation Husky*.[71] So, *Garb*
managed to retain his reputation as a reliable secret intelligence sourc
with the Germans, in spite of having done his bit to support the *Barclay*
Mincemeat deception plan covering the invasion of Sicily. This would prov
of immense use and benefit to the Allies when the need arose, a year later, t
'sell' the deception plan for the Normandy invasion to the German intel
ligence services and High Command.

Perhaps it is no wonder, then, that the Nazis' intelligence communit
swallowed *Mincemeat* whole: its deceptive message conformed to their ow
strategic expectations; it was presented to them in a highly convincin
fashion; and, without realizing the fact, they lacked a means of checkin
up on its authenticity which was not controlled by the very opponents wh
had drafted and dispatched that message in the first place. Indeed, it seeme
that only a great error on that enemy's part—in the form of a really seriou
breach of the security around the Allies' plans—could now threaten th
credibility of *Operation Mincemeat*. Yet, incredibly, exactly at that ver
moment (i.e., during the second week of May 1943) when the Nazi
intelligence analysts and warlords were falling for Major Martin's deceptiv
documents, there occurred a spectacular series of breaches in the securit
ring surrounding *Operation Husky*. The first of these happened at a very hig
level of the American government. On 11 May 1943, Colonel Frank Kno
the Secretary of the Navy in the Roosevelt administration, was giving a pres
conference in Washington. Knox was known for plain speaking and, as
newspaper proprietor, he was probably too used to talking to journalists t
be constantly on his guard with them.[72] In any case, whatever prompted h
indiscretion on that occasion, it was a truly breathtaking one. Asked whe
the Allies might be free to send convoys at will through the Mediterranean
Knox sensibly refused to give a precise date but affirmed that that da
would surely come. However, he could not resist adding a comment, whic
The New York Times reported, thus:

> Conceding that Axis possession of Sicilian and Cretan air fields remained a
> peril on the Mediterranean route, Mr. Knox added: 'Possession of Sicily by
> the Allies would obviously be a tremendous asset. So would possession of all
> the northern coast of the Mediterranean.'[73]

Colonel John Bevan, on reading reports of Knox's public statements in th
British press, instantly realized how 'undesirable' they were 'on grounds o
security and cover'. With a few unguarded words, it seemed that Secretar

ɔx had blown the entire *Barclay/Mincemeat* cover plan for *Husky*, whilst
ting the enemy to the real target for the forthcoming Anglo–American
ımer offensive in the Mediterranean theatre of war. With this prior
·lic warning of where the Allies' blow was set to fall, the Germans
ɪld have time to reinforce Sicily's defenders with their own forces on a
·e which might spell disaster for the invaders. Bevan was sufficiently
·raught over the potentially fatal consequences of this blunder to appeal
·he US military authorities to prevent any repetition of such 'specula-
ɪs' and public declarations in the future. All the embarrassed Americans
·ld do was to promise to keep up their efforts 'to inculcate security-
ıdedness among high officials'. Still, the strategic damage already seemed
·have been done.[74] Yet, over the next few weeks, Allied intelligence
·lysts could detect no signs that the Germans had seen through *Operation*
ıcemeat and were concentrating on the danger to Sicily. What appeared
ɪave rescued the Allies' operations—real and notional—from exposure
 time was the very unbelievable nature of Knox's gaffe; it seemed that
·h a blatant indiscretion must have been calculated to deceive! Such was
 conclusion of Propaganda Minister Goebbels, when he learned of the
·sode:

∢nox declares . . . that Sicily will be occupied soon. We show no interest in
ıll these baseless rumours and attempts at a smoke screen.[75]

·eed, it is possible that German staff officers and intelligence appraisers
·y even have regarded Knox's assertion as a ham-fisted attempt to counter
 damage done by the loss of the Allies' 'real' offensive plans in Spain.
·her way, the readiness with which the Germans dismissed Secretary
·ox's revelation about the next objective of the Western Allies in the
·diterranean shows how well-conceived and crafted *Operation Mincemeat*
·l been. The deception plan appeared more plausible to the Germans than
·accidental admission of the true Allied target, by a senior member of the
 Administration.

·Yet, it was not only the civilian politicians whose carelessness imperilled
·sky's security and, therefore, *Mincemeat's* credibility. Some professional
·diers also seemed to be doing their damnedest to compromise secrecy
·l, again, just at the time *Mincemeat's* message was seizing hold of the
·ention of the German High Command. Thus, on 16 May 1943, General
·lson, C.-in-C. Middle East, wrote to General Alan Brooke to inform the
·GS of 'a gross breach of security' committed by the General Staff Officer 1

(GSO1) of the British Airborne Division. The security authorities in C.
had been made aware of this senior paratroop officer's blunder on
morning of 15 May, when Lieutenant Wolff of the Free Czechoslo
forces had handed 'a copy of a signal of the highest secrecy' which had b
confided to the care of the Airborne Division's GSO1. This document w
telegram addressed to 'Force 545', the Eastern Task Force (British Eig
Army under General Montgomery) for the *Husky* invasion. The comm
nication gave away details for the airborne assault, which formed part of
Allied plan of attack against Sicily, as a clearly worried Wilson inform
Brooke:

> The signal in question refers to a date for projected operations, quotes the
> time of moonset and mentions the times for dropping para-troops. It also
> gives the availability of aircraft and gliders for such operations.[76]

Prompt investigation of this security leak revealed some very alarm
facts about the incident. Predictably it had occurred in the famous Sh
heard's hotel. With its officers-only admissions policy for military patro
Shepheard's cultivated an exclusive, club-like atmosphere, conducive
intimacy and indiscretion. This was especially so in its 'Long Bar', wh
the exclusion of female guests, produced an ethos of male clannishn
even more subversive of security consciousness. Indeed, the conventio
wisdom was that nobody belonging to this bibulous band of broth
could keep a military secret for very long.[77] In any case, in whate
part of Shepheard's the unfortunate GSO1 from the Airborne Divisi
had lost the tell-tale signal originally, it did the rounds of the establishm
for a full two days. During that time, between 13 and 15 May, offi
inquiries discovered that it had gone through numerous pairs of han
those of an Egyptian hotel employee, a Swiss hall porter, the Germ
manager of the hotel (who possessed an Uruguayan passport), a Sw
doctor, the latter's Polish secretary and, finally, the ADC (Lieuten.
Wolff) to a Czechoslovak General.[78]

For all his dismay at this turn of events, Dudley Clarke could not h
but regard this incident as a perfect example of 'the virtual impossibility'
preserving military secrets in a cosmopolitan city like Cairo in the mid
of a world war.[79] Still, the Office of Security Intelligence Middle East h
to try and assess the damage done by this lapse in security. Its age
interrogated all the individuals who had come into contact with t
top-secret document. Back in London, MI5 operatives also checked

on the allegiances not only of Lieutenant Wolff but also of his superior, General Gak of the Czechoslovak mission in Cairo. These 'most exhaustive inquiries' (as Dudley Clarke described them) appeared to prove that there had been no transmission of the sensitive information contained in the military signal to enemy spies. Indeed, one of the foreign nationals interviewed in the case offered the opinion that 'the document was probably planted in the hotel with intent to deceive'.[80] However, a fortnight's nervous scanning of the 'Ultra' decrypts and double-agents' traffic, until the end of May 1943, provided even more assurance that Operations *Husky* and *Mincemeat* had not been blown: no signs were detected that the Germans had got their hands on any real intelligence which was enabling them to sort out military fact from military fiction.[81] The close watch kept on enemy signal traffic in later May for any indication that Allied plans, real and covert, had been compromised was due to more than the paratroop officer's mistake; for another significant breakdown in the security for *Operation Husky* had occurred in mid May. This emerged when an Egyptian laundry worker (who could not read English) handed a British soldier a notebook, which he had found inside the pocket of a bush shirt belonging to a British officer. This 'Tommy' lost no time in turning the important-looking notebook over to the military authorities. This was just as well because the item—which had been negligently left in his shirt pocket by an officer belonging to Force 545—could have hopelessly compromised the Allies' operational plans, actual and feigned. The notebook 'contained the full date of a part of the "HUSKY" assault', and also identified 'the troops involved, the times and places of the landings and even the code-names of the beaches!'[82] Once more, however, the SIGINT gathered from German military and espionage radio traffic seemed to prove that *Husky* and *Mincemeat* had survived another monumental security scare. Still, as Dudley Clarke observed, these episodes 'left behind an uncomfortable feeling that more incidents of the kind might be happening, and that such luck as we had had so far might not hold for ever'.[83]

In truth, however, Britain's deception planners had never thought that they could keep the lid on *Operation Husky* right up to its appointed D-Day of 10 July 1943. They were sure that its secrecy would be breached decisively, with a consequent discrediting of its cover plans, not by individual officers' carelessness but by the deliberate order of the Allied commanders. The unavoidable problem, as they saw it, was that there would come a time when the Allies' material preparations to mount the actual operation—the invasion of Sicily—would give that real plan of campaign away. The growing concentration of Allied power on the island of Malta, for example, would be all too obvious to enemy reconnaissance flights and electronic eavesdropping. Axis planes flying from airfields in Sicily, only sixty miles away, could hardly miss the build-up of aircraft, troops, and *matériel* on the island. Equally, enemy signals personnel monitoring Allied radio traffic could not but notice the increased volume of communications from Malta, once the Allied invasion headquarters had been transferred there. Dudley Clarke and his colleagues certainly felt that these necessary measures for the launching of the real attack would be bound to disclose the central Mediterranean focus of the actual Anglo–American offensive: 'as huge new dumps began to cover the open fields of the island, as extra fighters crowded into its airfields, and as one by one new wireless stations came up on the air, we began to feel that the guilty evidence was piling up to an overwhelming degree'.[84] Of course, Sardinia had been included in the *Barclay/Mincemeat* cover plan to try and account for the strength of Allied forces in Eastern Algeria and Tunisia.[85] Moreover, 'A' Force did what it could to represent the surge in Allied military activity in the Central Mediterranean as the prelude to an invasion of that island, rather than Sicily. Thus, Dudley Clarke informed Bevan, on 20 May 1943, that his radio experts had devised a signal plan for *Operation Barclay* which was designed to make 'genuine HUSKY w/t traffic' appear to be 'dummy traffic specially designed to draw attention towards Husky-land' as only, apparently, an object of Allied deception plans.[86]

Such a double bluff might have had a chance of succeeding, if it had not been undermined by other material signs that the Allies really had Sicily firmly in their sights. Thus, at the Port of Sousse, on Tunisia's eastern coast and an obvious springboard for the invasion of Sicily, there was an unmistakable military concentration by mid June 1943: one whole army division with the landing craft necessary to transport it by sea as part of an amphibious invasion force. Not too far back inland, at Kairouan, 'two whole divisions of airborne troops, with their tell-tale gliders and transport planes', stood ready to join in the forthcoming attack.[87] Indeed, the intense Allied interest in Sicily had been flagged to the enemy even earlier—in March and April 1943—by the high numbers of Combined Operations Pilotage Parties (COPPS) caught in the act, reconnoitring potential invasion beaches on the island. The COPPS fared better in their forays into Sicily during late May to arly June, but these necessary preparations for the invasion, in Dudley Clarke's assessment, 'seemed to deal an almost fatal blow' to the Allies' eception plans. This was because the capture of the COPPS by the Italian orces in Sicily, should have immediately betrayed to the Axis the Anglo– mericans' real tactical and strategic designs on that island.[88]

However, it was another Allied preliminary to *Operation Husky* that most efinitely gave their game away to the enemy, according to the commander f 'A' Force. This was the capture of the small island of Pantellaria (which y more or less midway between Tunisia and Sicily) on 11 June 1943. This peration was deemed necessary because General Eisenhower had come ound to the view that Pantellaria's garrison should not be left in place with s radar installations, airfields, and underground aircraft hangars to monitor, nd maybe even molest, the *Husky* invasion convoys.[89] Britain's Mediter- nean deception planners thoroughly disapproved of this move because it nly made strategic sense if the Allies were bent on subsequently invading icily. From the day Pantellaria was taken, 'the enemy knew for certain that, some time and in some fashion, we were going to land in Sicily', Dudley Clarke lamented.[90] Yet, it was not only the seizure of Pantellaria but the way was reduced which appeared, literally, to 'blow' the *Barclay/Mincemeat* eception plans. To avoid any significant losses of the troops and *matériel* orely needed for *Husky* itself, 'Ike' decided 'to make the capture of antellaria a sort of laboratory to determine the effect of concentrated eavy bombing on a defended coastline'. Three-and-a half thousand Allied lanes dropped nearly 5,000 tons of bombs on the island during the first days f June. As a British amphibious invasion force bore down on Pantellaria, n the morning of 11 June, a further mass aerial bombardment was carried ut by one hundred American 'Flying Fortresses'. Actually, this campaign of turation bombing inflicted much more serious psychological distress than hysical damage on the defenders and their defences. The garrison surren- ered en masse, without inflicting a single casualty on the attackers.[91]

Yet, it seemed that the Pantellaria campaign would cost the Allies dear in rms of strategic surprise lost for the impending invasion of Sicily. The istained heavy bombing of Pantellaria combined with the progressive, pre- vasion softening-up of Sicily by Allied aerial attack to reveal, even more early, the Anglo–American intention to invade that island in the not too stant future. Although, during May, Allied forces had divided their aerial ombardments more or less equally between Sardinia and Sicily, the Air orce Commanders could not afford that luxury in June, as the countdown

to *Husky*'s D-Day began in earnest. They simply did not have enoug
aircraft to spare for 'cover' bombing. So, not only did the Allied air forc
bomb Pantellaria into submission in early June but, after it fell, they turne
the weight of their attacks against Sicily. In the remainder of June, the
launched a further twenty large-scale raids on *Husky*'s target, as opposed to
solitary attack on Sardinia. In Dudley Clarke's judgement, 'this wide di
crepancy in the distribution of the air attacks had its effect in aggravating th
damage to the "BARCLAY" Plan which had been caused by the prelim
inary seizure of PANTELLARIA'.[92]

Given all these solid signs of an Allied will to invade Sicily before to
long, it is no wonder that 'A' Force resolved to concentrate its efforts fro
mid June onwards, more on 'concealing the date of the "HUSKY" assau
rather than its destination'. Dudley Clarke and his colleagues console
themselves with the realization that the Axis High Command would n
have time to make significant changes to their existing troop deployment
during the few weeks remaining before *Husky* was launched on 10 July. S
'A' Force's priority now became to persuade the enemy that the invasion c
Sicily had been postponed until the end of July 1943.[93] This seemed a
appropriately modest ambition, given that Allied preparations for th
amphibious assault were now in plain sight. Certainly, such a limited go
seemed all that was attainable, in view of the altered strategic appreciation c
enemy dispositions produced by the JIC for the COS, on 16 June 1943:

> Present and projected Axis reinforcements indicate that the main object of
> their anxiety is now the Central and Western, rather than the Eastern
> Mediterranean. These fears will probably have increased since the capture
> of Pantellaria and adjacent islands, which, combined with our strategic
> bombing, has focussed attention on Sicily and Sardinia.[94]

Indeed, 'Ultra' revealed to the British the movement of the *Hermann Görir*
Panzer Division—admittedly previously earmarked for the defence c
Sicily—into that island, from 20 June to early July.[95] SIGINT also told c
an increase in the number of *Luftwaffe* fighter planes based in Sicily t
around 180, after the fall of Pantellaria.[96] So, it appeared that *Minceme*
lost its capacity to misinform and mislead the German High Command
once and for all, by later June 1943.

That development would have come as no surprise even to the deceptio
plan's most ardent advocates; they had always recognized that Major Marti
could have a finite afterlife. Ewen Montagu, for one, had wondere

ether it was really worthwhile including mention of the fictional Royal
arine's death in the official casualty lists. These lists were published in *The*
mes and that newspaper was regularly available in Lisbon, where local
wehr agents were amongst its most loyal readers. They might be relied
on to forward any additional evidence, appearing in England's newspaper
record, of the British courier's death (and previous existence) to Berlin.
t, Montagu also reckoned that the Germans should have made their basic
deployments in response to the *Mincemeat* deception by the time they
re notified of the press listing of the death (which would have to be
blished in early June, to conform to the normal five-week interval
tween a military fatality and its publication).[97] Montagu would have
derstood, also, that the visible progress of Allied preparations for the
cilian invasion, by early to mid June, might also render any further efforts
bolster Major Martin's credibility futile.

However, after some deliberation, he decided to go ahead and have
ajor Martin's name inscribed on the 'Roll of Honour'. After all, it did
t appear that such action would do any harm and it might even do some
od, in certain circumstances. For instance, if the D-Day for the invasion
d to be postponed, then even a long shot at extending the deceptive life of
e *Mincemeat* plan would have been more than justified.[98] Accordingly, the
ue of *The Times* for 4 June 1943 contained a statement from the Board of
dmiralty that amongst the casualties which had been sustained by the
yal Navy 'in meeting the general hazards of war' was 'T/Capt
/Major) William Martin' of the Royal Marines. This issue of the news-
per proved to be a very suitable one in which to draw attention to the
ficial notification of Major Martin's demise. For even the least observant
the Abwehr's agents in Portugal could not miss the 'Roll of Honour',
xtaposed as it was with *The Times'* obituary of the British actor, Leslie
oward.[99] The star of stage and screen had perished, along with all the other
ssengers, on board an unarmed civilian clipper, flying between Lisbon and
ymouth, which was shot down by German aircraft. The inclusion of
ajor Martin's name in that particular 'Roll of Honour' also proved
nducive to the deception planners' purpose for another reason. Two of
e other fatalities listed among the fallen naval officers were Rear Admiral
J. Mack and Captain Sir T. L. Beevor. Since it had already been officially
nounced that these two senior officers had lost their lives in an air
cident over the sea, enemy agents would naturally assume that Major
artin had died along with these individuals in the same incident, when

they saw his name listed with theirs. This was a fortuitous confirmation the Royal Marine's life and death, which rewarded Montagu for his ext effort in arranging for the inclusion of the courier's *nom de guerre* in t official casualty lists.[100]

Yet, the immediate result of this conscientious action was yet mo trouble for Montagu from the service bureaucrats. For Major Martin 'death notice' could attract attention at home, as well as abroad. Montag had tried to forestall any administrative inquisitiveness by arranging for t Deputy Adjutant General of the Royal Marines to pre-empt it. That offic warned off the relevant quarters within the Corps from taking any action ' respect of the notification of the death of Major William Martin' who h been 'detached on special service'. However, other naval record-keepe surfaced, in the months immediately succeeding the inclusion of Willia Martin's name in the published casualty list, with queries of their ow about the shadowy major. A special section of the Medical Director Ger eral's Department asked why they had not been informed officially of t Royal Marine officer's death. They also wanted to know how he had die so that they could register the correct details in their records. The Nav Wills Department, too, complained about not being notified of the office death and inquired, in addition, as to whether the deceased had made ar testamentary provisions. In Montagu's judgement these unwelcome inqui ies came nearest, of all the security scares they experienced concernir *Mincemeat*'s secrecy, to blowing the Operation. As before, Montagu acte promptly, in invoking the authority of the DNI to stifle the curiosity these naval bureaucrats about the circumstances of Major Martin's death.[1] His incentive for doing so, even in the late summer of 1943, was that— against all the odds and to their own amazement—the British deceptic planners were still managing to maintain a notional threat of invasion again Greece, weeks after *Husky*'s D-Day.[102]

Although Montagu later claimed that these further travails with Britain wartime bureaucracy caused him to regret including Major Martin's nan in the 'Roll of Honour', that action also turned out to be of definit assistance in reviving the *Mincemeat* plan's deceptive influence at a critic moment.[103] For, by the time the NID officer was fending off these admir istrative probes, the dead British messenger had secured a remarkable ext lease on his afterlife, from late June until at least late July 1943. Th extended his power to deceive the enemy well beyond the British deceptic planners' own expectations. In that context, the publication by *The Times* name in the casualty list provided convenient corroboration of his life death. However, it was not, in itself, the real source of Major Martin's rrection as an active agent of deception, against the German High nmand. His revived influence over the enemy's warlords arose from ther operation mounted by the British to substantiate the *Barclay/Mince-* threat to Greece. That action was code-named *Animals* and it was ertaken by the British Special Operations Executive, with some peration from the Greek Resistance. Such irregular warfare attacks in port of deception plans were very rare, because John Bevan did not ur them. The head of LCS did not believe SOE—with its myriad tacts with multiple underground groups in Nazi-occupied Europe—to ecure enough against penetration by enemy agents, for the top-secret k of strategic deception.[104]

However, the British Chiefs of Staff had overruled Bevan in the spring of 3, when they were considering the appropriate subversive policies to pt to further the Allies' planned offensive in the Mediterranean. Faced h the prospect of having to launch the largest amphibious assault in ory to date (i.e. *Operation Husky*), the Chiefs were quite prepared to st SOE's assistance in supporting the cover plan for the invasion of ly. So, in their 20 March directive to the SOE for 1943, they stipulated : Britain's irregular warriors should promote 'guerrilla activities and btage in Greece, Crete and the Dodecanese' in order 'to create a ersion to our offensive operations in the Central Mediterranean'.[105] e group charged with responsibility for the execution of this subversive tegy was the British Military Mission to Greece. This body was entirely creation of two individuals, in the studied opinion of the Cabinet ice's historian of SOE. They were Lieutenant Colonel (later Brigadier) C. Myers and Captain (later Major, then Colonel) C. M. Woodhouse— e of the strongest teams which S.O.E. ever sent out'. 'Eddie' Myers, the d of the Mission, was an engineer by training, and a sapper officer in the ular Army by profession. His second-in-command, 'Monty' Wood-se, was a brilliant young classical scholar from Oxford who spoke dern Greek.[106] Myers duly received advance warning in March 1943 to a for a possible severance of communications within Greece 'in con-ction with an attack elsewhere in the MEDITERRANEAN'.[107] Of rse, a campaign of sabotage against Axis lines of communication in ece, spearheaded by members of the SOE mission might offset, some degree at least, the negative impact the massing of the Allies'

conventional forces for the invasion of Sicily was having on their decep
plan for the Mediterranean. So, at the end of May 1943, Myers receive
order from SOE's Middle Eastern headquarters in Cairo, directing hir
launch *Operation Animals* to sever 'all main communications through
Greece at the end of June and for the first week in July'.[108] 'Mo
Woodhouse later defined the purpose of this campaign, thus:

> Our operations were to precede the landings in SICILY by a few weeks wit
> the object of diverting the enemy's attention towards Greece. The essence c
> the plan was to create the utmost havoc in the enemy's communication
> throughout the length and breadth of Greece, in order to deceive the enem
> into thinking that this was the preliminary to the invasion of Greece.[109]

On the military front, Myers' mission seemed perfectly placed to exec
such a countrywide disruption of roads, railways, and telephone lines. Si
parachuting into Greece at the end of September 1942, Woodhouse anc
had managed to place SOE liaison teams with local guerrilla bands throu
out the mountainous region of northern Greece. This organizatic
achievement arose, at least in part, from the propaganda value in a dee
remarkable daring, namely their success in leading a Greek guerrilla ass
against superior numbers on the Gorgopotamos railway viaduct on
night of 25–6 November 1942. Explosive charges laid by an SOE dem
tion party during the attack seriously damaged the viaduct, in the first m
act of sabotage committed in the name of a national resistance movemen
Nazi-occupied Europe during the Second World War. Given the pres
which the British Military Mission had already won in Greece and the
that their personnel were posted to guerrilla bands right across the moun
fastnesses of northern Greece, they seemed well capable of launchin
coordinated campaign of sabotage.[110] Moreover, when the order ca
through from Cairo, at the end of May 1943, Myers already had his p
ready for action, thanks to the advance notice received in March. All
needed to do was 'to send out some half a dozen signals by wireless',
teams of British saboteurs, more-or-less assisted by Greek resistance fight
would 'cut all communications on 21st June' and 'keep them cut by furt
demolitions until 14th July'.[111]

Politically, however, the ground was not so well prepared. The Gr
Resistance was far from being united, riven as it was by Left–Right id
logical splits and divisions between Republicans and Royalists. Of the cc
tending factions comprising occupied Greece's clandestine polity, it was

Communist Party (KKE), already hardened by years of persecution during the Metaxas dictatorship, which adapted best to the demands of underground subsistence and struggle against the Axis. Indeed, they created the strongest indigenous political and military organizations in wartime Greece: the National Liberation Front (EAM) and the National Popular Liberation Army (ELAS), both of which attracted many 'progressive' political and military figures into their ranks, along with thousands of peasant partisans.[112] Given their strength on the ground, it was clear to Woodhouse, for example, that Operation *Animals* 'could not be done without the cooperation of ELAS'.[113] However, that formation was not easily persuaded to take to the field to suit the strategic priorities of the Western Allies in the summer of 1943. Indeed, EAM–ELAS had a different agenda to pursue at that stage of the Second World War—one that derived from its own analysis of the trend of the global conflict. It seemed to the KKE strategists, who were the ones really calling the shots for ELAS, that the Axis might be on the verge of total defeat in south-eastern Europe. The recent reverses the fascist powers had suffered at Stalingrad and in Tunisia suggested that the KKE should concentrate on positioning itself for the internal political battle to replace a doomed occupation regime inside Greece, lest the British-backed Greek royal government-in-exile slip into the vacuum created by the apparently imminent Axis collapse in the Balkans. Of course, the very desire of the British Military Mission to Greece to instigate a widespread campaign of sabotage against Axis communications in Greece, during late June to early July 1943, suggested that an Allied invasion was on the way—a development which would clinch the rout of Axis forces in their country, precisely according to the KKE's analyses.[114] Myers and Woodhouse were secretly advised by SOE's Cairo headquarters that *Operation Animals* would be only a deceptive sideshow. However, they could not admit as much to the leaders of EAM–ELAS (or, for that matter, to any other guerrilla chiefs). So, they were unable to disabuse the Communists of their false hopes of an imminent Axis debacle in Greece.[115]

As a result, while Myers was striving during the spring and early summer of 1943 to forge the Greek resistance bands into a united force to fight the common foreign enemy, EAM–ELAS was actually turning its guns against fellow Greeks, as it sought to eliminate domestic rivals in its drive for national political supremacy. Alarmed at the outbreak of open civil war within the Greek resistance, Brigadier Myers attempted to cajole and coerce EAM–ELAS into cooperation with its ideological rivals in all-party talks sponsored by the British Military Mission.[116] Myers and Woodhouse had agreed on the wisest course to adopt towards such discussions, which were held in the first week of June: 'the best thing to do was to let everyone talk their heads off and see what would emerge'. The tactic did not work, however, as Woodhouse ruefully recorded:

> They talked continuously . . . They talked with us and without us and at us and over us and through us and sometimes they all sat and scowled in silence simultaneously.[117]

The sticking point in these and subsequent exchanges with EAM–ELAS was their demand to centralize the Greek national liberation struggle under a joint headquarters 'to control all guerrilla activity', a body they obviously intended to run.[118] Although the British Military Mission were very reluctant to yield to communist dictation, the matter was taken out of their hands. With the deadline of 21 June 1943 for the initiation of *Operation Animals* fast approaching, the imperatives of the cover plan overrode official British distaste for EAM's naked grab for power. On 18 June 1943, and under orders from British military headquarters in Cairo, Myers effectively assented to the ascendancy of EAM–ELAS over the Greek resistance, since he knew that 'any further delay might be fatal to ANIMALS'.[119]

However, whatever its political cost—and, as it turned out, the June deal represented no more than a temporary halt in Greece's eventual descent into civil war—*Operation Animals* proved to be a rip-roaring military success. It opened with one of the most spectacular acts of sabotage in wartime Europe, when a six-man team of British saboteurs, under the command of Captain Geoffrey Gordon-Creed, brought down the key railway viaduct at Asopos in Eastern Roumeli. They pulled off this *coup de force* on 21 June 1943, right under the noses of German sentries (one of whom they silently killed) and the roaming glare of enemy searchlights. In order to gain access to the bridge and set their explosives in place on its structure, the British attackers had had to scale down a supposedly impassable gorge, over jagged cliffs and through torrential waterfalls. Myers, himself, regarded this feat as the greatest example of 'endurance, of sheer "guts" and determination' he had ever encountered.[120] Indeed, the ELAS Command had refused to join in the attack on the Asopos viaduct, deeming it to be an impossible mission.[121] However, elsewhere in Eastern Greece, ELAS fighters joined in SOE-led attacks on Axis lines of communication, as did the more pro-Western guerrillas of Western Greece. The material damage these inflicted

as substantial: 44 major severances of road and railway lines and hundreds
'cuts to telephone wires. The military effects of these acts of sabotage were
'even greater import. Thus, the destruction of the Asopos railway viaduct
at the only railway line connecting Greece with the outside world' and
so 'bottled up a German Armoured Division (1st Panzer)' in the Pelopon-
se for three months, until a replacement bridge could be built, because
oving such a massive unit by road was not a practical possibility in the
gion.[122] However, as Woodhouse noted in his later assessment of this
ave of sabotage attacks, it was their psychological impact on the enemy
igh Command which was most critical:

> The task of getting reinforcements in time from Greece to Sicily became
> impossible, not only because the communications had broken down but
> because the scale of guerilla activity in Greece convinced the enemy until too
> late, as it was intended to do, that the Allied landings would take place in
> Greece.[123]

deed, as *Operation Mincemeat*'s principal protagonist lay silent in his grave
Spain, his Greek chorus was making such a song and dance at the other
ad of the Mediterranean, as to reawaken all the German High Command's
ars about that region's security. Not even the proliferating signs, during
te June to early July, of the Anglo–American intent to invade Sicily, could
ake the renewed German conviction that Greece was also in imminent
anger. The strategic implications of the Asopos attack immediately wor-
ed the Germans, as is clear from the urgent commission (in a radio message
ecrypted by Bletchley Park) Abwehr headquarters sent to its post in Athens
e morning after that daring act of sabotage. Germany's military spies in
reece were ordered to conduct 'a speedy reconnaissance' of the 'compos-
on, strength and armament of guerilla bands in Greece' and, also, 'any
scoverable plans of guerilla leaders suggesting [a] conjunction with pos-
ole Allied landings'.[124] The Joint Intelligence Sub-Committee also
etected something of a shift back towards Greece in the hierarchy of
erman concerns, soon after the opening of *Operation Animals*. While
ey advised the British Chiefs of Staff on 23 June that the Nazis still
onsidered Sicily to be 'the most likely first objective', they also were fearful
f an Allied invasion of Greece.[125] By the 7 July, the JIC found the trend of
erman anxiety towards the targets mentioned in the *Mincemeat* corres-
ondence to be even more pronounced. Sicily was still reckoned to be 'the
bjective for Allied attack in the very near future', but assaults on Sardinia

and Western Greece, 'either simultaneously with or immediately after, the attack on Sicily' were also feared.[126] A few days earlier, British Military Intelligence had produced an even more damning verdict on how *Operations Barclay, Mincemeat,* and *Animals* combined to distort the German High Command's strategic judgement by the end of June 1943:

> German interest is at present almost exclusively devoted to the <u>Mediterranean</u>. Fear of a <u>major attack in the Balkans</u> is the uppermost thought in the German mind, with emphasis on Western <u>Greece</u> but also, to a lesser degree, on the <u>Salonika</u> area. Expectation of a prior attack on the <u>Italian islands,</u> in particular on <u>Sicily</u>, is high with the possibility also of attacks on <u>Corsica</u> and the <u>Italian mainland</u>.[127]

The intercepted enemy signals which led the JIC and British Military Intelligence to reach such conclusions included the following decoded messages: an appreciation sent by the German C.-in-C. (East) to the C.-in-C. (South) reporting that 'the British are preparing a landing on the west coast of Greece' decrypts of the German C.-in-C.'s 'day reports' which 'showed him believing the concentrations of guerrillas in western Greece gave some support to rumours that the Allies intended to land there'; and a request from the Italian Supreme Command that 'the dispatch of German troops already earmarked for the defence of Cephallonia be expedited' in view of the 'increased possibility' of 'an Allied landing attempt on the west coast of Greece'.[128]

Of course, if the mutually reinforcing Allied deception plans were really to have a strategic impact on the enemy High Command during the crucial days leading up to *Husky*'s D-Day, then that influence should be reflected in German actions as well as their attitudes. Sure enough, SOE Middle East received intelligence reports indicating the transfer of at least one German 'commando' division from Serbia to Greece as a result of 'the demolition carried out' there 'in the latter part of June'.[129] The JIC, for its part reported on 14 July 1943 (in an analysis of the military situation in the Balkans which Churchill sent to Roosevelt in August) that there had been 'considerable increase in the Axis garrison of the mainland of Greece' during the immediately preceding weeks. The JIC, however, did concede that 'guerrilla action alone' could not account for 'the four additional German divisions' sent to Greece, during that period.[130] Yet, of course, *Operation Animals* had never been designed to work in isolation. Its purpose—clearly one that was fulfilled—was to reinforce and revitalize the spurious threat outlined in the correspondence carried by *Mincemeat*'s dead messenger.

After the Third Reich had surrendered in 1945, the British discovered a
ocument amongst the captured OKW records which confirmed their
e-*Husky* analysis of German strategic fixations. This item was a German
preme Command assessment of Allied offensive intentions in the
editerranean. It was issued under the name of Hitler's right-hand
an, Field Marshal Wilhelm Keitel, on 9 July 1943, to brief senior
erman commanders and their staff about the Anglo–American threat,
a what turned out to be the very eve of *Operation Husky*. This OKW
sessment exposed the depth of misjudgements concerning the military
ents about to unfold in the Mediterranean and also the success of British
ceptions in clouding their strategic vision. With Axis reconnaissance
anes already having spotted some of the convoys making up the Allied
vasion fleet bound for Sicily, it is no surprise that Keitel should identify
e seizure of that island as 'probably' the Anglo–Americans' first objective.[131]
owever, clearly influenced by the *Brimstone* component of *Operation
incemeat*, he claimed that Sardinia was just as imminently menaced, with
orsica not far behind. Yet, the full extent to which the British deception
anners had come to hold Keitel and the OKW in their thrall was only
vealed when the Field Marshal proceeded to define the primary danger
at he saw looming in the Mediterranean in mid summer 1943. Accepting
ot only Dudley Clarke's long-term inflation of the Allied order of battle,
at also the more recent creation of Twelfth Army Group, Keitel was clearly
rsuaded that 'the enemy forces concentrated in French N. Africa after
e capture of Tunisia were so powerful' that they surpassed 'what would
required for a large-scale landing in SICILY and SARDINIA'. So, he
sumed—now, clearly under *Mincemeat*'s sway—that 'a part of these forces'
d been 'transferred to the Eastern Mediterranean to be prepared for the
nding in Greece'.

Such a venture, he contended, would also make more strategic sense for
e Allies—once Sicily was in the bag—than an invasion of peninsular Italy:

In view of the efficient and undamaged communications system on the
Italian mainland, the enemy must reckon there with rapid and powerful
countermeasures by the German and Italian forces. On the Greek mainland
supplies are entirely dependent on one railway—1300 kilometres in length,
menaced by partisans and of very small capacity. The Greeks and Serbs will
support the enemy into whose lap the Peloponnese and also Crete and the
Dodecanese will fall without a fight, like a ripe plum, if he once succeeds in
reaching the SALONICA-ATHENS railway.

The political effect on HUNGARY and RUMANIA and the possibility of being able to make an effective attack on the Rumanian oilfields from N. GREECE also argue in favour of a landing in GREECE, in which case the EPIRUS may perhaps appear to be in even greater danger than the Peloponnese.[132]

Keitel's expression of the Nazis' paranoia about the Balkans proves how astute the British had been to prey upon Hitler's insecurity there. The Führer and his military advisers were easily distracted by Balkan bogeymen as the greatest armada in history sailed through rough seas to carefully selected landing sites in south-eastern Sicily. While all minds in the Anglo–American Command were focused as one on getting the troops safely ashore in Sicily, the minds of the German commanders were largely elsewhere, and so were most of their fighting men.

Epilogue

t 10.00 p.m. on the night of 8 July 1943, a submarine rose through the
surface of the Mediterranean Sea off the southern coast of Sicily. HMS
…aph, as ever under the capable command of Lieutenant N. L. A. Jewell,
…s undertaking yet another clandestine mission on behalf of the Allied war
…ort. In fact, the British submarine had already taken up an offensive patrol
…ion for *Operation Husky* in the Gulf of Gela on D-Day minus 3 (7 July).
…ell and some of his crew had spent the daylight hours of 8 July in close-up
…onnaissance of one of the designated landing sites through the periscope
…heir submerged craft. The object of their scrutiny was 'Blue Beach', one
…he landing sites for the American 'CENT Force', near the Sicilian fishing
…n of Scoglitti. Jewell dutifully informed 'CENT Force's' Commander,
…ar Admiral Alan G. Kirk, US Navy, by coded radio message, of the details
…he Italian defences at sea (such as minefields) and on land (such as barbed-
…e entanglements and gun emplacements) which he had detected during
…offshore surveillance. However, it was only when night fell that *Seraph*
…gan executing one part of its main mission for the amphibious invasion.
…r appointed role was to act as a 'Beacon Submarine', ensuring the
…curate location of the transports off the invasion beaches', in both the
…erican and British sectors. One way to mark these crucial rendezvous
…nts for the invasion convoys was to lay type FH–830 sonic buoys, which
…t out ASDIC signals, on which the incoming ships could home in.
…However, as Jewell and his sailors set about laying the sonic buoy, the
…pper's concentration on the task in hand was interrupted suddenly, as one
…his look outs gave the following alarm: 'E-boat on port quarter, sir.' When
…ell turned to look in that direction he saw that the enemy vessel had come
…actically alongside' his own boat, without either craft noticing the other in
…e surrounding fog until then. Having got over his surprise, the captain of
…e speedy and well-armed German motor torpedo boat challenged the

unidentified submarine by flashing his navigation lights. Doubtless, he h
refrained from shooting on sight because he reckoned that a submarine lyi
that far inshore must be an Axis boat. Correctly giving priority to his missi
to guide in the invading forces, Jewell grabbed the chance to avoid a fig
On his urgent orders, *Seraph* crash-dived, virtually onto the sea bed of t
shallow coastal waters. Literally scraping the bottom, the British boat slipp
away before the enemy could make up their minds what to do—since
submarine belonging to any navy which was challenged in so abrupt
manner would be likely to take evasive action. Returning to the scene h
an hour later, Jewell found that the E-boat had gone and, this time arou
he was able to lay the sonic buoy on the appointed spot.[1]

Still, Jewell's navigational services for *Operation Husky* were far from ov
once he had lowered the type FH-830 buoy onto the bottom of the sea. F
with fifteen British convoys sailing from points as far separated as the Cly
and Port Said, and an additional seven American convoys from No
African ports also making for Sicily's coastline, the Allied Naval Comma
knew they would need every assistance to reach the correct 'release po
tions' from which their flotillas of landing craft could run in to th
designated invasion beaches. So, three of the Royal Navy's S-class subm
ines (*Safari* and *Shakespeare*, along with *Seraph*) and four of its U-cl
submarines (*Unrivalled*, *Unison*, *Unseen*, and *Unruffled*) were assigned to
as surface markers for the American Western and British Eastern Ta
Forces, respectively. These 'Beacon Submarines' provided the incomi
invasion convoys with a 'final check' on the accuracy of their courses a
generally ensured that they attained the correct release positions.[2] Inde
General George Patton, the Commander of the US Seventh Army bei
transported by the Western Task Force, had informed Lieutenant Jew
in person—and in typically brusque fashion—that the British submarin
must hold their marking positions during the hours of darkness precedi
H-Hour for *Operation Husky*'s amphibious assault. As thousands of shi
converged on the selected landing grounds on Sicily's southern and easte
coasts, the Beacon Submarines would play a vital role in pointing the ma
individual attacking forces at their allocated beaches for the final run-in.[3]

Patton's imperious order to stay put, until the US Navy hove into vie
turned out to be a dangerous commission, however, for Jewell and his me
For, just as the distant throb of incoming ships' engines became audible
board HMS *Seraph*, late in the night of 9 July 1943, their own boat w
illuminated by searchlights from the Sicilian coast. Alerted by their radar

he approach of the invaders' ships, the Italians were seeking to pinpoint their
position. Since *Seraph* was the only immediately visible target on the sea's
surface the defenders' searchlight beams began to play on the vulnerable craft.
Normally, the submariners' response to such unwelcome attention, while
caught on the surface, would be to seek the safety of their natural element
and slip beneath the waves. Yet, mindful of his orders to keep his boat on the
surface as a visible beacon for the Allied invasion shipping, Jewell knew that
discretion could not be the better part of valour on this occasion.[4] Despite the
risk of being hit by the enemy's coastal batteries, he stuck to his post and *Seraph*
rendered invaluable navigational service to that part of *Husky*'s invasion fleet
steaming into the Gulf of Gela. This was because two separate invading forces,
code-named 'CENT' and 'DIME', respectively, 'were somewhat cramped for
sea room' and 'it was deemed essential that these forces be accurately fixed and
mutual interferences avoided'.[5] Thus, Admiral Kirk commanding 'CENT'
Force from on board the USS *Ancon* reported sighting *Seraph*'s beacon, and the
enemy searchlights playing around the submarine, at 11.16 p.m. on 9 July. The
American destroyer, USS *Cowie*, which was the escort vessel assigned 'to effect
rendezvous' with *Seraph* 'during the approach phase of the operation', also had
no difficulty picking up its beacon. The *Cowie* managed to establish direct
contact with Jewell's boat at 11.18 p.m. on that eve-of-invasion night.
Another US destroyer, the *Tillman*, detected HMS *Seraph* on its radar screen
at 11.33 p.m., and proceeded to exchange blinker signals with her.[6] Even with
Seraph's invaluable navigational assistance, Admiral Kirk had difficulty in
keeping CENT Force's ships clear not only of DIME Force but also the
convoy carrying the 1st Canadian Division to its Eastern Task Force landing
grounds. Accordingly, he fell behind schedule in assembling his transports in
'approach disposition' and had to postpone the initial landings on the beaches
on either side of Scoglitti by an hour, until 3.45 a.m. on 10 July.[7] Still, the
American sailors appreciated how vital *Seraph*'s guidance had been in such
congested waters and the risks her crew had run to help them. They made their
gratitude clear to the embarrassed officers and men of HMS *Seraph* before the
British submarine was given leave to retire to Malta. As the first US destroyer,
with long lines of landing craft trailing in its wake, rounded the *Seraph* in the
early hours of 10 July, her crew saluted, with loud cheers, the bravery displayed
by Jewell and his men, in holding their exposed position. Not long afterwards,
Jewell was hailed by a 'four-ringed captain' from a landing craft. He turned out
to be Admiral Kirk's Chief of Staff, whom the 'CENT Force' commander had
sent to thank Lieutenant Jewell 'personally in his name for a great job of work'.[8]

Despite the heroics of the 'Beacon Submarines', many of the landing craft ran into trouble, due to heavy surf, uncharted sandbanks, and inexperienced crews.[9] Still, crucially, almost everywhere, the resistance the invaders encountered was much less than they expected and its intensity was generally less than they feared. To the naval commander of the Eastern Task Force, Admiral Sir Bertram Ramsay, the Sicilian coastline, as dawn broke on D-Day, looked 'sleepy and peaceful', with 'surprisingly poor' opposition being offered to the amphibious assault in that sector of *Operation Husky*.[10] Only in one of the Americans' three invasion areas—the beaches opposite the plain of Gela— did an Allied force, the 1st US Infantry Division, come under serious counter-attack on 10 and 11 July. Even there, although its frontline units were outnumbered and heavily outgunned by elements of the German *Hermann Göring* Division and the Italian *Livorno* Division, the 'Big Red One' beat back the Axis forces' attempt to break through to the landing beaches, with help from pockets of American paratroopers, naval gunfire, and the timely arrival of small numbers of Sherman tanks.[11] It was an opportunity to hurl the invaders back into the sea that never came again for Sicily's Axis defenders. By 12 July, the build-up of Allied power on the island was already assuming massive proportions, with 80,000 men, 7,000 vehicles, 300 tanks, and 900 heavy guns ashore.[12] The continuous flow of Allied men and *matériel* was substantial enough even to shake the conviction of many amongst the German top-level staff and intelligence evaluation officers that the Sicilian incursion was but the forerunner of an even greater Allied thrust into the Balkans. Thus, on 12 July, the OKW informed subordinate commanders that there was 'little possibility of additional landings in the Greek area before the end of the Sicilian operation' because the Anglo–Americans seemed to have employed all their available forces in the latter attack.[13]

However, it was apparently solid evidence, in the form of battlefield intelligence gathered by the Germans during the early weeks of conflict in Sicily, which pushed the analysts of Foreign Armies West to a similar conclusion. The first of these items of information which suggested that the Allies had definitely changed the plan of attack outlined in the Nye–Alexander letter was the discovery that the British 5th Division was fighting in Sicily. Of course, in General Nye's letter to General Alexander, that unit had been identified as the main force going to land 'on the beach south of CAPE ARAXOS' in the Peloponnese. The location of this particular British Army formation in Egypt, at the time the *Mincemeat* documents were being

ommunicated to the enemy, made it seem a likely candidate for this assault
n German-occupied Greece. However, in fact, the 5th Division had sailed
om Port Said on board a 'Fast Assault' convoy on 6 July 1943, arriving in
me to land on beaches at Cassibile, as part of the amphibious assault
ounted by *Husky*'s Eastern Task Force on D-Day. The 5th Division's
esence in Sicily undoubtedly contradicted the notion that the Anglo–
mericans were about to launch a large-scale attack on Greece, to coincide
ore or less with their Sicilian venture. Equally at odds with the vision of
ture Anglo–American strategy contained in Major Martin's official cor-
spondence was another German battlefield discovery in Sicily. This find
as an official military document specifying the code name for the Allied
vasion of Sicily as '*Operation Husky*'. FHW had to admit, in a report of
5 July, that in the documents found on the body of the British courier, the
ode name *Husky* had 'stood for the British operation planned against
Greece (Kalamata and Araxos)'. However, FHW did not conclude
om this switch of operational code name that they had been wrong to
ndorse Major Martin's papers as genuine articles. Indeed, openly confess-
ng errors of judgement was rare in the cut-throat world inhabited by Nazi
ermany's rival intelligence services, which fiercely competed among
hemselves for recognition and resources. Instead, FHW maintained that
he Allies must have changed their minds, and decided to abandon their
arlier plan for 'a simultaneous two-pronged operation in the Western and
astern Mediterranean in favour of the operation in Sicily'. FHW could
nly speculate as to the cause of the alleged alteration in the Anglo–
mericans' offensive design: they imagined that it might have been due
o a lack of British confidence in the Americans' ability to conduct the
Western Mediterranean attack all on their own. Whatever the reason for
he change of plan and code name, it seemed clear that the assault on Greece
ad been 'given up' for the moment, and that the invasion of Sicily was now
he main operation', although a thrust into the Balkans might come later.[14]

Yet, for all the material and documentary evidence now to hand reveal-
ng the degree of Allied commitment to their Sicilian expedition, one
erman grand strategist was far from convinced that that meant the imme-
iate danger to the Balkans had passed. Adolf Hitler's profound anxiety
bout the vulnerability of the German position in that area was now
xacerbated by his growing doubts about the Italians' military stamina.
ny precipitate Italian withdrawal from the war could have disastrous
onsequences in south-eastern Europe, where they provided most of the

occupying forces. Given these preoccupations, a Führer Directive issued on
26 July (the day after the latest FHW assessment) revived the threatening
strategic scenario within the Mediterranean theatre which Keitel had
delineated in his appreciation of 9 July:

> *Directive No. 48*
> *Command and defence measures in the South-east*
> I. *The enemy's measures in the Eastern Mediterranean*, in conjunction with the
> attack on Sicily, indicate that he will shortly begin landing operations against
> our strong line in the Aegean, Peloponnese-Crete-Rhodes, and against the
> west coast of Greece with offshore Ionian islands.
>
> Should the operations of the enemy extend from Sicily to the mainland of
> Southern Italy, we must also reckon with an assault on the east coast of the
> Adriatic, north of the straits of Otranto.
>
> The enemy's conduct of operations is also based on the bandit movement,
> which is increasingly organized by him in the interior of the South-east
> area.[15]

So, the Allied threat to Greece continued to dominate Hitler's strategic
appreciation of the Mediterranean theatre of war over two weeks after the
invasion of Sicily—and for much beyond that time, too, as future SIGINT
would reveal to the Anglo–American planning and deception staff.
Yet, there are commentators who deny that Hitler's fixation with the
Balkans in general and Greece, in particular, had anything to do with the
influence of Britain's deception planners. Prominent amongst those who
doubt *Operation Mincemeat*'s effectiveness as a deception plan is the late
General Walter Warlimont, deputy chief of the OKW operations staff. His
basic contention was that Hitler's anxieties about South-Eastern Europe
predated the British attempt—primarily via Major Martin's fabricated
documents—to pose a mock menace to that region. He advanced as
proof for this argument Hitler's own statement to Admiral Dönitz, on
14 May 1943, about the British courier's papers: 'the discovery of the
British orders [referring to the papers found on 'Martin'] strengthens the
conviction that Sardinia and Peloponnese will be the main targets' (Warlimont's English translation of Hitler's original statement in German).
Hitler's carefully chosen words do seem to imply that the *Kurierfund* in
Spain merely served to substantiate 'what he himself had predicted for many
months as the Allies' next move'. So, according to Warlimont, the intention of *Mincemeat*'s planners to divert German grand strategic forebodings in
the Mediterranean theatre towards Greece was frustrated 'by the sheer

ony of history that Hitler was already convinced of what the deception
as supposed to suggest'.[16]

However, Warlimont's negative verdict on *Operation Mincemeat* is based
n a misunderstanding of the nature of British strategic deception efforts
uring the Second World War. The deception planners had come to
alize, over the course of that conflict, that it was impossible to cultivate
fear in the mind of the enemy which had not already taken root there,
ontaneously. Thanks to the Trojan work of the Bletchley Park code-
eakers, British deception planners were able to peer into the enemy's
oubled psyche and identify those preoccupations ripe for exploitation for
cceptive purposes. Therefore, there was nothing ironical or coincidental
oout *Operation Mincemeat*'s targeting of Hitler's obsession with south-
stern Europe. It was a *ruse de guerre* precisely designed to work by
ompounding the Führer's pre-existing fears and fancies. Another former
ember of the OKW's staff showed a much better understanding of the
npact *Operation Mincemeat* had on the minds of the German High Com-
and, when he came to reflect on the matter in the post-war period. In
)43, Dr Percy Ernst Schramm, a historian of considerable reputation, had
een placed in charge of compiling the official diary of the *Wehrmachtführ-
ngsstab*.[17] In a study on German operations in south-eastern Europe
cluded in the later published version of the OKW's operations staff war
ary which he edited, Schramm conceded that the German Supreme
ommand had been concerned about an Allied move into the Balkans,
nce the autumn of 1942. This worry naturally increased, after the defeat of
e Axis forces in Tunisia freed up large forces to make mischief for the
scist powers elsewhere in the Mediterranean theatre. Still, as he also
bserved, *Operation Mincemeat*'s deceptive documents—news of which
ached Berlin on the virtual eve of the Axis capitulation in Tunisia—
ave the Allied threat to south-eastern Europe 'a new appearance'. The
rect result of Major Martin's revelations, and the antics of his Greek
iorus, was the strengthening of German forces and defences, not only in
e Peloponnese but also in the rest of Greece 'where now as well the
icreasingly disruptive activity of the [guerrilla] bands made itself felt'.[18]

Of course, the fact that Hitler already had to be on the path to self-
eception before the British could compound and complete his progress
owards strategic delusion in the Mediterranean theatre makes it impossible
) quantify the effect of *Operation Mincemeat* upon German military decision-
aking with absolute precision. It will never be possible to determine

exactly how much of the indisputable increase in German forces stationed
the Balkans, between March and *Husky*'s D-Day of 10 July 1943, may k
attributed to the influence of Allied deception efforts. That increase w
substantial, with the number of German divisions in South-Eastern Europ
as a whole, expanding from eight to eighteen during that period, and th
share of this total assigned to Greece going up from one division to eigh
divisions.[19] This sizeable troop transfer arose from an inextricable mix
German miscalculation, British misinformation, and Greek mayhem. How
ever, it is not just the numerical imbalance between the German forc
allocated to Greece and Sicily, respectively—with only two German div
sions present on the Italian island when it was invaded—which proves th
success of *Barclay/Mincemeat* in affecting German deployments in the Med
terranean in the run-up to the launching of *Operation Husky*. After all, th
primary brief given to Britain's deception planners by the Anglo–America
High Command in the Spring of 1943, in relation to *Husky,* had been '
retard the reinforcement of Sicily by German Troops', via simultaneou
threats to Corsica and Sardinia in the Western, and to Greece, in the Easter
Mediterranean.[20] The aim of this deception plan was to disperse the Germar
across the northern coastline of the Mediterranean, a purpose which Allie
force headquarters in that theatre of war judged to have been achieved whe
they reported on the influence of strategic cover and deception plans on re
operations there during 1943:

> The deception plan in force before the landing on SICILY not only caused
> the enemy to dissipate his forces in countries which we had no intention of
> attacking, but also to misplace his forces defending the real objective, with
> the result that the landing was practically unopposed.[21]

Actually, Allied diversionary threats may have had less to do with the initi
location of the 15th Panzer Grenadier Division in Western Sicily than th
Allied Force Headquarters staff assumed, since the German C.-in-C
'South', Kesselring, had reasons of his own for placing the unit there.
However, the role of *Operation Mincemeat*, in particular, in detaining Germa
forces or diverting their reinforcements elsewhere, cannot be gainsaid. Foi
as the author of the official British history on the campaign in Sicily and Ital
in 1943–4, Brigadier C. J. C. Molony notes, 'the margin between success an
failure was narrow' for *Operation Husky*. Certainly, the Anglo–American
eventually would commit half a million soldiers sailors, and airmen to th
fight to drive a little over 60,000 German troops from Sicily. Howeve

ing the most critical stage of the amphibious assault, when the invaders
had 'one foot in the sea and one on the shore', they were very vulnerable
ny concentrated counter-attack by the island's defenders—as the Ameri-
s' experience at Gela demonstrated. During that delicate phase of the
ck, as Molony again comments, 'the Allies had simply not had the means
providing sufficient reserves to overcome anything greater than a slight
-back'.[23] In a contest of such fine margins, the fact that the 1st Panzer
vision was kicking its heels in Greece rather than lending critical mass to
ily's protectors was sufficient alone to justify all the effort expended in
veloping and executing the *Mincemeat* deception plan. Moreover, the
cess of *Mincemeat* in preventing a lethal concentration of enemy firepower
Italy not only during *Husky*'s initial assault phase, but also during the
sequent campaign on the island, was not lost on Britain's chief deception
nners. When the time came to prepare a cover plan for the invasion of
rmandy in 1944, they would focus a major part of their deceptive efforts
the post-D-Day phase of *Operation Overlord*.

Still, it has to be acknowledged that the conduct of the campaign in
ily itself, like the one on the Italian mainland after it, left a lot to be
sired. Poor strategic vision, operational lethargy, and intense rivalries—
th national and personal—amongst the Allied commanders resulted in
bulk of the enemy forces escaping to fight another day.[24] Yet, in spite of
excessively methodical nature of the Allied way of making war in Sicily
Italy, the Anglo–American campaign there did achieve some notable
ns, especially on the grand strategical plane and, particularly, as a result of
eration Husky. For a start, the invasion of Sicily led to the overthrow of
Fascist regime in Italy and Mussolini's fall from political power on 25
y, when he was repudiated by both the majority of his fellow senior
scists and the King of Italy, Victor Emmanuel III. That political trans-
mation inside Italy also led to a complete volte-face in the international
na and the break-up of the Axis alliance with Nazi Germany. Although
government which succeeded Mussolini's dictatorship, under the lead-
hip of Marshal Badoglio, professed loyalty to the Axis war effort, it
retly negotiated an armistice with the Allies and deserted Hitler's Ger-
ny in early September 1943.[25]

The military consequences of *Operation Husky* were no less far-reaching.
13 July 1943, in one of the most pivotal decisions of the entire Second
orld War in Europe, Hitler suspended his massive tank offensive in the
rsk salient on the Eastern Front. Not only the ferocity of the Red Army's

resistance during the previous eight days of battle, but, also, the impact
the Sicilian landings upon Hitler's strategic calculations account for t
uncharacteristic readiness to go on to the defensive.[26] Haunted by the fe
of a Western Allied invasion into the Balkans—so recently reawakened
Major Martin's revelations—the Führer was inclined to see *Operation Hu.*
as a prelude to a further Anglo–American adventure in south-eastern E
ope (as his later 'Directive' of 26 July would testify). So, he wanted to
able to transfer sizeable formations, such as the II SS Panzer Corps, from
Russian Front to fortify Fascist Italy, as a defensive barrier for the Balka
where he saw looming the most immediate danger to Nazi Germany.[27] T
massive Soviet counter-offensive launched north and south of the Ku
salient in mid July would upset, if not entirely wreck, Hitler's plans for
orderly redeployment of Wehrmacht units to the Central Mediterrane
However, Hitler eventually found out that there was a more lasting, a
more injurious, legacy from his strategic response to the converging crises
Kursk and *Husky* in July 1943. Having once surrendered the offensi
initiative to the Soviets under those twin pressures, he found that he v
never able to regain it.[28] The Western Allies' summer offensive in 1943 h
attained—with a little help from their deception specialists—their ma
strategic goal of reducing German military pressure on the Soviets.

   The British were not privy to the conference of 13 July 1943 in t
'Wolf's Lair', where Hitler announced his decision to go on to the defensi
at Kursk, nor did they learn, at the time, his rationale for doing
However, they could not fail to notice, as SIGINT continued to flow
to their Commands from Bletchley Park, that the Führer remained fearful
an Allied attack against the Balkans, long after the start of the Sicili
campaign.[29] This allowed them, in Dudley Clarke's words, 'to go on cryi
"wolf" over the BALKANS in a long succession of plans which continu
until the Allied bridgehead had been firmly established in NORMANDY
year later'.[30] Moreover that bridgehead was strongly established by then n
least because the Allies (as already noted above) had learned an invaluab
lesson from implementing the *Barclay/Mincemeat* plan for *Husky*. This w
that the enemy could be induced to go on believing in the threat to
notional target, even after an actual objective had been really attacked. T
insight permitted the formulation of a deception plan for *Operation Overl*
whose primary purpose was to persuade the German High Command th
the Normandy landings were a 'diversionary manoeuvre', designed to dra
away German reserves. When that goal was accomplished, according to t

deception planners' version of events, the main invasion force would then strike in the Pas de Calais area, where Hitler—as was known courtesy of the Ultra' secret—expected the major blow to fall. The British double agent Garbo played a key part, with his misleading messages to the Germans, in keeping the German Fifteenth Army on guard east of the river Seine against an attack that would never come, while the Allies steadily built up an irresistible power in Normandy.[31]

Therefore, *Operation Mincemeat* produced results of real use and benefit to the anti-fascist Grand Alliance: it helped to ensure the success of the Allied invasion of Sicily and thereby to destroy Mussolini's regime and the Axis alliance; it helped weaken Hitler's resolve and, thereby, to blunt the Wehrmacht's offensive spirit on the Russian Front; and it showed how the German High Command might be deceived on an even grander scale when the time came to invade France. Given the thousands of lives which *Mincemeat* saved amongst *Husky*'s invading troops and the millions of people whose liberation from Nazi oppression it advanced, it is no wonder that many of those involved in its development and execution received formal recognition for these services from their grateful superiors. Thus, although the Americans had been frustrated in their earlier desire to give Lieutenant Jewell an US decoration, Generals Eisenhower and Clark seized the opportunity presented by the submariner's 'extraordinary fidelity and exceptionally meritorious conduct in the performance of outstanding service to the Government of the United States as commanding officer of a British submarine during the assault on the Island of Sicily'. That citation was for the award to Lieutenant N. L. A. Jewell of the US Legion of Merit. Not to be outdone, the British authorities also gave Jewell a DSC for his gallant conduct of 'operation patrols' in the Mediterranean.[32]

Mincemeat's prime mover and principal proponent were also recognized for their exceptional contributions to this covert operation—and it was the head of LCS who made sure that they were not forgotten. With characteristic generosity, Colonel John Bevan wrote several letters to his fellow service bureaucrats to propose that Charles Cholmondeley and Ewen Montagu receive appropriate honorific reward. One of his letters, written on 21 August 1943, made the following points:

> From the evidence at present available it would seem that Operation MINCEMEAT proved a considerable success and influenced German dispositions in the Mediterranean prior to HUSKY. I have already personally

congratulated Lt. Cdr. Montagu and Flt. Lieut. C. Cholmondeley on the success for which they were primarily and almost entirely responsible.

. . . I am writing this line to suggest that you might possibly consider recommending these two officers for some decoration as a reward for their ingenuity and extremely hard work in connection with this operation. I believe that Cholmondeley was originally responsible for the idea of MINCEMEAT, and though he was very active in arranging certain details of its execution it was, however, largely due to Lt. Cdr. Montagu's tireless energy in organising the operation that it achieved such results. If it is felt that some recognition should be made for these services, I would suggest that both officers should receive a similar decoration, since each seems to have played equally vital parts in the plot.[33]

Bevan's advocacy ensured that both Cholmondeley and Montagu were awarded the military OBE for their work in championing *Operation Mincemeat*.[34] Moreover, if the 'backroom boys' were remembered, so were the fighters in the field. Every single member of the SOE team which sabotaged the Asopos railway viaduct was decorated for his part in that audacious attack. Thus, not only the two trained Commando officers and the two Royal Engineers who had undertaken the operation were honoured but so were two of the escaped prisoners of war who swelled the ranks of the British Military Mission to Greece and had joined in the act of sabotage: Lance-Corporal Charlie Mutch, a New Zealander, and Sergeant Michael Khouri, a Palestinian Arab (who had already been decorated for bravery in the earlier Gorgopotamos attack).[35]

There was one prominent participant in *Operation Mincemeat*, however, who received no medal or even a mention in dispatches. Of course, Glyndwr Michael's involvement in the deception scheme was not a matter of his own volition and his service to the cause was entirely posthumous. Still, the Commonwealth War Graves Commission did add an inscription in 1998 to the tombstone on the Royal Marine's grave in Huelva's Catholic Cemetery, to the effect that Glyndwr Michael had 'served as Major William Martin, RM'.[36] Now, under his own name, at last, this Welshman's unique contribution to *Operation Mincemeat* may be recognized properly. Without his passive cooperation, British deception planners could not have inflicted a body blow on Hitler's war effort in the Mediterranean, let alone helped turn the 'Hinge of Fate' so decisively against the Nazis.

Appendix

The Real Identity of the Corpse that Duped the Nazis

here are some authors who claim that the team implementing *Operation Mincemeat* made a dramatic alteration to their deception plan, at a very late stage in their work. These writers contend that, as the date for the Operation's launch drew near, the deception planners—or their superiors—decided that Glyndwr Michael's mortal remains were not suitable, after all, to play the part of the courier in the subterfuge. Allegedly, they came to appreciate that the deceased Welsh labourer had not been physically fit enough to pass as a Royal Marine officer and, also, to realize that the fact that he had not died by drowning would be exposed in any post-mortem. The sceptics' candidate for the role of *Mincemeat's* messenger is one of the sailors who died when HMS *Dasher*, an American-built escort (aircraft) carrier was destroyed in an accidental explosion and fire on 27 March 1943, while in the Firth of Clyde.[1] Quite how one of the unfortunate victims of this disaster could fill Major Martin's boots at such short notice is not really explained, given that it had taken a couple of months to equip and outfit Glyndwr Micheal for the job. Certainly, obtaining the requisite identity card, with a credible photographic likeness of its bearer, would have been a very tall order within the few weeks that elapsed between the sinking of HMS *Dasher* and the sailing of HMS *Seraph*.

The assertion that the Welshman was deemed unfit, ultimately, to play the key posthumous part in *Operation Mincemeat* raises other questions, too. Why, for example, should Ewen Montagu identify *Mincemeat's* corpse-courier as Glyndwr Michael in the official record of the Operation which he submitted to his superiors on 27 April 1943, only a few weeks after the homeless labourer was allegedly replaced in that role by a deceased member of HMS *Dasher's* crew?[2] Again, why would Montagu repeat that

identification in his post-war account of this deception plan for the offic
records of Naval Intelligence Division?[3] The best the doubters can do
explain away this documentary confirmation of *Mincemeat*'s messenger
Glyndwr Michael is to allege some sort of government cover-up—su
posedly to conceal the official expropriation of the body of one of tl
Dasher disaster's victims for use in the deception scheme. The Briti
authorities' supposed reluctance to acknowledge that they stole the bo
in question is compounded by their allegedly having done so in the face
a request from the deceased's grieving widow that he be returned to tl
family's place of residence for burial.[4]

However, this contention that the British government has suppress
Major Martin's true identity to avoid admitting that they expropriated tl
individual's body is not supported by the facts of the case. As alrea
explained, Montagu and Cholmondeley had stipulated that only the bo
of a man with 'no friends and relatives to claim him' could be used in tl
deception.[5] Indeed, according to the draft summary which Montagu pr
pared in July 1945, for inclusion in the secret internal history of MI
Bentley Purchase was specifically 'asked to collect and retain a suitab
unclaimed body' to serve as the Operation's dead messenger.[6] What ma
Glyndwr Michael so eminently eligible to play the part was his soc
isolation, in general, and his estrangement from his family, in particul
Abandoning him for a less marginalized member of society would ha
meant dealing with the kinds of awkward questions from the decease
nearest and dearest that they were determined to dodge for securi
reasons. Moreover, given the apparent improprieties involved in getti
hold of Glyndwr Michael's body for *Operation Mincemeat*, how would the
authorities save face by concealing another such acquisition beneath tl
first one?

Of course, in defining the characteristics of a suitable corpse-courie
Montagu and company had specified other prerequisites, in addition to h
being a loner. These further stipulations were that the body had to belong
someone 'who could pass as a Staff Officer' and also 'who had died fro
reasonably undetectable causes'.[7] It is Glyndwr Michael's alleged failure
match this military and medical profile that would have made it necessary,
is asserted by some authors, to replace his body late in the day with that of
real active-service type who had actually died by drowning. Yet, this is
mistaken conclusion drawn from false assumptions. For a start, the assertic
that the Welshman's gaunt physique contradicted his notional status as a sta

ficer ignores the fact that such military professionals came in all shapes and
es. The contrast between General Bernard Law Montgomery's slight
me and the massive figure of General Henry Maitland ('Jumbo') Wilson
veals the wide range of physical specimens to be found within the
mmand and staff echelons of the British Army during the Second
orld War. A scrawny physique was not incompatible with being a man-
-arms, especially a desk-bound one. Since staff officers did not have to be
the peak of physical fitness to pass muster, then neither would *Mincemeat*'s
urier, as Montagu fully understood.[8] That is why Glyndwr Michael's
mewhat emaciated appearance did not disqualify him from playing a
votal part in the deception plan.

However, the objection that Glyndwr Michael was medically unfit for
s designated role in *Mincemeat* might seem more serious, especially as it has
en endorsed by one of the people centrally involved in the execution of
e Operation, namely, the Commanding Officer of HMS *Seraph*. The
yal Navy's own newspaper, *Navy News*, invited Captain Bill Jewell in late
96, to comment upon the discovery made by Roger Morgan, among
cently released government records, of the name and cause of death of
incemeat's courier.[9] Although he had not been given any personal details at
e time about the individual whose body he had transported to Huelvan
aters in late April 1943, Jewell expressed real doubts about the official
cord's revelations:

I don't believe the claims about the body's identity—he says the man they
chose killed himself with poison, but no one with any sense would use a body
in which poison could be found . . . It had to look like he had drowned.[10]

et, as already explained, Glyndwr Michael's real cause of death did not
squalify him from serving as *Mincemeat*'s moribund messenger—at least
cording to the best medical advice available when the Welshman's corpse
as selected for the role, at the end of January 1943. Moreover, the medical
xpert responsible for that choice had not changed his mind on its aptness,
ven after the remains had been consigned to a grave in Spain. The
oroner, Dr William Bentley Purchase, made this point clear to Ewen
lontagu at a meeting which they had on 27 May 1943. The reason for their
ncounter was the concern raised by one of Britain's deception planners that
e corpse-courier—whose body had been interred in Huelva earlier that
onth—still might be exhumed 'with a view to a more thorough aut-
psy'.[11] Montagu had turned to Bentley Purchase for medical advice on this

issue, because Sir. Bernard Spilsbury had been temporarily incapacitated
a recent stroke.[12] Of course, in seeking the Coroner's medical couns
Montagu was hardly getting second best: Bentley Purchase, himself, wa
distinguished lecturer and author in the field of forensic medicine.[13] One
his future publications on the subject would be an edition of the standa
textbook, *Aids to Forensic Medicine and Toxicology*.[14] Drawing on his ov
very considerable expertise, Bentley Purchase was able to assure the Briti
deception planners that there was no real prospect of their *ruse de gue*
being exposed by any further examination of the dead-and-buried courie
remains. Montagu reported the coroner's reasoning to Colonel Bevan,
28 May 1943:

> MINCEMEAT took a minimal dose of a rat poison containing phosphorus.
> This dose was not sufficient to kill him outright and its only effect was so to
> impair the functioniong of the liver that he died a little time afterwards. The
> amount of phosphorus that he took was almost certainly so small that it
> would have taken a first rate post mortem, even at that stage, to trace the
> cause of death.
>
> Apart from the smallness of the dose the next point is that phosphorus is
> not one of the poisons readily traceable after long periods, such as arsenic,
> which invades the roots of the hair, etc., or strychnine. In addition, any
> investigator would have the difficulty that there is normally a certain amount
> of phosphorus in the human body . . .
>
> Mr. Bentley Purchase's view is that any attempt to find the cause of death
> at this stage would not be a question for a pathologist but rather one for a
> highly skilled medico-criminal-chemist who would have to weigh all the
> chemical compositions of every organ before he could come to any conclu-
> sion, and even then Mr. Bentley Purchase would bet heavily against this
> chemist or anyone else being able to determine the cause of death with
> sufficient certainty to go through the witness box. He was confident that no
> one would at this stage be able to deny the presumption that the man had
> drowned, and far less that he could deny that the man had been killed by
> shock through an aeroplane crash and then been immersed in water.[15]

This restatement, in late May 1943, of the opinion that an individual wh
had died from the effects of phosphorus poisoning might be depicted
having expired in or on the ocean, does more than demonstrate th
consistency of the medical advice which informed the implementation
Operation Mincemeat from first to last. It also provides irrefutable proof that
was Glyndwr Michael—and not a drowned victim of the HMS *Dash*
tragedy, or anybody else—who served as the deceased courier in th

eption scheme. After all, the fundamental premise of the conversation
veen Montagu and Bentley Purchase on 27 May was the possibility that
additional autopsy of the actual body already interred in Spain might
ay the British deception. Therefore, it follows that the corpse under
ussion had to be the one actually employed in *Operation Mincemeat*.
in, the whole point of the talk between the Naval Intelligence officer
the Coroner was to assess the risk that such further post-mortem
estigation of the particular body buried in Spain might reveal the true
se of the corpse-courier's death as phosphorus poisoning rather than
wning or shock. Thus, it equally follows that the mortal remains, by then
est in that Spanish grave, must have been those of Glyndwr Michael
en though he is referred to only by the code name 'MINCEMEAT' in
ntagu's report on the conversation).[16] This conclusion is unavoidable,
e the cause of death (phosphorus poisoning), the mode of death (liver
age), and the manner of death (suicide) attributed to the code-named
son, who was the subject of the conversation between Montagu and
tley Purchase on 27 May 1943, fit the Welshman's case perfectly. It was
ndwr Michael who had died by taking phosphorus-based rat poison and
sequently succumbing to fatal liver damage.[17] Thus, the real identity of
man whose mortal remains deceived the Nazi High Command seems
blished beyond reasonable doubt. It was a *Man of Harlech* who answered
call of 'bright-eyed freedom'.[18]

Notes

Unless otherwise indicated, all the archival sources cited in the endnotes to work are held by the National Archives of the United Kingdom at K Richmond, Surrey.

PROLOGUE

1. Monthly log of HM Submarine *Seraph* (for month of April 1943), entry Thursday 29 April 1943, ADM 173/18038; Jewell, Norman Limbury Auch leck ('Bill'), 1991 interview, Imperial War Museum Sound Archive, ref. 122 reel 3.

2. Rear Admiral David Scott, *Action Reply: Reminiscences of a naval career* (typesc memoirs), 47, Royal Naval Museum Library (Portsmouth); Report on *Opera Mincemeat* from the Commanding Officer, HM Submarine *Seraph* to the I ector of Naval Intelligence, 30 April 1943, WO 106/5921.

3. Official Record of 'Operation Mincemeat', dated 27 April 1943, submitted by Cdr Ewen Montagu, RNVR, and Flt Lt Charles Cholmondeley, RAFVR, pa 28 and 55, the Papers of Captain E. E. S. Montagu, Department of Docume Imperial War Museum, Box 1, 97/45/1.

   There are two different versions extant of the official record of *Opera Mincemeat*. The one cited immediately above is a Crown copyright docum to be found in the Montagu Papers, held by the Department of Document the Imperial War Museum. Although dated 27 April 1943, it has an addend carrying the story of the deception operation forward to 29 May 1943. It a incorporates revisions to its text submitted by Colonel John Bevan, head of London Controlling Section (Britain's central body, during the Second Wc War, for developing and coordinating strategic deception plans) in 1945. (! Bevan's letters of 3 June 1945 to Lt Cdr E. E. S. Montagu and to Major J. Masterman, respectively, and the actual text of Bevan's amendments, dated April 1945, to paras. 11, 13, 14, and 15 to the original record, in CAB 154/(

   The second version of the official record of *Operation Mincemeat* inclu an appreciation of 'Documents in the German Admiralty (OKM) archi captured at Tambach' in 1945, apparently providing 'proof of success Mincemeat'. This unsigned and undated document, although it covers a longer period than the one produced in April–May 1943, is largely an abridgement of the earlier version, but it also reproduces some of that draft's text. It was drawn up by Lt Cdr Montagu for the war records of the Naval Intelligence Division, where it may be found in the United Kingdom's National Archives at ADM 223/794 (with another copy located among the official records of the London Controlling Section at CAB 154/112, in the National Archives). This later version of the official record of *Operation Mincemeat* is also a Crown copyright document.

4. Ibid., para. 32; Ewen Montagu, *The Man Who Never Was* (London: Evans Brothers, 1965), but the edition cited here, and throughout this book, is the one published by J. P. Lippincott Company of New York in 1954, 107.

5. Scott, *Action Reply*, 46.

6. Jewell interview, IWM Sound Archive, ref. 12278, reel 3.

7. *Operation Mincemeat*, paras. 57–8, Montagu Papers, Box 1, 97/45/1.

8. Jewell interview, IWM Sound Archive, ref. 12278, reel 3; Scott, *Action Reply*, 47; Terence Robertson, *The Ship with Two Captains* (London: Evans Brothers, 1957), 21, 71, 125, 142.

9. Montagu, *The Man Who Never Was*, 108–9.

10. 'Operation Mincemeat', from CO *Seraph* to DNI, 30 April 1943, WO 106/5921.

11. Ibid.; Montagu, *The Man Who Never Was*, 109; Ian Colvin, *The Unknown Courier* (London: William Kimber, 1953), 165; 'Operation Mincemeat', para. 44, Montagu Papers, Box 1, 97/45/1; photographs of corpse taken in Hackney Mortuary on 17 April 1943, WO 106/5921.

12. *The Annotated Book of Common Prayer*, edited by the Rev. John Henry Blunt (London: Rivingtons, 1872), 295, 369; Montagu, *The Man Who Never Was*, 109; Jewell interview, IWM Sound Archive, ref. 12278, reel 3.

13. 'Operation Mincemeat', from CO *Seraph* to DNI, 30 April 1943; Addendum 1, (para. J: 'The Launching of the Body') appended by Montagu, on 29 May 1943, to 'Operation Mincemeat', Montagu Papers, Box 1, 97/45/1; Scott, *Action Reply*, 47–8.

CHAPTER 1

1. Inter-Services Security Board's report (n.d., but of 2 October 1942), 'Enquiry into possibility of compromise of Operation TORCH as a result of accident to CATALINA F.P.119 on 26 September 1942', accompanying minute of 6 October 1942 from General H. L. Ismay (Chief of Staff to the Minister of Defence and military Deputy Secretary to the War Cabinet) to the Prime Minister, Winston Churchill, PREM 3/439/17; telegram no. 532, 4 October 1942, from General F. N. Mason-MacFarlane, Governor and C.-in-C. Gibraltar, to the War Office, ibid; Note (n.d.) enclosed with letter from Ismay to General Dwight D. Eisenhower, 29 September 1942, CAB 121/496.

2. ISSB report on 'Possibility of compromise of Operation TORCH', PREM 3/439, 17; Clamorgan's Official 'Departure Form' for the Catalina flight, 30 July 1942, CAB 121/496; Sir Charles Hambro (Executive Director of the Special Operatio Executive) to the ISSB, 24 October 1942, ibid.; Chairman of the ISSB, to th Secretary of the Chiefs of Staff Committee, 29 October 1942, ibid. Clamorgan's fal surname is spelled 'Marsil' in some of the documents contained in CAB 121/496

3. Mason-MacFarlane's telegram no. 532, 4 October 1942, PREM 3/439/17.

4. See, e.g., F. H. Hinsley et al., *British Intelligence in the Second World War: i influence on strategy and operations*, ii (London: HMSO, 1981), 463; Micha Howard, *British Intelligence in the Second World War*, v: *Strategic Decepti* (London: HMSO, 1990), 55–6.

5. Hinsley et al., *British Intelligence in the Second World War*, ii, 471–2; Arthu Layton Funk, *The Politics of TORCH: The Allied landing and the Algerian putsc 1942* (Lawrence/Manhattan/Wichita: University of Kansas Press, 1974), 98 100, 107; Michael Howard, *Grand Strategy*, iv: *August 1942–September 19* (London: HMSO, 1972), xix–xx; Douglas Porch, *The Path to Victory: T. Mediterranean theater in World War II* (New York: Farrar, Straus and Girou: 2004), 329, 331–2, 343.

6. Eden reported the Prime Minister's concern to his own private secretary, Olive Harvey, who recorded it in his diary entry for 2 October 1942: see John Harve (ed.), *The War Diaries of Oliver Harvey, 1941–1945* (London: Collins, 1978), 16

7. Winston S. Churchill, *The Second World War*, iv: *The Hinge of Fate* (Londo Folio Society edn, 2000), 487.

8. See, e.g., Carlo D'Este, *Eisenhower: A soldier's life* (New York: Henry Hol 2002), 340.

9. 'LIGHTFOOT: General Plan of Eighth Army', 14 September 1942 (th master plan for the Alamein offensive developed by Lt Gen. Bernard La Montgomery, GOC-in-C. Eighth Army), quoted in full by Nigel Hamilto *Monty*, i: *The making of a general, 1887–1942*, 2nd edn (Toronto: Fleet Book 1982), 732–41. See also Nigel Hamilton, *Monty*, ii: *Master of the battlefield, 1942 1944*, 2nd edn (London: Sceptre, 1987), 63–6 and Martin Blumenson, 'Rom mel' in Correlli Barnett (ed.), *Hitler's Generals* (London: Weidenfeld an Nicolson, 1989), 302, 304–5.

10. Hamilton, *Monty*, i, 745.

11. Churchill, *Hinge of Fate*, 442.

12. Alex Danchev and Daniel Todman (eds.), *War Diaries, 1939–1945: Field Marsh Lord Alanbrooke* (London: Weidenfeld and Nicolson, 2001), 325.

13. Harry C. Butcher, *Three Years with Eisenhower: The personal diary of Captain Harr C. Butcher, USNR, Naval Aide to General Eisenhower, 1942 – 1945* (London: Willia Heinemann, 1946), 89. See also Oliver Harvey's diary entry for 5 October 194 (Lord Harvey of Tasburgh Diaries and Papers, Add. 56399, British Library).

14. Clark to MacFarlane, 14 September 1942, Annex I to copy of the ISSB 'Enquiry into possibility of compromise of Operation TORCH', CAB 121/496

HQ Naval Commander-in-Chief, Expeditionary Force to Commander Parry, Chief of Staff to Flag Officer Commanding North Atlantic, 21 September 1942, Annex II, ibid.

Ismay to Eisenhower, 29 September 1942, CAB 121/496.

Telegram no. 529, 1 October 1942, from Mason-MacFarlane to War Office, Annex V to ISSB 'Enquiry', ibid.; diary entry for 5 October 1942, Harvey Diaries and Papers, Add. 56399.

See, e.g., Denis Smyth, 'Reflex reaction: Germany and the onset of the Spanish Civil War' in Paul Preston (ed.), *Revolution and War in Spain* (London: Methuen, 1984), 243–4; Denis Smyth, 'The Moor and the money-lender: Politics and profits in Anglo–German relations with Francoist Spain, 1936–1940' in Marie-Luise Recker (ed.), *Von der Konkurrenz zur Rivalität: Das Britische-Deutsche Verhältnis in den Ländern der Europäischen Peripherie, 1919–1939* (Stuttgart: Franz Steiner, 1986), 158–60; and Paul Preston, 'Italy and Spain in Civil War and World War' in Sebastian Balfour and Paul Preston (eds.), *Spain and the Great Powers in the Twentieth Century* (London: Routledge, 1999), 151–2, 171–4.

See, e.g., Denis Smyth, *Diplomacy and Strategy of Survival: British policy and Franco's Spain, 1940–41* (Cambridge: Cambridge University Press, 1986), 39, 83–94, 101–4, 112–4, 133–5, 164–8, 229–30; Denis Smyth, 'Screening "Torch": Allied counter-intelligence and the Spanish threat to the secrecy of the Allied invasion of French North Africa in November 1942', *Intelligence and National Security*, 4/2 (1989), 335–53; Ralph Erskine, 'Eavesdropping on "Bodden": ISOS v. the Abwehr in the Straits of Gibraltar', *Intelligence and National Security*, 12/3 (1997), 110–29; and F. H. Hinsley and C. A. G. Simkins, *British Intelligence in the Second World War*, iv: *Security and Counter-Intelligence* (London: HMSO, 1990), 102, 104–5, 107–10, 159–62.

Extracts from minutes of the meetings of the Chiefs of Staff Committee, 29 September (COS (42) 131st mtg (o), Min. 1) and 30 September 1942 (COS (42) 132nd mtg (o), Min. 3), CAB 121/496; Minutes of meeting of the Inter-Services Security Board, 29 September 1942 (ISSB (42) 688th mtg, Min. 2 (b), WO 283/7). On the functioning of the Chiefs of Staff Committee within Churchill's wartime government, see J. R. M. Butler, *Grand Strategy*, ii: *September 1939–June 1941* (London: HMSO, 1957), 247–50, 356–7, 557, 561–2.

Hinsley and Simkins, *British Intelligence in the Second World War*, iv, 247–8.

Liddell Diaries (kept by Guy Liddell, Director of the Security Service's B Division, during the Second World War) vi, KV 4/190.

ISSB (42) 690th mtg, 30 September 1942, WO 283/7.

ISSB report on 'Enquiry into the possibility of compromise of Operation TORCH', PREM 3/439/17; Mason-MacFarlane's telegrams no. 521, 28 September, and no. 526 29 September 1942, ibid.; telegram no. 498, 28 September 1942 from VACNA to Admiralty, ibid.

ISSB report on 'Enquiry into the possibility of compromise of Operation TORCH', PREM 3/439/17.

25. Ibid.

26. COS (42) 136th mtg (o), Min. 11, 3 October 1942, CAB 79/57.

27. See, e.g., Ralph Erskine, 'Breaking Air Force and Army Enigma' in Ra
    Erskine and Michael Smith (eds.), *Action This Day: Bletchley Park from
    breaking of the Enigma code to the birth of the modern computer* (London: Bant
    2001), 47–61; Ralph Erskine, 'Breaking German Naval Enigma on both side
    the Atlantic', in ibid., 174–84; Derek Taunt, 'Hut 6 from the inside', in ibid., 83
    Michael Smith, 'How it began: Bletchley Park goes to war' in B. Jack Co
    land (ed.), *Colossus: The secrets of Bletchley Park's codebreaking computers* (Oxf
    Oxford University Press, 2006), 21–35; Stephen Budiansky, 'Colossus, Co
    breaking and the digial age', in ibid., 52–63; Hinsley et al., *British Intelligence in
    Second World War*, iii: Pt II (London: HMSO, 1988), 945–59; Stuart Miln
    Barry, 'Hut 6: Early days' in F. H. Hinsley and Alan Stripp (eds.), *Codebreak
    The inside story of Bletchley Park* (Oxford: Oxford University Press, 1993), 92
    Peter Twinn, 'The Abwehr Enigma', in ibid., 123–4; F. H. Hinsley, 'An in
    duction to Fish', in ibid., 141–3; Jack Good, 'Engima and Fish', in ibid., 16c
    Paul Gannon, *Colossus: Bletchley Park's greatest secret* (London: Atlantic, 2006), 65
    139–55, 160–71, 213–70, 283–6; Hugh Sebag-Montefiore, *Enigma: The b
    for the code* (London: Weidenfeld and Nicolson, 2000), 55–8, 71–82, 94–1
    118–19, 142–3, 149–53; R. A. Ratcliff, *Delusions of Intelligence: Engima, Ultra
    the end of secure ciphers* (Cambridge: Cambridge University Press, 2006), 25
    Ralph Erskine, 'The Poles reveal their secrets: Alastair Denniston's account
    the July 1939 meeting at Pyry', *Cryptologia*, 30/4 (2006), 294–305.

28. Hinsley and Stripp (eds.), *Codebreakers*, v.

29. Jack Copeland, 'The German Tunny machine' in Copeland (ed.), *Colos.
    36–42.

30. See, e.g., Peter Hilton, 'Living with Fish: Breaking Tunny in the Newmanry.
    the Testery', in ibid., 189–97; Donald Michie, 'Codebreaking and Coloss
    ibid., 223–45; Gil Hayward, 'Operation Tunny' in Hinsley and Stripp (e
    Codebreakers, 174–92; Shaun Wylie, 'Breaking Tunny and the birth of Coloss
    in Erskine and Smith (eds.), *Action This Day*, 317–41; Donald Michie, 'Colos
    and the breaking of the wartime "Fish" codes', *Cryptologia*, 26/1 (2002), 17–.

31. Alan Stripp, 'The Enigma machine: Its mechanism and use' in Hinsley a
    Stripp (eds), *Codebreakers*, 83–8.

32. Hinsley, 'Introduction to Fish', 143; Gannon, *Colossus*, 71–2; Ratcliff, *De
    sions*, 25.

33. Milner-Barry, 'Hut 6: Early days', 92; Erskine, 'Breaking Air Force and Ar
    Enigma', 61, 67–76; Ratcliff, *Delusions*, 23–9.

34. Erskine, 'Breaking German Naval Enigma', 174–96; Sebag-Montefiore, *Enig
    69–78, 95–101, 118–19, 122–53, 159–60, 185–99, 211–24, 227–36; J. Da
    Brown, 'The Battle of the Atlantic, 1941–1943: Peaks and troughs' in Timo
    J. Runyan and Jan M. Copes (eds.), *To Die Gallantly: The Battle of the Atla
    (Boulder: Westview Press, 1994), 137–57.

Philip H. J. Davies, 'From amateurs to professionals: GC&CS and Institution-building in Sigint' in Erskine and Smith (eds.), *Action This Day*, 400; Hinsley and Stripp (eds.), *Codebreakers*, v.

See, e.g., Gordon Welchman, *The Hut Six Story: Breaking the Enigma codes*, 2nd edn (Harmondsworth: Penguin Books, 1984), 58, 121, 126–7, 136–7, 159–61; William Millward, 'Life in and out of Hut 3' in Hinsley and Stripp (eds.), *Codebreakers*, 19–23; Ralph Bennett, 'The duty officer, Hut 3', in ibid., 30–7; Rodney M. Brunt, 'Special documentation systems at the Government Code and Cypher School, Bletchley Park, during the Second World War', *Intelligence and National Security*, 21/1 (2006), 129–48.

Hinsley and Stripp (eds.), *Codebreakers*, vii.

Sebag-Montefiore, *Enigma*, 112–13.

Ibid., 103.

Penelope Fitzgerald, *The Knox Brothers*, 2nd edn (Washington, DC: Counter-point, 2000), 127–8, 134–6; Mavis Batey, 'Breaking Italian Naval Enigma' in Erskine and Smith (eds.), *Action This Day*, 96–7; Patrick Beesly, *Room 40: British Naval Intelligence, 1914–1918* (San Diego: Harcourt, Brace, Jovanovich, 1982), 252–70.

Fitzgerald, *Knox Brothers*, 161, 189, 192, 229; Mavis Batey, entry on 'Knox (Alfred) Dillwyn 1884–1943', *Oxford Dictionary of National Biography,* herein-after cited as *ODNB* (Oxford: Oxford University Press, 2004–7), <http://www.oxforddnb.com>; Mavis Batey, 'Breaking Italian Naval Enigma', 102; Sebag-Montefiore, *Enigma*, 103–4.

Fitzgerald, *Knox Brothers*, 59.

Quoted by Sebag-Montefiore, *Enigma*, 113.

Mavis Batey, 'Dilly Knox: A reminiscence of this pioneer Enigma cryptana-lyst', *Cryptologia*, 32/2 (2008), 123–5; Keith Batey, 'How Dilly Knox and his girls broke the Abwehr Enigma' in Erskine and Smith (eds.), *Action This Day*, 303–8; Peter Twinn, 'The Abwehr Enigma' in Hinsley and Stripp (eds.), *Codebreakers*, 123–5, 127–9; Frank Carter, 'The Abwehr Enigma machine', <http://www.BletchleyPark.org.uk>.

Ralph Erskine, 'Introduction' to Keith Batey, 'How Dilly Knox and his girls broke the Abwehr Enigma', 302; Erskine, 'Eavesdropping on "Bodden"', 111; Hinsley and Simkins, *British Intelligence in the Second World War,* iv, 181–2.

Batey, 'How Dilly Knox and his girls broke the Abwehr Enigma', 303, 308–10; Twinn, 'Abwehr Enigma', 129–30; Fitzgerald, *Knox Brothers*, 248–50.

Hinsley and Simkins, *British Intelligence in the Second World War*, iv, 108.

Ibid., 159. The Abwehr in Spain had an additional twenty subsections oper-ating in that country's harbours: David Kahn, *Hitler's Spies: German Military Intelligence in World War II* (London: Hodder and Stoughton, 1978), 243.

See, e.g., Kenneth Benton, 'The ISOS years: Madrid 1941–3', *Journal of Contemporary History*, 30/3 (1995), 372–3, 379; Howard, *Strategic Deception*, 47; Hinsley et al., *British Intelligence in the Second World War*, ii, 668. Actually, the weight of the Allied strategic bombing offensive forced the Abwehr to evacuate its main offices, in April 1943, from downtown Berlin to the site of the German Army's headquarters at Zossen, twenty miles south of the Reich's capital: Kahn, *Spies*, 238.

50. On the solution of the Abwehr's hand ciphers, see, e.g., Hinsley et al., *British Intelligence in the Second World War*, i (London: HMSO, 1979), 120; Hinsley et al., *British Intelligence in the Second World War*, ii, 20; Hinsley and Simkins, *British Intelligence in the Second World War*, iv, 73, 89, 182; Henry Dryden, 'Recollections of Bletchley Park, France, and Cairo' in Hinsley and Stripp (eds.), *Codebreakers*, 201. Another veteran codebreaker, Oliver Strachey, originally headed the team which made the critical break into the Abwehr's hand ciphers, so its product was dubbed ISOS (Intelligence Services Oliver Strachey). However, once the Abwehr Enigma was added to Bletchley Park's list of scalps—although its product was distinguished from the hand-ciphered traffic by the designation ISK—for reasons of security the term 'ISOS' was applied to all decrypted messages transmitted by the Nazi secret intelligence services: Hinsley and Simkins, *British Intelligence in the Second World War*, iv, 108, fn†.

51. ISOS 40296, Madrid to Cadiz, 28/9/42, HW 19/38; ISOS 40297, Cadiz to Madrid, 29/9/42, ibid.; ISK 18414, Madrid to Berlin, 28/9/42, HW 19/102.

52. Ismay's minute of 6 October 1942 for the Prime Minister (covering a copy of the ISSB report into the Catalina crash) with Churchill's initials, penned on 7 October, thereon, PREM 3/439/17.

53. ISK 19690, Madrid to Berlin, 30/9/42, HW 19/104; *Liddell Diaries*, 2 October 1942, vi, KV 4/190.

54. ISSB (42) 706th mtg, Min. 9, 20 October 1942, WO 283/8; Chairman ISSB to Secretary, COS, 21 October 1942, CAB 121/496; COS (42) 156th mtg (o) Min. 5, 22 October 1942, CAB 79/57. Actually, the British had suspected, as early as 4–5 October, that the documents on the person of the Free French agent, Marcil, might have fallen into hostile hands. Telegram no. 532, 4 October 1942, from Mason-MacFarlane to War Office, PREM 3/439/17; ISSB (42) 693rd mtg, Min. 5, 5 October 1942, WO 283/7. See, also, para. 3 of Ismay's minute of 6 October 1942 to Churchill, PREM 3/439/17.

55. ISSB (42) 706th mtg, Min. 9, 20 October 1942, WO 283/8.

56. Chairman ISSB to Secretary, COS, 6 October 1942, CAB 121/496; Chairman ISSB to Secretary, COS, 29 October 1942, with Appendix A, 'List of documents salvaged from the wrecked Catalina', ibid.

57. Chairman ISSB to Secretary, COS, 29 October 1942, with Appendix B, 'Translation of Document 1 ("Meeting held on 22nd September, 1942")', CAB 121/496. On Dewavrin, see, e.g., Guy Perrier, *Le Colonel Passy et les Services Secrets de la France Libre* (Paris: Hachette, 1999), passim; and David de Young de la Marck, 'De Gaulle, Colonel Passy and British Intelligence 1940–42', *Intelligence and National Security*, 18/1 (2003), 21–40.

Chairman ISSB to Secretary, COS, 29 October 1942, CAB 121/496; ISSB (42) 713th mtg, 29 October 1942, WO 283/8.
'Recent intelligence affecting Operation "Torch" ', report by the Joint Intelligence Sub-Committee, 3 November 1942, JIC (42) 432 (o) (Final), CAB 154/69.
Hinsley et al., *British Intelligence in the Second World War*, ii, 478–81; Howard, *Strategic Deception*, 55–63; Lt Cdr Ewen Montagu, 'Machinery of deception outside NID: W-Board, Twenty Committee & London Controlling Section', 18 September 1945, ADM 223/794; *Liddell Diaries*, 6, 11 November 1942, vi KV4/190; Kahn, *Hitler's Spies*, 472–8; Ralph Erskine, 'From the archives: A Bletchley Park assessment of German intelligence on TORCH', *Cryptologia*, 13/2 (1989), 135–8, Smyth, 'Screening "Torch" ', 350–3.
Quoted by Martin Gilbert, *Road to Victory: Winston S. Churchill, 1941–1945* (Toronto: Stoddart, 1986), 247.
The official record of *Operation Mincemeat*, submitted under the names of both Charles Cholmondeley and Ewen Montagu (but more likely to have been drafted by the latter) on 27 April 1943, recognized the former's primary role in instigating the hoax, and the latter's prominent part in implementing it:

Flight Lieutenant Cholmondeley, R.A.F.V.R., brought up for consideration . . . Plan TROJAN HORSE . . . The general scheme was to drop a body with important documents which had been specially prepared from an aircraft, thereby planting them on the enemy . . . From then on the operation was devised and all preparations made by Lt. Commander Montagu with the assistance of Flight Lieutenant Cholmondeley and some of the staff of B.I.A. Section of M.I.5. ['Operation Mincemeat', paras. 1 and 4, Montagu Papers, Box 1, 97/45/1]

Guy Liddell, Director of the Security Service's B Division (responsible for countering enemy espionage) came to a similar conclusion on the division of labour and honours for *Operation Mincemeat*, in his diary entry for 6 February 1943:

Plan Mincemeat is in the making . . . The idea was conceived by Charles Cholmondeley and is being developed by him and Euan (sic) Montagu. [*Liddell Diaries*, vii, KV 4/191]

'Plan TROJAN HORSE', CAB 154/67. The copy of the plan held in the Cabinet Office records is undated but the one to be found in the Montagu Papers (Box 1, 97/45/1) at the Imperial War Museum is dated 31 October 1942.
'Tar' Robertson to David Mure, 24 April 1979, quoted by Thaddeus Holt, *The Deceivers: Allied military deception in the Second World War* (New York: Scribner, 2004), 370.
Montagu, *The Man Who Never Was*, 17–19.
'Plan TROJAN HORSE', CAB 154/67.

67. See, e.g., J. C. Masterman, *The Double-Cross System in the War of 1939 to 1*
    (New Haven: Yale University Press, 1972), 10–11, 63–7; Hinsley and Simk
    British Intelligence in the Second World War, iv, 98–101; Howard, *Strategic De*
    tion, 8–10; Michael Smith, 'Bletchley Park, Double Cross and D-Day'
    Erskine and Smith (eds.), *Action This Day*, 282–5; 'Machinery of decept
    outside N.I.D.: W. Board, Twenty Committee & London Controlling Secti
    18 September 1945, 3, ADM 223/794.

68. Howard, *Strategic Deception*, 15, 20–1; Smith, 'Bletchley Park, Double C
    and D-Day', 286–7; Hinsley and Simkins, *British Intelligence in the Second W*
    War, iv, 126–30.

69. Howard, *Strategic Deception*, 57–9, 62–3; Masterman, *Double-Cross System*, 109–
    'Machinery of deception outside N.I.D.: W-Board, Twenty Committee
    London Controlling Section', 18 September 1945, 7, ADM 223/794.

70. Masterman, *Double-Cross System*, 137.

71. Twenty Committee (42) 96th mtg, Min. 4, 5 November 1942, KV 4/65.

72. Hugh Trevor-Roper, 'Foreword' to Ewen Montagu, *Beyond Top Secret U*
    (New York: Coward, McCann & Geoghan, 1978), 10.

CHAPTER 2

1. David Mure, *Master of Deception: Tangled webs in London and the Middle 1*
   (London: William Kimber, 1980), 195: See, also, 'Tar' Robertson to Da
   Mure, 24 April 1979, The Private Papers of D. W. A. Mure, Department
   Documents, Imperial War Museum, Box 2, 67/321/2.

2. Mure, *Master of Deception*, 195; Dennis Wheatley, *The Deception Planners:*
   secret war (London: Hutchinson, 1980), 152; 'Mr. Charles Cholmondel
   obituary written by The Hon. Ewen S. Montagu, *The Times*, 23 June 198

3. Michael Smith, *Foley: The spy who saved 10,000 Jews* (London: Hodder
   Stoughton, 1999), 240–3; Nigel West (ed.), *The Guy Liddell Diaries*, i: 19
   1942 (London: Routledge, 2005), 251. Foley's predecessor as MI6 representat
   on the Twenty Committee was Felix Cowgill, head of the spy servi
   counter-espionage department, Section V. As a former officer in the Ind
   police force, Cowgill's professional priorities could strike his MI5 contact
   'narrow and petty' and provoke them to fury. See, e.g., West (ed.), *Lid*
   Diaries, i, 238.

4. Smith, *Foley*, 20–2, 63–6, 80–2, 87, 97–9, 109–12, 118–19, 121–39, 150
   154–5, 157–61, 163–5, 168–71.

5. Ibid., 169–71, 173–5, 188–96, 201; West (ed.), *Liddell Diaries*, i, 77–8.

6. Smith, *Foley*, 244.

7. Ibid., 217–36, 277.

8. Ibid., 244.

9. Anthony Powell, *The Military Philosophers* (Chicago: University of Chica
   Press edition, 1995), 39.

0. Lt Gen. Sir Ian Jacob, 'Memoir' in Sir John Wheeler-Bennett (ed.), *Action This Day: Working with Churchill* (London: Macmillan, 1968), 195–6.

1. Smith, *Foley*, 244.

2. Ismay to Churchill, 14 April 1943, PREM 3/227/6. General the Rt Hon. Lord Ismay, 'Foreword' to Montagu, *The Man Who Never Was*, 12.

3. Ewen Montagu, *Beyond Top Secret Ultra,* 149

4. 'Hon Ewen Montagu: Organizer of wartime hoax', obituary, *The Times*, 20 July 1985; M. R. D. Foot, 'Montagu, Ewen Edward Samuel (1901–1985)', rev., *ODNB* <http://www.oxforddnb.com>; Chandrika Paul, 'Montagu, Edwin Samuel (1879–1934), *ODNB* <http://www.oxforddnb.com>.

5. Montagu, *Beyond Top Secret Ultra*, 16–17, 19–24, 27, 29–30, 33–5, 46–51, 75–84, 96; 'J.H.G' (Admiral John Godfrey), 'Deception: N.I.D. 12', (undated), ADM 223/478; Hinsley, *British Intelligence in the Second World War*, ii, 650–1.

6. 'J.H.G.', 'Deception: N.I.D. 12', ADM 223/478.

7. Montagu, *Beyond Top Secret Ultra*, 150. See, also, 106–7 therein.

8. Ibid., 140–1, and Hugh Trevor-Roper, 'Foreword' in ibid., 9–11.

9. Ibid., 82.

0. Ibid., 55, 120–1.

1. Ibid., 164.

2. Ibid., 136–8, 164–5; 'Historical record of deception in the war against Germany and Italy' (Narrative by Sir Ronald Wingate), i, 104, CAB 154/100 (copy also in DEFE 24/48); Lt Cdr Ewen Montagu's Memorandum on 'Deception', 1 March 1943, para. 5 (c), ADM 223/794.

3. 'Operation Mincemeat', para. 3, Montagu Papers, Box 1, 97/45/1.

4. Howard, *Strategic Deception*, x.

5. 'Operation Mincemeat', para. 3, Montagu Papers, Box 1, 97/45/1; Twenty Committee (42), 96th mtg, 5 November 1942, Min. 4, KV 4/65.

6. Masterman, *Double-Cross System*, 137.

7. Richard Davenport-Hines (ed.), *Letters from Oxford: Hugh Trevor-Roper to Bernard Berenson* (London: Weidenfeld & Nicolson, 2006), 292.

8. Montagu, *Beyond Top Secret Ultra,* 48, 144–5.

9. Montagu, *The Man Who Never Was*, 27.

0. Colin Evans, *The Father of Forensics: The groundbreaking cases of Sir Bernard Spilsbury and the beginnings of modern CSI* (New York: Berkeley Books, 2006), 63.

1. Douglas G. Browne and Tom Tullett, *Bernard Spilsbury: His life and cases* (New York: Dorset Press, 1951), 361.

2. See, e.g., Andrew Rose, *Lethal Witness: Sir Bernard Spilsbury, honorary pathologist* (London: Sutton, 2007), 41–2, 114–17.

3. George Orwell, 'Decline of the English murder' in John Early (ed.), *George Orwell: Essays* (New York: Knopf, 2002), 1029.

4. Rose, *Lethal Witness*, 241.

35. Evans, *Father of Forensics*, 121.

36. Ibid., 15-16, 25, 309; Rose, *Lethal Witness*, 21.

37. Michael A. Green, 'Is Sir Bernard Spilsbury dead?' in Alistair R. Brownlie (ed.), *Crime Investigation, Art or Science?: Patterns in a labyrinth* (Edinburgh: Scottish Academic Press, 1984), 24.

38. Quoted by Evans, *Father of Forensics*, 63.

39. Rose, *Lethal Witness*, 114.

40. Ibid., 117.

41. Evans, *Father of Forensics*, 122, 139; Rose, *Lethal Witness*, 117-18.

42. Rose, *Lethal Witness*, 123.

43. Evans, *Father of Forensics*, 145.

44. Ibid., 90.

45. Rose, *Lethal Witness*, 31, 113, 258.

46. Ibid., 104.

47. Evans, *Father of Forensics*, 26-7.

48. Quoted by Christmas Humphreys, 'Spilsbury, Sir Bernard Henry (1877-1947)', *The Dictionary of National Biography: 1941–1950*, ed. L. G. Wickham Legg and E. T. Williams (Oxford: Oxford University Press, 1959), 816.

49. Ibid., 815–16; Evans, *Father of Forensics*, 27, 116-17; Rose, *Lethal Witness* 269–70.

50. Quoted by Rose, *Lethal Witness*, 96.

51. Ibid., 149.

52. Ibid., 188; Green, 'Is Spilsbury dead?', 25.

53. Montagu, *The Man Who Never Was*, 27-8.

54. Obituary of Bernard Spilsbury, *The Lancet*, 250/6487 (27 December 1947), 965

55. Quoted by Rose, *Lethal Witness*, 232-3.

56. Twenty Committee (42) 97th mtg, 12 November 1942, Min. 2 and 98th mtg, 19 November 1942, Min. 1 (b), KV4/65.

57. Montagu, *Beyond Top Secret Ultra*, 145.

58. Montagu, *The Man Who Never Was*, 27-8.

59. 'Operation Mincemeat', para. 5, Montagu Papers, Box 1, 97/45/1.

60. Inteviews with Dr Noel McAuliffe, Forensic Pathology Unit (Ministry of Community Safety and Correctional Services), Office of the Chief Coroner for Ontario, Toronto, 18 October 2007 and 13 May 2009; Evans, *Father of Forensics*, 44-6.

61. 'Operation Mincemeat', para. 5, Montagu Papers, Box 1, 97/45/1; Montagu, *The Man Who Never Was*, 28.

62. Montagu, *The Man Who Never Was*, 28.

63. Twenty Committee (42) 99th mtg, 26 November 1942, Min. 3 (b), KV 4/65; Rose, *Lethal Witness*, 211; Evans, *Father of Forensics*, 148; Browne and Tullett, *Spilsbury*, 400; 'Sir W. Bentley Purchase', obituary, *The Times*, 28 September 1961; Robert Jackson, *Coroner: The biography of Sir Bentley Purchase* (London: Harrap, 1963) 49–50.

Twenty Committee (42), 99th mtg, 26 November 1942, Min. 3(b), KV 4/65.

Twenty Committee (42) 100th mtg, 3 December, Min. 2 (a) and 101st mtg, 10 December 1942, Min. 2, KV 4/65.

Jackson, *Coroner*, 28; 'Sir W. Bentley Purchase', obituary, *The Times*, 28 September 1961.

Twenty Committee (42) 101st mtg, 10 December, Min. 2 and 102nd mtg, 17 December 1942, Min. 2, KV 4/65; 'Operation Mincemeat', para. 9, Montagu Papers, Box 1, 97/45/1; Jackson, Coroner, 147–8.

'Operation Mincemeat', para. 6, Montagu Papers, Box 1, 97/45/1.

Four-page extract from earlier draft of *The Man Who Never Was*, Montagu Papers, Box 1, 97/45/1.

Montagu, *The Man Who Never Was*, 28–9.

Interview with Dr Noel McAuliffe, Forensic Pathology Unit (Ministry of Community Safety and Correctional Services), Office of the Chief Coroner of Ontario, Toronto, 13 May, 2009.

Montagu, *The Man Who Never Was*, 28–9.

'Operation Mincemeat', para. 8, Montagu Papers, Box 1, 97/45/1; 'Operation Mincemeat', 1, ADM 223/794; Reference Sheet on 'Mincemeat' from Lt Cdr Montagu, NID, 12 to Colonel Bevan, 28 May 1943, CAB 154/67.

Reference Sheet on 'Mincemeat', Montagu to Bevan, 28 May 1943, paras. 2, 3, and 4, CAB 154/67.

'Operation Mincemeat', para. 8, Montagu Papers, Box 1, 97/45/1.

Sydney Smith, *Forensic Medicine: A text-book for students and practioners*, 8th edn (London: J. & A. Churchill, 1943, reprinted 1945), 487–8; Francis Camps, 'Smith, Sir Sydney Alfred (1883–1969)', rev. Brenda M. White, *ODNB* <http://www.oxforddnb.com>; Rose, *Lethal Witness*, 146–51, 153–83, 229–32; Sir Sydney Smith, *Mostly Murder* (London: Harrap, 1959; New York: Dorset Press, 1973), 150–65, 196–204.

Reference Sheet on 'Mincemeat', Montagu to Bevan, 28 May 1943, para. 5, CAB 154/67; Smith, *Forensic Medicine*, 269.

'Operation Mincemeat', para. 8, Montagu Papers, Box 1, 97/45/1.

Montagu, *The Man Who Never Was*, 30.

Powell, *Military Philosophers*, 2; Anthony Powell, *To Keep the Ball Rolling: The memoirs of Anthony Powell* (Harmondsworth, Middlesex: Penguin, 1983), 17–18, 295.

Roger Morgan, 'The Second World War's best kept secret revealed', *After the Battle*, 94 (November 1996), 31–2; John Ezard, '"Man Who Never Was" finds an identity', *Guardian Weekly*, 10 November 1996.

Montagu, *The Man Who Never Was*, 30.

'Operation Mincemeat', paras. 8 and 9, Montagu Papers, Box 1, 97/45/1.

Glyndwr Michael's death certificate reproduced in Morgan, 'Second World War's best kept secret', 32.

Morgan, 'Second World War's best kept secret', 31–2.

86. 'Operation Mincemeat' (Plan), para. 4 (i), Twenty Committee, 4 Februa
    1943, CAB 154/65; Twenty Committee (43) 108th mtg, 4 February 194
    Min. 8, KV 4/65.
87. 'Operation Mincemeat', (Plan), para. 4 (i), Twenty Committee, 4 Februa
    1943, CAB 154/67; Twenty Committee (43) 108th mtg, 4 February 194
    Min. 8, KV 4/65.
88. 'Operation Mincemeat', paras. 6 and 8, Montagu Papers, Box 1, 97/45/1.
89. Sir Harold Parker to D. P. Reilly, 8 December 1950, DEFE 28/22.
90. Sir Harold Parker to the Hon. Ewen E. S. Montagu, 20 December 195
    DEFE 28/23.
91. Montagu to Parker, 7 January 1951, Montagu Papers, Box 1, 97/45/1.
92. J. A. Drew to 'Secretary', 29 October 1952, DEFE 28/23. Drew's official ti
    was 'Director of Forward Plans', Ministry of Defence. See Richard J. Aldric
    The Hidden Hand: Britain, America and Cold War secret intelligence (Woodsto
    & New York: Overlook Press, 2001), 504.
93. Directorate of Forward Plans 'Draft' for 'Secretary, J.I.C.', January 195
    DEFE 28/23.
94. 'J.A.D.' (John A. Drew) draft telegram, 2 January 1953, DEFE 28/23; J.
    Drew's memo on 'Operation Mincemeat', to 'Secretary', 3 January 195
    DEFE 28/23.
95. Drew to Captain G. M. Liddell, 6 January 1953, DEFE 28/23.
96. See the two drafts of Montagu's first chapter, 'The birth of an idea' in DEF
    28/23 and Montagu, *The Man Who Never Was*, 30.
97. General N. C. D. Brownjohn to Major General Sir John Noble Kenned
    11 March 1953, DEFE 28/23.
98. Extract from earlier draft of *The Man Who Never Was*, Montagu Papers, B
    1, 97/45/1.
99. Montagu, *The Man Who Never Was*, 91-3; 'Sir W. Bentley Purchase', obitu
    ary, *The Times*, 28 September 1961.
100. John D. Cantwell, *The Second World War: A guide to documents in the Pub*
    Record Office (Kew: PRO, 1998), 7.
101. Montagu, *The Man Who Never Was*, 32.
102. 'Operation Mincemeat' (Plan), para. 1 (i), Twenty Committee, 4 Februa
    1943, CAB 154/67.
103. Ibid., para. 1(ii); Howard, *Strategic Deception*, ix.
104. 'Operation Mincemeat' (Plan), para. 3, Twenty Committee, 4 February 194
    CAB 154/67.
105. Ibid., para. 4 (ii).
106. Ibid., para. 4 (iii) and (iv).
107. Ibid., para. 5 (i).
108. Ibid., para. 5 (ii).
109. Twenty Committee (43), 108th mtg, 4 February 1943, Min. 8, KV 4/65.
110. Ibid.

1. 'Operation Mincemeat' (Plan), para. 2 (ii) (f), Twenty Committee, 4 February 1943.
2. Maurice Matloff, *Strategic Planning for Coalition Warfare, 1943–1944* (Washington DC: Office of the Chief of Military History, Department of the Army, 1959), 26.
3. Twenty Committee (43) 108th mtg, 4 February 1943, Min. 8, KV 4/65.
4. Powell, *The Military Philosophers*, 40.

CHAPTER 3

1. 'Conduct of the War in 1943', *Memorandum by the Combined Chiefs of Staff*, CCS 155/1, 19 January 1943, printed as Appendix III (D) in Howard, *Grand Strategy,* iv, 621–2.
2. See, e.g., Samuel Eliot Morison, *History of United States Naval Operations in World War II,* ix: *Sicily–Salerno–Anzio, January 1942–June 1944* (Boston: Little, Brown, 1954), 7–9; Howard, *Grand Strategy*, iv, 241–55; Matloff, *Strategic Planning*, 19–37; Porch, *Path to Victory*, 415–17; Danchev and Lodman (eds.), *Alanbrooke War Diaries, 1939–1945*, 358–68; Carlo D'Este, *Bitter Victory: The battle for Sicily, July–August 1943* (London: Collins, 1988), 31–52.
3. Matloff, *Strategic Planning*, 21–5; Howard, *Grand Strategy*, iv, 252–4.
4. D'Este, *Bitter Victory*, 153; Carlo D'Este, *World War II in the Mediterranean, 1942–1945* (Chapel Hill: Algonquin Books, 1990), 57; Porch, *Path to Victory*, 426.
5. Quoted by Rick Atkinson, *The Day of Battle: The war in Sicily and Italy, 1943–1944* (New York: Henry Holt, 2007), 54.
6. Eisenhower's Cable no. 7892, 20 March 1943, to The Combined Chiefs of Staff and British Chiefs of Staff, in Alfred D. Chandler et al. (eds.), *The Papers of Dwight David Eisenhower: The war years,* ii (Baltimore: Johns Hopkins, 1970), 1045–8. See, also, D'Este, *Bitter Victory*, 84–5.
7. 'Historical record of deception', (Wingate), i, 128–33, CAB 154/100.
8. See, e.g., '"A" Force Narrative War Diary' (by Brigadier Dudley W. Clarke), iii (1 Jan. to 31 Dec. 1943), 65, CAB 154/3; Howard, *Strategic Deception*, 87; Atkinson, *Day of Battle*, 52; Sir David Hunt, *A Don at War*, rev. edn (London: Frank Cass, 1990), 187.
9. 'Historical record of deception' (Wingate), i, 135, CAB 154/100.
10. Ibid., 10
11. Ibid., 9.
12. 'Services of ULTRA to L.C.S. and "A" Force' (undated—but clearly post-war—and unsigned document), HW 41/142.
13. Howard, *Strategic Deception*, 26–7, 243; Holt, *Deceivers*, 188–9.

14. 'Machinery of Deception outside N.I.D., W. Board, Twenty Committee and London Controlling Section' (assessment by Lt Cdr Ewen Montagu (18 September 1945), 8, ADM 223/794.

15. Report on 'Meeting held in Major Robertson's room at 16.30 hours on 10.2.43' about 'Operation Mincemeat', by Flt Lt Charles C. Cholmondeley 11 February 1943, CAB 154/67.

16. Ibid.

17. Quoted by Montagu in his memo on 'Deception', 1 March 1943, para. 1 ADM 223/794; See, also, Howard, Strategic Deception, 86.

18. Montagu, 'Deception', 1 March 1943, para. 1, ADM 223/794.

19. Ibid., para. 2.

20. Ibid., para. 5.

21. Masterman, Double-Cross System, 109–10; Smyth, 'Screening "Torch"', 33. 'Machinery of Deception' (Montagu), 18 September 1945, 7, ADM 223/794

22. Montagu, 'Deception', 1 March 1943, para. 5, ADM 223/794

23. Ibid., para. 6.

24. Ibid., para. 4.

25. Ibid., paras. 7–8.

26. Entry on 'Rushbrooke, Edmund Gerald Noel' in 'Royal Navy (RN) Officer 1939–1945', <http://www.unithistories.com/officers/RN_officersR2.html> Correlli Barnett, Engage the Enemy More Closely: The Royal Navy in the Second World War (London: Hodder and Stoughton, 1991), 504–9.

27. Montagu, Beyond Top Secret Ultra, 165.

28. Entry on 'Rushbrooke, Edmund Noel', in 'Royal Navy (RN) Officers, 1939–1945 <http://www.unithistories.com/officers/RN_officersR2.html>.

29. Wheatley, Deception Planners, 42.

30. Reprinted as Appendix 3 in Howard, Strategic Deception, 243.

31. Ibid. See, also, Wheatley, Deception Planners, 91.

32. John P. Campbell, 'Bevan, John Henry' (1894–1978), ODNB <http://www oxforddnb.com>; Holt, Deceivers, 182–5.

33. Wheatley, Deception Planners, 60.

34. Ibid.

35. Howard, Strategic Deception, 56–7.

36. 'Machinery of Deception' (Montagu), 18 September 1945, 9, ADM 223/794.

37. Howard, Strategic Deception, 57.

38. Holt, Deceivers, 195.

39. Wheatley, Deception Planners, 80.

40. Ibid., 61–2; Howard, Strategic Deception, 56.

41. Holt, Deceivers, 184–5; Campbell, 'Bevan, John Henry (1894–1978)', ODNB <http://www.oxforddnb.com>; Wheatley, Deception Planners, 60.

42. Wheatley, Deception Planners, 80; Holt, Deceivers, 194; Howard, Strategic Deception, 56.

Wheatley, *Deception Planners*, 80–2.

Twenty Committee (43) 110th mtg, 18 February 1943, Min. 7, KV 4/65.

Porch, *Path to Victory*, 401.

Letter from Colonel John Bevan to Major T. A. Robertson re 'Operation Mincemeat', 12 February 1943, CAB 154/67. See, also, 'Operation Mincemeat', para. 11, Montagu Papers, Box 1, 97/45/1.

Porch, *Path to Victory*, 384–7.

Ibid., 354–7; Hinsley et al., *British Intelligence in the Second World War*, ii, 487–505.

Reinhard Stumpf, 'Der Krieg im Mittelmeerraum 1942/43: Die Operationen in Nordafrika und im Mittleren Mittelmeer' in Horst Boog et al., *Der Globale Krieg: Die Ausweitung zum Weltkrieg und der Wechsel der Initiative, 1941–1943 (Das Deutsche Reich und der Zweite Weltkrieg)*, Band 6 (Stuttgart: Deutsche Verlags-Anstalt, 1990), 736–7.

Porch, *Path to Victory*, 381–91, 402–3; Hinsley et al., *British Intelligence in the Second World War*, ii, 586–97.

Porch, *Path to Victory*, 404–12.

Howard, *Grand Strategy*, v, 364–8; Omar N. Bradley and Clay Blair, *A General's Life* (New York: Simon and Schuster, 1983), 160.

Howard, *Strategic Deception*, 71–3.

'Historical Record of Deception' (Wingate), i, 133, CAB 154/100; 'Deception Policy: 1943', Minute by Controlling Officer, LCS (43) (P) 2 (Final), 2 February 1943, War Cabinet, Chiefs of Staff Committee, CAB 81/83; 'Deception Policy 1943—Part I: Germany and Italy', Minute by the Controlling Officer and Annexes, LCS (43) (P) 3 (revise) (also COS (43) 179 (0)), 7 April, 1943, War Cabinet, CAB 81/83.

'Historical record of deception' (Wingate), i, 133.

See, e.g., Howard, *Grand Strategy*, 362, 364; Matloff, *Strategic Planning*, 68–70, 72–6.

Chandler (ed.), *Eisenhower Papers: The war years*, ii, 959–61.

Letter from Bevan to Robertson re 'Operation Mincemeat', 12 February 1943, CAB 154/67.

Twenty Committee (43) 111th mtg, 25 February 1943, Min. 2 (viii), KV 4/65.

CHAPTER 4

Montagu, 'Deception', 1 March 1943, para. 5 (m), ADM 223/794. Wheatley describes Dudley Clarke as the 'Great Deceiver' in his *Deception Planners*, 97.

Montagu, 'Deception', 1 March 1943, para. 7, ADM 223/794.

Howard, *Strategic Deception*, 32–3; Ian Beckett, 'Wavell' in John Keegan (ed.), *Churchill's Generals* (London: Weidenfeld and Nicolson, 1991), 71.

'Some notes on the organisation of deception in the United States Forces', by Brigadier D. W. Clarke, Commander 'A' Force, 30 October 1944, RG 319

(Records of the Army Staff: Records of the Office of the Assistant Chief
Staff, G-3, Operations—Special Correspondence Maintained by the T
Secret Control Office, 1943–1952: Cover and Deception Folders 70–8
NM-3, Entry 101, Box 4, Folder 77, US National Archives and Reco
Administration.

5. Howard, *Strategic Deception*, 35–6; Holt, *Deceivers*, 27–8, 31–2; West (e
   Liddell Diaries, i, 180–1.

6. Holt, *Deceivers*, 32; Howard, *Strategic Deception*, 36.

7. Holt, *Deceivers*, 32.

8. ' "A" Force Narrative War Diary' (by Brigadier Dudley W. Clarke), ii (1 J
   to 31 Dec. 1942), 34, CAB 154/2.

9. Ibid., 35.

10. 'Historical record of deception' (Wingate), i, 92, CAB 154/100.

11. Howard, *Strategic Deception*, 44.

12. ' "A" Force War Diary' (Clarke), ii, 40.

13. Ibid., 41, 45–9.

14. Ibid., 48.

15. Ibid.

16. Quoted by Holt, *Deceivers*, 14.

17. Holt, *Deceivers*, 42–3.

18. Entries for 23 October and 11 November 1941, *Liddell Diaries*, iv, KV 4/1

19. Nigel West and Oleg Tsarev, *The Crown Jewels: The British secrets at the hear
    the KGB Archives* (New Haven: Yale University Press, 1998), Appendix
    The Philby Reports, 307–9.

20. Entry for 11 November 1941, *Liddell Diaries*, iv, KV 4/188.

21. Ibid., Entries for 11 November and 12 December 1941; Holt, *Deceivers*, 43

22. Montagu, 'Deception', 1 March 1943, para. 7, ADM 223/794.

23. ' "A" Force War Diary' (Clarke), ii, 108–15; CAB 154/2; Howard, *Strat*
    Deception, 65–7.

24. Howard, *Strategic Deception*, 36–7, 68, 84; ' "A" Force War Diary' (Clarke),
    122, CAB 154/2.

25. ' "A Force War Diary' (Clarke), ii, 39–40, CAB 154/2.

26. Ibid., 48.

27. 'Some notes on the organisation of deception' (Clarke), 30 October 19
    RG 319, NM-3, Entry 101, Box 4, Folder 77, NARA.

28. ' "A" Force War Diary' (Clarke), ii, 132, CAB 154/2; Holt, *Deceivers*, 331–

29. 'Deception Policy: 1943', Minute by Controlling Officer, LCS (43) (P)
    (Final), 2 February 1943, CAB 81/83; ' "A" Force War Diary' (Clarke),
    55–8, 63–4, CAB 154/3; 'Precis of Plan "Barclay" ', by Controlling Offic
    LCS (43), 4, 24 April, 1943, CAB 81/77.

30. ' "A" Force War Diary' (Clarke), iii, 68–9, CAB 154/3.

31. 'Plan "Barclay" (Approved Version)', (signed by D. W. Clarke), 10 April 19
    Para. 3, CAB 81/77.

32. 'Precis of Plan Barclay', LCS (43) 4 (by Controlling Officer), 24 April 1943, para. 4 (a), CAB 81/77.

33. 'Plan "Barclay" (Appoved Version)', 10 April 1943, para. 6 (a) (i), CAB 81/77; '"A" Force War Diary' (Clarke), iii, 71, CAB 154/3; Howard, *Strategic Deception*, 43, 86.

34. F. W. Deakin, 'The Myth of an Allied landing in the Balkans during the Second World War (with particular reference to Yugoslavia)' in Phyllis Auty and Richard Clogg (eds.), *British Policy Towards Wartime Resistance in Yugoslavia and Greece* (London: Macmillan, 1975), 102.

35. Ibid.; Helmut Heiber and David M. Glantz (eds.), *Hitler and His Generals: Military conferences, 1942–1945* (New York: Enigma Books, 2002–3), 119–20, 832 (notes, 367, 368); Gannon, *Colossus*, 204–5; Smyth, *Diplomacy and Strategy*, 112.

36. Hinsley et al., *British Intelligence in the Second World War*, iii: Pt I (London: HMSO, 1984), 7.

37. 'Hitler as seen by source', 24 May 1945, 6, HW 13/58.

38. Ibid.

39. Howard, *Strategic Deception*, 67–8, 90.

40. Ibid., 90.

41. Entry for 30 January 1943, *Liddell Diaries*, vii, KV 4/191.

42. '"A" Force War Diary' (Clarke), ii, 8–17, CAB 154/2.

43. 'Plan "Barclay" (Approved Version)', 10 April 1943, paras. 35–9, CAB 81/77; '"A" Force War Diary' (Clarke), iii, 73–4, 81–2, CAB 154/3.

44. '"A" Force War Diary' (Clarke), ii, 122, CAB 154/2; '"A" Force War Diary' (Clarke), iii, 59, CAB 154/3.

45. '"A" Force War Diary' (Clarke), iii, 59–62, CAB 154/3; Holt, *Deceivers*, 149–50.

46. Holt, *Deceivers*, 36–8, 40; Hinsley and Simkins, *British Intelligence in the Second World War*, iv, 165–6; 'Historical record of deception' (Wingate), i, 30–1, CAB 154/100.

47. Holt, *Deceivers*, 38; Howard, *Strategic Deception*, 36–7.

48. '"A" Force War Diary' (Clarke), ii, 93, CAB 154/2.

49. Hinsley and Simkins, *British Intelligence in the Second World War*, iv, 166.

50. Ibid., 167; '"A" Force War Diary' (Clarke), ii, 111, CAB 154/2.

51. '"A" Force War Dairy' (Clarke), iii, 115, CAB 154/3.

52. Ibid., 115–16.

53. Ibid., 45.

54. Ibid.

55. Ibid., 45–6.

56. Ibid., 46.

57. Ibid.

58. Ibid.

59. Ibid., 46–7.

60. Ibid., 47–8.

61. Ibid., 48.
62. Ibid., 44.
63. Howard, *Strategic Deception*, 20-1.
64. Admittedly one German effort to plant a 'stay-behind' agent in Tunis, in the spring of 1943, backfired and actually gifted one of the greatest of all the Mediterranean double-cross agents, code-named *Gilbert* (a French army officer, André Latham), to the anti-Nazi camp. However, his case did not become productive until after the *Husky* landings in July 1943 (Holt, *Deceivers*, 358-61; '"A" Force War Diary' (Clarke), iii, 125-35).
65. Howard, *Strategic Deception*, 84.

CHAPTER 5

1. Montagu, *The Man Who Never Was*, 43.
2. Ibid., 44, 51.
3. Bevan to Robertson on 'Operation Mincemeat', 12 February 1943, CAB 154/67.
4. Ibid.
5. Montagu to Robertson on 'Mincemeat', 16 February 1943, WO 106/5921.
6. Ibid.
7. Bevan to Robertson on 'Operation Mincemeat', 12 February 1943, CAB 154/67.
8. 'Operation Mincemeat', para. 13 (as amended by Col. J. H. Bevan), Montagu Papers, Box 1, 97/45/1; '"A" Force War Diary' (Clarke), iii, 53, 63, CAB 154/3; Holt, *Deceivers*, 338. On Bevan's changes to the Montagu–Cholmondeley report of 27 April 1943, cf. his letter of 3 June 1945 to J. C. Masterman and the amended text of paras. 11 and 13-15 (dated 10 April 1945), CAB 154/67.
9. '"A" Force War Diary' (Clarke), iii, 68-9, CAB 154/3; Holt, *Deceivers*, 338; Howard, *Strategic Deception*, 85; 'Plan "Barclay" (Approved Version)', 10 April 1943, para. 35, CAB 81/77.
10. 'Operation Mincemeat', para. 13 (Montagu's earlier draft: replaced in final version of report by Bevan's amended version), Montagu Papers, Box 1, 97/45/1; telegram from 'Chaucer' for Goldbranson for Galveston; L/2035, 30 March 1943, CAB 154/67; '"A" Force War Diary' (Clarke), III, 76, CAB 154/3; 'Operation Mincemeat': dropping of a body and documents (undated memo, apparently arising out of Bevan-Clarke meeting in March 1943), WO 169/24912.
11. 'Operation Mincemeat', para. 11 (as amended by Col. J. H. Bevan), Montagu Papers, Box 1, 97/45/1.
12. Telegram from Chaucer for Goldbranson for Galveston, L/2035, 30 March 1943, CAB 154/67; Bevan's manuscript memo to Wingate (undated, but probably of very late March 1943), CAB 154/67.

. 'Operation Mincemeat', para. 14 (as amended by Col. J. H. Bevan), Montagu Papers, Box 1, 97/45/1.

. 'Machinery of Deception' (Montagu), 18 September 1943, 8, ADM 223/794.

. Bevan's manuscript memo to Wingate (undated but probably of very late 30 March 1943), CAB 154/67.

. Mure, *Master of Deception*, 194–200; Holt, *Deceivers*, 332.

. Ibid., 'Foreword' by Colonel Nöel Wild, 10, 12; Holt, *Deceivers*, 217.

. Quoted by John P. Campbell, 'A retrospective on John Masterman's *The Double-Cross System*', *International Journal of Intelligence and CounterIntelligence*, 18/2 (2005), 335.

. ' "A" Force War Diary' (Clarke), iii, 77, CAB 154/3.

. 'Operation Mincemeat', para. 13 (as amended by Col. J. H. Bevan), Montagu Papers, Box 1, 97/45/1; telegram no. 869 from Galverston for Chaucer, 1 April 1943 and 870 from ADVANCE HQ 'A' Force for War Cabinet Offices for Hatfield, 1 April 1943, CAB 154/67.

. Montagu, *The Man Who Never Was*, 51.

. Ibid.; Bevan's minute to Brigadier Hollis, 5 April 1943 and Bevan's minute to Montagu et al., 5 April 1943, CAB 154/67; copy of Directors of Plans' memo 43/427 for Group Captain Vintras (and with his manuscript comment thereon), 5 April 1943, CAB 154/67.

. 'Operation Mincemeat', Para. 12, Montagu Papers, Box 1, 97/45/1.

. Ibid., para. 13 (as amended by Col. J. H. Bevan); Bevan to Hollis, 5 April 1943, CAB 154/67; copy of Directors of Plans' memo 43/427 for Group Captain Vintras (and with his manuscript comment thereon), 5 April 1943, CAB 154/67.

. 'Operation Mincemeat' (by Col. J. H. Bevan), 4 April 1943, CAB 154/67. For the actual text of the 'Draft Letter from V.C.I.G.S. to General Alexander', notionally dated 23 April 1943, see 'Annex "A" ' to the document specified in note 26 immediately below.

. Bevan to General Nye re 'Operation Mincemeat', para. 1(b)(i), 8 April 1943, CAB 154/67.

. Ibid., 'Annex B': 'Note on OPERATION "Mincemeat" ' re 'C.O.S. Meeting to be held on 7 April 1943', War Office, 6 April 1943, CAB 154/67.

. Montagu, *The Man Who Never Was*, 51; 'Operation Mincemeat' para. 14 (as amended by Col. J. H. Bevan), Montagu Papers, Box 1, 97/45/1.

. Bevan to Nye re 'Operation Mincemeat', 8 April 1943, CAB 154/67.

. Ibid., 'Annex C': 'Most Secret and Personal Draft Letter from V.C.I.G.S. to General Alexander', para. 1(c)(ii), notionally dated 23 April 1943, CAB 154/67.

. Bevan to Nye, re 'Operation Mincemeat', 8 April 1943, Annex B, para. (d), CAB 154/67.

. On Bevan's strict adhesion to the established procedures for drafting military documents, see Wheatley, *Deception Planners*, 62–3.

33. Bevan to Nye, Re 'Operation Mincemeat', 8 April 1943, 'Annex C', para.
    CAB 154/67.
34. Ibid., 'Annex B''.
35. Twenty Committee (43), 117th mtg, 8 April 1943, Min. 2, KV 4/66.
36. Ibid.
37. 'Operation Mincemeat', para. 14 (as amended by Col. J. H. Bevan), Montagu
    Papers, Box 1, 97/45/1.
38. 'Draft Letter from V.C.I.G.S. to General Alexander (3rd Draft)', notionall
    dated 23 April 1943, para. 1(a)–(b), CAB 154/67.
39. Bevan to Nye, re 'Operation "Mincemeat"', 10 April 1943, CAB 154/67.
40. Montagu, *The Man Who Never Was*, 51.
41. 'Lt.-Gen. Sir Archibald Nye: Distinguished Career in Army and Common
    wealth', obituary, *The Times*, 15 November 1967 and 'Sir Archibald Nye
    obituary by 'J.C.S.', *The Times*, 17 November 1967; Anthony Farrar-Hockley
    'Nye, Sir Archibald Edward', *ODNB* <http://www.oxforddnb.com>.
42. Bevan to Hollis re 'Operation "Mincemeat"', 12 April 1943, CAB 154/67.
43. 'Operation Mincemeat', para. 14 (Original drafted by Lt Cdr E. E. S. Montagu
    Montagu Papers, Box 1, 97/45/1.
44. Montagu, *The Man Who Never Was*, 52.
45. '"A" Force War Diary' (Clarke), iii, 76–7.
46. COS (43) 74th mtg, 13 April 1943, Min. 10, CAB 79/60; Bevan to Nye r
    'Operation "Mincemeat"', 13 April 1943, CAB 154/67.
47. WO 106/5921.
48. Bevan to Nye, re 'Operation "Mincemeat"', 13 April 1943, CAB 154/67.
49. Nye to Bevan, 14 April 1943, CAB 154/67.
50. Montagu, *Beyond Top Secret Ultra*, 147.
51. Montagu, *The Man Who Never Was*, 54.
52. Ibid., 55.
53. Bevan to Hollis, re 'Operation "Mincemeat"', 12 April 1943, CAB 154/67.
54. Ibid.
55. Mountbatten to Admiral Sir A. B. Cunningham, notionally dated 21 Apri
    1943, WO 106/5921; Montagu, *The Man Who Never Was*, 55.
56. 'Operation Mincemeat', para. 14 (as amended by Col. J. H. Bevan), Montagu
    Papers, Box 1, 97/45/1 and CAB 154/67 (10 April, 1945); Montagu, *The Ma
    Who Never Was*, 55–6.
57. 'Operation Mincemeat', 3, ADM 223/794.
58. 'Operation Mincemeat', para. 15, Montagu Papers, Box 1, 97/45/1; 'Note o
    Three Letters', 1, 21 May 1943, ibid; Interview with ms. p. Davies, 15/2/2010
59. Ewen Montagu, *The Man Who Never Was: The story of Operation Mincemeat
    Cadet Edition (London: Evans Brothers, 1965), 45, 70–1, 127.
60. War Office 'Note on Operation "Mincemeat"', 6 April 1943, Annex B
    to Bevan's letter to Nye, re 'Operation Mincemeat', 8 April 1943, CA
    154/67.

CHAPTER 6

1. Cholmondeley report on meeting (of 10 February 1943) about 'Operation Mincemeat', 11 February 1943, CAB 154/67.
2. 'Operation Mincemeat', para. 33(i), Montagu Papers, Box 1, 97/45/1.
3. Ibid., para. 33(ii).
4. Ibid., para. 34; Montagu, *The Man Who Never Was*, 58.
5. Montagu, *Beyond Top Secret Ultra*, 147.
6. Ibid.; Montagu, *The Man Who Never Was*, 58.
7. Montagu, *The Man Who Never Was*, 58; Montagu, *Beyond Top Secret Ultra*, 147.
8. Montagu, *The Man Who Never Was*, 59; Montagu, *Beyond Top Secret Ultra*, 147–8.
9. Montagu, *The Man Who Never Was*, 59; Montagu, *Beyond Top Secret Ultra*, 148.
10. Montagu, *The Man Who Never Was*, 59; 'Operation Mincemeat', para. 35, Montagu Papers, Box 1, 97/45/1.
11. 'Operation Mincemeat', para. 37, Montagu Papers, Box 1, 97/45/1; Montagu, *The Man Who Never Was*, 72; Gieves 'Sale Note', no. 5038, 7 April 1943, WO 106/5921; Ben Fenton, 'Found: The fiancée who never was', *Electronic Telegraph*, no. 524, 29 October 1996.
12. Ibid.; 'Clothing' list, WO 106/5921.
13. Masterman, *Double-Cross System*, 134.
14. Wild, 'Foreword' to Mure, *Master of Deception*, 11–12.
15. Montagu, *Beyond Top Secret Ultra*, 138.
16. Obituary of 'Mr. H. A. L. Fisher', *The Times*, 19 April 1940.
17. Ibid.; Editorial (leader on 'H. A. L. Fisher', ibid.; A. Ryan, 'Fisher, Herbert Albert Laurens (1865–1940)', *ODNB* <http://www.oxforddnb.com>.
18. Ryan, 'Fisher', *ODNB*; *The Times* Obituary, 19 April 1940.
19. *The Times* editorial/leader, 19 April 1940; *The Times*, obituary, 19 April 1940.
20. Ryan, 'Fisher', *ODNB*.
21. Henry Hardy (ed.), *Letters, 1928–1946: Isaiah Berlin* (New York: Cambridge University Press, 2004), 707–8.
22. Masterman, *Double-Cross System*, 134.
23. *The Times* editorial/leader, 19 April 1940.
24. Montagu, *The Man Who Never Was*, 72.
25. Ibid., 'Cadet Edition', 70–1.
26. Montagu, *The Man Who Never Was*, 61–2.
27. 'Operation Mincemeat', para. 38, Montagu Papers, Box 1, 97/45/1.
28. Ibid.
29. Alan Stripp, 'Introduction' to 1996 paperback edn of *The Man Who Never Was* (Oxford: Oxford University Press, 1996), 7.
30. Montagu, *The Man Who Never Was*, 59, 62.
31. 'Martin, William Hynd Norrie', Royal Navy (RN) Officers, 1939–1945, <http://www.unithistories.com/officers/RN>; 'Memoirs of Commander

William Hynd Martin' (1986), Appendix II: 'The Man Who Never Wa
Story', The Papers of Commander W. H. N. Martin, Department of Docu
ments, Imperial War Museum, 98/1/1.

32. 'Operation Mincemeat', para. 38, Montagu Papers, Box 1, 97/45/1. O
course, Montagu may also have altered the third initial in Major Martin'
name to keep the Germans and other Royal Marines confused between an
amongst the several officers on the Navy List with the surname 'Martin' (c
Montagu, Beyond Top Secret Ultra, 48 and Man Who Never Was, 62).

33. 'Memoirs of Command William Hynd Norrie Martin', Appendix II: 'Th
Man Who Never Was Story', Commander W. H. N. Martin Papers, 98/1/1

34. 'Operation Mincemeat', para. 38, Montagu Papers, Box 1, 97/45/1; Photo
graph of pp. 2–3 of Major William Martin's Identity Card, WO 106/5921.

35. 'Operation Mincemeat', paras. 38–9, Montagu Papers, Box 1, 97/45/1
Montagu, The Man Who Never Was, 62–3.

36. 'Operation Mincemeat', para. 38, Montagu Papers, Box 1, 97/45/1; Montagu
The Man Who Never Was, 63.

37. Montagu, The Man Who Never Was, 63.

38. Ibid., 63; 'Operation Mincemeat', para. 38, Montagu Papers, Box 1, 97/45/1

39. Montagu, The Man Who Never Was, 60.

40. Ibid.

41. Ibid., 60–1; Box 1, 'Operation Mincemeat', para. 39, Montagu Papers, Box 1
97/45/1.

42. 'Operation Mincemeat', para. 39, Montagu Papers, Box 1, 97/45/1.

43. Montagu, The Man Who Never Was, 61.

44. Ben Macintyre, Agent Zigzag (New York: Harmony Books, 2007), 117–19
Fenton, 'Found: The fiancée who never was'.

45. Masterman, Double-Cross System, 21–3.

46. Macintyre, Agent Zigzag, 119.

47. Reed did commit one serious blunder, however, in monitoring Chapman'
radio traffic with his Abwehr contacts back in France. On 27 December 1942
he failed to spot that Chapman had omitted, evidently accidentally, the routin
set of letters (five 'Fs') that assured the Abwehr that he had not been appre-
hended by the British. Although the Zigzag case survived this 'howler' o
Reed's part, 'Tar' Robertson was not amused by this potentially fatal sin o
omission (Macintyre, Agent Zigzag, 129–33).

48. Hinsley and Simkins, British Intelligence in the Second World War, iv, 120, 219
Macintyre, Agent Zigzag, 136–8; Twenty Committee (43), 106th mtg, 2
January 1943, Min. 6, KV 4/65.

49. Macintyre, Agent Zigzag, 133–4, 152–8; Hinsley and Simkins, British Intelligenc
in the Second World War, iv, 219.

50. Quoted in Macintyre, Agent Zigzag, 157.

51. Ibid., 117.

52. Montagu, The Man Who Never Was, 61.

'Operation Mincemeat', para. 39, Montagu Papers, Box 1, 97/45/1.

Montagu, *The Man Who Never Was*, 61.

Ibid., 63–4.

Ibid.; Entry on 'Combined Operations' in I. C. B. Dear and M. R. D. Foot (eds.), *Oxford Companion to World War II* (Oxford: Oxford University Press, 1995), 254; Brigadier C. J. C. Molony, et al., *The Mediterranean and the Middle East* (*History of the Second World War: United Kingdom Military Series*), v: *The Campaign in Sicily, 1943 and the Campaign in Italy, 3rd September 1943 to 31st March, 1944* (London: HMSO, 1973), 66–8.

Philip Ziegler, 'Mountbatten, Louis Francis Albert Victor Nicholas', First Earl Mountbatten of Burma (1900–1979)', *ODNB* <http://www.oxforddnb.com>.

See, e.g., ibid.; Robin Neillands, *The Dieppe Raid: The story of the disastrous 1942 expedition* (London: Aurum, 2005; paperback edn, 2006), 79–83, 108–26, 267, 272–9; Brian Loring Villa, *Unauthorized Action: Mountbatten and the Dieppe raid* (Toronto: Oxford University Press, 1989), 62–73, 232–47.

Gilbert, *Road to Victory*, 210–12; Danchev and Todman (eds.), *Alanbrooke War Diaries*, 317.

Ibid., 236–7.

Ibid., 356–7. See, also, Loring Villa, *Unauthorized Action*, 171–3.

'Operation Mincemeat', para. 45, Montagu Papers, Box 1, 97/45/1; Montagu, *The Man Who Never Was*, 64.

WO 106/5921.

Montagu, *The Man Who Never Was*, 65–6.

Ibid., 66; Montagu, *Beyond Top Secret Ultra*, 148–9.

Howard, *Grand Strategy*, iv, 184–8, 347–8; Molony, *Mediterranean and the Middle East*, v, 861; David Hunt, 'Alexander, Harold Rupert Leofric George, First Earl Alexander of Tunis (1891–1969), *ODNB* <http://www.oxforddnb.com>.

'Operation Mincemeat', para. 44, Montagu Papers, Box 1, 97/45/1; Cholmondeley's report of meeting about 'Operation Mincemeat', on 10 February 1943, CAB 154/67; Montagu, *The Man Who Never Was*, 66–7.

'Operation Mincemeat', para. 44, Montagu Papers, Box 1, 97/45/1.

Cholmondeley's report of meeting about 'Operation Mincemeat' on 10 February 1943, CAB 154/67.

Bevan to T. A. Robertson re 'Operation Mincemeat', 12 February 1943, CAB 154/67.

'Operation Mincemeat', para. 37, Montagu Papers, Box 1, 97/45/1.

Ibid., para. 46.

Saunders, Hillary St. George, *Combined Operations: The official story of the Commandos, with a foreword by Vice-Admiral Lord Louis Mountbatten, Chief of Combined Operations* (New York: Macmillan 1943); Charles Morgan and Lord Ruffside, 'Mr. H. St. George Saunders: A generous spirit', obituary, *The Times*,

29 December 1951; 'Hilary Saunders, 1989–1951', <http://www.xs4all.nl/
embden11/Engels/saunders.htm>.

74. Montagu, *Beyond Top Secret Ultra*, 49–50, 96, 99.

75. D. McLachlan, *Room 39: Naval intelligence in action, 1939–45* (London: We
denfeld and Nicolson, 1968), 65–71.

76. *Combined Operations* (US edition, 1943) back jacket and back flap; Micha
Davie (ed.), *The Diaries of Evelyn Waugh* (London: Weidenfeld and Nicholso
1976; paperback edn, London: Penguin, 1979), 532–5; Martin Stannar
'Waugh, Evelyn Arthur St. John (1903–1966)', *ODNB* <http://ww
oxforddnb.com>.

77. 'Operation Mincemeat', para. 46, Montagu Papers, Box 1, 97/45/1.

78. WO 106/5921.

79. 'Operation Mincemeat', para. 47, Montagu Papers, Box 1, 97/45/1; Montag
Beyond Top Secret Ultra, 149.

80. 'Operation Mincemeat', para. 49, Montagu Papers, Box 1, 97/45/1; Montag
The Man Who Never Was, 69.

81. Cholmondeley's report of meeting about 'Operation Mincemeat' on 10 Februa
1943, CAB 154/67.

82. Ibid.

83. 'Operation Mincemeat', para. 49, Montagu Papers, Box 1, 97/45/1; Montag
The Man Who Never Was, 69–70.

84. 'Operation Mincemeat': Operation Orders, drafted by Lt Cdr E. E. S. Mo
tagu, 31 March 1943, para. 5, WO 106/5921; Montagu, *The Man Who Nev
Was*, 37–41.

85. Montagu, *The Man Who Never Was*, 69–71.

86. 'Operation Mincemeat', para. 49, Montagu Papers, Box 1, 97/45/1; 'Ope
ation Mincemeat': Operation Orders, 31 March 1943, para. 5; Montagu, *T
Man Who Never Was*, 70.

87. 'Operation Mincemeat', para. 49, Montagu Papers, Box 1, 97/45/1.

88. Montagu, *The Man Who Never Was*, 74.

CHAPTER 7

1. Montagu, *The Man Who Never Was*, 74–5; Montagu, *Beyond Top Secret Ultr
149.

2. 'Operation Mincemeat', para. 41, Montagu Papers, Box 1, 97/45/1; 'Person
Documents and Articles in Pockets', WO 106/5921; 'Operation Mincemea
7, ADM 223/794.

3. 'Operation Mincemeat', para. 41, Montagu Papers, Box 1, 97/45/1; 'Ope
ation Mincemeat', 7, ADM 223/794; Montagu, *The Man Who Never W
76–7.

4. Montagu, *The Man Who Never Was*, 77–8.

5. Ibid., 78.

6. WO 106/5921.

7. 'Operation Mincemeat', para. 41, Montagu Papers Box 1, 97/45/1; Montagu, *The Man Who Never Was*, 78–9.

8. Montagu, *The Man Who Never Was*, 72–3.

9. Ibid., 71–2; 'Operation Mincemeat', para. 41, Montagu Papers, Box 1, 97/45/1; 'Personal Documents and Articles in Pockets' and 'Combined Operations Headquarters' pass no. 649, made out to Major W. Martin, RM, WO 106/5921.

10. Montagu, *The Man Who Never Was*, 75–6; 'Personal Documents and Articles in Pockets': bill-cum-receipt from Naval and Military Club, 24 April 1943 and undated letter of invitation to the Cabaret Club, WO 106/5921.

11. Holt, *Deceivers*, 132; J. C. Masterman, *On the Chariot Wheel: An autobiography* (London: Oxford University Press, 1975), 219; John Curry, *The Security Service 1908–1945: The official history*, Introduction by Christopher Andrew (Kew, Surrey: Public Record Office, 1999), 247.

12. West (ed.), *Guy Liddell Diaries*, i, 106 (entry for 15 October, 1940).

13. KV 4/429. Actually, there is no trace of the article mentioned by Marriott in any issue of *The Field* published between the outbreak of the Second World War in early September 1939 and early January 1943. So, he may have misremembered the actual title of the journal in which he originally read it or, perhaps, brought to mind a piece published many years before.

14. See, e.g., 'Colonel Richard Meinertzhagen', obituary, *The Times*, 19 June 1967.

15. See, e.g., M. R. D. Foot, 'Meinertzhagen, Richard (1878–1967), *ODNB* <http://www.oxforddnb.com>.

16. Anthony Bruce, *The Last Crusade: The Palestine campaign in the First World War* (London: John Murray, 2002), 111–16.

17. Quoted by Yigal Sheffy, 'Institutionalized deception and perception reinforcement: Allenby's campaigns in Palestine', *Intelligence and National Security*, 5/2 (1990), 182.

18. Ibid., 189.

19. T. E. Lawrence, *Seven Pillars of Wisdom: A triumph* (London: Jonathan Cape, 1935; Folio Edition, London, 2000), 320.

20. Ibid.

21. See, e.g., Brian Garfield, *The Meinertzhagen Mystery: The life and legend of a colossal fraud* (Washington, DC: Potomac Books, 2007), 5–8; Yigal Sheffy, 'The spy who never was: An intelligence myth in Palestine, 1914–18', *Intelligence and National Security*, 14/3 (1999), 128; John Seabrook, 'Ruffled Feathers: Uncovering the Biggest Scandal in the Bird World', *The New Yorker*, 82/15 (2006), 51–61.

22. Garfield, *Meinertzhagen Mystery*, 26–7.

23. Quoted ibid., 33.

24. Ibid., 31

25. 'Ten years ago: The capture of Beersheba. A triumph of surprise', *The Times*, 31 October 1927.

26. Garfield, *Meinertzhagen Mystery*, 31–7.
27. Bruce, *Last Crusade*, 128–70; Trevor Wilson, *The Myriad Faces of War: Britain and the Great War* (Cambridge: Cambridge University Press, 1986), 501.
28. Sheffy, 'Institutionalized deception', 195.
29. Ibid.
30. Bruce, *Last Crusade*, 126–7, 135–7.
31. Sheffy, 'Institutionalized deception', 195–6.
32. Michael Handel, 'Introduction: Strategic and operatonal deception in historical perspective', in idem (ed.), *Strategic and Operational Deception in the Second World War* (London: Frank Cass, 1987), 60–6; H. O. Dovey, 'The false going map at Alam Halfa', *Intelligence and National Security*, 4/1 (1989), 165–8; Hinsley et al., *British Intelligence in the Second World War*, ii, 416.
33. Marriott to Bevan, 6 January 1943, KV 4/429.
34. Ibid.; Montagu, *The Man Who Never Was*, 75.
35. Montagu, *The Man Who Never Was*, 75–6.
36. Marriott to Bevan, 6 January 1943, KV 4/429.
37. Ben Fenton, 'Found: The fiancée who never was', *Electronic Telegraph*, 29 October 1996; Montagu, *The Man Who Never Was*, 80.
38. 'Operation Mincemeat', 7, ADM 223/794; Fenton, 'Found: The fiancée who never was'; Montagu, *The Man Who Never Was*, 80–1.
39. Obituary of Colonel William Gerard Leigh, <http://www.telegraph.co.uk/news/obituaries/3118034/Colonel-William-Gerard-Leigh.html>, 1 October 2008; Fenton, 'Found: The fiancée who never was'.
40. Montagu, *The Man Who Never Was*, 80.
41. Ibid., 81.
42. Ibid.; 'Operation Mincemeat', 8, ADM 223/794; Fenton, 'Found: The fiancée who never was'; Martin Vander Weyer, 'The real Moneypenny is alive and kicking', *Daily Telegraph*, 10 May 1997; Samantha Weinberg, 'Licensed to thrill', *Times Online*, 11 November 2006; 'Lady Ridsdale', obituary, 17 December 2009, <http://www.telegraph.co.uk>; 'Dame Paddy Ridsdale: Conservative grande dame', obituary, *The Times*, 19 December 2009.
43. 'Operation Mincemeat', 8, ADM 223/794.
44. Montagu, *The Man Who Never Was*, 81.
45. WO 106/5921.
46. Ibid.
47. See, e.g., 'Operation Mincemeat', para. 43, Montagu Papers, Box 1, 97/45/1.
48. Montagu, *The Man Who Never Was*, 81.
49. Ibid., 82; Fenton, 'Found: The fiancée who never was'; 'Operation Mincemeat', para. 42, Montagu Papers, Box 1, 97/45/1.
50. Montagu, *The Man Who Never Was*, 82.
51. Montagu, 'Postscript', *The Man Who Never Was* (Cadet Edition), 127.
52. Ibid.
53. 'Operation Mincemeat', 7–8, ADM 223/794.

. Ibid., 7.
. WO 106/5921. Again, to ensure that this missive from Major Martin's father looked like a genuine piece of handwriting, the last three letters of the word 'uninhabitable' contained in its text, are all but obliterated by an ink blot—such as an aged, unsteady hand might so easily make.
. Ibid.
. Montagu, *The Man Who Never Wa*s, 84.
. Ibid. It is tempting to speculate that Montagu himself was the author of these letters, since he had both the native irreverence and legal knowledge necessary to write them.
. WO 106/5921; Montagu, *The Man Who Never Was*, 79–80.
. 'Operation Mincemeat', 7, ADM 223/794.
. WO 106/5921.
. Ibid.; Montagu, *The Man Who Never Was*, 86–7.
. 'Operation Mincemeat', 7, ADM 223/794.
. See, e.g., Smith, 'Bletchley Park', 287–8 and Howard, *Strategic Deception*, 20–1. The Jeweller's bill is in WO 106/5921.
. Montagu, *The Man Who Never Was*, 86.
. Montagu, *The Man Who Never Was*, Cadet Edition, 70–1.
. Ibid.
. Montagu, *The Man Who Never Was*, 87–8; Martin Fletcher and Dominic Kennedy, 'MI5 agents snatched body of Man Who Never Was', *The Times*, 19 March 2002.
. ' "A" Force War Diary' (Clarke), iii, 77, CAB 154/3.
. Montagu, *The Man Who Never Was*, 74–5.
. Fenton, 'Found: The fiancée who never was'.

CHAPTER 8

1. Twenty Committee (43), 108th mtg, 4 February 1943, Min. 8, KV4/65.
2. 'Operation Mincemeat',1, ADM 223/794.
3. Ibid., 1.
4. 'Operation Mincemeat', para. 17, Montagu Papers, Box 1, 97/45/1.
5. Ibid., para. 17.
6. Hinsley and Simkins, *British Intelligence in the Second World War*, iv, 159–62; Curry, *Security Service*, 236–7; Manuel Ros Agudo, *La Guerra Secreta de Franco (1939–1945)* (Barcelona: Crítica, 2002), 206–60; 'Spanish Assistance to the German Navy', A report submitted by E. G. N. Rushbrooke, Director of Naval Intelligence, 10 January 1946, FO 371/60331, Z 094/8/G 41.
7. Hinsley and Simkins, *British Intelligence in the Second World War*, iv, 160.
8. Ros Agudo, *La Guerra Secreta*, 232–36, 243.
9. Smyth, 'Screening "Torch" ', 335.
10. Hinsley et al., *British Intelligence in the Second World War*, ii, 719.

11. Smith, 'Bletchley Park, Double Cross and D-Day', 287; Erskine, 'Eavesdrop ping on "Bodden"', 111.
12. Erskine, 'Eavesdropping on "Bodden"', 111–13.
13. Hinsley et al., *British Intelligence in the Second World War*, ii, 719.
14. Ibid. 'R.I.S. Note no.1', issued by the recently-established Radio Intelligen Service on 5 June 1943, attached global significance to German monitoring Allied air and sea transports in the Gibraltar strait:

   > The keystone of the Abwehr reporting system is the observation of ships and aircraft in the Straits of Gibraltar; if this were disrupted, the Abwehr presentation of the enemy order of battle would be hopelessly incomplete and inaccurate; this explains the extraordinary importance which Canaris attaches to his relations with highly-placed Spaniards.

   (Quoted by E. D. R. Harrison, 'British radio security and intelligence, 193 43', *English Historical Review*, CXXIV/506 (2009), 87.)
15. Montagu, *The Man Who Never Was*, 33.
16. Montagu, *Beyond Top Secret Ultra*, 144; 'Operation Mincemeat', para. 1 Montagu Papers, Box 97/45/1.
17. 'Operation Mincemeat', para. 18, Montagu Papers, Box 1, 97/45/1; Ca tain Alan Hillgarth, 'The Naval Attaché to Spain and Naval Intelligenc (undated but post-war), Pt II, Section V: 'Relations with S.I.S. and S.O. and covert intelligence', para. 5 and 'Miscellaneous points', paras. 11–1 ADM 223/490.
18. Interview with Captain Alan Hillgarth, RN, 27 January 1977, Ballinderry, C Tipperary, Ireland.
19. Viscount Templewood, *Ambassador on Special Mission* (London: Collins, 1946 211; Hillgarth, 'The Naval Attaché to Spain and Naval Intelligence', Pt I 'Miscellaneous points', paras. 13–14, ADM 223/490.
20. Denis Smyth, 'Hillgarth, Alan Hugh (1899–1978)', *ODNB* <http://www oxforddnb.com>; McLachlan, *Room 39*, 195; Smyth, *Diplomacy and Strateg* 190–1; 'Spanish assistance to the German Navy', FO 371/60331, Z 094/8/ 41; Hillgarth, 'The Naval Attaché to Spain and Naval Intelligence', Pt I Section II: 'Security', paras. 3–4, ADM 223/490.
21. 'Operation Mincemeat', para. 18, Montagu Papers, Box 1, 97/45/1.
22. Telegram no. 532, 4 October 1942, from Governor & C.-in-C. Gibraltar t the War Office, PREM 3/439/17; telegram no. 498, 28 September 1942, fro VACNA to the Admiralty, ibid.; 'Enquiry into the possibility of compromi of Operation TORCH', (n.d., but of 2 October 1942), para. 2, ibid.
23. See, e.g., McLachlan, *Room 39*, 194–6.
24. 'Operation Mincemeat', para. 18, Montagu Papers, Box 1, 97/45/1.
25. Ibid.
26. Jesus Ramírez Copeiro del Villar, *Espías y Neutrales: Huelva en la II Guer Mundial* (Huelva: Jesus Ramírez Copeiro del Villar, 1996), 78–9.

. Charles E. Harvey, *The Rio Tinto Company: An economic history of an international mining concern, 1873–1954* (Penzance, Cornwall: Alison Hodge, 1981), 52.

. Ibid., 130–6, 177–82; Smyth, *Diplomacy and Strategy*, 90–1.

. 'Operation Mincemeat', para. 18, Montagu Papers, Box 1, 97/45/1.

. Ibid.; Ramírez Copeiro, *Espías y Neutrales*, 306; José María Irujo, *La Lista Negra: Los espías nazis protegidos por Franco y la Iglesia* (Madrid: Aguilar, 2003), 91.

. Hinsley and Simkins, *British Intelligence in the Second World War*, iv, 159.

.. Ramírez Copeiro, *Espías y Neutrales*, 62, 307–9, 323–40; Irujo, *La Lista Negra*, 91.

. Ramírez Copeiro, *Espías y Neutrales*, 424.

.. Ibid., 55, 356–8.

. Ibid., 359–61; 'Operation Mincemeat', para. 18, Montagu Papers, Box 1, 97/45/1.

.. Bevan to Montagu, re 'Operation Mincemeat', 1 March 1943, CAB 154/67.

. 'Operation Mincemeat', para. 18, Montagu Papers, Box 1, 97/45/1.

. Ibid., para. 23.

.. Ibid.; 'Operation Mincemeat': Operation Orders drafted by Lt Cdr E. E. S. Montagu, 31 March 1943, Section 3 and Appendix (of 22 March 1943), WO 106/5921; Montagu, *The Man Who Never Was*, 33–4.

). 'Reference Sheet' on 'Mincemeat', from Montagu to Bevan, 26 March 1943, CAB 154/67.

.. 'Operation Mincemeat': Operation Orders (Montagu), 31 March 1943, Section 3, WO 106/5921.

.. 'Operation Mincemeat', para. 24, Montagu Papers, Box 1, 97/45/1.

.. Ibid., para. 19.

.. Ibid., para 22.

.. Ibid., para. 19.

.. Ibid.

.. Ibid., para. 21.

.. Ibid., para 20.

). Ibid.

). Ros Agudo, *La Guerra Secreta*, 208–9.

.. 'Operation Mincemeat', para. 20, Montagu Papers, Box 1, 97/45/1.

.. Hinsley et al., *British Intelligence in the Second World War*, ii, 6402.

.. Ros Agudo, *La Guerra Secreta*, 208–9. The German failure to read these coded communications was all the more striking in that their Spanish collaborators made sure that copies of all the British telegrams were delivered into their hands: Hillgarth, 'The Naval Attaché to Spain and Naval Intelligence', Pt II, Section IV: 'Communications', para. 3, ADM 223/490).

.. Hinsley et al., *British Intelligence in the Second World War*, ii, 633 (footnote).

.. 'Operation Mincemeat', para. 20, Montagu Papers, Box 1, 97/45/1.

.. McLachlan, *Room 39*, 182–3.

57. Smyth, 'Hillgarth, Alan Hugh (1899–1978)', *ODNB*.

58. Private information.

59. Smyth, 'Hillgarth, Alan Hugh (1899–1978)', *ODNB*; Patrick Beesly, *V* *Special Admiral: The life of Admiral J. H. Godfrey, CB* (London: Hamish Hami ton, 1980), 92.

60. Beesly, *Very Special Admiral*, 143–4; Hillgarth, 'The Naval Attaché to Spain a Naval Intelligence', Pt I, Section I: 'The importance of the maintenance of naval attaché in Spain', para. 8, ADM 223/490.

61. Smyth, 'Hillgarth, Alan Hugh (1899–1978)', *ODNB*; Smyth, *Diplomacy a Strategy*, 190–1; Charles B. Burdick, ' "Moro": The resupply of Germa submarines in Spain, 1939–1942', *Central European History*, 3/3 (1970).

62. McLachlan, *Room 39*, 197–8; Ros Agudo, *La Guerra Secreta*, 239–43; M Memorandum on (Enemy) 'Sabotage' in Spain, December 1943, Anne Section I: 'Spanish military guard on the *Olterra*', ADM 223/490.

63. Smyth, *Diplomacy and Strategy*, 26–7.

64. Ibid., 27–9.

65. Ibid., 28–30.

66. Ibid., 28, 35–6; David Stafford, *Roosevelt and Churchill: Men of secrets* (Londo Little Brown, 1999), 82.

67. Denis Smyth, ' "Les Chevaliers de Saint-George": La Grande-Bretagne et Corruption des généraux espagnols (1940–1942)', *Guerre Mondiales et Confl Contemporains*, No 162/April (1991), 29–37, 46–54.

68. Smyth, *Diplomacy and Strategy*, 38–9; Beesly, *Very Special Admiral*, 143– W. J. M. Mackenzie, *The Secret History of SOE: The Special Operations Executiv 1940–1945* (London: St Ermin's Press, 2000), 241–2; Hillgarth, 'The Naval Attach to Spain and naval intelligence', Pt II, Section V: 'Relations with S.I.S., S.O. and Covert Intelligence', para. I, ADM 223/490.

69. Kim Philby, *My Silent War* (New York: Grove, 1968), 66–7; Benton, 'Th ISOS years', 382; Desmond Bristow (with Bill Bristow), *A Game of Moles: T deceptions of an MI6 officer* (London: Little, Brown & Co., 1993), 185.

70. Philby, *My Silent War*, 66.

71. Keith Jeffery, *The Secret History of MI6* (New York: Penguin, 2010), 404–5.

72. Private information.

73. 'Operation Mincemeat', meeting held in Major Robertson's Room, 10 Februar 1943, CAB 154/67.

74. Bevan to Robertson, re 'Operation Mincemeat', 12 February 1943, CAB 154/6

75. 'Operation Mincemeat', brief given to Captain Lambe, Director of Plan Admiralty, by Lt Cdr Montagu, 12 March 1943, paras. 1 and 4(a), WO 106 5921; 'Operation Mincemeat', para. 26, Montagu Papers, Box 1, 97/45/1.

76. 'Operaton Mincemeat', Montagu's brief to Lambe, 12 March 1943, para. 4(c WO 106/5921.

77. Ibid., para. 4(d).

78. Ibid., para. 4(b).

. Ibid.

. Ibid.

. Ibid.

. Ibid., para. 5.

. Montagu, *The Man Who Never Was*, 35–6; 'Operation Mincemeat', paras. 28, 52, Montagu Papers, Box 1, 97/45/1; Montagu to Bevan, re 'Mincemeat', 26 March 1943, CAB 154/67.

. 'Operation Mincemeat', Montagu's brief to Lambe, 12 March 1943, para. 4(b), WO 106/5921.

. Obituary of 'Sir Charles Lambe', *The Times*, 31 August 1960; AJP, 'Sir Charles Lambe' (Obituaries), *The Times*, 7 September 1960; M. of B., 'Admiral of the Fleet: Sir Charles Lambe' (obituaries), *The Times*, 2 September 1960; William Davis, 'Lambe, Sir Charles Edward (1900–1960), *ODNB* <http://www. oxforddnb.com>.

. William Davis, 'Lambe, Sir Charles Edward (1900–1960), *ODNB*.

. See Ch. 5, p. 81 above and note 13.

. See, e.g., memo from LCS (sent at Bevan's request) to Group Captain Vintras (the Air Ministry's Director of Plans) with the latter's manuscript reply thereon, 5 April 1943, CAB 154/67.

. 'Operation Mincemeat', Montagu's brief to Lambe, 12 March 1943, para. 6, WO 106/5921; 'Operation Mincemeat', para. 26, Montagu Papers, Box 1, 97/45/1.

. 'Operation Mincemeat', para. 27(iii), Montagu Papers, Box 1, 97/45/1.

. Ibid., para. 27(i).

. Montagu, *The Man Who Never Was*, 35; Scott, *Action Reply*, 44.

. 'Operation Mincemeat', para. 27(iv), Montagu Papers, Box 1, 97/45/1.

. Ibid., para. 28; Montagu, *The Man Who Never Was*, 36; 'Operation Mincemeat', Operation Orders (Montagu), 31 March 1943, Section 2, WO 106/5921.

. Montagu to Bevan, re 'Mincemeat', 26 March 1943, CAB 154/67.

. 'Operation Mincemeat', para. 28, Montagu Papers, Box 1, 97/45/1; Scott, *Action Reply*, 44.

. 'Operation Mincemeat', para. 28, Montagu Papers, Box 1, 97/45/1; 'Operation Mincemeat', Operation Orders (Montagu), 31 March 1943, Section 2, WO 106/5921; Diagram of Container, WO 106/5921.

. 'Operation Mincemeat', Operation Orders (Montagu), 31 March 1943, Section 2, WO 106/5921.

. Ibid., Section 2, 10; 'Operation Mincemeat', para. 32, Montagu Papers, Box 1, 97/45/1.

. 'Operation Mincemeat', para. 29, Montagu Papers, Box 1, 97/45/1.

. Ibid., paras. 29 and 60; 'Operation Mincemeat', Operation Orders, 31 March 1943, Sections 4–5, WO 106/5921.

. 'Operation Mincemeat', para. 27 (ii), Montagu Papers, Box 1, 97/45/1; Montagu to Bevan re 'Mincemeat', 26 March 1943, CAB 154/67.

. Montagu to Bevan re 'Mincemeat', 26 March 1943, CAB 154/67.

104. Robertson, *The Ship With Two Captains*, 29–31; Porch, *Path to Victory*, 343, 357–8.
105. Eisenhower to Harry Cecil Butcher, 2 September 1942, Chandler (e *Eisenhower Papers*, i, 526–7.
106. Butcher, *Three Years*, 123.
107. Ibid., 127–30; Robertson, *The Ship With Two Captains*, 39–52; 'A see mission': an address by Lieutenant N. L. A. Jewell, MBE, LM, RN to Empire Club of Canada, 28 May 1944, <http://speeches.empireclub.org/
108. Butcher, *Three Years*, 130.
109. Porch, *Path to Victory*, 357–8.
110. Robertson, *The Ship With Two Captains*, 53.
111. Butcher, *Three Years*, 130.
112. Robertson, *The Ship With Two Captains*, 55, 63–9.
113. D'Este, *Eisenhower*, 344–5; Butcher, *Three Years*, 137–8; Porch, *Path to Victo* 366; Eisenhower to Giraud, 6 November 1942 in Chandler (ed.), *Eisenho Papers*, i, 656–8.
114. Robertson, *The Ship With Two Captains*, 69–70.
115. Ibid., 56–61; Butcher, *Three Years*, 122, 133.
116. Robertson, *The Ship With Two Captains*, 62, 71–90; Butcher, *Three Years*, 140 Jewell, 'Secret mission'; Bill Jewell, Accession Number 12278, Sound Ar ive, IWM Reel Number 2.
117. Butcher, *Three Years*, 141–6; Stephen E. Ambrose, *The Supreme Comman The war years of General Dwight D. Eisenhower* (London: Cassell, 1971), 114– Giraud changed his tune somewhat on 8 November 1942—the D-Day *Operation Torch*—when first reports indicated that the invasion of North Af was succeeding, despite French military opposition. As early as the follow day, however, Eisenhower had become thoroughly disenchanted with the se serving attitudes he encountered amongst senior French commanders, Gira included, as *Torch* was launched—a fact he admitted to an assistant: 'It isn't operation that's wearing me down—it's the petty intrigue and the necessity dealing with little, selfish, conceited worms that call themselves men': A brose, *Supreme Commander*, 116–19; Eisenhower to Walter Bedell Smi 9 November 1942, Chandler (ed.), *Eisenhower Papers*, ii, 677.
118. D'Este, *Eisenhower*, 347, 418–19; Porch, *Path to Victory*, 366, 382; Jean-Lo Crémieux-Brilhac, *La France Libre: de L'Appel du 18 Juin à la Libération* (Pa Gallimard, 1996), 455–82, 553–81.
119. Robertson, *The Ship With Two Captains*, 92.
120. Ibid., 104–8; Butcher, *Three Years*, 191.
121. Robertson, *The Ship With Two Captains*, 121–3.
122. Scott, *Action Reply*, 43.
123. Robertson, *The Ship With Two Captains*, 19; Robert Hutchinson, *Jap Submarines: War beneath the waves, from 1776 to the present day* (Londo HarperCollins, 2001), 74.

24. Innis McCartney, *British Submarines, 1939–45* (Botley, Oxfordshire: Osprey, 2006), 7.

25. Robertson, *The Ship With Two Captains*, 114–21; Bill Jewell, Accession Number 12278, Reel 3, Sound Archive, IWM.

26. John Parker, *The Illustrated World Guide to Submarines* (London: Hermes House, 2007), 145.

27. 'Operation Mincemeat', para. 27(ii), Montagu Papers, Box 1, 97/45/1.

28. Ibid., para. 30; Robertson, *The Ship With Two Captains*, 123; Montagu, *The Man Who Never Was*, 36–7.

29. 'Operation Mincemeat': Operation Orders (Montagu), 31 March 1943, Sections 1–2, WO 106/5921.

30. Alex May, 'Jewell, Norman Limbury Auchinleck (Bill) (1913–2004)', *ODNB* <http://www.oxforddnb.com>; Bill Jewell, Accession Number 12278, Reel 3, Sound Archive, IWM.

31. 'Operation Mincemeat', Operation Orders (Montagu), 31 March 1943, Sections 3, 5, 8, and 10.

32. Robertson, *The Ship With Two Captains*, 19–21; 'Captain Bill Jewell' (Obituary), *The Times*, 25 August 2004.

33. 'Operation Mincemeat', para. 55, Montagu Papers, Box 1, 97/43/1.

34. 'Operation Mincemeat': Operation Orders (Montagu), 31 March 1943, Section 10, WO 106/5921.

35. Montagu to Bevan, re 'Mincemeat', 26 March 1943, CAB 154/67.

36. Note for Col. Bevan, informing him of Montagu's phone-call to the effect that the 'departure of Mincemeat has been postponed to 17 April', 1 April 1943, CAB 154/67; 'Operation Mincemeat', para. 31, Montagu Papers, Box 1, 97/45/1.

37. 'Operation Mincemeat', para. 31, Montagu Papers, Box 1, 97/45/1.

38. COS (43) 74th mtg, 13 April 1943, Min. 10, CAB 79/60.

39. COS (43) 76th mtg, 14 April 1943, Min. 8, CAB 79/60.

40. Montagu, *Beyond Top Secret Ultra*, 145–50.

41. Ismay to Churchill, 14 April 1943, PREM 3/227/6.

42. Montagu, *Beyond Top Secret Ultra*, 149–150; David Stafford, *Churchill and Secret Service* (London: John Murray, 1997), 6–7; F. H. Hinsley, 'Churchill and the use of special intelligence' in Robert Blake and Wm. Roger Louis (eds.), *Churchill* (New York: Norton, 1993), 407–25; Carlo D'Este, *Warlord: A life of Winston Churchill at war, 1874–1945* (New York: HarperCollins, 2008), 458.

43. 'Mincemeat', undated, Manuscript Memo, signed by 'John H. Bevan, Controlling Officer', CAB 154/67; Gilbert, (citing Randolph Churchill's 'Interview with Mr. John Bevan', 9 May 1967) in *Road to Victory*, 405.

44. 'Mincemeat' (Bevan MS Memo), CAB 154/67; Gilbert, *Road to Victory*, 405.

45. Montagu, *The Man Who Never Was*, 90; Montagu, *Beyond Top Secret Ultra*, 143; Stripp, 'Introduction', *The Man Who Never Was*, paperback edn (Oxford: Oxford University Press, 1996), 4.

46. 'Mincemeat' (Bevan MS Memo), CAB 154/67.

147. Ibid.
148. Ibid.
149. Ambrose, *Supreme Commander*, 177–83.
150. Butcher, *Three Years*, 238–9.
151. Porch, *Path to Victory*, 408–12.
152. Eisenhower to John Sheldon Doud Eisenhower, 8 April 1943 in Chandle (ed.), *Eisenhower Papers*, ii, 1083–4; Atkinson, *Army at Dawn*, 465.
153. Howard, *Grand Strategy*, iv, 368; Ambrose, *Supreme Commander*, 207–8.
154. D'Este, *Bitter Victory*, 85–6; Howard, *Grand Strategy*, iv, 369; Ambrose *Supreme Commander*, 208. So, although—as Carlo D'Este notes—'Eisenhowe probably never saw Churchill's stinging minute', he was soon made aware the indignation he had provoked amongst the Anglo–American warlord (*Bitter Victory*, 87).
155. Howard, *Grand Strategy*, iv, 369.
156. Ibid., 369–70; Ambrose, *Supreme Commander*, 208.
157. See, e.g., Eisenhower to George Catlett Marshall, 13 May 1943 in Chandle (ed.), *Eisenhower Papers*, ii, 1129.
158. Cypher telegram no. L/2061 from Chaucer to Goldbranson (repeated t Galveston), 15 April 1943, CAB 154/67.
159. 'Operation Mincemeat': Operation Orders (Montagu), 31 March 1943, Sec tion 8, WO 106/5921.
160. Cypher telegram no. 4589 from Advanced Quarters for Chaucer, undate (but received at 16.20 p.m. on 17 April 1943), CAB 154/67.
161. Bevan to Brigadier Hollis (Secretary of the Chiefs of Staff Committee), 1 April 1943, CAB 154/67.
162. 'Operation Mincemeat', para. 48, Montagu Papers, Box 1, 97/45/1; Mon tagu, *The Man Who Never Was*, 97.
163. Montagu, 'Postscript' to Cadet Edition of *The Man Who Never Was*, 126.

CHAPTER 9

1. Letter from Ivor Leverton to the *Daily Telegraph*, 13 August 2002; Kim Janssen 'Undertaker who had a key role in plot that tricked the Nazis', obituary of Ivo Leverton, *Camden New Journal*, 9 September 2002; Roger Morgan, 'The ma who almost is', *After the Battle*, 54 (1986), 10; Jackson, *Coroner*, 56.
2. 'Operation Mincemeat', para. 9, Montagu Papers, Box 1, 97/45/1; 'Oper ation Mincemeat', 1, ADM 223/794; Morgan, 'The man who almost is', 11
3. 'Operation Mincemeat', para. 10, Montagu Papers, Box 1, 97/45/1; 'Oper ation Mincemeat', 1, ADM 223/794.
4. Interview with Dr Noel McAuliffe, Toronto, 16 July 2009. See, also, Achin Th. Schäfer and Jens D. Kaufmann, 'What happens in freezing bodies Experimental study of histological tissue change caused by freezing injuries' *Forensic Science International*, 102/2–3 (1999), 149–58.

'Operation Mincemeat', 9, ADM 223/794; 'Operation Mincemeat', para. 48, Montagu Papers, Box 1, 97/45/1; Montagu, *The Man Who Never Was*, 96.

Montagu, *The Man Who Never Was*, 92–3; 'Sir W. Bentley Purchase', obituary, *The Times*, 28 September 1961.

'Operation Mincemeat', 9, ADM 223/794; 'Operation Mincemeat', para. 48, Montagu Papers, Box 1, 97/45/1.

Montagu, *The Man Who Never Was*, 91–3.

'Operation Mincemeat', 9, ADM 223/794; 'Operation Mincemeat', para. 51, Montagu Papers, Box 1, 97/45/1; Photographs of the body, WO 106/5921.

'Operation Mincemeat', 9, ADM 223/794; 'Operation Mincemeat', para. 50, Montagu Papers, Box 1, 97/45/1.

Montagu, *The Man Who Never Was*, 96.

Ibid., 94–5; 'Strike a New Note' (Review), *The Times*, 19 March 1943; 'Mr. Sid Field', obituary, *The Times*, 4 February, 1950; 'Operation Mincemeat', 8, ADM 223/794, 'Operation Mincemeat', para. 43, Montagu Papers, Box 1, 97/45/1.

Invoice-receipt from the Naval and Military Club, 24 April 1943, WO 106/5921.

Montagu, *The Man Who Never Was*, 79, 94–5.

Ibid., 9; Montagu, *The Man Who Never Was*, 97; Terry Crowdy, *Deceiving Hitler: Double cross and deception in World War II* (Botley, Oxford: Osprey, 2008), 66; Morgan, 'The man who almost is', 16.

Montagu, *The Man Who Never Was*, 98.

Ibid., 97–8.

Ibid., 98.

Naval Cypher Message from NID 12 to Capt. S.3, 16 April 1943, ADM 223/478. The date of this message shows that Montagu and company knew they would have to set out for Scotland the following day, if the *Mincemeat* courier were to make his scheduled departure from Scotland on 19 April, and a timely landfall in Spain. However, the receipt of Eisenhower's agreement to the deception, on the Saturday afternoon of 17 April, meant that the Operation could be launched without any fear or its being cancelled while Major Martin was en route to Huelva.

Montagu, *The Man Who Never Was*, 98–9.

'Operation Mincemeat', 9, ADM 223/794; 'Operation Mincemeat', para. 54, Montagu Papers, Box 1, 97/45/1.

Brian Lavery, *Churchill's Navy: The ships, men and organisation* (London: Conway, 2006), 212.

Montagu, *The Man Who Never Was*, 99–100; 'Operation Mincemeat': Operation Orders (Montagu), 31 March 1943, Section 4, WO 106/5921.

Scott, *Action Reply*, 44; 'Operation Mincemeat', 9, ADM 223/794; 'Operation Mincemeat', paras. 55–8, Montagu Papers, Box 1, 97/45/1; Montagu, *The Man Who Never Was*, 100–1.

Montagu, *The Man Who Never Was*, 101.

26. Scott, *Action Reply*, 44.
27. Ibid., 45; Monthly log of HM Submarine 'SERAPH' (April 1943), 19 Ap ADM 173/18038; Montagu, *The Man Who Never Was*, 101.
28. Scott, *Action Reply*, 45.
29. Ibid., 45; Monthly log of HM Submarine 'SERAPH' (April 1943), 19 Apr ADM 173/18038; <http://www.oldships.org.uk>.
30. Scott, *Action Reply*, 45; Robertson, *The Ship With Two Captains*, 23–5.
31. Scott, *Action Reply*, 46; Monthly Log of HM Submarine 'SERAPH' (Apr 1943), 21 April, ADM 173/18038.
32. Monthly log of HM Submarine 'SERAPH' (April 1943), 21 April, ADM 17 18038; Scott, *Action Reply*, 46.
33. Hutchinson, *Submarines*, 74.
34. Scott, *Action Reply*, 46.
35. Ibid., 46; Monthly log of HM Submarine 'SERAPH' (April, 1943), 22 Apr ADM 173/18038.
36. Monthly log of HM Submarine 'SERAPH' (April, 1943), 23 April, 25 Apr 28 April, ADM 173/18038.
37. Ibid., 29 April; Scott, *Action Reply*, 47; 'Operation Mincemeat': Operati Orders (Montagu), 31 March 1943, Section 3, WO 106/5921.
38. Scott, *Action Reply*, 47; Message from NID 12 to FOIC Gibraltar, 29 Ap 1943, ADM 223/478.
39. Monthly log of HM Submarine 'SERAPH' (April, 1943), 29 April, ADM 17 18038; Scott, *Action Reply*, 47.
40. 'Operation Mincemeat' (Addendum 1, 29 May 1943), para. 62, Monta Papers, Box 1, 97/45/1; 'Operation Mincemeat', 11, ADM 223/794.
41. 'Operation Mincemeat', from CO 'SERAPH' to DNI (for Lt Cdr The H E. E. S. Montagu, RNVR personal), 30 April 1943, WO 106/5921.
42. 'Operation Mincemeat': Operation Orders (Montagu), 31 March 1943, Se tion 3, WO 106/5921.
43. Scott, *Action Reply*, 57.
44. Ibid., 47; 'Operation Mincemeat', from CO 'SERAPH' to DNI, 30 Ap 1943, WO 106/5921.
45. Scott, *Action Reply*, 47.
46. Ibid., 47; 'Operation Mincemeat', from CO 'SERAPH' to DNI, 30 Ap 1943, WO 106/5921.
47. Report by agent *Andros*, 8 June 1943, Montagu Papers, Box 1, 97/45/1; Rafa Romero, 'La Historia de un Pescador que cogío el Cadáver del "Hombre q nunca existío"', *La Vanguardia*, 24 July, 1989. See, also, the undated (but *c.*m June 1943) handwritten letter from Captain Alan Hillgarth to the DN accompanying the report by *Andros* who was clearly a prominent member Hillgarth's personal network of spies inside Franco's Spain. This letter is also the Montagu Papers (Box 1, 97/45/1), as is the undated 'Agent's Report

German Attempts in Spain to Get the Documents' which is a summary of the full *Andros* report of 8 June.

. *Andros* report, 8 June 1943, 1, Montagu Papers, Box 1, 97/45/1.

. Ramírez, *Espías y Neutrales*, 409, 411.

. 'Operation Mincemeat', 3, ADM 223/794.

. *Andros* report, 8 June 1943, 1, Montagu Papers, Box 1, 97/45/1, Ramírez, *Espías y Neutrales*, 409–10, 414.

. Montagu to Bevan, re 'Mincemeat', 26 March 1943, CAB 154/67.

. 'Operation Mincemeat', 11, ADM 223/794; 'Operation Mincemeat', Addendum 1, 29 May 1943, para. 61, Montagu Papers, Box 1, 97/45/1.

. Ramírez, *Espías y Neutrales*, 412; Abwehr Report, 'Drowned English courier picked up at Huelva', 22 May 1943, to Lt Col. (Alexis) Freiherr von Roenne, Chief of the Foreign Armies West, Intelligence Evaluation Branch of the German Army's High Command (hereinafter FHW), from 'Four documents extracted from the Abwehr file dealing with the Mincemeat case, and bearing the initials of Admiral Doenitz (11th May to 22nd May, 1943)', Appendix B, 'Historical record of deception' (Wingate), ii, 392, CAB 154/101.

. Rose, *Lethal Witness*, 252–3, 256; Evans, *Father of Forensics*, 296.

. Evans, *Father of Forensics*, 291; Rose, *Lethal Witness*, 22–30; 125–39, 162–83; Robin Mckie, 'Science that hanged Crippen uncovered', *The Guardian Weekly*, 22 August 2008; David Jones, 'Was Dr. Crippen really innocent?', *Mail Online*, 19 October 2007; Chris Irvine, 'Dr. Crippen could win posthumous pardon', *Telegraph.co.uk*, 7 June 2009; Ben McIntyre, 'Sir Bernard Spilsbury, Britain's first forensic scientist', *Times Online*, 2 January 2009.

. Rose, *Lethal* Witness, xx.

. Ibid., 229–32, 241–50.

. 'Operation Mincemeat', Addendum 1, para. 61, Montagu Papers, Box 1, 97/45/1; 'Operation Mincemeat', 11, ADM 223/794.

. Montagu to Bevan, Re 'Mincemeat', 28 May 1943, para. 5, CAB 154/67.

. Montagu, The *Man Who Never Was*, 36, 92; 'Operation Mincemeat', Addendum 1, para. 61, Montagu Papers, Box 1, 97/45/1; 'Operation Mincemeat', 11, ADM 223/794.

. Abwehr report on 'Drowned English courier', 22 May 1943 to von Roenne (FHW), Appendix B, 'Historical record of deception' (Wingate), ii, 392, CAB 154/101.

. Abwehr report on 'Drowned English courier picked up at Huelva', 15 May 1943, to von Roenne (FHW), Appendix B, 'Historical record of deception' (Wingate), ii, 389, CAB 154/101.

. Montagu, *The Man Who Never Was*, 135–7.

. Abwehr report on 'Drowned English courier', 22 May 1943, to von Roenne (FHW), Appendix B, 'Historical record of deception' (Wingate), ii, 392, CAB 154/101.

. Ibid.; Edward Smith to Montagu, 6 May 1969, Montagu Papers, Box 1, 97/45/1.

. Montagu to Bevan, re 'Mincemeat', 28 May 1943, para. 5, CAB 154/67.

68. Smith, *Forensic Medicine*, 269, 273; Interview with Dr Noel McAuliffe, Toronto, 13 May 2009; Brian Lane, *The Encyclopedia of Forensic Science* (London: Headline, 1992; 1993 edn), 226–8.
69. Montagu to Bevan, re 'Mincemeat', 28 May 1943, para. 5, CAB 154/67.
70. Interview with Dr Noel McAuliffe, Toronto, 16 July 2009.
71. Abwehr report on 'drowned English courier', 22 May 1943, to von Roenne (FHW), Appendix B, 'Historical record of deception' (Wingate), ii, 392, CAB 154/101.
72. Ibid.
73. Major William Martin's 'Naval Identity Card No. 148228', WO 106/5921.
74. Interview with Dr Noel McAuliffe, Toronto, 16 and 28 July 2009; Lane, *Encyclopedia of Forensic Science*, 533–6.
75. *Andros* report, 8 June 1943, 1, Montagu Papers, Box 1, 97/45/1; Ramírez, *Espías y Neutrales*, 412, 419, 420.
76. Ramírez, *Espías y Neutrales*, 417.
77. NA Madrid to DNI, no. 011843, 2 May 1943, ADM 223/478; NA Madrid to Admiralty for DNI, no. 021738, 2 May 1943, ADM 223/478.
78. *Andros* report, 8 June 1943, i, Montagu Papers, Box I, 97/45/1; 'Agent's report on German attempts in Spain to get the documents' (Appendix III), Montagu Papers, Box 1, 97/45/1; Holt, *Deceivers*, 848.
79. Pekka Saukko and Bernard Knight, *Knight's Forensic Pathology*, 3rd edn (London: Arnold, 2004), 64. See, also, Cyril John Polson, D. J. Gee and Bernard Knight, *The Essentials of Forensic Medicine*, 4th edn (Oxford: Pergamon, 1985), 5.
80. Ramírez, *Espías y Neutrales*, 415.
81. Ibid., 422; 'Questions from Mr. Ian Colvin put to Mr. Haselden, Late Vice Consul at Huelva' (undated but *c*.March 1953, with the latter's answers duly entered thereon), DEFE 28/25. When Haselden sought official approval to send his answers back to Colvin, it was not forthcoming because it was not deemed 'fitting for an officer who was in the Government service at the time to answer a questionnaire of this nature' (Minute Sheet, 'Vice Consul Huelva/Colvin', 22/4 (1953), Ibid.).
82. Ramírez, *Espías y Neutrales*, 422; *Andros* report, 8 June 1943, 2, Montagu Papers, Box 1, 97/45/1.
83. NA Madrid to DNI, no. 081012, 8 May 1943, ADM 223/478.
84. 'Mr Drew (Message from Mr Montagu)—Op. 'Mincemeat', 15 May 1953, DEFE 28/23; 'Operation Mincemeat', 3–4, ADM 223/794, 'Operation Mincemeat', paras. 18–19, Montagu Papers, Box 1, 97/45/1.
85. Ramírez, *Espías y Neutrales*, 422.
86. 'Operation Mincemeat', 3, ADM 223/794.
87. *Andros* report, 2, 8 June 1943, Montagu Papers, Box 1, 97/45/1.
88. Ibid.; Ramírez, *Espías y Neutrales*, 42–7.
89. *Andros* report, 3, 8 June 1943, Montagu Papers, Box 1, 97/45/1.

Ibid., 2.

Abwehr report on 'Drowned English courier', 22 May 1943, to von Roenne (FHW), Appendix B, 'Historical record of deception' (Wingate), ii, 392, CAB 154/101.

Andros report, 3, 8 June 1943, Montagu Papers, Box 1, 97/45/1.

Ros Agudo, La Guerra Secreta, 210–18; Kahn, Hitler's Spies, 243, 246–7; Heinz Höhne, Canaris (London: Secker and Warburg, 1979), 427.

Charles B. Burdick, Germany's Military Strategy and Spain in World War II (Syracuse, New York: Syracuse University Press, 1968), 25 (footnote 29).

Höhne, Canaris, 196, 240.

Reinhard R. Doerries, Hitler's Last Chief of Intelligence: Allied interrogations of Walter Schellenberg (London: Frank Cass, 2003), 21, 96–8.

Ibid., 97–8.

Mark Seaman (introduction), Garbo: The Spy Who Saved D-Day (Richmond, Surrey: Public Record Office, 2000), 69; Kahn, Hitler's Spies, 356–7; Ros Agudo, La Guerra Secreta, 212.

Seaman (intro.), Garbo, 8–29.

Ibid., 70.

Ibid., 128.

Andros report, 3–4, 8 June 1943, Montagu Papers, Box 1, 97/45/1.

Raymond L. Proctor, entry on 'Vigón Suerodiaz, Juan (1880–1959)' in James W. Cortada (ed.), Historical Dictionary of the Spanish Civil War (London: Greenwood Press, 1982), 473–4; Stanley G. Payne, Politics and the Military in Modern Spain (Stanford: Stanford University Press, 1967), 428; Paul Preston, Franco: A biography (London: HarperCollins, 1993), 349; Höhne, Canaris, 424.

Andros report, 4, 8 June 1943, Montagu Papers, Box 1, 97/45/1.

Ibid.

Ros Agudo, La Guerra Secreta, 207–8.

Andros report, 4, 8 June 1943, Montagu Papers, Box 1, 97/45/1; Gerald R. Kleinfeld and Lewis A. Tambs, Hitler's Spanish Legion: The Blue Division in Russia (Carbondale and Edwardsville: Southern Illinois University Press, 1979), 34, 189.

Andros report, 8 June 1943, Montagu Papers, Box 1, 97/45/1; 'Operation Mincemeat', 14, ADM 223/794; Payne, Politics and the Military, 432.

Stanley G. Payne, Franco and Hitler: Spain, Germany and World War II (New Haven: Yale University Press, 2008), 245.

Abwehr report on 'Drowned English courier', 22 May 1943 to von Roenne (FHW), Appendix B, 'Historical record of deception' (Wingate), ii, 392, CAB 154/101; Klaus-Jörg Ruhl, Spanien im Zweiten Weltkrieg: Franco, die Falange und das 'Dritte Reich' (Hamburg: Hoffmann und Campe, 1975), 221.

Abwehr report on 'Drowned English courier picked up at Huelva', 15 May 1943, to von Roenne (FHW), Appendix B, 'Historical record of deception' (Wingate), ii, 388–9; Abwehr report on 'Drowned English courier', 22 May

1943, to von Roenne (FHW), Appendix B, 'Historical record of decepti (Wingate), ii, 391; Ros Agudo, *La Guerra Secreta*, 232.

112. Fundación Nacional Francisco Franco, *Documentos Inéditos para la Historic Generalísimo Franco*, tomo iv, (Madrid: Azor, 1994), 223–5.

113. Burdick, *Germany's Military Strategy*, 24–5, 67, 106–7, 150–1.

114. Enemy Documents Section, Appreciation 14, Pt 1: 'Axis Plans and Policie the Mediterranean May–September 1943', 4–5, CAB 146/28.

115. ISK 44720, Madrid to Berlin, 10/5/43, HW 19/120; ISK 46257, Berlin Madrid, 13/5/43, HW 19/120; Ros Agudo, *La Guerra Secreta*, 213.

116. Montagu, *The Man Who Never Was*, 134; Montgu, *Beyond Top Secret Ultra*, 1

117. Ruhl, *Spanien im Zweiten Weltkrieg*, 221.

118. Montagu, *The Man Who Never Was*, 95, 102–4; 'The Gargoyle Cl <http://www.museumoflondon.org.uk>.

119. FOS to Capt. (S) 3, Repeated Admiralty, C.-in-C. Western Approacl HQCC, C.-in-C. Plymouth, FOIC Gibraltar, no. 151451, 15 April 19 ADM 223/478.

120. FOIC Gibraltar to FOS, no. 161237, ADM 223/478.

121. DNI to FOIC Gibraltar, NA Madrid, repeated FOS, no. 171128, 17 A 1943, ADM 223/478; NA Madrid to DNI, no. 191109, 19 April 1943, AI 223/478; S.O. (I) Gibraltar to DNI, no. 191155, 19 April 1943, ADM 2 478; NA Madrid to DNI, no. 192123, 20 April 1943, ADM 223/794.

122. John Winton, *Cunningham* (London: John Murray, 1998), 279.

123. See, e.g., NA Madrid to DNI, no. 192123, 20 April 1943, ADM 223/47￼

124. DNI to NA Madrid, no. 202056, 20 April 1943, ADM 223/478; NA Mac to DNI, 221600, 22 April 1943, ADM 223/478; FOC Gibraltar to 1 Madrid, repeated DNI no. 241916, 24 April 1943, ADM 223/478; 1 Madrid to FOIC Gibraltar, repeated, DNI, no. 250953, 25 April 19 ADM 223/478; FOIC Gibraltar to DNI, repeated NA Madrid, no. 2911 29 April 1943, ADM 223/478; FOIC Gibraltar to DNI, repeated NA Mad no. 291626, 29 April 1943, ADM 223/478.

125. Telegram to DSO Gibraltar, reference: P. 63/B.I.A., 22 April 1943, AI 223/478; NID 12 (approved by DNI) to FOIC Gibraltar, no. 291929, April 1943, ADM 223/478; Bristow, *Game of Moles*, 55; West (ed.), *Lid Diaries*, i, 178, 235.

126. NID 12 (approved by DNI) to FOIC Gibraltar, no. 291929, 29 April 19 ADM 223/478.

127. HM Submarine P. 219 'SERAPH' to FOC Gibraltar, repeated FOC S marines, no. 300648, 30 April 1943, ADM 223/478.

128. CO, HM Submarine 'SERAPH' to DNI, Copy to FOS, 30 April 1943, W 106/5921; Montagu, *The Man Who Never Was*, 104.

129. NA Madrid to Admiralty for DNI, no. 021738, 2 May 1943, ADM 223/4

130. 'Operation Mincemeat', Appendix II: 'Miscellaneous security precautions England', ADM 223/794.

31. Ibid.

32. Ibid.; Hillgarth, 'The Naval Attaché to Spain and Naval Intelligence', Pt II, Section IV: 'Communications', para. 3, ADM 223/490.

33. 'Operation Mincemeat', Appendix II, ADM 223/794.

34. Ibid.

35. NA Madrid to Admiralty for DNI, no. 021738, 2 May 1943, ADM 223/478.

36. Ibid.

37. 'Operation Mincemeat', 3, ADM 223/794.

38. NA Madrid to Admiralty for DNI, no. 021518, 3 May 1943, ADM 223/478.

39. NA Madrid to DNI, no. 081012, 8 May 1943, ADM 223/478.

40. Hillgarth, 'The Naval Attaché to Spain and Naval Intelligence', Pt I, Section II: 'Choice of Naval attaché', para. 3, ADM 223/490.

41. DNI (NID 12) to NA Madrid, no. 870, 6 May 1943, ADM 223/478.

42. NA Madrid to DNI, no. 051823, 6 May 1943, ADM 223/478; NA Madrid to DNI, no. 171914, undated (?15 May 1943), ADM 223/478.

43. NA Madrid to DNI, no. 11925, 12 May 1943, ADM 223/478; NA Madrid to Admiralty for DNI, no. 112011, 12 May 1943, ADM 223/478.

44. NA Madrid to DNI, no. 171914, undated (?15 May 1943), ADM 223/478.

45. DNI to NA Madrid, no. 874/101555, 10 May 1943, ADM 223/478.

46. 'Note on three letters', 1, 21 May 1943, Montagu Papers, Box 1, 97/45/1.

47. NA Madrid to Admiralty for DNI, no. 112011, 12 May 1943, ADM 223/478.

48. Ibid.; DNI to NA Madrid, no. 877/181213, 18 May 1943, ADM 223/478; NA Madrid to DNI, no. 191412, 18 May 1943 (mutilated group in para. B repeated in follow-up, undated message), ADM 223/478.

49. 'Note on three letters', 1–3, 21 May 1943, Montagu Papers, Box 1, 97/45/1; 'Operation Mincemeat', 12, ADM 223/794, 'Operation Mincemeat', para. 75, Montagu Papers, Box 1, 97/45/1.

50. Ibid. 3–4.

51. Abwehr report on 'Drowned English courier', 15 May 1943, to von Roenne (FHW), Appendix B, 'Historical record of deception (Wingate), ii, 388–9.

52. 'Operation Mincemeat', para. 75, Montagu Papers, Box 1, 97/45/1; 'Operation Mincemeat', 12, ADM 223/794.

53. 'Operation Mincemeat', para. 77, Montagu Papers, Box 1, 97/45/1.

54. Ibid.

55. Hinsley et al., *British Intelligence in the Second World War*, iii: Pt I, 78: Geoffrey P. Megargee, *Inside Hitler's High Command* (Lawrence, Kansas: University Press of Kansas, 2000), 172; Walter Warlimont, *Inside Hitler's Headquarters, 1939–45* (London: Weidenfeld and Nicolson, 1964), Presidio Press edition (Novato California, undated), 219.

56. CX/MSS/2571/T4, 14 May 1943, ADM 223/478. This document, alone, disproves the claim made by General Walter Warlimont, deputy chief of the German Armed Forces Command Staff, that to 'the best' of his 'recollection' the *Mincemeat* documents never reached 'the Staff of the German High

Command': (General der Artillerie Walter Warlimont, retired, 'The ma
who never was', *An Cosantoir: The Irish Defence Journal*, June 1973, 184).
157. 'Operation Mincemeat', para. 77, Montagu Papers, Box 1, 97/45/1; 'Oper
ation Mincemeat', 14, and Appendix: 'Facts from Special Intelligence indi
cating the success of Operation Mincemeat', ADM 223/794.
158. Quoted by Howard, *Grand Strategy*, iv, 370.
159. 'General Sir Leslie Hollis', obituary, *The Times*, 10 August 1963.
160. 'Precis of Plan "Barclay"', LCS (43) 4, Section 2: 'Objects of the plan', 2
April 1943, CAB 81/77.

CHAPTER 10

1. *Liddell Diaries*, 31 May 1943, vii, KV4/191.
2. Trevor-Roper, 'German Intelligence Service' (1945), para. 29, CAB 154/10;
Kahn, 'Introduction', *Final Solution of the Abwehr*, xiii–xiv; Howard, *Strateg
Deception*, 50.
3. Howard, *Strategic Deception*, 45.
4. Ibid., 51; Kahn, *Hitler's Spies*, 462–78; E. Montagu, NID 12, 'Abweh
developments', 13 August 1943, ADM 223/296.
5. Trevor-Roper, 'German Intelligence Service' (1945), para. 40.
6. ISK 44720, Madrid to Berlin, 10/5/43, HW 19/120; ISK 46257, Berlin t
Madrid, 13/5/43, HW 19/120.
7. Chef Abwehr I to Wehrmachtführungsstab, etc., no. 2282/43, 9 May 1943
File AL 1780, EDS Collection (Groups of German Documents ex Enem
Documents Section of the Cabinet Office), IWM.
8. Werner Rahn and Gerhard Schreiber (eds.), *Kriegstagebuch der Seekriegsleitun
1939–1945*, Teil A, Band 45: *Mai 1943* (Berlin: Mittler, 1994), 127–8. Th
inclusion of this item amongst the entries for 7 May 1943 appears to be
chronological error, since other records seem to show that the first (summary
report of the Nye–Alexander letter did not reach Berlin until 9 May 1943.
9. EDS, Appreciation 14, Pt I: 'Axis Plans and Policies in the Mediterranea
May–September 1943', 5–6, CAB 146/28.
10. Fremde Heere West Appreciation, no. 874/43, 9 May 1943, File AL 1780
EDS Collection, IWM.
11. Kahn, *Hitler's Spies*, 424.
12. FHW report on 'Discovery of the English courier' to Wehrmachtführungsstab
11 May 1943, Appendix B, 'Historical record of deception' (Wingate), ii, 386–8
13. Ibid., para. III(iv), 387.
14. Ibid.
15. FHW Appreciation no. 874/43, 9 May 1943, File AL 1780, EDS Collection
IWM.
16. FHW report, 'Discovery of English courier', 11 May 1943, Appendix B
'Historical record of deception' (Wingate), ii, para. IV, 386–8. In the post-wa

official British translation of this passage from the FHW report in question the German word *Abwehr* is rendered as 'Abwehr' (i.e., the German military intelligence service). However, it is clear from the context that the term should be given its more general meaning of 'defence', here.

. The German Navy's intelligence analysts were sufficiently persuaded by this FHW assessment to accept that 'the genuineness of captured documents' was 'above suspicion' but still rather illogically thought that there was a 'slight' possibility that they might have been planted on them. (Comments written in Berlin on 14 May 1943 about the Nye–Alexander letter, 'for perusal by Admiral DONITZ' in extract from documents in 'Kriegstagebuch 1 skl. Teil C/1943/Heft XIV', NID 12, 10 July 1945, CAB 154/67.)

. CX/MSS/2571/T4, 14 May 1943, ADM 223/478.

. OKW signal no. 661055/43, 12 May 1943, in Walther Hubatsch (ed.), *Kriegstagebuch des Oberkommandos der Wehrmacht (Wehrmachtführungsstab)*, Band III, *1. Januar 1943–31. Dezember 1943* (Herrsching: Manfred Pawlak, 1982), 1429.

. Ibid., 1430–1; EDS Appreciation 14, Pt I, 'Axis plans and policies in the Mediterranean, May–September 1943', 8–9, CAB 146/28.

. Warlimont, *Inside Hitler's Headquarters*, 172–3. The name is usually translated into English as 'Wolf's Lair', but *Schanze* might be rendered more accurately as 'entrenchment' or 'redoubt'.

. F. W. Deakin, *The Brutal Friendship* (London: Weidenfeld and Nicholson, 1962); revised two-volume edn, i: *The Brutal Friendship: Mussolini, Hitler and the fall of Italian fascism* (Harmondsworth, Middlesex: Penguin, 1966), 315–17.

. 'Report to the Fuehrer at Headquarters, Wolfsschanze, May 14 1943, at 1730', in *Fuehrer Conferences on Naval Affairs*, 1990 edn., with a Foreword by Jak P. Mallman Showell (London: Greenhill Books), 327–30.

. Ibid., 327.

. Quoted by Deakin, *Brutal Friendship*, 383.

. Ibid., 383–5.

. Heiber and Glantz (eds.), *Hitler and His Generals*, 119–20.

. Ibid., 120–5.

. Ibid., 125–6.

. Ibid., 129.

. Samuel W. Mitcham Jr, *The Panzer Legions: A guide to the German Army tank divisions of World War II and their commanders* (Mechanicsburg, Pennsylvania: Stackpole Books, 2007), 40.

. CX/MSS/2607/T17, 21/5/43, HW 1/1700.

. CX/MSS/2623/T18, 25/5/43, HW 1/1705.

. CX/MSS/2693/T42, 7/6/43, HW 1/1722.

. Montagu to Bevan, Reference sheet on 'Operation Mincemeat', para. 4, 8 June 1943, CAB 154/67.

. Montagu, 'Operation Mincemeat', Appendix: 'Facts from special intelligence indicating the success of Operation Mincemeat', ADM 223/794.

37. Colonel D. W. Clarke, 'Amendment no. 1 to Plan "BARCLAY" (Approve Version)', Note by Commander 'A' Force, para. 4, 20 May 1943, copy David Mure Papers, 67/321/3, IWM.

38. ' "A" Force War Diary' (Clarke), iii, 78, CAB 154/3.

39. 'Recent intelligence affecting operations in the Mediterranean', JIC (43) 2 (O) Final, 19 May 1943, paras. 2 and 4–5, CAB 81/115.

40. 'The G.A.F. and Husky', ADM 223/209.

41. Ibid. Hinsley et al., *British Intelligence in the Second World War*, iii: Pt 1, 81–3

42. Batey, 'Dilly Knox', 125–6.

43. Harrison, 'British radio security', 63–93; P. R. J. Winter, 'A higher form intelligence: Hugh Trevor-Roper and wartime British Secret Service', *Intel gence and National Security*, 22/6 (2007), 848–9, 851–71.

44. 'The Abwehr and Allied intentions', para. 1, May 1943, CAB 154/96. A though this report is not attributed to any department or agency, it seems cle that it could only have been produced by Trevor-Roper's unit. See, als Harrison, 'British radio security', 86).

45. 'Allied landing plans', para. 2, RIS, HRT-R/IR, 1 June, 1943. CAB 154/67

46. Ibid., 'Post-script'.

47. Deakin, *Brutal Friendship*, 386; Montagu, 'Operation Mincemeat', para. 7 Montagu Papers, Box 1, 97/45/1.

48. 'The Abwehr and Allied intentions, para. 2, May 1943, CAB 154/96.

49. Of course, Montagu had to take administrative precautions to ensure that ar 'Ultra' decrypts, which actually mentioned the enemy's acquisition of high level correspondence lost in an air crash would receive restricted circulation. order to avoid a security 'flap' and 'numerous enquiries on security grounds to what had been lost and how it came to be lost', such signals were to be reported only to 'C' (the Head of MI6) and Montagu, himself: Montagu Frank Brich, Esq. (for Cdr. Travis, Director of Bletchley Park), 30 April 194 HW 20/546.

50. ISK 46257, Berlin to Madrid, 13/5/43, HW 19/120.

51. ISK 46259, Madrid to Berlin, 14/5/43, HW 19/120.

52. Ibid.

53. ISK 46262, Berlin to Madrid, 15/5/43, HW 19/120.

54. Bevan to Dudley Clarke, no. 909, 16 May 1943, CAB 154/67.

55. Dudley Clarke to Bevan, no. KN 211, 20 May 1943, CAB 154/67.

56. Bevan to Dudley Clarke, no. L/651, 21 May 1943, CAB 154/67.

57. Montagu to Bevan re 'Mincemeat', 28 May 1943, CAB 154/67.

58. Montagu, *The Man Who Never Was*, 115–16; DNI to NA Madrid, no. 878, 2 May 1943, ADM 223/478; Ramírez, *Espías y Neutrales*, 426.

59. DNI to NA Madrid, no. 878, 21 May 1943, ADM 223/478; Montagu, T Man Who Never Was, 116. Of course, both the notional dates of birth ar death, given for Major Martin on the tombstone, differed from Glyndw Michael's real ones.

50. 'Operation Mincemeat', 11–12, ADM 223/794.

51. Montagu, *The Man Who Never Was*, 116; Photographs of William Martin's tombstone in WO 106/5921.

52. Montagu, *The Man Who Never Was*, 116.

53. Abwehr report on 'Drowned English courier', 22 May 1943, to von Roenne (FHW), Appendix B, 'Historical record of deception' (Wingate), ii, 391, CAB 154/101.

54. Ros Agudo, *La Guerra Secreta*, 252–3.

55. Abwehr report on 'Drowned English courier', 22 May 1943, to von Roenne (FHW), Appendix B, 'Historical record of deception' (Wingate), ii, 391, CAB 154/101.

56. Ibid., 392.

57. Ibid.

58. Colvin, *Unknown Courier*, 175–6.

59. Elke Fröhlich (ed.), *Die Tagebücher von Joseph Goebbels*, Teil II, *Diktate, 1941–1945*, Band 8, *April–Juni 1943* (Munich: K. G. Saur, 1993), 361–2.

60. 'Garbo', message received 7 June 1943, CAB 154/67.

1. Seaman (intro.), *Garbo*, 134–6; Masterman, *Double-Cross System*, 117, 129–30. Another prominent agent in the double-cross system, *Brutus* (code name for Roman Garby-Czerniawski) was also asked by his Abwehr controllers to find out whether any Greeks were accompanying the Canadian units earmarked for transfer to the Middle East (*Liddell Diaries*, 31 May 1943, vii, KV 4/191). On the origins of the *Brutus* case, see Hinsley and Simkins, *British Intelligence in the Second World War*, iv, 117–19.

2. 'Colonel Frank Knox', obituary, *The Times*, 29 April 1944.

3. 'Knox looks to use of Mediterranean route; Discounts Axis air threat to shipping now', *The New York Times*, 12 May 1943.

4. 'Cover plans and security', Minute by the controlling officer (of LCS, Col. John Bevan), submitted to the Chiefs of Staff: attached to Hastings to Churchill, 21 July 1943, PREM 3/117.

5. Fröhlich (ed.), *Die Tagebücher von Joseph Goebbels*, Teil II, Band 8, 285. See, also, ' "A" Force War Diary' (Clarke), iii, 91, CAB 154/3.

6. 'Extract from D.O. letter to C.I.G.S. from General Wilson dated 16 May 43', CAB 154/67; Dudley Clarke to Bevan, no. KN 211, 20 May 1943, CAB 154/67; Molony, *Mediterranean and Middle East*, v, 7.

7. Artemis Cooper, *Cairo in the War, 1939–1945* (London: Hamish Hamilton, 1989), 37, 120.

8. ' "A" Force War Diary' (Clarke), iii, 97, CAB 154/3.

9. On SIME, see Hinsley and Simkins, *British Intelligence in the Second World War*, iv, 150–3, 188–90.

10. ' "A" Force War Diary' (Clarke), iii, 97–8, CAB 154/3; ISSB to Secretary, Joint Intelligence Sub-Committee, re 'Operation HUSKY Breach of Security', undated, CAB 154/67.

81. 'Extract from D.O. letter to C.I.G.S. from General Wilson dated 16 May 43, CAB 154/67.
82. '"A" Force War Diary' (Clarke), iii, 98, CAB 154/3.
83. Ibid.
84. '"A" Force War Diary', (Clarke), iii, 66; CAB 154/3; D'Este, Eisenhower 431.
85. Montagu, The Man Who Never Was, 48–9.
86. Dudley Clarke to Bevan, no. KN 211, 20 May 1943, CAB 154/3.
87. '"A" Force War Diary' (Clarke), iii, 66, 103.
88. Ibid., 66, 80; Hinsley et al., British Intelligence in the Second World War, iii: Pt 86–7.
89. Albert N. Garland and Howard McGaw Smyth, Sicily and the Surrender of Italy (Washington, DC: Center of Military History, United States Army, 1993), 69–70; D'Este, Eisenhower, 429; Molony, Mediterranean and Middle East, v, 49.
90. '"A" Force War Diary', (Clarke), iii, 66.
91. Garland and Smyth, Sicily and the Surrender of Italy, 70–2; Hinsley et al., British Intelligence in the Second World War, iii: Pt I, 84–5.
92. '"A" Force War Diary' (Clarke), iii, 79.
93. Ibid., 103; Howard, Grand Strategy, iv, 466–7.
94. 'Recent intelligence affecting operations in the Mediterranean', JIC (43) 25 (o) Final, para. 1, CAB 81/115. Noted at COS (43) 122 and mtg (o), Min. 8, 17 June 1943, CAB 79/61.
95. Hinsley et al., British Intelligence in the Second World War, iii: Pt I, 75–6.
96. 'The G.A.F. and Husky', ADM 223/209.
97. Montagu, The Man Who Never Was, 118–19.
98. Ibid., 119.
99. 'Mr. Leslie Howard: Distinguished film and stage actor', obituary, The Times, 4 June 1943; Gilbert, Road to Victory, 426.
100. Montagu, The Man Who Never Was, 119–20.
101. Ibid., 120–2; 'Operation Mincemeat', Appendix II, para. 4, ADM 223/794.
102. See, e.g., Howard, Strategic Deception, 93–4.
103. Montagu, The Man Who Never Was, 119.
104. M. R. D. Foot, 'Foreword' in Mackenzie, Secret History of SOE, xviii; M. R. D. Foot, Memories of an S.O.E. Historian (Barnsley, South Yorkshire: Pen & Sword, 2008), 172–3.
105. 'Special Operations Executive Directive for 1943', COS (43) 142 (o), para. 20, 20 March 1943, CAB 80/68.
106. Mackenzie, Secret History of SOE, 450.
107. Extracts from a Report by Brigadier Edmond Myers, DSO, September 1943, entitled 'Inside Greece: A review', 6, HS 8/897.
108. Ibid., 11.
109. Colonel C. M. Woodhouse, DSO, OBE, 'History of the Allied Military Mission in Greece, September 1942 to December 1944', 65, HS 7/154.

0. Myers, 'Inside Greece', 1–5, HS 8/897; Mackenzie, *Secret History of SOE*, 450–8; Brigadier E. C. W. Myers, *Greek Entanglement*, revised edn (Gloucester: Alan Sutton, 1985), 69–87, 110–24.

1. Myers, 'Inside Greece', 11, HS 8/897.

2. John L. Hondros, 'The Greek Resistance, 1941–1944', in John O. Iatrides (ed.), *Greece in the 1940s: A nation in crisis,* (Hanover and London: University Press of New England, 1981), 37–45.

3. Woodhouse, 'Allied Military Mission to Greece', 65, HS 7/154.

4. See, e.g., Mackenzie, *Secret History of SOE*, 455–7.

5. Woodhouse, 'Allied Military Mission to Greece, 74, 81–2, HS 7/154.

6. See, e.g., C. M. Woodhouse, *The Struggle for Greece, 1941–1949*, 2nd edn (Chicago: Ivan R. Dee, 2003), 31–4.

7. Woodhouse, 'Allied Military Mission to Greece', 65, HS 7/154.

8. Mackenzie, *Secret History of SOE*, 458–9.

9. Woodhouse, 'Allied Military Mission to Greece', 79, HS 7/154.

0. Myers, 'Inside Greece', 9–11, HS 8/897; Myers, *Greek Entanglement*, 169–86.

1. Woodhouse, 'Allied Military Mission to Greece', 74, HS 7/154; SOE War Diaries: Middle East and Balkans, Apr.–June 1943, 678–9, HS 7/269.

2. Woodhouse, 'Allied Military Mission to Greece', 75, 79, HS 7/154; Myers, 'Inside Greece', 11–12, HS 8/897; 'Recent activities and present strengths (July 1943) of opposing forces in Yugoslavia, Albania and Greece', Report by the Joint Intelligence Sub-Committee, 14 July 1943 (with accompanying memo of 13 August 1943 from Churchill to Roosevelt), Annex E: 'Analysis of Guerrilla activities in Greece from May–July 1943', 8–9, President's secretary files, <http://www.fdrlibrary.marist.edu/psf>.

3. Woodhouse, 'Allied Military Mission to Greece', 79, HS 7/154.

4. 'Abwehr operational material: Central Mediterranean', no. 387, 22 June 1943, CAB 154/77.

5. 'Recent intelligence affecting operations in the Mediterranean', JIC (43), 262 (o), 23 June 1943, CAB 81/115. Noted at COS (43) 136th mtg, Min. 6 (o), 24 June 1943, CAB 79/62.

6. 'Recent intelligence affecting operations in the Mediterranean', JIC (43), 277 (o) (Final), 7 July 1943, CAB 81/115. Noted at COS (43) 150th mtg (o), Min. 14 (o), CAB 79/62.

7. 'The OKW and Allied intentions, June 1943', 3 July 1943, CAB 154/96. This paper was produced by the German Section, M114, of British Military Intelligence.

8. 'Operation "Husky" ', ADM 223/209; Hinsley et al., *British Intelligence in the Second World War*, iii: Pt I, 78; CX/MSS/2849/T16, 5/7/43, DEFE 3/824. See, also, Woodhouse, 'Summer 1943', 125.

9. 'S.O.E. War Diaries: Middle East and Balkans, July–Sep. 1943', 895–6, HS 7/270.

130. 'Recent activities and present strengths (July 1943) of opposing forces Yugoslavia, Albania and Greece', Pt II, 'Greece', 5, President's secreta files, <http://www.fdrlibrary.marist.edu.psf>.

131. Hinsley et al., *British Intelligence in the Second World War*, iii: Pt I, 80; Garla and Smyth, *Sicily and the Surrender of Italy*, 110–11.

132. 'O.K.W. most immediate telegram of 9th July, 1943, on Allied intentions the Mediterranean', Appendix B, 'Historical record of deception' (Wingat ii, 396, CAB 154/101.

EPILOGUE

1. Robertson, *The Ship With Two Captains*, 135; Vice Admiral H. K. Hewitt, U Navy, Naval Commander, Western Task Force, 'Action report Weste Naval Task Force, the Sicilian Campaign: Operation "Husky" July–Augu 1943', 37–8, File no. A16-3/N31, Serial: 00872, United States Naval Admi istration in World War Two, <http://ibiblio.org/hyperwar/USN/Adm Hist/I48.3-Sicily/index.html>; Jewell interview, IWM Sound Archive, r 12278, reel 3. In the latter interview Jewell remembered the E-boat arrivi on the scene just *after Seraph's* crew had set the sonic buoy on the seabed.

2. Bernard Ireland, *Jane's Naval History of World War II* (London: HarperColli 1998), 132; 'Action report Western Naval Task Force' (Hewitt), 37; Corre Barnett, *Engage The Enemy*, 643–4; Molony, *Mediterranean and Middle East*, v, 5

3. Robertson, *The Ship With Two Captains*, 134; Jewell interview, IWM Sou Archive, ref. 12278, reel 3.

4. Robertson, *The Ship With Two Captains*, 137.

5. 'Action report Western Naval Task Force' (Hewitt), 37.

6. Ibid., 3, 37, 113; Morison, *Sicily—Salerno—Anzio*, 64, 128.

7. Morison, *Sicily—Salerno—Anzio*, 126–7, 129–37.

8. Robertson, *The Ship With Two Captains*, 138–9.

9. See, e.g., D'Este, *Bitter Victory*, 257–8; Morison, *Sicily—Salerno—Anzio*, 133–

10. Barnett, *Engage The Enemy*, 644–5.

11. D'Este, *Bitter Victory*, 282–302; Garland and Smith, *Sicily and the Surrender Italy*, 147–74.

12. Howard, *Grand Strategy*, 468.

13. '"A" Force War Diary' (Dudley Clarke), iii, 113, CAB 154/3.

14. Howard, *Strategic Deception*, 92; Molony, *Mediterranean and Middle East*, v, 52, 5

15. H. R. Trevor-Roper (ed.), *Hitler's War Directives* (London: Pan Books, 1966), 21

16. Walter Warlimont, 'The Man Who Never Was', *An Cosantoir*, June 197 184. See, also, Klaus-Jürgen Muller, 'A German Perspective on Allied Dece tion Operations in the Second World War', *Intelligence and National Securi* 2/3 (1987), 310–15.

17. 'Dr. Percy Ernst Schramm Dead; Published Nazi Command Diary', obituar *New York Times*, 14 November 1970.

8. Percy E. Schramm (ed.), *Kriegstagebuch des Oberkommandos der Wehrmacht (Wehrmachtführungsstab)*, Band IV, *I. Januar 1944–22. Mai 1945* (Herrsching: Manfred Pawlak, 1982), 601–3.

9. Hinsley et al., *British Intelligence in the Second World War*, iii: Pt I, 80.

10. 'Plan "BARCLAY" (Approved Version)', paras. 3, 18, 10 April 1943, CAB 81/77.

11. COS (44) 16 (O), Annex: 'Report by Allied Force Headquarters, North Africa', Section III: 'Conclusions', para. 1, 8 January 1944, CAB 80/78.

12. See, e.g., D'Este, *Bitter Victory*, 198–9.

13. Molony, *Mediterranean and Middle East*, v, 66–8; D'este, Bitter Victory, 579.

14. See, e.g., Brian Holden Reid, 'The Italian Campaign, 1943–45: A reappraisal of Allied generalship' in John Gooch (ed.), *Decisive Campaigns of the Second World War* (London: Frank Cass, 1990), 128–61; and Michael Howard, 'The Second World War in Italy: Was it worth it?', *Times Literary Supplement*, 25 June 2008; Michael Howard, *Captain Professor: The memoirs of Sir Michael Howard* (London: Continuum, 2008), 85–6.

15. See, e.g., D'Este, *Eisenhower*, 445.

16. David M. Glantz and Jonathan M. House, *The Battle of Kursk* (Lawrence: University of Kansas Press, 1999), 151, 217–18, 264.

17. Garland and Smith, *Sicily and the Surrender of Italy*, 213.

18. Glantz and House, *Kursk*, 223, 238, 277–81.

19. Howard, *Strategic Deception*, 93–4.

20. '"A" Force War Diary' (Clarke), iii, 113, CAB 154/3.

21. See, e.g., Howard, *Strategic Deception*, 103, 111, 187–93.

22. Robertson, *The Ship With Two Captains*, 185–6.

23. Bevan to Colonel C. R. W. Lamplough, RM, DNI, Admiralty, 21 August 1943, CAB 154/67. See, also, Bevan to Commodore E. G. N. Rushbrooke, 30 August 1943 and Bevan to Air Marshal F. F. Inglis, 4 September 1943 (both in CAB 154/67).

24. Montagu, *The Man Who Never Was*, 151.

25. Myers, 'Inside Greece', 10, HS 8/897; Myers, *Greek Entanglement*, 181–2. The Palestinian Arab Sergeant's surname is given as 'Shibly' in SOE War Diaries: Middle East and Balkans, Apr.–June 1943, 678–9, HS 7/269.

26. Giles Trimlett, 'Poppy tribute in Spain for 'man who never was', *The Times*, 13 November 1998.

APPENDIX

1. John Steele and Noreen Steele, *The Secrets of HMS Dasher*, 4th edn (Glendaruel: Argyll Publishing, 2004), 211, 214–18, 223; Klaus Gottlieb, 'The Mincemeat postmortem: Forensic aspects of World War II's boldest counterintelligence operation', *Military Medicine*, 174/1 (2009), 94–5; Jürgen Rohwer, *Chronology of the War at Sea, 1939–1945: The naval history of World War Two*, 3rd rev. edn (Annapolis, Maryland: Naval Institute Press, 2005), 241.

2. 'Operation Mincemeat', para. 8, Montagu Papers, Box 1, 97/45/1.
3. 'Operation Mincemeat', 1, ADM 223/794.
4. Steele, *Secrets*, 215–16, 221, 223, 226–7.
5. 'Operation Mincemeat', para. 6, Montagu Papers, Box 1, 97/45/1.
6. 'Mincemeat', draft prepared for compiler of MI6 History, 24 July 1945, Montagu Papers, Box 1, 97/45/1.
7. 'Operation Mincemeat', para. 6, Montagu Papers, Box 1, 97/45/1.
8. Montagu, *The Man Who Never Was*, 30.
9. 'Deception still a mystery', *Navy News*, December 1996, 9; Ezard, ' "Man Who Never Was" finds an identity', *Guardian Weekly*, 10 November 1996; Ben Fenton, 'The man who was "The Man Who Never Was" is revealed', *Daily Telegraph*, 28 October 1996.
10. *Navy News*, December 1996. See, also, 'Grave doubts add to wartime mystery', *Navy News*, January 1997, 15.
11. Telegram no. KN 211, from 'Dowager' (Col. Dudley Clarke) to 'Chaucer' (Col. Bevan), para. 4, 20 May 1943, CAB 154/67.
12. Rose, *Lethal Witness*, 256.
13. 'Sir W. Bentley Purchase', obituary, *The Times*, 28 September 1961.
14. Sir W. Bentley Purchase, *Aids to Forensic Medicine and Toxicology*, 13th edn (London: Ballière, Tindall and Cox, 1960).
15. Montagu to Bevan, re 'Mincemeat', 28 May 1943, paras. 2, 3, 7, CAB 154/67.
16. Ibid., para. 2.
17. 'Operation Mincemeat', 1, ADM 223/794. On the distinct medical meanings of the terms 'cause', 'mode' and 'manner' of death, see Saukko and Knight, *Knight's Forensic Pathology*, 3rd edn, 55.
18. The quotation is taken from John Oxenford's lyrics for *Men of Harlech*. Oxenford's version was published in 1873.

Bibliography

UNPUBLISHED SOURCES

Official British Government Records:

A) UK National Archives:

CABINET OFFICE

CAB 79	War Cabinet, Chiefs of Staff Committee: Minutes of meetings.
CAB 80	War Cabinet, Chiefs of Staff Committee: Memoranda.
CAB 81	War Cabinet, Chiefs of Staff Committees and Sub-Committees.
CAB 121	War Cabinet and Cabinet Office: Special Secret Information Centre: Files.
CAB 146	Cabinet Office: Historical Section, Enemy Documents Section: Files and papers.
CAB 154	London Controlling Section: Correspondence and papers.
PREM 3	Operations Papers: Files of the Prime Minister's Office kept at the War Cabinet offices, dealing with defence and operational subjects.

ADMIRALTY

ADM 1	Admiralty and Secretariat papers.
ADM 223	Naval Intelligence papers.

DEFENCE, MINISTRY OF

DEFE 28	Ministry of Defence: Directorate of Forward Plans: Registered files.

ECONOMIC WARFARE, MINISTRY OF

HS 7	Special Operations Executive: Histories and war diaries: Registered files.
HS 8	Ministry of Economic Warfare, Special Operations Executive and successors: Records.

FOREIGN OFFICE

FO 371	Foreign Office: General correspondence: Political.

GOVERNMENT CODE AND CYPHER SCHOOL

HW 1   Government Code and Cypher School: Signals intelligence passed t
            the Prime Minister, messages, and correspondence.
HW 13   Government Code and Cypher School: Second World War intelli
            gence summaries based on SIGINT.
HW 19   Government Code and Cypher School: ISOS Section and ISK Sec
            tion: Decrypts of German Secret Service (Abwehr and Sicherheits
            dienst) messages (ISOS, ISK, and other series).

THE SECURITY SERVICE (MI5)

KV 4   The Security Service: Policy (Pol F Series) files.

WAR OFFICE

WO 106   Directorate of Military Operations and Intelligence.
WO 169   War of 1939 to 1945, war diaries, Middle East forces.
WO 283   Inter-Services Security Board: Minutes of meetings.

(B) Imperial War Museum:

EDS Collection   Groups of copied German documents ex Enen
                                Documents Section of the Cabinet Office's
                                Historical Section.
Crown Copyright Documents   Department of Documents, Imperial War
in the papers of Captain   Museum, ref. 97/45/1.
E. E. S. Montagu, RN

Official United States Government Records:

US National Archives And Records Administration

RG 319   Records of the Army Staff: Records of the Office of the Assistant Chie
            of Staff, G-3, Operations-Special Correspondence maintained by th
            Top Secret Control Office, 1943–1952: Cover and Deception folders

Private Collections

Lord Harvey of Tasburgh,   British Library, Add. 56398.
Diaries and Papers
The papers of Commander   Department of Documents, Imperial
W. H. N. Martin, RN   War Museum, ref. 98/1/1.
The papers of D. W. A. Mure   Department of Documents, Imperial
                                War Museum, ref. 67/321/1–3.

ear Admiral David Scott   *Action Reply: Reminiscences of a naval*
                                        career (typescript memoirs), Royal
                                        Naval Museum Library, Ports-
                                        mouth.
'he Templewood papers (papers   University Library, Cambridge.
f Rt Hon. Sir Samuel Hoare, later
iscount Templewood)

PUBLISHED SOURCES

ooks

gudo, Manuel Ros, *La Guerra Secreta de Franco (1939–1945)* (Barcelona: Crítica,
    2002).
kten zur Deutschen Auswärtigen Politik, 1918–1945, Serie E: 1941–1945, Band VI:
    1.Mai bis 30.September 1943 (Göttingen: Vandenhoeck and Ruprecht, 1979).
ldrich, Richard J., *The Hidden Hand: Britain, America and Cold War secret intelligence*
    (Woodstock and New York: Overlook Press, 2001).
mbrose, Stephen E., *The Supreme Commander: The war years of General Dwight D.*
    Eisenhower (London: Cassell, 1971).
ndrew, Christopher, *The Defence of the Realm: The authorized history of MI5*
    (Toronto: Viking Canada, 2009).
tkinson, Rick, *An Army at Dawn: The war in North Africa, 1942–1943* (New York:
    Henry Holt, 2002).
—— *The Day of Battle: The war in Sicily and Italy, 1943–1944* (New York: Henry
    Holt, 2007).
uty, Phyllis and Richard Clogg (eds.), *British Policy towards Wartime Resistance in*
    Yugoslavia and Greece (London: Macmillan, 1975).
alfour, Sebastian and Paul Preston (eds.), *Spain and the Great Powers in the Twentieth*
    Century (London: Routledge, 1999).
arnett, Correlli, (ed.), *Hitler's Generals* (London: Weidenfeld and Nicolson, 1989).
—— *Engage the Enemy More Closely: The Royal Navy in the Second World War*
    (London: Hodder and Stoughton, 1991).
eesley, Patrick, *Very Special Admiral: The life of Admiral J. H. Godfrey, CB* (London:
    Hamish Hamilton, 1980).
—— *Room 40: British Naval Intelligence, 1914–1918* (San Diego: Harcourt, Brace,
    Jovanovich, 1982).
ishop, Chris, *Order of Battle: German panzers in WWII* (St Paul, Minnesota:
    Zenith, 2008).
lake, Robert and William Roger Louis (eds.), *Churchill* (New York: Norton, 1993).
lunt, John Henry (ed.), *Annotated Book of Common Prayer* (London: Rivingtons,
    1872).
oog, Horst et al., *Der Globale Krieg: Die Austweitung zum Weltkrieg und der Wechsel*
    der Initiative, 1941–1943 (Stuttgart: Deutsche Verlags-Anstalt, 1990).

Bowen, Wayne, *Spaniards and Nazi Germany: Collaboration in the new order* (Columbia Missouri: University of Missouri Press, 2000).

Bradley, Omar N. and Clay Blair, *A General's Life* (New York: Simon an Schuster, 1983).

Bristow, Desmond (with Bill Bristow), *A Game of Moles: The deceptions of an MI officer* (London: Little, Brown and Co., 1993).

Browne, Douglas G. and Tom Tullett, *Bernard Spilsbury: His life and cases* (New York: Dorset Press, 1951).

Brownlie, Alistair R. (ed.), *Crime Investigation, Art or Science?: Patterns in a labyrinth* (Edinburgh: Scottish Academic Press, 1984).

Bruce, Anthony, *The Last Crusade: The Palestine campaign in the First World War* (London: John Murray, 2002).

Burdick, Charles, *Germany's Military Strategy and Spain in World War II* (Syracuse New York: Syracuse University Press, 1968).

Burns, Jimmy, *Papa Spy: Love, faith and betrayal in wartime Spain* (London: Blooms bury, 2009).

Butcher, Harry C., *Three Years with Eisenhower: The personal diary of Captain Harry C. Butcher, USNR, Naval Aide to General Eisenhower, 1942–1945* (London: William Heinemann, 1946).

Butler, J. R. M., *Grand Strategy*, ii: *September 1939–June 1941* (London: HMSO, 1957).

Cantwell, John D., *The Second World War: A guide to documents in the Public Record Office* (Kew: PRO, 1998).

Chandler, Alfred D. et al. (eds.), *The Papers of Dwight David Eisenhower: The war years*, 2 vols. (Baltimore: Johns Hopkins, 1970).

Churchill, Winston S., *The Second World War*, iv: *The Hinge of Fate* (London: Folio Society edn, 2000).

Colvin, Ian, *The Unknown Courier* (London: William Kimber, 1953).

Cooper, Artemis, *Cairo in the War, 1939–1945* (London: Hamish Hamilton, 1989).

Cooper, Sir Duff, *Operation Heartbreak* (London: Rupert Hart-Davis, 1950).

Copeland, B. Jack et al., *Colossus: The secrets of Bletchley Park's code-breaking computer* (Oxford; Oxford University Press, 2006).

Cortada, James W. (ed.), *Historical Dictionary of the Spanish Civil War* (London Greenwood Press, 1982).

Crémieux-Brilhac, Jean-Louis, *La France Libre: de L'Appel du 18 Juin à la Libération* (Paris: Gallimard, 1996).

Crowdy, Terry, *Deceiving Hitler: Double cross and deception in World War II* (Botley Oxford: Osprey, 2008).

Cruickshank, Charles, *Deception in World War II* (Oxford: Oxford University Press 1979).

Curry, John, *The Security Service 1908–1945: The official history* (Kew, Surrey: Public Record Office, 1999).

Danchev, Alex and Daniel Todman (eds.), *War Diaries, 1939–1945: Field Marshal Lord Alanbrooke* (London: Weidenfeld and Nichlson, 2001).

niel, Donald and Katherine Herbig (eds.), *Strategic Military Deception* (New York: Pergamon, 1982).

venport-Hines, Richard (ed.), *Letters from Oxford: Hugh Trevor-Roper to Bernard Berenson* (London: Weidenfeld and Nicholson, 2006).

vie, Michael (ed.), *The Diaries of Evelyn Waugh* (London: Weidenfeld and Nicolson, 1976; paperback edn, London: Penguin, 1979).

akin, F. W., *The Brutal Friendship* (London: Weidenfeld and Nicholson, 1962); revised two-volume edn, i: *The Brutal Friendship: Mussolini, Hitler and the fall of Italian fascism* (Harmondsworth, Middlesex: Penguin, 1966).

ar, I. C. B. and M. R. D. Foot (eds.), *Oxford Companion to World War II* (Oxford: Oxford University Press, 1995).

Este, Carlo, *Bitter Victory: The battle for Sicily, July–August 1943* (London: Collins, 1988).

— *World War II in the Mediterranean, 1942–1945* (Chapel Hill: Algonquin Books, 1990).

— *Eisenhower: A soldier's life* (New York: Henry Holt, 2002).

— *Warlord: A life of Winston Churchill at war, 1874–1945* (New York: Harper-Collins, 2008).

erries, Reinhard R., *Hitler's Last Chief of Intelligence: Allied interrogations of Walter Schellenberg* (London: Frank Cass, 2003).

rly, John (ed.), *George Orwell's Essays* (New York: Knopf, 2002).

kine, Ralph and Michael Smith (eds.), *Action This Day: Bletchley Park from the breaking of the Enigma code to the birth of the modern computer* (London: Bantam, 2001).

ans, Colin, *The Father of Forensics: The groundbreaking cases of Sir Bernard Spilsbury and the beginning of modern CSI* (New York: Berkeley Books, 2006).

zgerald, Penelope, *The Knox Brothers* (Washington, DC: Counterpoint, 2000).

ot, M. R. D., *Memories of an S.O.E. Historian* (Barnsley: Pen and Sword, 2008).

ɔhlich, Elke (ed.), *Die Tagebücher von Joseph Goebbels*, Teil II, *Diktate*, 1941–1945, Band 8, *April–Juni 1943* (Munich: K. G. Saur, 1993).

ehrer *Conferences on Naval Affairs, 1939–1945* (London: Greenhill Books, 1990).

ndación Nacional Francisco Franco, *Documentos Inéditos para la Historia del Generalísimo Franco*, Tomo, iv (Madrid: Azor, 1994).

nk, Arthur Layton, *The Politics of TORCH: The Allied landing and the Algerian putsch, 1942* (Lawrence/Manhatten/Wichita: University of Kansas Press, 1974).

nnon, Paul, *Colossus: Bletchley Park's greatest secret* (London: Atlantic, 2006).

rfield, Brian, *The Meinertzhagen Mystery: The life and legend of a colossal fraud* (Washington, DC: Potomac Books, 2007).

rland, Albert N. and Howard McGaw Smyth, *Sicily and the Surrender of Italy* (Washington, DC: Center of Military History, United States Army, 1993).

lbert, Martin, *Road to Victory: Winston S. Churchill, 1941–1945* (Toronto: Stoddart, 1986).

antz, David M. and Jonathan M. House, *The Battle of Kursk* (Lawrence: University of Kansas Press, 1999).

Gooch, John (ed.), *Decisive Campaigns of the Second World War* (London: Frank Ca 1990).

Green, Jack and Alessandro Massignani, *The Naval War in the Mediterrane* (London: Chatham Publishing, 1998).

Hamilton, Nigel, *Monty,* i: *The making of a general, 1887–1942* (Toronto: Fle Books, 1982).

—— *Monty,* ii: *Master of the battlefield, 1942–1944* (London: Sceptre, 1987).

Handel, Michael (ed.), *Strategic and Operational Deception in the Second World W* (London: Frank Cass, 1987).

Hardy, Henry (ed.), *Letters, 1928–1946: Isaiah Berlin* (New York: Cambrid University Press, 2004).

Harvey, Charles E., *The Rio Tinto Company: An economic history of an internatio mining concern, 1873–1954* (Penzance: Alison Hodge, 1981).

Harvey, John (ed.), *The War Diaries of Oliver Harvey, 1941–1945* (London: Colli 1978).

Heiber, Helmut and David M. Glantz (eds.), *Hitler and His Generals: Milit conferences, 1942–1945* (New York: Enigma Books, 2002).

Hinsley, F. H. et al., *British Intelligence in the Second World War: Its influence on strate and operations,* i (London: HMSO, 1979).

—— *British Intelligence in the Second World War: Its influence on strategy and operatio* ii (London: HMSO, 1981).

—— *British Intelligence in the Second World War: Its influence on strategy and operatio* iii, Pt I (London: HMSO, 1984).

—— *British Intelligence in the Second World War,* iii, Pt II (London: HMSO, 198

Hinsley, F. H. and C. A. G. Simkins, *British Intelligence in the Second World War,* Security and Counter-Intelligence (London: HMSO, 1990).

Hinsley, F. H. and Alan Stripp (eds), *Codebreakers: The inside story of Bletchley P* (Oxford: Oxford University Press, 1993).

Höhne, Heinz, *Canaris* (London: Secker and Warburg, 1979).

Holt, Thaddeus, *The Deceivers: Allied military deception in the Second World W* (New York: Scribner, 2004).

Howard, Michael, *Grand Strategy,* iv: *August 1942–September 1943* (London: HMS(1972).

—— *British Intelligence in the Second World War,* v: *Strategic Deception* (Londc HMSO, 1990).

—— *Captain Professor: The memoirs of Sir Michael Howard* (London: Continuum, 200

Hubatsch, Walther (ed.), *Kriegstagebuch des Oberkommandos der Wehrmacht (We machtführungsstab),* Band iii, *1.Januar 1943–31.Dezember 1943* (Herrsching: Ma fred Pawlak, 1982).

Hunt, Sir David, *A Don at War,* rev. edn (London: Frank Cass, 1990).

Hutchinson, Robert, *Jane's Submarines: War beneath the waves, from 1776 to the pres day* (London: HarperCollins, 2001.

atrides, John O. (ed.), *Greece in the 1940s: A nation in crisis* (Hanover and London: University Press of New England, 1981).

reland, Bernard, *Jane's Naval History of World War II* (London: HarperCollins, 1998).

rujo, José María, *La Lista Negra: Los espías nazis protegidos por Franco y la Iglesia* (Madrid: Aguilar, 2003).

ackson, Robert, *Coroner: The biography of Sir Bentley Purchase* (London: Harrap, 1963).

effery, Keith, *The Secret History of MI6* (New York: Penguin, 2010).

Kahn, David, *Hitler's Spies: German military intelligence in World War II* (London: Hodder and Stoughton, 1978).

—— *The Final Solution of the Abwehr* (New York: Garland, 1989), Introduction.

Kam, Ephraim, *Surprise Attack: The victim's perspective* (Cambridge, Massachusetts: Harvard University Press, 1988; 2004 edn).

Keegan, John (ed.), *Churchill's Generals* (London: Weidenfeld and Nicolson, 1991).

Kleinfeld, Gerald R. and Lewis A. Tambs, *Hitler's Spanish Legion: The Blue Division in Russia* (Carbondale and Edwardsville: Southern Illinois University Press, 1979).

Lane, Brian, *The Encyclopedia of Forensic Science* (London: Headline, 1992).

Latimer, Jon, *Deception in War* (London: John Murray, 2001).

Lavery, Brian, *Churchill's Navy: The ships, men and organisation* (London: Conway, 2006).

Lawrence, T. E., *Seven Pillars of Wisdom: A triumph* (London: Jonathan Cape, 1935; London: Folio edn, 2000).

Louis, William Roger (ed.), *Adventures with Britannia: Personalities, politics and culture in Britain* (Austin: University of Texas Press, 1995).

Macintyre, Ben, *Agent Zigzag* (New York: Harmony Books, 2007).

Mackenzie, W. J. M., *The Secret History of SOE: The Special Operations Executive, 1940–1945* (London: St Ermin's Press, 2000).

Masterman, J. C., *The Double-Cross System in the War of 1939 to 1945* (New Haven: Yale University Press, 1972).

—— *On the Chariot Wheel: An autobiography* (London: Oxford University Press, 1975).

Matloff, Maurice, *Strategic Planning for Coalition Warfare, 1943–1944* (United States Army in World War II), (Washington, DC: Office of the Chief of Military History, Department of the Army, 1959).

McCartney, Innis, *British Submarines, 1939–45* (Botley, Oxfordshire: Osprey, 2006).

McLachlan, Donald, *Room 39: Naval intelligence in action, 1939–45* (London: Weidenfeld and Nicolson, 1968).

Mitcham, Jr, Samuel W., *German Order of Battle, iii: Panzer, Panzer Grenadier and Waffen SS Divisions in World War II* (Menchanicsburg, Pennsylvania: Stackpole Books, 2007).

—— *The Panzer Legions: A guide to the German army tank divisions of World War II and their commanders* (Menhanicsburg, Pennsylvania: Stackpole Books, 2007).

Molony, Brigadier C. J. C. et al., *The Mediterranean and the Middle East (History of the Second World War: United Kingdom Military Series)*, v: *The Campaign in Sicily, 1943 and the Campaign in Italy, 3rd September 1943 to 31st March, 1944* (London: HMSO, 1973).

Montagu, Ewen, *The Man Who Never Was* (New York: J. P. Lippincott Company, 1954).

—— *The Man Who Never Was: The story of Operation Mincemeat*, Cadet Edition (London: Evans Brothers, 1965).

—— *Beyond Top Secret Ultra* (New York: Coward, McCann and Geoghegan, 1978).

—— *The Man Who Never Was* (Oxford: Oxford University Press, 1996).

Morison, Samuel Eliot, *History of United States Naval Operations in World War II*, ix: *Sicily—Salerno—Anzio, January 1942–June 1944* (Boston: Little, Brown, 1954).

Mure, David, *Practise to Deceive* (London: William Kimber, 1977).

—— *Master of Deception: Tangled webs in London and the Middle East* (London: William Kimber, 1980).

Myers, E. C. W., *Greek Entanglement*, rev. edn (Gloucester: Alan Sutton, 1985).

Neillands, Robin, *The Dieppe Raid: The story of the disastrous 1942 expedition* (London: Aurum, 2005; paperback edn, 2006).

Paillole, Colonel Paul, *Fighting the Nazis: French military intelligence and counter intelligence, 1935–1945* (New York: Enigma Books, 2003).

Papastratis, Procopis, *British Policy Towards Greece during the Second World War 1941–1944* (Cambridge: Cambridge University Press, 1984).

Parker, John, *The Illustrated World Guide to Submarines* (London: Hermes House, 2007).

Payne, Stanley G., *Politics and the Military in Modern Spain* (Stanford: Stanford University Press, 1967).

—— *The Franco Regime, 1936–1975* (Madison, Wisconsin: University of Wisconsin Press, 1987).

—— *Franco and Hitler: Spain, Germany and World War II* (New Haven: Yale University Press, 2008).

Perrier, Guy, *Le Colonel Passy et les Services Secrets de la France Libre* (Paris: Hachette, 1999).

Philby, Kim, *My Silent War* (New York: Grove, 1968).

Polson, Cyril John, D. J. Gee, and Bernard Knight, *The Essentials of Forensic Medicine*, 4th edn (Oxford: Pergamon, 1985).

Porch, Douglas, *The Path to Victory: The Mediterranean theater in World War War II* (New York: Farrar, Straus and Giroux, 2004).

Powell, Anthony, *To Keep the Ball Rolling: The memoirs of Anthony Powell* (Harmondsworth, Middlesex: Penguin, 1983).

—— *The Military Philosophers* (Chicago: University of Chicago Press, 1995).

Preston, Paul, *Franco: A biography* (London: HarperCollins, 1993).

— (ed.), *Revolution and War in Spain* (London: Methuen, 1984).

ırchase, Sir W. Bentley, *Aids to Forensic Medicine and Toxicology*, 13th edn (London: Ballière, Tindall and Cox, 1960).

hn, Werner and Gerhard Schreiber (eds.), *Kriegstagebuch der Seekriegsleitung 1939–1945*, Teil A, Band 45: *Mai 1943* (Berlin: Mittler, 1994).

mírez Copeiro del Villar, Jesús, *Espías y Neutrales: Huelva en la Segunda Guerra Mundial* (Huelva: Ramírez Copeiro, 1996).

tcliff, R. A., *Delusions of Intelligence: Enigma, Ultra and the end of secure ciphers* (Cambridge: Cambridge University Press, 2006).

·cker, Marie-Luise (ed.), *Von der Konkurrenz zur Rivalität: Das Britische-Deutsche Verhältnis in den Ländern der Europäischen Peripherie, 1919–1939* (Stuttgart: Franz Steiner, 1986).

ıbertson, Terence, *The Ship With Two Captains* (London: Evans Brothers, 1957).

ıhwer, Jürgen, *Chronology of the War at Sea, 1939–1945: The naval history of World War Two*, 3rd rev. edn (Annapolis, Maryland: Naval Institute Press, 2005).

ıse, Andrew, *Lethal Witness: Sir Bernard Spilsbury, honorary pathologist* (London: Sutton, 2007).

ıhl, Klaus-Jörg, *Spanien im Zweiten Weltkrieg: Franco, die Falange und das 'Dritte Reich'* (Hamburg: Hoffmann und Campe, 1975).

ınyan, Timothy J. and Jan M. Copes, *To Die Gallantly: The Battle of the Atlantic* (Boulder: Westview Press, 1994).

ıukko, Pekka and Bernard Knight, *Knight's Forensic Pathology*, 3rd edn (London: Arnold, 2004).

ıunders, Hillary St George, *Combined Operations: The official story of the Commandos, with a foreword by Vice-Admiral Lord Louis Mountbatten, Chief of Combined Operations* (New York: Macmillan, 1943).

hramm, Percy E. (ed.), *Kriegstagebuch des Oberkommandos der Wehrmacht (Wehrmachtführungsstab)*, Band IV, *1. Januar 1944–22. Mai 1945* (Herrsching: Manfred Pawlak, 1982).

aman, Mark, *Garbo: The Spy Who Saved D-Day* (Richmond, Surrey: Public Record Office, 2000), Introduction.

bag-Montefiore, Hugh, *Enigma: The battle for the code* (London: Weidenfeld and Nicolson, 2000).

·rrano Suñer, Ramón, *Entre el Silencio y la Propaganda, la Historia come fue: Memorias* (Barcelona: Planeta, 1977).

nith, Michael, *Foley: The spy who saved 10,000 Jews* (London: Hodder and Stoughton, 1999).

nith, Sydney, *Forensic Medicine: A text-book for students and practioners* (London: J. and A. Churchll, 1943).

— *Mostly Murder* (London: Harrap, 1959).

ınyth, Denis, *Diplomacy and Strategy of Survival: British policy and Franco's Spain, 1940–41* (Cambridge: Cambridge University Press, 1986).

Smyth, Denis, (ed.), *British Documents on Foreign Affairs: Reports and papers from Foreign Office confidential print*, Pt III: *From 1940 through 1945*, Series F: Euro, xii–xix (Bethesda, Maryland: University Publications of America, 1998).

Stafford, David, *Churchill and Secret Service* (London: John Murray, 1997).

—— *Roosevelt and Churchill: Men of secrets* (London: Little Brown, 1999).

Steele, John and Noreen Steele, *The Secrets of HMS Dasher* (Glendaruel: Arg, Publishing, 2004).

Suárez, Luis, *España, Franco y la Segunda Guerra Mundial: Desde 1939 Hasta 19* (Madrid: Actas, 1997).

Templewood, Viscount, *Ambassador on Special Mission* (London: Collins, 1946).

Trevor-Roper, Hugh (ed.), *Hitler's War Directives* (London: Pan Books, 1966).

Tusell, Javier, *Franco, España y la II Guerra Mundial: Entre el Eje y la Neutralid* (Madrid: Temas de Hoy, 1995).

Villa, Brian Loring, *Unauthorized Action: Mountbatten and the Dieppe raid* (Toront Oxford University Press, 1989).

Warlimont, Walter, *Inside Hitler's Headquarters, 1939–45* (London: Weidenfeld a Nicholson, 1964).

Welchman, Gordon, *The Hut Six Story: Breaking the Enigma codes* (Harmondswort Penguin Books, 1984).

West, Nigel (ed.), *The Guy Liddell Diaries*, i: *1939–1942*; ii: *1942–1945* (Londo Routledge, 2005).

West, Nigel and Oleg Tsarev, *The Crown Jewels: The British secrets at the heart of KGB archives* (New Haven: Yale University Press, 1998).

Wheatley, Dennis, *The Deception Planners: My secret war* (London: Hutchinso 1980).

Wheeler-Bennett, Sir John (ed.), *Action This Day: Working with Churchill* (Londo Macmillan, 1968).

Wickham Legg, L. G. and E. T. Williams (eds.), *The Dictionary of National Bic raphy: 1941–1950* (Oxford: Oxford University Press, 1959).

Wilson, Trevor, *The Myriad Faces of War: Britain and the Great War* (Cambridg Cambridge University Press, 1986).

Winton, John, *Cunningham* (London: John Murray, 1998).

Woodhouse, C. M., *Apple of Discord: A survey of recent Greek politics in th international setting* (London: Hutchinson, 1948).

—— *The Struggle for Greece, 1941–1949*, 2nd edn (Chicago: Ivan R. Dee, 2003).

Young, Martin and Robbie Stamp, *Trojan Horses: Deception operations in the Seco World War* (London: Bodley Head, 1991).

Articles and Essays

Batey, Keith, 'How Dilly Knox and his girls broke the Abwehr Engima' in Ral Erskine and Michael Smith (eds.), *Action This Day: Bletchley Park from the breaki of the Enigma Code to the birth of the modern computer* (London: Bantam, 200 301–16.

ey, Mavis, 'Breaking Italian Naval Enigma' in Ralph Erskine and Michael Smith
(eds.), *Action This Day: Bletchley Park from the breaking of the Enigma Code to the
birth of the modern computer* (London: Bantam, 2001), 94–109.

— 'Dilly Knox: A reminiscence of this pioneer Enigma cryptanalyst', *Cryptologia*, 32/2 (2008), 104–30.

ckett, Ian, 'Wavell' in John Keegan (ed.), *Churchill's Generals* (London: Weidenfeld and Nicolson, 1991), 70–88.

nnett, Ralph, 'The duty officer, Hut 3' in F. H. Hinsley and Alan Stripp (eds.),
Codebreakers: The inside story of Bletchley Park (Oxford: Oxford University Press,
1993), 30–40.

nton, Kenneth, 'The ISOS Years: Madrid 1941–3', *Journal of Contemporary
History*, 30/3 (1995), 355–410.

own, J. David, 'The Battle of the Atlantic, 1941–1943: Peaks and troughs' in
Timothy J. Runyan and Jan M. Copes (eds.), *To Die Gallantly: The Battle of the
Atlantic* (Boulder: Westview, 1994), 137–57.

unt, Rodney M., 'Special documentation systems at the government Code and
Cypher School, Bletchley Park, during the Second World War', *Intelligence and
National Security*, 21/1 (2006), 129–48.

diansky, Stephen, 'Colossus, code-breaking and the digital age' in B. Jack
Copeland et al., *Colossus: The secrets of Bletchley Park's code-breaking computers*
(Oxford: Oxford University Press, 2006), 52–63.

rdick, Charles B., '"Moro": The resupply of German submarines in Spain,
1939–1942', *Central European History*, 3/3 (1970), 256–84.

mpbell, John P., 'A retrospective on John Masterman's *The Double-Cross System*', *International Journal of Intelligence and Counterintelligence*, 18/2 (2005), 320–53.

opeland, B. Jack, 'The German Tunny machine', in B. Jack Copeland et al.,
Colossus: The secrets of Bletchley Park's code-breaking computers (Oxford: Oxford
University Press, 2006), 36–51.

vies, Philip H. J., 'From amateurs to professionals: GC&CS and institution-
building in Sigint' in Ralph Erskine and Michael Smith (eds.), *Action This Day:
Bletchley Park from the breaking of the Enigma code to the birth of the modern computer*
(London: Bantam, 2001), 386–402.

eakin, F. W., 'The myth of an Allied landing in the Balkans during the Second
World War (with particular reference to Yugoslavia)' in Phyllis Auty and
Richard Clogg (eds.), *British Policy towards Wartime Resistance in Yugoslavia and
Greece* (London: Macmillan, 1975), 93–116.

ovey, H. O., 'The false going map at Alam Halfa', *Intelligence and National Security*,
4/1 (1989), 165–8.

yden, Henry, 'Recollections of Bletchley Park, France, and Cairo' in F. H.
Hinsley and Alan Stripp (eds.), *Codebreakers: The inside story of Bletchley Park*
(Oxford: Oxford University Press, 1993), 195–208.

skine, Ralph, 'From the archives: A Bletchley Park assessment of German
intelligence on TORCH', *Cryptologia*, 13/2 (1989), 135–42.

Erskine, Ralph, 'Eavesdropping on "Bodden": ISOS v. the Abwehr in the Straits
    Gibraltar', *Intelligence and National Security*, 12/3 (1997), 110–29.
—— 'Breaking Air Force and Army Enigma' in Ralph Erskine and Mich
    Smith (eds.), *Action This Day: Bletchley Park from the breaking of the Enig*
    code to the birth of the modern computer (London: Bantam, 2001), 47–76.
—— 'Breaking German Naval Enigma on both sides of the Atlantic' in Ra
    Erskine and Michael Smith (eds.), *Action This Day: Bletchley Park from*
    breaking of the Enigma code to the birth of the modern computer (London: Banta
    2001), 174–96.
—— 'The Poles reveal their secrets: Alastair Denniston's account of the July 19
    meeting at Pyry', *Cryptologia*, 30/4, (2006), 294–305.
Good, Jack, 'Enigma and Fish' in F. H. Hinsley and Alan Stripp (eds.), *Co*
    breakers: The inside story of Bletchley Park (Oxford: Oxford University Pre
    1993), 149–66.
Gottlieb, Klaus, 'The Mincemeat postmortem: Forensic aspects of World War I
    boldest counterintelligence operation', *Military Medicine*, 174/1 (2009), 93–9.
Green, Michael A., 'Is Sir Bernard Spilsbury dead?' in Alistair R. Brownlie (ed
    Crime Investigation, Art or Science?: Patterns in a labyrinth (Edinburgh: Scott
    Academic Press, 1984), 23–6.
Handel, Michael, 'Introduction: Strategic and operational deception in histori
    perspective', in idem (ed.), *Strategic and Operational Deception in the Second Wo*
    War (London: Frank Cass, 1987), 1–91.
Harrison, E. D. R., 'British radio security and intelligence, 1939–43', *Engl*
    Historical Review, CXXIV/506 (2009), 53–93.
Hayward, Gil, 'Operation Tunny', in F. H. Hinsley and Alan Stripp (eds.), *Co*
    breakers: The inside story of Bletchley Park (Oxford: Oxford University Press, 199
    175–92.
Hilton, Peter, 'Living with Fish: Breaking Tunny in the Newmanry and t
    Testery' in B. Jack Copeland et al., *Colossus: The secrets of Bletchley Park's co*
    breaking computers (Oxford: Oxford University Press, 2006), 189–203.
Hinsley, F. H., 'An introduction to Fish', in Hinsley, F. H. and Alan Stripp (eds
    Codebreakers: The inside story of Bletchley Park (Oxford: Oxford University Pre
    1993), 141–8.
—— 'Churchill and the use of special intelligence' in Robert Blake and Willia
    Roger Louis (eds.), *Churchill* (New York: Norton, 1993), 407–26.
Howard, Michael, 'Reflections on strategic deception' in William Roger Lou
    (ed.), *Adventures with Britannia: Personalities, politics and culture in Britain* (Austi
    University of Texas Press, 1995), 235–45.
—— 'The Second World War in Italy: Was it worth it?', *Times Literary Supplemen*
    25 June 2008.
Jacob, Agnes, 'When corpses speak . . .', *Doctor's Review*, August 1998, 97–9.
Marck, David de Young de la, 'De Gaulle, Colonel Passy and British intelligenc
    1940–42', *Intelligence and National Security*, 18/1 (2003), 21–40.

ward, William, 'Life in and out of Hut 3', in F. H. Hinsley and Alan Stripp eds.), *Codebreakers: The inside story of Bletchley Park* (Oxford: Oxford University 'ress, 1993), 17–29.

ner-Barry, Stuart, 'Hut 6: Early days' in F. H. Hinsley and Alan Stripp (eds.), *Codebreakers: The inside story of Bletchley Park* (Oxford: Oxford University Press, 993), 89–99.

:hie, Donald, 'Colossus and the breaking of the wartime "Fish" codes', *Crypto-gia*, 26/1, (2002), 17–58.

— 'Codebreaking and Colossus' in B. Jack Copeland et al., *Colossus: The secrets of Bletchley Park's code-breaking computers* (Oxford: Oxford University Press, 2006), 23–46.

rgan, Roger, 'The man who almost is', *After the Battle*, 54 (1986), 1–25.

— 'The Second World War's best kept secret revealed', *After the Battle*, 94, November (1996), 31–3.

ller, Klaus-Jürgen, 'A German perspective on Allied deception operations in the econd World War', *Intelligence and National Security*, 2/3 (1987), 301–26.

well, George, 'Decline of the English murder' in John Carey (ed.), *George Orwell: Essays* (New York and London: Knopf, 2002), 1028–32.

ston, Paul, 'Italy and Spain in Civil War and World War' in Sebastian Balfour nd Paul Preston (eds.), *Spain and the Great Powers in the Twentieth Century* London: Routledge, 1999), 151–84.

d, Brian Holden, 'The Italian Campaign, 1943–45: A reappraisal of Allied generalship' in John Gooch (ed.), *Decisive Campaigns of the Second World War* London: Frank Cass, 1990), 128–61.

äfer, Th. Achim and Jens D. Kaufman, 'What happens in freezing bodies? Experimental study of histological tissue change caused by freezing injuries', *Forensic Science International*, 102/2–3 (1999), 149–58.

brook, John, 'Ruffled feathers: Uncovering the biggest scandal in the Bird World', *The New Yorker*, 82/15, 51–61.

ffy, Yigal, 'Institutionalized deception and perception reinforcement: Allen-by's campaigns in Palestine', *Intelligence and National Security*, 5/2 (1990), 73–236.

— 'The spy who never was: An intelligence myth in Palestine, 1914–18', *Intelligence and National Security*, 14/3 (1999), 123–42.

ith, Michael, 'Bletchley Park, double cross and D-Day' in Ralph Erskine and Michael Smith (eds.), *Action This Day: Bletchley Park from the breaking of the enigma code to the birth of the modern computer* (London: Bantam, 2001), 278–300.

— 'How it began: Bletchley Park goes to war' in B. Jack Copeland et al., *Colossus: The secrets of Bletchley Park's code-breaking computers* (Oxford: Oxford University Press, 2006), 18–35.

yth, Denis, ' "Les Chevaliers de Saint-George: La Grande-Bretagne et La Corruption des généraux espagnols (1940–1942)', *Guerre Mondiales et Conflits Contemporains*, 162/Avril (1991), 29–54.

Smyth, Denis, 'The Moor and the money-lender: Politics and profits in Ang
German relations with Francoist Spain, 1936–1940' in Marie-Luise Recker (e
*Von der Konkurrenz zur Rivalität: das Britishche-Deutsche Verhältnis in den Länd
der Europäischen Peripherie, 1919–1939* (Stuttgart: Franz Steiner, 1986), 143–74.
—— 'Reflex reaction: Germany and the onset of the Spanish Civil War', in P
Preston (ed.), *Revolution and War in Spain* (London: Methuen, 1984), 243–65
—— 'Screening "Torch": Allied counter-intelligence and the Spanish threat
the secrecy of the Allied invasion of French North Africa in November 194
Intelligence and National Security, 4/2 (1989), 335–56.
Stripp, Alan, 'The Enigma machine: Its mechanism and use' in F. H. Hinsley a
Alan Stripp (eds.), *Codebreakers: The inside story of Bletchley Park* (Oxford: Oxf
University Press, 1993), 83–8.
Stumpf, Reinhard, 'Der Krieg im Mittelmeerraum 1942/43: Die Operationen
Nordafrika und im Mittleren Mittelmeer' in Horst Boog et al., *Der Globale Kr
Die Austweitung zum Weltkrieg und der Wechsel der Initiative, 1941–1943, (L
Deutsche Reich und der Zweite Weltkrieg)* (Stuttgart: Deutsche Verlag-Anst
1990), 569–757.
Taunt, Derek, 'Hut 6 from the inside' in Ralph Erskine and Michael Smith (ed
*Action This Day: Bletchley Park from the breaking of the Enigma Code to the birth of
modern computer* (London: Bantam, 2001), 77–93.
Twinn, Peter, 'The Abwehr Engima' in F. H. Hinsley and Alan Stripp (ed
Codebreakers: The inside story of Bletchley Park (Oxford: Oxford University Pr
1993), 123–31.
Warlimont, Walter, 'The man who never was', *An Cosantoir: The Irish Defe
Journal*, June 1973, 183–93.
Winter, P. R. J., 'A higher form of intelligence: Hugh Trevor-Roper and warti
British Secret Service', *Intelligence and National Security*, 22/6 (2007), 847–80.
Wylie, Shaun, 'Breaking Tunny and the birth of Colossus' in Ralph Erskine a
Michael Smith (eds.), *Action This Day: Bletchley Park from the breaking of
Enigma Code to the birth of the modern computer* (London: Bantam, 2001), 317–

Newspapers and Journals

Camden New Journal (London)
Daily Mail (London)
Daily Telegraph (London)
Guardian Weekly (London)
The Lancet (London)
Navy News (Portsmouth)
The New York Times (New York)
The Times (London)
The Times Literary Supplement (London)
La Vanguardia (Barcelona)

nline Sources

http://ibiblio.org/hyperwar/USN/Admin-Hist/148.3-Sicily/index.html>
http://speeches.empireclub.org/>
http://www.BletchleyPark.org.uk>
http://www.dailymail.co.uk>
http://www.fdrlibrary.marist.edu/psf>
http://www.museumoflondon.org.uk>
http://www.oldships.org.uk>
http://www.oxforddnb.com>
http://www.telegraph.co.uk>
http://www.timesonline.co.uk>
http://www.unithistories.com/officers/RN>
http://www.xs4all.nl/~embden11/Engels/saunders.htm>

INTERVIEWS

uthor's interview with Captain Alan Hillgarth, RN, 27 January 1977, Ballinderry,
   Co. Tipperary, Ireland.
ral history interview with Captain Norman Limbury Auchinleck ('Bill') Jewell,
   RN, 10 March 1991, IWM Sound Archive, London, ref. 12278, reels 2 and 3.
uthor's interviews with Dr Noel McAuliffe, MD, DMJ (Path.), 18 October 2007,
   13 May 2009, 16 July 2009, and 28 July 2009, Toronto, Ontario, Canada.
uthor's telephone interview with Mrs. Patricia Davies (née Trehearne),
   15 February 2010.

Index